BUSINESS ETHICS

PROBLEMS

PRINCIPLES

PRACTICAL APPLICATIONS

Third Edition

Keith W. Krasemann

Copley Custom Textbooks

An imprint of XanEdu Publishing, Inc.

ISBN13: 978-1-58152-694-3
ISBN10: 1-58152-694-6

Acknowledgments:
pp. 4–10, 362–364: As appeared in *Harvard Business Review*, May/June 1997.
Copyright © 1997 by Harvard Business School Publishing. Reprinted by
permission of Harvard Business School Publishing.
pp. 17–24: Copyright © 1970 by the New York Times Co. Reprinted by
permission.
pp. 25–36: As appeared in *Ethical Issues in Business: A Philosophical Approach*
edited by Thomas Donaldson and Patricia Werhane. Copyright 2002 by
Edward R. Freeman. Reprinted by permission of the author.
pp. 37–47: From *A Primer on Business Ethics* by Tibor Machan and James
Chesher. Copyright © 2002 by Rowman & Littlefield Publishers, Inc.
Reprinted by permission.
pp. 48–52: From *Karl Marx: Early Writings, The Economic and Philosophic
Manuscripts of 1844* translated by T. B. Bottomore. Copyright © 1963 by
McGraw-Hill, Inc. Reprinted by permission.
pp. 53–64: From *Social Philosophy* by Joel Feinberg. Copyright © 1973 by
Prentice Hall, Inc., a division of Pearson Education.
pp. 65–74: Reprinted by permission of the publisher from *A Theory of Justice*
by John Rawls, pp. 10–15, 52–56. Cambridge, Mass.: The Belknap Press of
Harvard University Press, Copyright © 1971, 1999 by the President and
Fellows of Harvard College.

Copley Custom Textbooks
An imprint of XanEdu Publishing, Inc.
138 Great Road
Acton, MA 01720
800-562-2147

In memory of my sister, Lynn Lundwall

Contents

Appendixes

Preface

At the dawn of a new millennium, businesses face unprecedented challenges. Social and technological change is occurring in a way, and at a speed, that is without precedent. Radical, rapid, and revolutionary change and increased complexity are constants with which all businesses and corporations must deal. Major challenges in the twenty-first century include international competition, new technologies, demands for increased quality, employee motivation, management of a diverse, knowledge-based workforce, and ethical problems. How businesses respond to these challenges will determine their success and whether, in fact, they survive.

These challenges provide opportunities to rethink and re-conceptualize the ways in which business is conducted. The new century holds innumerable possibilities for making business better. This book is written with the belief that true success in any human endeavor must have a solid moral and ethical foundation. Because of the international scope of business, moral theories and ethical perspectives from both Western and non-Western cultures are included.

For fourteen years I have enjoyed a wonderful relationship with Copley Custom Textbooks. I want to thank Lucy Miskin for her professionalism and thoroughness as a publisher and for her kindness as a friend.

Finally, I wish to express my gratitude to Peggy Qin for the inspiration and support that made this book possible.

KWK

Sycamore, Illinois
November 11, 2009

Introduction

Introduction

What makes a human life good? How can I lead a good life? What does life require of me? What kinds of human institutions are needed to support individuals in their quest for goodness? The above questions reflect basic concerns of ethics. Normative thinking about how we, as human beings, are to dwell in the world constitutes that branch of philosophy called "ethics." Ethics is thinking philosophically about the moral dimension of human existence. Ethics examines the nature of good and evil, the concept of right, the essence of justice and personal integrity. Ethics deals with the conduct and character of life.

Business ethics deals with the conduct and character of business. It is applied ethics. Business ethics applies ethics and practical understanding about what is good and right to a wide range of institutions, economies, technologies, traditions, and practices that make up the world of business. Since the world of business affects all of our lives, it is hoped that by thinking deeply about those standards that ought to govern business activities and attempting to put our highest values into practice, that our lives will be enriched and our character ennobled.

For some, the term "business ethics" is an oxymoron. To use the term is, as the figure of speech implies, nothing more than "wise folly." After all, "business is business." Business is about profit, not about ethics. But, business is not merely a moneymaking enterprise; it is also a human enterprise and, therefore, ought to embody our deepest human values. In fact, business ethics is a necessary precondition for a flourishing business enterprise and for true business success.

This book is divided into three parts—Part I: "Problems in Business Ethics" deals with basic problems of social responsibility and economic justice. It also deals with the problem of moral relativism in the international marketplace. Part II: "Ethical Principles and Moral Theories" is concerned primarily with the nature of moral reasoning and a consideration of the theoretical grounds for moral obligation. The principles discussed here are essential for the reasoned analysis of ethical problems in business. Part III: "Practical Applications of Business Ethics" brings theoretical, abstract ethical principle, and moral theories to the flesh and blood, practical world of business. Suggestions for creating ethical corporate structures, teaching ethical decision making, and corporate social responsibility are among the topics discussed.

Business Ethics: Problems, Principles, Practical Applications begins with a story, "The Parable of the Sadhu." The "Parable" is about a mountain climber's ethical dilemma; but it was written to call attention to the ever present moral dilemmas that must be confronted daily in the business world. The "Parable" is about life and death. It is a story about ambition and the dominant metaphor suggests a link to "climbing the corporate ladder," or pursuing one's own personal objectives. "Getting to the top" is equated with success. The story shows that often people display sincerity and good intentions; yet choose to pursue selfish courses of action.

In the narrative teamwork breaks down; no one is willing to take final responsibility to ensure the rescue of the Sadhu. Rationalization occurs and the mountain climbing group, in the end, proceeds according to agreed upon shared objectives. Despite the discussion of values, such as time, effort, expense, human life, and personal safety, no decisive action is taken to complete the Sadhu's rescue. Although one could argue that the problem was due to a failure on the part of the group to have established shared values to balance shared objectives; nevertheless, the virtues that translate abstract values to concrete action were absent.

This book is written with the belief that corporate leaders and business managers want to make the right ethical choices but need help to better reconcile human obligations with commitments to the bottom line.

The Parable of the Sadhu

Bowen H. McCoy

It was early in the morning before the sun rose, which gave them time to climb the treacherous slope to the pass at 18,000 feet before the ice steps melted. They were also concerned about their stamina and altitude sickness, and felt the need to press on. Into the chance collection of climbers on that Himalayan slope an ethical dilemma arose in the guise of an unconscious, almost naked sadhu, an Indian holy man. Each climber gave the sadhu help but none made sure he would be safe. Should somebody have stopped to help the sadhu to safety? Would it have done any good? Was the group responsible? Since leaving the sadhu on the mountain slope, the author, who was one of the climbers, has pondered these issues. He sees many parallels for business people as they face ethical decisions at work.

Last year, as the first participant in the new six-month sabbatical program that Morgan Stanley has adopted, I enjoyed a rare opportunity to collect my thoughts as well as do some traveling. I spent the first three months in Nepal, walking 600 miles through 200 villages in the Himalayas and climbing some 120,000 vertical feet. On the trip my sole Western companion was an anthropologist who shed light on the cultural patterns of the villages we passed through.

During the Nepal hike, something occurred that has had a powerful impact on my thinking about corporate ethics. Although some might argue that the experience has no relevance to business, it was a situation in which a basic ethical dilemma suddenly intruded into the lives of a group of individuals. How the group responded I think holds a lesson for all organizations no matter how defined.

The Sadhu

The Nepal experience was more rugged and adventuresome than I had anticipated. Most commercial treks last two or three weeks and cover a quarter of the distance we traveled.

My friend Stephen, the anthropologist, and I were halfway through the 60-day Himalayan part of the trip when we reached the high point, an 18,000-foot pass over a crest that we'd have to traverse to reach the village of Muklinath, an ancient holy place for pilgrims.

Six years earlier I had suffered pulmonary edema, an acute form of altitude sickness, at 16,500 feet in the vicinity of Everest base camp, so we were understandably concerned about what would happen at 18,000 feet. Moreover, the Himalayas were having their wettest spring in 20 years; hip-deep powder and ice had already driven us off one ridge. If we failed to cross the pass, I feared that the last half of our "once in a lifetime" trip would be ruined.

The night before we would try the pass, we camped at a hut at 14,500

4

feet. In the photos taken at that camp, my face appears wan. The last village we'd passed through was a sturdy two-day walk below us, and I was tired.

During the late afternoon, four backpackers from New Zealand joined us, and we spent most of the night awake, anticipating the climb. Below we could see the fires of two other parties, which turned out to be two Swiss couples and a Japanese hiking club.

To get over the steep part of the climb before the sun melted the steps cut in the ice, we departed at 3:30 A.M. The New Zealanders left first, followed by Stephen and myself, our porters and Sherpas, and then the Swiss. The Japanese lingered in their camp. The sky was clear, and we were confident that no spring storm would erupt that day to close the pass.

At 15,500 feet, it looked to me as if Stephen were shuffling and staggering a bit, which are symptoms of altitude sickness. (The initial stage of altitude sickness brings a headache and nausea. As the condition worsens, a climber may encounter difficult breathing, disorientation, aphasia, and paralysis.) I felt strong, my adrenaline was flowing, but I was very concerned about my ultimate ability to get across. A couple of our porters were also suffering from the height, and Pasang, our Sherpa sirdar (leader), was worried.

Just after daybreak, while we rested at 15,500 feet, one of the New Zealanders, who had gone ahead, came staggering down toward us with a body slung across his shoulders. He dumped the almost naked, barefoot body of an Indian holy man—a sadhu—at my feet. He had found the pilgrim lying on the ice, shivering and suffering from hypothermia. I cradled the sadhu's head and laid him out on the rocks. The New Zealander was angry. He wanted to get across the pass before the bright sun melted the snow. He said, "Look, I've done what I can. You have porters and Sherpa guides. You care for him. We're going on!" He turned and went back up the mountain to join his friends.

I took a carotid pulse and found that the sadhu was still alive. We figured he had probably visited the holy shrines at Muklinath and was on his way home. It was fruitless to question why he had chosen this desperately high route instead of the safe, heavily traveled caravan route through the Kali Gandaki gorge. Or why he was almost naked and with no shoes, or how long he had been lying in the pass. The answers weren't going to solve our problem.

Stephen and the four Swiss began stripping off outer clothing and opening their packs. The sadhu was soon clothed from head to foot. He was not able to walk, but he was very much alive. I looked down the mountain and spotted below the Japanese climbers marching up with a horse.

Without a great deal of thought, I told Stephen and Pasang that I was concerned about withstanding the heights to come and wanted to get over the pass. I took off after several of our porters who had gone ahead.

On the steep part of the ascent where, if the ice steps had given way, I would have slid down about 3,000 feet, I felt vertigo. I stopped for a breather, allowing the Swiss to catch up with me. I inquired about the sadhu and Stephen. They said that the sadhu was fine and that Stephen was just behind. I set off again for the summit.

Stephen arrived at the summit an hour after I did. Still exhilarated by victory, I ran down the snow slope to congratulate him. He was suffering from altitude sickness, walking 15 steps, then stopping, walking 15 steps, then stopping, Pasang accompanied him all the way up. When I reached them, Stephen glared at me and said: "How do you feel about contributing to the death of a fellow man?"

I did not fully comprehend what he meant.

"Is the sadhu dead?" I inquired.

"No," replied Stephen, "but he surely will be!"

After I had gone, and the Swiss had departed not long after, Stephen had remained with the sadhu. When the Japanese had arrived, Stephen had asked to use their horse to transport the sadhu down to the hut. They had refused. He had then asked Pasang to have a group of our porters carry the sadhu. Pasang had resisted the idea, saying that the porters would have to exert all their energy to get themselves over the pass. He had thought they could not carry a man down 1,000 feet to the hut, reclimb the slope, and get across safely before the snow melted. Pasang had pressed Stephen not to delay any longer.

The Sherpas had carried the sadhu down to a rock in the sun at about 15,000 feet and had pointed out the hut another 500 feet below. The Japanese had given him food and drink. When they had last seen him he was listlessly throwing rocks at the Japanese party's dog, which had frightened him.

We do not know if the sadhu lived or died.

For many of the following days and evenings Stephen and I discussed and debated our behavior toward the sadhu. Stephen is a committed Quaker with deep moral vision. He said, "I feel that what happened with the sadhu is a good example of the breakdown between the individual ethic and the corporate ethic. No one person was willing to assume ultimate responsibility for the sadhu. Each was willing to do his bit just so long as it was not too inconvenient. When it got to be a bother, everyone just passed the buck to someone else and took off. Jesus was relevant to a more individualistic stage of society, but how do we interpret his teaching today in a world filled with large, impersonal organizations and groups?"

I defended the larger group, saying, "Look, we all cared. We all stopped and gave aid and comfort. Everyone did his bit. The New Zealander carried him down below the snow line. I took his pulse and suggested we treat him for hypothermia. You and the Swiss gave him clothing and got him warmed up. The Japanese gave him food and water. The Sherpas carried him down to the sun and pointed out the easy trail toward the hut. He was well enough to throw rocks at a dog. What more could we do?"

"You have just described the typical affluent Westerner's response to a problem. Throwing money—in this case food and sweaters—at it, but not solving the fundamentals!" Stephen retorted.

"What would satisfy you?" I said. "Here we are, a group of New Zealanders, Swiss, Americans, and Japanese who have never met before and who are at the apex of one of the most powerful experiences of our lives. Some years the pass is so bad no one gets over it. What right does an almost naked pilgrim who chooses the wrong trail have to disrupt our lives? Even the Sherpas had no interest in risking the trip to help him beyond a certain point."

Stephen calmly rebutted, "I wonder what the Sherpas would have done if the sadhu had been a well-dressed Nepali, or what the Japanese would have done if the sadhu had been a well-dressed Asian, or what you would have done, Buzz, if the sadhu had been a well-dressed Western woman?"

"Where, in your opinion," I asked instead, "is the limit of our responsibility in a situation like this? We had our own well-being to worry about. Our Sherpa guides were unwilling to jeopardize us or the porters for the sadhu. No one else on the mountain was willing to commit himself beyond certain self-imposed limits."

Stephen said, "As individual Christians or people with a Western ethical tradition, we can fulfill our obligations in such a situation only if (1) the sadhu dies in our care, (2) the sadhu demonstrates to us that he could undertake the two-day walk down to the village, or (3) we carry the sadhu for two days down to the village and convince someone there to care for him."

"Leaving the sadhu in the sun with food and clothing, while he demonstrated hand-eye coordination by throwing a rock at a dog, comes close to fulfilling items one and two," I answered. "And it wouldn't have made sense to take him to the village where the people appeared to be far less caring than the Sherpas, so the third condition is impractical. Are you really saying that, no matter what the implications, we should, at the drop of a hat, have changed our entire plan?"

The Individual vs. the Group Ethic

Despite my arguments, I felt and continue to feel guilt about the sadhu. I had literally walked through a classic moral dilemma without fully thinking through the consequences. My excuses for my actions include a high adrenaline flow, a superordinate goal, and a once-in-a-lifetime opportunity—factors in the usual corporate situation, especially when one is under stress.

Real moral dilemmas are ambiguous, and many of us hike right through them, unaware that they exist. When, usually after the fact, someone makes an issue of them, we tend to resent his or her bringing it up. Often, when the full import of what we have done (or not done) falls on us, we dig into a defensive position from which it is very difficult to emerge. In rare circumstances we may contemplate what we have done from inside a prison.

Had we mountaineers been free of physical and mental stress caused by the effort and the high altitude, we might have treated the sadhu differently. Yet isn't stress the real test of personal and corporate values? The instant decisions executives make under pressure reveal the most about personal and corporate character.

Among the many questions that occur to me when pondering my experience are: What are the practical limits of moral imagination and vision? Is there a collective or institutional ethic beyond the ethics of the individual? At what level of effort or commitment can one discharge one's ethical responsibilities?

Not every ethical dilemma has a right solution. Reasonable people often disagree; otherwise there would be no dilemma. In a business context, however, it is essential that managers agree on a process for dealing with dilemmas.

The sadhu experience offers an interesting parallel to business situations. An immediate response was mandatory. Failure to act was a decision in itself. Up on the mountain we could not resign and submit our résumés to a headhunter. In contrast to philosophy, business involves action and implementation—getting things done. Managers must come up with answers to problems based on what they see and what they allow to influence their decision-making processes. On the mountain, none of us but Stephen realized the true dimensions of the situation we were facing.

One of our problems was that as a group we had no process for developing a consensus. We had no sense of purpose or plan. The difficulties of dealing with the sadhu were so complex that no one person could handle it. Because it did not have a set of preconditions that could guide its action to an acceptable resolution, the group reacted instinctively as individuals. The cross-cultural nature of the group added a further layer of complexity. We had no leader with whom we could all identify and in whose purpose we believed. Only Stephen was willing to take charge, but he could not gain adequate support to care for the sadhu.

Some organizations do have a value system that transcends the personal values of the managers. Such values, which go beyond profitability, are usually revealed when the organization is under stress. People throughout the organization generally accept its values, which, because they are not presented as a rigid list of commandments, may be somewhat ambiguous. The stories people tell, rather than printed materials, transmit these conceptions of what is proper behavior.

For 20 years I have been exposed at senior levels to a variety of corporations and organizations. It is amazing how quickly an outsider can sense the tone and style of an organization and the degree of tolerated openness and freedom to challenge management.

Organizations that do not have a heritage of mutually accepted, shared values tend to become unhinged during stress, with each individual bailing out for himself. In the great takeover battles we have witnessed during past years, companies that had strong cultures drew the wagons around them and fought it out, while other companies saw executives, supported by their golden parachutes, bail out of the struggles.

Because corporations and their members are interdependent, for the corporation to be strong the members need to share a preconceived notion of what is correct behavior, a "business ethic," and think of it as a positive force, not a constraint.

As an investment banker I am continually warned by well-meaning lawyers, clients, and associates to be wary of conflicts of interest. Yet if I were to run away from every difficult situation, I wouldn't be an effective investment banker. I have to feel my way through conflicts. An effective manager can't run from risk either; he or she has to confront and deal with risk. To feel "safe" in doing this, managers need the guidelines of an agreed-on process and set of values within the organization.

After my three months in Nepal, I spent three months as an executive-in-residence at both Stanford Business School and the Center for Ethics and Social Policy at the Graduate Theological Union at Berkeley. These six months away from my job gave me time to assimilate 20 years of business experience. My thoughts turned often to the meaning of the leadership role in any large organization. Students at the seminary thought of themselves as antibusiness. But when I questioned them they agreed that they distrusted all large organizations, including the church. They perceived all large organizations as impersonal and opposed to individual values and needs. Yet we all know of organizations where peoples' values and beliefs are respected and their expressions encouraged. What makes the difference? Can we identify the difference and, as a result, manage more effectively?

The word "ethics" turns off many and confuses more. Yet the notions of shared values and an agreed-on process for dealing with adversity and change—what many people mean when they talk about corporate culture—seem to be at the heart of the ethical issue. People who are in touch with their own core beliefs and the beliefs of others and are sustained by them can be more comfortable living on the cutting edge. At times, taking a tough line or a decisive stand in a muddle of ambiguity is the only ethical thing to do. If a manager is indecisive and spends time trying to figure out the "good" thing to do, the enterprise may be lost.

Business ethics, then, has to do with the authenticity and integrity of the enterprise. To be ethical is to follow the business as well as the cultural goals of the corporation, its owners, its employees, and its customers. Those who cannot serve the corporate vision are not authentic business people and, therefore, are not ethical in the business sense.

At this stage of my own business experience I have a strong interest in organizational behavior. Sociologists are keenly studying what they call corporate stories, legends, and heroes as a way organizations have of transmitting the value system. Corporations such as Arco have even hired consultants to perform an audit of their corporate culture. In a company, the leader is the person who understands, interprets, and manages the corporate value system. Effective managers are then action-oriented people who resolve conflict, are tolerant of ambiguity, stress, and change, and have a strong sense of purpose for themselves and their organizations.

If all this is true, I wonder about the role of the professional manager who moves from company to company. How can he or she quickly absorb the values and culture of different organizations? Or is there, indeed, an art of management that is totally transportable? Assuming such fungible managers do exist, is it proper for them to manipulate the values of others?

What would have happened had Stephen and I carried the sadhu for two days back to the village and become involved with the villagers in his care? In four trips to Nepal my most interesting experiences occurred in 1975 when I lived in a Sherpa home in the Khumbu for five days recovering from altitude sickness. The high point of Stephen's trip was an invitation to participate in a family funeral ceremony in Manang. Neither experience had to do with climbing the high passes of the Himalayas. Why were we so reluctant to try the lower path, the ambiguous trail? Perhaps because we did not have a leader who could reveal the greater purpose of the trip to us.

Why didn't Stephen with his moral vision opt to take the sadhu under his personal care? The answer is because, in part, Stephen was hard-stressed physically himself, and because, in part, without some support system that involved our involuntary and episodic community on the mountain, it was beyond his individual capacity to do so.

I see the current interest in corporate culture and corporate value systems as a positive response to Stephen's pessimism about the decline of the role of the individual in large organizations. Individuals who operate from a thoughtful set of personal values provide the foundation for a corporate culture. A corporate tradition that encourages freedom of inquiry, supports personal values, and reinforces a focused sense of direction can fulfill the need for individuality along with the prosperity and success of the group. Without such corporate support, the individual is lost.

That is the lesson of the sadhu. In a complex corporate situation, the individual requires and deserves the support of the group. If people cannot find such support from their organization, they don't know how to act. If such support is forthcoming, a person has a stake in the success of the group, and can add much to the process of establishing and maintaining a corporate culture. It is management's challenge to be sensitive to individual needs, to shape them, and to direct and focus them for the benefit of the group as a whole.

For each of us the sadhu lives. Should we stop what we are doing and comfort him; or should we keep trudging up toward the high pass? Should I pause to help the derelict I pass on the street each night as I walk by the Yale Club en route to Grand Central Station? Am I his brother? What is the nature of our responsibility if we consider ourselves to be ethical persons? Perhaps it is to change the values of the group so that it can, with all its resources, take the other road.

Part I

Problems in Business Ethics

Part I: Problems in Business Ethics

The problems in business ethics are both old and new. Problems of ethics are problems of the human condition and, as such, these problems are perennial. However, because of the unprecedented rate, complexity, and scope of radical change, new problems in the area of applied ethics abound. This section examines basic problems that must be faced by individuals and corporations in a diverse world of global economies. Specifically, Part I focuses on problems of social responsibility, economic justice, and cultural relativism.

According to Milton Friedman,

> There is only one social responsibility of business . . . to use its resources and engage in activities designed to increase its profits so long as it stays within the rules of the game, which is to say, engages in open and free competition without deception or fraud.

In a free-market economy, Friedman argued, the primary responsibility of those who run corporations is to make as much money as possible.

In "The Social Responsibility of Business Is to Increase Its Profits," Friedman invokes the law of agency that, in a general sense, specifies the legal duties of individuals to their principals. Roughly, an agent has an obligation to act solely for the benefit of the principal in all matters relating to his agency. Thus, a corporate executive has a duty to act on behalf of the stockholders in order to garner maximum profits. It is the political institution and not business that is responsible to foster "social" objectives.

Friedman's influential essay has presented a formidable challenge for proponents of corporate social responsibility. But, Friedman understood the corporation primarily as a legal entity. Is it not also a moral entity? Furthermore, legality is not morality. Although a fundamental principle of business ethics requires willing compliance with the law, ethics goes beyond the law. Moral individuals within and associated with corporations must be motivated to comply with ethical standards because they respect things that are right, rather than by fear of the law. What moral responsibilities might a corporation have that extend beyond the scope of its legal obligations? In addition to the stockholders of a corporation, what other stakeholders is a corporation morally responsible to?

In the "Stakeholder Theory of the Modern Corporation" R. Edward Freeman identifies other stakeholders to whom corporations have obligations. Freeman challenges the assumption of the primacy of the stockholder and seeks to transform our understanding of the modern corporation. He states, "My thesis is that I can revitalize the concept of managerial capitalism by replacing the notion that managers have the duty to stockholders with the concept that managers bear a fiduciary relationship to stakeholders." For Freeman the central question around which the true notion of the firm is to be reconceptualized is: "For whose benefit and at whose expense should the firm be managed?"

In "Capitalism" Tibor R. Machan and James E. Chesher present a discussion of the political/economic arrangement of human societies. The term "capitalism" they contend,

> refers to that feature of a human community whereby citizens are understood to have the basic right to make their own decisions concerning what they will do with their labor and property. Thus capitalism includes freedom of trade and contract, free movement of labor, and protection of property rights against both criminal and official intrusiveness.

Alternatives to capitalist societies, namely managed economies and market socialism, are also considered.

Supporters of capitalism highlight its role in the creation of wealth, and its contributions to human progress and political liberty. The capitalist system, it is believed, "rewards hard work, ingenuity, industry, entrepreneurship, and personal or individual responsibility, and this is all to the good."

In contrast, Karl Marx believed that capitalism leads inevitably to the immiseration of workers. Marxists criticize capitalism for destroying the intrinsic value of human labor. Workers are viewed, and thus treated, instrumentally as a means of production. In "Alienated Labor," Marx argues that workers should not be alienated from the value of their labor by capitalist systems of private ownership. Modern political (capitalist) economy results in four forms of alienation or estrangement. It alienates the laborer from the product of his/her labor; it alienates the laborer from his/her life (proper) activity and thus changes the entire act of production. Furthermore, it alienates the laborer from his species-life or essential being and it alienates people from each other.

In Marxist thought, and by extension socialist theories, priority is given to basic human needs such as the need for food, health care, and education. Marxist theories stress the distinction of social benefits and burdens by appealing to the criteria of need and ability. The Marxist principle of distributive justice states: "From each according to his abilities, to each according to his needs."

The problem of **Distributive Justice** asks how a society ought to allocate wealth, resources and benefits along with corresponding burdens and responsibilities. In other words, who should get what? How much should they get? And, why? Is there a just way to distribute the goods and materials of society? In "Distributive Justice," Joel Feinberg explains and analyzes five different principles that have been put forth as criteria to achieve justice in distribution. These principles are equality, need, merit, contribution, and effort. These principles are fundamental for assessing the ethical character of a particular economy.

In "Justice as Fairness," John Rawls presents an egalitarian theory of distributive justice. An egalitarian is one who embraces the principle of equality. Rawls articulates his guiding idea as follows:

> [T]he principles of justice for the basic structure of society are the objects of the original agreement. They are the principles that free and rational persons concerned to further their own interests would accept in an initial position of equality as defining the fundamental terms of their association. These principles are used to regulate all further agreements; they specify the kinds of social cooperation that can be entered into and the forms of government that can be established. This way of regarding the principles of justice I call justice as fairness.

Rawls' position is rooted in the choices that rational individuals would make in the hypothetical situation of equal liberty.

Rawls sets forth two basic principles of justice. The first is called the "Principle of Equal Liberty." This principle states: [E]ach person is to have an equal right to the most extensive basic liberty compatible with a similar liberty for others." The second principle is known as the "Difference Principle":

Social and economic inequalities are to be arranged so that they are both (a) reasonably expected to be everyone's advantage, and (b) attached to positions and offices open to all. . . .

He argues against utilitarianism because it sacrifices the welfare of some individuals for the public good.

Libertarian theories of justice emphasize individual rights and personal freedoms. Among the freedoms advocated by libertarians is the freedom to accumulate wealth. Their criteria for distributive justice emphasize merit and contribution; i.e., those who contribute the most to society should receive the greatest compensation.

In "The Entitlement Theory," Robert Nozick presents a popular libertarian theory. Nozick focuses on two principles: justice in acquisition and justice in transfer. Here is what Nozick says:

1. A person who acquires a holding in accordance with the principle of justice in acquisition is entitled to that holding.
2. A person who acquires a holding in accordance with the principle of justice in transfer, from someone else entitled to that holding, is entitled to that holding.
3. No one is entitled to a holding except by (repeated) applications of 1 and 2.

In other words, a distribution is just if everyone is entitled to the holdings they, in fact, have under the distribution. Nozick's theory is based upon historical principles of justice rather than the end-result, end-state, or time-slice principles of welfare economics.

International business has generated ethical controversy for centuries. Today, the world's major corporations are multinationals. Multinational corporations maintain operations in various "host" nations. Concerned business leaders, politicians, lawyers, ethicists, economists, and activists want to make international business better. In "Values in Tension: Ethics Away from Home," Thomas Donaldson presents the general views that govern current approaches to international business ethics and offers three guiding principles to help managers make distinctions "between practices that are merely different and those that are wrong." Donaldson asks, "How can companies answer the toughest question in global business ethics: what happens when a host country's ethical standards seem lower than the home country's?

One view of the international situation claims that no culture's ethics are better than any others. This view is generally known as cultural relativism but is also referred to as ethical or moral relativism or cultural particularism. Relativism is the view that there are many standards of morality—not just one. Hence, morality is culturally conditioned and varies from place to place, from society to society, and from historical time to historical time. However, Donaldson maintains that "cultural relativism is morally blind. There are fundamental values that cross cultures, and companies must uphold them."

At the opposite extreme is the view of ethical absolutism or cultural universalism. "Absolutism," says Donaldson, is "the theory behind ethical imperialism." Ethical imperialism directs individuals around the world to do exactly as they do at home. Donaldson critiques this view and shows why it is not adequate to serve as a global standard.

Between the extremes of relativism and absolutism Donaldson offers three guiding principles to balance the extreme positions: respect for core human values, respect for local traditions, and the belief that context matters when deciding moral issues.

The Social Responsibility of Business Is to Increase Its Profits

Milton Friedman

When I hear businessmen speak eloquently about the "social responsibilities of business in a free-enterprise system," I am reminded of the wonderful line about the Frenchman who discovered at the age of 70 that he had been speaking prose all his life. The businessmen believe that they are defending free enterprise when they declaim that business is not concerned "merely" with profit but also with promoting desirable "social" ends; that business has a "social conscience" and takes seriously its responsibilities for providing employment, eliminating discrimination, avoiding pollution and whatever else may be the catchwords of the contemporary crop of reformers. In fact they are—or would be if they or anyone else took them seriously—preaching pure and unadulterated socialism. Businessmen who talk this way are unwitting puppets of the intellectual forces that have been undermining the basis of a free society these past decades.

The discussion of the "social responsibilities of business" are notable for their analytical looseness and lack of rigor. What does it mean to say that "business" has responsibilities? Only people can have responsibilities. A corporation is an artificial person and in this sense may have artificial responsibilities, but "business" as a whole cannot be said to have responsibilities, even in this vague sense. The first step toward clarity to examining the doctrine of the social responsibility of business is to ask precisely what it implies for whom.

Presumably, the individuals who are to be responsible are businessmen, which means individual proprietors or corporate executives. Most of the discussion of social responsibility is directed at corporations, so in what follows I shall mostly neglect the individual proprietors and speak of corporate executives.

In a free-enterprise, private-property system, a corporate executive is an employee of the owners of the business. He has direct responsibility to his employers. That responsibility is to conduct the business in accordance with their desires, which generally will be to make as much money as possible while conforming to the basic rules of the society, both those embodied in law and those embodied in ethical custom. Of course, in some cases his employers may have a different objective. A group of persons might establish a corporation for an eleemosynary purpose—for example, a hospital or a school. The manager of such a corporation will not have money profit as his objectives but the rendering of certain services.

In either case, the key point is that, in his capacity as a corporate executive, the manager is the agent of the individuals who own the corporation or establish the eleemosynary institution, and his primary responsibility is to them.

Needless to say, this does not mean that it is easy to judge how well he is performing his task. But at least the criterion of performance is straightforward, and the persons among whom a voluntary contractual arrangement exists are clearly defined.

Of course, the corporate executive is also a person in his own right. As a person, he may have many other responsibilities that he recognizes or assumes voluntarily—to his family, his conscience, his feelings of charity, his church, his clubs, his city, his country. He may feel impelled by these responsibilities to devote part of his income to causes he regards as worthy, to refuse to work for particular corporations, even to leave his job, for example, to join his country's armed forces. If we wish, we may refer to some of these responsibilities as "social responsibilities." But in these respects he is acting as a principal, not an agent; he is spending his own money or time or energy, not the money of his employers or the time or energy he has contracted to devote to their purposes. If these are "social responsibilities," they are the social responsibilities of individuals, not of business.

What does it mean to say that the corporate executive has a "social responsibility" in his capacity as businessman? If this statement is not pure rhetoric, it must mean that he is to act in some way that is not in the interest of his employers. For example, that he is to refrain from increasing the price of the product in order to contribute to the social objective of preventing inflation, even though a price increase would be in the best interests of the corporation. Or that he is to make expenditures on reducing pollution beyond the amount that is in the best interests of the corporation or that is required by law in order to contribute to the social objective of improving the environment. Or that, at the expense of corporate profits, he is to hire "hardcore" unemployed instead of better qualified available workmen to contribute to the social objective of reducing poverty.

In each of these cases, the corporate executive would be spending someone else's money for a general social interest. Insofar as his actions in accord with his "social responsibility" reduce returns to stockholders, he is spending their money. Insofar as his actions raise the price to customers, he is spending the customers' money. Insofar as his actions lower the wages of some employees, he is spending their money.

The stockholders or the customers or the employees could separately spend their own money on the particular action if they wished to do so. The executive is exercising a distinct "social responsibility," rather than serving as an agent of the stockholders or the customers or the employees, only if he spends the money in a different way than they would have spent it.

But if he does this, he is in effect imposing taxes, on the one hand, and deciding how the tax proceeds shall be spent, on the other.

This process raises political questions on two levels: principle and consequences. On the level of political principle, the imposition of taxes and the expenditure of tax proceeds are governmental functions. We have established elaborate constitutional, parliamentary and judicial provisions to control these functions, to assure that taxes are imposed so far as possible in accordance with the preferences and desires of the public—after all, "taxation without representation" was one of the battle cries of the American Revolution. We have a system of checks and balances to separate the legislative function of imposing taxes and enacting expenditures from the executive function of collecting taxes and administering expenditure programs and from the judicial function of mediating disputes and interpreting the law.

Here the businessman—self-selected or appointed directly or indirectly by stockholders—is to be simultaneously legislator, executive and jurist. He is to decide whom to tax by how much and for what purpose, and he is to spend the proceeds—all this guided only by general exhortations from on high to restrain inflation, improve the environment, fight poverty and so on and on.

The whole justification for permitting the corporate executive to be selected by the stockholders is that the executive is an agent serving the interests of his principal. This justification disappears when the corporate executive imposes taxes and spends the proceeds for "social" purposes. He becomes in effect a public employee, a civil servant, even though he remains in name an employee of a private enterprise. On grounds of political principle, it is intolerable that such civil servants—insofar as their actions in the name of social responsibility are real and not just window dressing—should be selected as they are now. If they are to be civil servants, then they must be elected through a political process. If they are to impose taxes and make expenditures to foster "social" objectives, then political machinery must be set up to make the assessment of taxes and to determine through a political process the objectives to be served.

This is the basic reason why the doctrine of "social responsibility" involves the acceptance of the socialist view that political mechanisms, not market mechanisms, are the appropriate way to determine the allocation of scarce resources to alternative uses.

On the grounds of consequences, can the corporate executive in fact discharge his alleged "social responsibilities"? On the one hand, suppose he could get away with spending the stockholders' or customers' or employees' money. How is he to know how to spend it? He is told that he must contribute to fighting inflation. How is he to know what action of his will contribute to that end? He is presumably an expert in running his company—in producing a product or selling it or financing it. But nothing about his selection makes him an expert on inflation. Will his holding down the price of his product reduce inflationary pressure? Or, by leaving more spending power in the hands of his customers, simply divert it elsewhere? Or, by forcing him to produce less because of the lower price, will it simply contribute to shortages? Even if he could answer these questions, how much cost is he justified in imposing on his stockholders, customers and employees for this social purpose? What is his appropriate share and what is the appropriate share of others?

And, whether he wants to or not, can he get away with spending his stockholders', customers' or employees' money? Will not the stockholders fire him? (Either the present ones or those who take over when his actions in the name of social responsibility have reduced the corporation's profits and the price of its stock.) His customers and his employees can desert him for other producers and employers less scrupulous in exercising their social responsibilities.

This facet of "social responsibility" doctrine is brought into sharp relief when the doctrine is used to justify wage restraint by trade unions. The conflict of interest is naked and clear when union officials are asked to subordinate the interest of their members to some more general purpose. If union officials try to enforce wage restraint, the consequence is likely to be wildcat strikes, rank-and-file revolts and the emergence of strong competitors for their jobs. We thus have the ironic phenomenon that union leaders—at least in the U.S.—have objected to Government interference with the market far more consistently and courageously than have business leaders.

The difficulty of exercising "social responsibility" illustrates, of course, the great virtue of private competitive enterprise—it forces people to be responsible for their own actions and makes it difficult for them to "exploit" other people for either selfish or unselfish purposes. They can do good—but only at their own expense.

Many a reader who has followed the argument this far may be tempted to remonstrate that it is all well and good to speak of Government's having the responsibility to impose taxes and determine expenditures for such "social" purposes as controlling pollution or training the hard-core unemployed, but that the problems are too urgent to wait on the slow course of political processes, that the exercise of social responsibility by businessmen is a quicker and surer way to solve pressing current problems.

Aside from the question of fact—I share Adam Smith's skepticism about the benefits that can be expected from "those who affect to trade for the public good"—this argument must be rejected on the grounds of principle. What it amounts to is an assertion that those who favor the taxes and expenditures in question have failed to persuade a majority of their fellow citizens to be of like mind and that they are seeking to attain by undemocratic procedures what they cannot attain by democratic procedures. In a free society it is hard for "evil" people to do "evil," especially since one man's good is another's evil.

I have, for simplicity, concentrated on the special case of the corporate executive, except only for the brief digression on trade unions. But precisely the same argument applies to the newer phenomenon of calling upon stockholders to require corporations to exercise social responsibility (the recent G.M. crusade for example). In most of these cases, what is in effect involved is some stockholders trying to get other stockholders (or customers or employees) to contribute against their will to "social" causes favored by the activists. Insofar as they succeed, they are again imposing taxes and spending the proceeds.

The situation of the individual proprietor is somewhat different. If he acts to reduce the returns of his enterprise in order to exercise his "social responsibility," he is spending his own money, not someone else's. If he wishes to spend his money on such purposes, that is his right, and I cannot see that there is any objection to his doing so. In the process, he, too, may impose costs on employees and customers. However, because he is far less likely than a large corporation or union to have monopolistic power, any such side effects will tend to be minor.

Of course, in practice the doctrine of social responsibility is frequently a cloak for actions that are justified on other grounds rather than a reason for those actions.

To illustrate, it may well be in the long-run interest of a corporation that is a major employer in a small community to devote resources to providing amenities to that community or to improving its government. That may make it easier to attract desirable employees, it may reduce the wage bill or lessen losses from pilferage and sabotage or have other worthwhile effects. Or it may be that, given the laws about the deductibility of corporate charitable contributions, the stockholders can contribute more to charities they favor by having the corporation make the gift than by doing it themselves, since they can in that way contribute an amount that would otherwise have been paid as corporate taxes.

In each of these—and many similar—cases, there is a strong temptation to rationalize these actions as an exercise of "social responsibility." In the present climate of opinion, with its widespread aversion to "capitalism," "profits," and the "soulless corporation" and so on, this is one way for a corporation to generate goodwill as a by-product of expenditures that are entirely justified in its own self-interest.

It would be inconsistent of me to call on corporate executives to refrain from this hypocritical window-dressing because it harms the foundations of a free society. That would be to call on them to exercise a "social responsibility"! If our institutions, and the attitudes of the public make it in their self-interest to cloak their actions in this way, I cannot summon much indignation to renounce them. At the same time, I can express admiration for those individual proprietors or owners of closely held corporations or stockholders of more broadly held corporations who disdain such tactics as approaching fraud.

Whether blameworthy or not, the use of the cloak of social responsibility, and the nonsense spoken in its name by influential and prestigious businessmen, does clearly harm the foundations of a free society. I have been impressed time and again by the schizophrenic character of many businessmen. They are capable of being extremely far-sighted and clearheaded in matters that are internal to their businesses. They are incredibly shortsighted and muddle-headed in matters that are outside their businesses but affect the possible survival of business in general. This shortsightedness is strikingly exemplified in the calls from many businessmen for wage and price guidelines or controls or income policies. There is nothing that could do more in a brief period to destroy a market system and replace it by a centrally controlled system than effective governmental control of prices and wages.

The short-sightedness is also exemplified in speeches by businessmen on social responsibility. This may gain them kudos in the short run. But it helps to strengthen the already too prevalent view that the pursuit of profits is wicked and immoral and must be curbed and controlled by external forces. Once this view is adopted, the external forces that curb the market will not be the social consciences, however highly developed, of the pontificating executives; it will be the iron fist of Government bureaucrats. Here, as with price and wage controls, businessmen seem to me to reveal a suicidal impulse.

The political principle that underlies the market mechanism is unanimity. In an ideal free market resting on private property, no individual can coerce any other, all cooperation is voluntary, all parties to such cooperation benefit or they need not participate. There are no values, no "social" responsibilities in any sense other than the shared values and responsibilities of individuals. Society is a collection of individuals and of the various groups they voluntarily form.

The political principle that underlies the political mechanism is conformity. The individual must serve a more general social interest—whether that be determined by a church or a dictator or a majority. The individual may have a vote and say in what is to be done, but if he is overruled, he must conform. It is appropriate for some to require others to contribute to a general social purpose whether they wish to or not.

Unfortunately, unanimity is not always feasible. There are some respects in which conformity appears unavoidable, so I do not see how one can avoid the use of the political mechanism altogether.

But the doctrine of "social responsibility" taken seriously would extend the scope of the political mechanism to every human activity. It does not differ in philosophy from the most explicitly collectivist doctrine. It differs only by professing to believe that collectivist ends can be attained without collectivist means. That is why, in my book *Capitalism and Freedom*, I have called it a "fundamentally subversive doctrine" in a free society, and I have said that in such a society, "there is one and only one social responsibility of business—to use its resources and engage in activities designed to increase its profits so long as it stays within the rules of the game, which is to say, engages in open and free competition without deception or fraud."

Stakeholder Theory
of the Modern Corporation

R. Edward Freeman

INTRODUCTION

> Corporations have ceased to be merely legal devices through which the private business transactions of individuals may be carried on. Though still much used for this purpose, the corporate form has acquired a larger significance. The corporation has, in fact, become both a method of property tenure and a means of organizing economic life. Grown to tremendous proportions, there may be said to have evolved a "corporate system"—which has attracted to itself a combination of attributes and powers, and has attained a degree of prominence entitling it to be dealt with as a major social institution.[1]

Despite these prophetic words of Berle and Means (1932), scholars and managers alike continue to hold sacred the view that managers bear a special relationship to the stockholders in the firm. Since stockholders own shares in the firm, they have certain rights and privileges, which must be granted to them by management, as well as by others. Sanctions, in the form of "the law of corporations," and other protective mechanisms in the form of social custom, accepted management practice, myth, and ritual, are thought to reinforce the assumption of the primacy of the stockholder.

The purpose of this article is to pose several challenges to this assumption, from within the framework of managerial capitalism, and to suggest the bare bones of an alternative theory, *a stakeholder theory of the modern corporation*. I do not seek the demise of the modern corporation, either intellectually or in fact. Rather, I seek its transformation. In the words of Neurath, we shall attempt to "rebuild the ship, plank by plank, while it remains afloat."[2]

My thesis is that I can revitalize the concept of managerial capitalism by replacing the notion that managers have a duty to stockholders with the concept that managers bear a fiduciary relationship to stakeholders. Stakeholders are those groups who have a stake in or claim on the firm. Specifically I include suppliers, customers, employees, stockholders, and the local community, as well as management in its role as agent for these groups. I argue that the legal, economic, political, and moral challenges to the currently received theory of the firm, as a nexus of contracts among the owners of the factors of production and customers, require us to revise this concept. That is, each of these stakeholder groups has a right not to be treated as a means to some end, and therefore must participate in determining the future direction of the firm in which they have a stake.

25

The crux of my argument is that we must reconceptualize the firm around the following question: For whose benefit and at whose expense should the firm be managed? I shall set forth such a reconceptualization in the form of a *stakeholder theory of the firm*. I shall then critically examine the stakeholder view and its implication for the future of the capitalist system.

THE ATTACK ON MANAGERIAL CAPITALISM

The Legal Argument

The basic idea of managerial capitalism is that in return for controlling the firm, management vigorously pursues the interests of stockholders. Central to the managerial view of the firm is the idea that management can pursue market transactions with suppliers and customers in an unconstrained manner.

The law of corporations gives a less clearcut answer to the question: In whose interest and for whose benefit should the modern corporation be governed? While it says that the corporation should be run primarily in the interests of the stockholders in the firm, it says further that the corporation exists "in contemplation of the law" and has personality as a "legal person," limited liability for its actions, and immortality, since its existence transcends that of its members. Therefore, directors and other officers of the firm have a fiduciary obligation to stockholders in the sense that the "affairs of the corporation" must be conducted in the interest of the stockholders. And stockholders can theoretically bring suit against those directors and managers for doing otherwise. But since the corporation is a legal person, existing in contemplation of the law, managers of the corporation are constrained by law.

Until recently, this was no constraint at all. In this century, however, the law has evolved to effectively constrain the pursuit of stockholder interests at the expense of other claimants on the firm. It has, in effect, required that the claims of customers, suppliers, local communities, and employees be taken into consideration, though in general they are subordinated to the claims of stockholders.

For instance, the doctrine of "privity of contract," as articulated in *Winterbottom v. Wright* in 1842, has been eroded by recent developments in products liability law. Indeed, *Greenman v. Yuba Power* gives the manufacturer strict liability for damage caused by its products, even though the seller has exercised all possible care in the preparation and sale of the product and the consumer has not bought the product from nor entered into any contractual arrangement with the manufacturer. Caveat emptor has been replaced, in large part, with caveat venditor.[3] The Consumer Product Safety Commission has the power to enact product recalls, and in 1980 one U.S. automobile company recalled more cars than it built. Some industries are required to provide information to customers about a product's ingredients, whether or not the customers want and are willing to pay for this information.[4]

The same argument is applicable to management's dealings with employees. The National Labor Relations Act gave employees the right to unionize and to bargain in good faith. It set up the National Labor Relations Board to enforce these rights with management. The Equal Pay Act of 1963 and Title VII of the Civil Rights Act of 1964 constrain management from discrimination in hiring practices; these have been followed with the Age Discrimination in Employment Act of 1967.[5] The emergence of a body of administrative case law arising from labor-management disputes and the historic settling of discrimination claims with large employers such as AT&T have caused the emergence of a body of practice in the corporation that is consistent with the legal guarantee of the rights of the employees. The law has protected the due process rights of those employees who enter into collective bargaining agreements with management. As of the present, however, only 30 percent of the labor force are participating in such agreements; this has prompted one labor law scholar to propose a statutory law prohibiting dismissals of the 70 percent of the work force not protected.[6]

The law has also protected the interests of local communities. The Clean Air Act and Clean Water Act have constrained management from "spoiling the commons." In an historic case, *Marsh v. Alabama*, the Supreme Court ruled that a company-owned town was subject to the provisions of the U.S. Constitution, thereby guaranteeing the rights of local citizens and negating the "property rights" of the firm. Some states and municipalities have gone further and passed laws preventing firms from moving plants or limiting when and how plants can be closed. In sum, there is much current legal activity in this area to constrain management's pursuit of stockholders' interests at the expense of the local communities in which the firm operates.

I have argued that the result of such changes in the legal system can be viewed as giving some rights to those groups that have a claim on the firm, for example, customers, suppliers, employees, local communities, stockholders, and management. It raises the question, at the core of a theory of the firm: In whose interest and for whose benefit should the firm be managed? The answer proposed by managerial capitalism is clearly "the stockholders," but I have argued that the law has been progressively circumscribing this answer.

The Economic Argument

In its pure ideological form managerial capitalism seeks to maximize the interests of stockholders. In its perennial criticism of government regulation, management espouses the "invisible hand" doctrine. It contends that it creates the greatest good for the greatest number, and therefore government need not intervene. However, we know that externalities, moral hazards, and monopoly power exist in fact, whether or not they exist in theory.

Further, some of the legal apparatus mentioned above has evolved to deal with just these issues.

The problem of the "tragedy of the commons" or the free-rider problem pervades the concept of public goods such as water and air. No one has an incentive to incur the cost of clean-up or the cost of nonpollution, since the marginal gain of one firm's action is small. Every firm reasons this way, and the result is pollution of water and air. Since the industrial revolution, firms have sought to internalize the benefits and externalize the costs of their actions. The cost must be borne by all, through taxation and regulation; hence we have the emergence of the environmental regulations of the 1970s.

Similarly, moral hazards arise when the purchaser of a good or service can pass along the cost of that good. There is no incentive to economize, on the part of either the producer or the consumer, and there is excessive use of the resources involved. The institutionalized practice of third-party payment in health care is a prime example.

Finally, we see the avoidance of competitive behavior on the part of firms, each seeking to monopolize a small portion of the market and not compete with one another. In a number of industries, oligopolies have emerged, and while there is questionable evidence that oligopolies are not the most efficient corporate form in some industries, suffice it to say that the potential for abuse of market power has again led to regulation of managerial activity. In the classic case, AT&T, arguably one of the great technological and managerial achievements of the century, was broken up into eight separate companies to prevent its abuse of monopoly power.

Externalities, moral hazards, and monopoly power have led to more external control on managerial capitalism. There are de facto constraints, due to these economic facts of life, on the ability of management to act in the interests of stockholders.

A STAKEHOLDER THEORY OF THE FIRM

The Stakeholder Concept

Corporations have stakeholders, that is, groups and individuals who benefit from or are harmed by, and whose rights are violated or respected by, corporate actions. The concept of stakeholders is a generalization of the notion of stockholders, who themselves have some special claim on the firm. Just as stockholders have a right to demand certain actions by management, so do other stakeholders have a right to make claims. The exact nature of these claims is a difficult question that I shall address, but the logic is identical to that of the stockholder theory. Stakes require action of a certain sort, and conflicting stakes require methods of resolution.

Freeman and Reed (1983)[7] distinguish two senses of *stakeholder*. The "narrow definition" includes those groups who are vital to the survival and success of the corporation. The "wide-definition" includes any group or individual who can affect or is affected by the corporation. I shall begin with a modest aim: to articulate a stakeholder theory using the narrow definition.

Stakeholders in the Modern Corporation

Figure 1 depicts the stakeholders in a typical large corporation. The stakes of each are reciprocal, since each can affect the other in terms of harms and benefits as well as rights and duties. The stakes of each are not univocal and would vary by particular corporation. I merely set forth some general notions that seem to be common to many large firms.

Owners have financial stake in the corporation in the form of stocks, bonds, and so on, and they expect some kind of financial return from them. Either they have given money directly to the firm, or they have some historical claim made through a series of morally justified exchanges. The firm affects their livelihood or, if a substantial portion of their retirement income is in stocks or bonds, their ability to care for themselves when they can no longer work. Of course, the stakes of owners will differ by type of owner, preferences for money, moral preferences, and so on, as well as by type of firm. The owners of AT&T are quite different from the owners of Ford Motor Company, with stock of the former company being widely dispersed among 3 million stockholders and that of the latter being held by a small family group as well as by a large group of public stockholders.

Employees have their jobs and usually their livelihood at stake; they often have specialized skills for which there is usually no perfectly elastic market. In return for their labor, they expect security, wages, benefits, and meaningful work. In return for their loyalty, the corporation is expected to provide for them and carry them through difficult times. Employees are expected to follow the instructions of management most of the time, to speak favorably about the company, and to be responsible citizens in the local communities in which the company operates. Where they are used as means to an end, they must participate in decisions affecting such use. The evidence that such policies and values as described here lead to productive company-employee relationships is compelling. It is equally compelling to realize that the opportunities for "bad faith" on the part of both management and employees are enormous. "Mock participation" in quality circles,

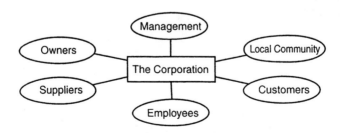

FIGURE 1. A Stakeholder Model of the Corporation.

singing the company song, and wearing the company uniform solely to please management all lead to distrust and unproductive work.

Suppliers, interpreted in a stakeholder sense, are vital to the success of the firm, for raw materials will determine the final product's quality and price. In turn the firm is a customer of the supplier and is therefore vital to the success and survival of the supplier. When the firm treats the supplier as a valued member of the stakeholder network, rather than simply as a source of materials, the supplier will respond when the firm is in need. Chrysler traditionally had very close ties to its suppliers, even to the extent that led some to suspect the transfer of illegal payments. And when Chrysler was on the brink of disaster, the suppliers responded with price cuts, accepting late payments, financing, and so on. Supplier and company can rise and fall together. Of course, again, the particular supplier relationships will depend on a number of variables such as the number of suppliers and whether the supplies are finished goods or raw materials.

Customers exchange resources for the products of the firm and in return receive the benefits of the products. Customers provide the lifeblood of the firm in the form of revenue. Given the level of reinvestment of earnings in large corporations, customers indirectly pay for the development of new products and services. Peters and Waterman (1982)[8] have argued that being close to the customer leads to success with other stakeholders and that a distinguishing characteristic of some companies that have performed well is their emphasis on the customer. By paying attention to customers' needs, management automatically addresses the needs of suppliers and owners. Moreover, it seems that the ethic of customer service carries over to the community. Almost without fail the "excellent companies" in Peters and Waterman's study have good reputations in the community. I would argue that Peters and Waterman have found multiple applications of Kant's dictum, "Treat persons as ends unto themselves," and it should come as no surprise that persons respond to such respectful treatment, be they customers, suppliers, owners, employees, or members of the local community. The real surprise is the novelty of the application of Kant's rule in a theory of good management practice.

The local community grants the firm the right to build facilities and, in turn, it benefits from the tax base and economic and social contributions of the firm. In return for the provision of local services, the firm is expected to be a good citizen, as is any person, either "natural or artificial." The firm cannot expose the community to unreasonable hazards in the form of pollution, toxic waste, and so on. If for some reason the firm must leave a community, it is expected to work with local leaders to make the transition as smoothly as possible. Of course, the firm does not have perfect knowledge, but when it discovers some danger or runs afoul of new competition, it is expected to inform the local community and to work with the community to overcome any problem. When the firm mismanages its relationship with the local community, it is in the same position as a citizen who commits a crime. It has violated the implicit social contract with the community and should expect to be distrusted and ostracized. It should not be surprised when punitive measures are invoked.

I have not included "competitors" as stakeholders in the narrow sense, since strictly speaking they are not necessary for the survival and success of the firm; the stakeholder theory works equally well in monopoly contexts. However, competitors and government would be the first to be included in an extension of this basic theory. It is simply not true that the interests of competitors in an industry are always in conflict. There is no reason why trade associations and other multi-organizational groups cannot band together to solve common problems that have little to do with how to restrain trade. Implementation of stakeholder management principles, in the long run, mitigates the need for industrial policy and an increasing role for government intervention and regulation.

The Role of Management

Management plays a special role, for it too has a stake in the modern corporation. On the one hand, management's stake is like that of employees, with some kind of explicit or implicit employment contract. But, on the other hand, management has a duty of safeguarding the welfare of the abstract entity that is the corporation. In short, management, especially top management, must look after the health of the corporation, and this involves balancing the multiple claims of conflicting stakeholders. Owners want higher financial returns, while customers want more money spent on research and development. Employees want higher wages and better benefits, while the local community wants better parks and day-care facilities.

The task of management in today's corporation is akin to that of King Solomon. The stakeholder theory does not give primacy to one stakeholder group over another, though there will surely be times when one group will benefit at the expense of others. In general, however, management must keep the relationships among stakeholders in balance. When these relationships become imbalanced, the survival of the firm is in jeopardy.

When wages are too high and product quality is too low, customers leave, suppliers suffer, and owners sell their stocks and bonds, depressing the stock price and making it difficult to raise new capital at favorable rates. Note, however, that the reason for paying returns to owners is not that they "own" the firm, but that their support is necessary for the survival of the firm, and that they have a legitimate claim on the firm. Similar reasoning applies in turn to each stakeholder group.

A stakeholder theory of the firm must redefine the purpose of the firm. The stockholder theory claims that the purpose of the firm is to maximize the welfare of the stockholders, perhaps subject to some moral or social constraints, either because such maximization leads to the greatest good or because of property rights. The purpose of the firm is quite different in my view.

"The stakeholder theory" can be unpacked into a number of stakeholder theories, each of which has a "normative core," inextricably linked

31

to the way that corporations should be governed and the way that managers should act. So, attempts to more fully define, or more carefully define, a stakeholder theory are misguided. Following Donaldson and Preston, I want to insist that the normative, descriptive, instrumental, and metaphorical (my addition to their framework) uses of 'stakeholder' are tied together in particular political constructions to yield a number of possible "stakeholder theories." "Stakeholder theory" is thus a genre of stories about how we could live. Let me be more specific.

A "normative core" of a theory is a set of sentences that includes among others, sentences like:

(1) Corporations ought to be governed . . .
(2) Managers ought to act to . . .

where we need arguments or further narratives which include business and moral terms to fill in the blanks. This normative core is not always reducible to a fundamental ground like the theory of property, but certain normative cores are consistent with modern understandings of property. Certain elaborations of the theory of private property plus the other institutions of political liberalism give rise to particular normative cores. But there are other institutions, other political conceptions of how society ought to be structured, so that there are different possible normative cores.

So, one normative core of a stakeholder theory might be a feminist standpoint one, rethinking how we would restructure "value-creating activity" along principles of caring and connection.[9] Another would be an ecological (or several ecological) normative cores. Mark Starik has argued that the very idea of a stakeholder theory of the *firm* ignores certain ecological necessities.[10] Exhibit 1 is suggestive of how these theories could be developed.

In the next section I shall sketch the normative core based on pragmatic liberalism. But, any normative core must address the questions in columns A or B, or explain why these questions may be irrelevant, as in the ecological view. In addition, each "theory," and I use the word hesitantly, must place the normative core within a more full-fledged account of how we could understand value-creating activity differently (column C). The only way to get on with this task is to see the stakeholder idea as a metaphor. The attempt to prescribe one and only one "normative core" and construct "a stakeholder theory" is at best a disguised attempt to smuggle a normative core past the unsophisticated noses of other unsuspecting academics who are just happy to see the end of the stockholder orthodoxy.

If we begin with the view that we can understand value-creation activity as a contractual process among those parties affected, and if for simplicity's sake we initially designate those parties as financiers, customers, suppliers, employees, and communities, then we can construct a normative core that reflects the liberal notions of autonomy, solidarity, and fairness as articulated by John Rawls, Richard Rorty, and others.[11] Notice that building these moral notions into the foundations of how we understand value creation and contracting requires that we eschew separating the "business" part of the

EXHIBIT 1. A Reasonable Pluralism

	A. Corporations ought to be governed . . .	**B.** Managers ought to act . . .	**C.** The background disciplines of "value creation" are . . .
Doctrine of Fair Contracts	. . . in accordance with the six principles.	. . . in the interests of stakeholders.	—business theories —theories that explain stakeholder behavior
Feminist Standpoint Theory	. . . in accordance with the principles of caring/connection and relationships.	. . . to maintain and care for relationships and networks of stakeholders.	—business theories —feminist theory —social science understanding of networks
Ecological Principles	. . . in accordance with the principle of caring for the earth.	. . . to care for the earth.	—business theories —ecology —other

process from the "ethical" part, and that we start with the presumption of equality among the contractors, rather than the presumption in favor of financier rights.

The normative core for this redesigned contractual theory will capture the liberal idea of fairness if it ensures a basic equality among stakeholders in terms of their moral rights as these are realized in the firm, and if it recognizes that inequalities among stakeholders are justified if they raise the level of the least well-off stakeholder. The liberal ideal of autonomy is captured by the realization that each stakeholder must be free to enter agreements that create value for themselves, and solidarity is realized by the recognition of the mutuality of stakeholder interests.

One way to understand fairness in this context is to claim *à la* Rawls that a contract is fair if parties to the contract would agree to it in ignorance of their actual stakes. Thus, a contract is like a fair bet, if each party is willing to turn the tables and accept the other side. What would a fair contract among corporate stakeholders look like? If we can articulate this ideal, a sort of corporate constitution, we could then ask whether actual corporations measure up to this standard, and we also begin to design corporate structures which are consistent with this Doctrine of Fair Contracts.

Imagine if you will, representative stakeholders trying to decide on "the rules of the game." Each is rational in a straightforward sense, looking out for its own self-interest. At least *ex ante*, stakeholders are the relevant parties since they will be materially affected. Stakeholders know how economic activity is organized and could be organized. They know general facts about the way the corporate world works. They know that in the real world there are or could be transaction costs, externalities, and positive costs of contracting. Suppose they are uncertain about what other social institutions exist, but they know the range of those institutions. They do not know if

33

government exists to pick up the tab for any externalities, or if they will exist in the nightwatchman state of libertarian theory. They know success and failure stories of businesses around the world. In short, they are behind a Rawls-like veil of ignorance, and they do not know what stake each will have when the veil is lifted. What groundrules would they choose to guide them?

The first groundrule is "The Principle of Entry and Exit." Any contract that is the corporation must have clearly defined entry, exit, and renegotiation conditions, or at least it must have methods or processes for so defining these conditions. The logic is straightforward: each stakeholder must be able to determine when an agreement exists and has a chance of fulfillment. This is not to imply that contracts cannot contain contingent claims or other methods for resolving uncertainty, but rather that it must contain methods for determining whether or not it is valid.

The second groundrule I shall call "The Principle of Governance," and it says that the procedure for changing the rules of the game must be agreed upon by unanimous consent. Think about the consequences of a majority of stakeholders systematically "selling out" a minority. Each stakeholder, in ignorance of its actual role, would seek to avoid such a situation. In reality this principle translates into each stakeholder never giving up its right to participate in the governance of the corporation, or perhaps into the existence of stakeholder governing boards.

The third groundrule I shall call "The Principle of Externalities," and it says that if a contract between A and B imposes a cost on C, then C has the option to become a party to the contract, and the terms are renegotiated. Once again the rationality of this condition is clear. Each stakeholder will want insurance that it does not become C.

The fourth groundrule is "The Principle of Contracting Costs," and it says that all parties to the contract must share in the cost of contracting. Once again the logic is straightforward. Any one stakeholder can get stuck.

A fifth groundrule is "The Agency Principle" that says that any agent must serve the interests of all stakeholders. It must adjudicate conflicts within the bounds of the other principals. Once again the logic is clear. Agents for any one group would have a privileged place.

A sixth and final groundrule we might call "The Principle of Limited Immortality." The corporation shall be managed as if it can continue to serve the interests of stakeholders through time. Stakeholders are uncertain about the future but, subject to exit conditions, they realize that the continued existence of the corporation is in their interest. Therefore, it would be rational to hire managers who are fiduciaries to their interest and the interest of the collective. If it turns out the "collective interest" is the empty set, then this principle simply collapses into the Agency Principle.

Thus, the Doctrine of Fair Contracts consists of these six groundrules or principles:

(1) The Principle of Entry and Exit
(2) The Principle of Governance
(3) The Principle of Externalities
(4) The Principle of Contracting Costs
(5) The Agency Principle
(6) The Principle of Limited Immortality

Think of these groundrules as a doctrine which would guide actual stakeholders in devising a corporate constitution or charter. Think of management as having the duty to act in accordance with some specific constitution or charter.

Obviously, if the Doctrine of Fair Contracts and its accompanying background narratives are to effect real change, there must be requisite changes in the enabling laws of the land. I propose the following three principles to serve as constitutive elements of attempts to reform the law of corporations.

The Stakeholder Enabling Principle

Corporations shall be managed in the interests of its stakeholders, defined as employees, financiers, customers, employees, and communities.

The Principle of Director Responsibility

Directors of the corporation shall have a duty of care to use reasonable judgment to define and direct the affairs of the corporation in accordance with the Stakeholder Enabling Principle.

The Principle of Stakeholder Recourse

Stakeholders may bring an action against the directors for failure to perform the required duty of care.

Obviously, there is more work to be done to spell out these principles in terms of model legislation. As they stand, they try to capture the intuitions that drive the liberal ideals. It is equally plain that corporate constitutions which meet a test like the doctrine of fair contracts are meant to enable directors and executives to manage the corporation in conjunction with these same liberal ideals.

Notes

1. Cf. A. Berle and G. Means, *The Modern Corporation and Private Property* (New York; Commerce Clearing House, 1932), 1. For a reassessment of Berle and Means' argument after 50 years, see *Journal of Law and Economics* 26 (June 1983), especially G. Stigler and C. Friedland, "The Literature of Economics: The Case of Berle and Means," 237–68; D. North, "Comment on Stigler and Friedland," 269–72; and G. Means, "Corporate Power in the Marketplace," 467–85.

2. The metaphor of rebuilding the ship while afloat is attributed to Neurath by W. Quine, *Word and Object* (Cambridge: Harvard University Press, 1960), and W. Quine and J. Ullian, *The Web of Belief* (New York: Random House, 1978). The point is that to keep the ship afloat during repairs we must replace a plank with one that will do a better job. Our argument is that stakeholder capitalism can so replace the current version of managerial capitalism.

3. See R. Charan and E. Freeman, "Planning for the Business Environment of the 1980s," *The Journal of Business Strategy* 1 (1980): 9–19, especially p. 15 for a brief account of the major developments in products liability law.

4. See S. Breyer, *Regulation and Its Reform* (Cambridge: Harvard University Press, 1983), 133, for an analysis of food additives.

5. See I. Millstein and S. Katsh, *The Limits of Corporate Power* (New York: Macmillan, 1981), Chapter 4.

6. Cf. C. Summers, "Protecting All Employees Against Unjust Dismissal," *Harvard Business Review* 58 (1980): 136, for a careful statement of the argument.

7. See E. Freeman and D. Reed, "Stockholders and Stakeholders: A New Perspective on Corporate Governance," in C. Huizinga, ed., *Corporate Governance: A Definitive Exploration of the Issues* (Los Angeles: UCLA Extension Press, 1983).

8. See T. Peters and R. Waterman, *In Search of Excellence* (New York: Harper and Row, 1982).

9. See, for instance, A. Wicks, D. Gilbert, and E. Freeman, "A Feminist Reinterpretation of the Stakeholder Concept," *Business Ethics Quarterly*, Vol. 4, No. 4, October 1994; and E. Freeman and J. Liedtka, "Corporate Social Responsibility: A Critical Approach," *Business Horizons*, Vol. 34, No. 4, July–August 1991, pp. 92–98.

10. At the Toronto workshop Mark Starik sketched how a theory would look if we took the environment to be a stakeholder. This fruitful line of work is one example of my main point about pluralism.

11. J. Rawls, *Political Liberalism*, (New York: Columbia University Press, 1993); and R. Rorty, "The Priority of Democracy to Philosophy" in *Reading Rorty: Critical Responses to Philosophy and the Mirror of Nature (and Beyond)*, ed. Alan R. Malachowski, (Cambridge, MA: Blackwell, 1990).

Capitalism

Tibor R. Machan and James E. Chesher

Capitalism is the political economic system in which the institution of the right to private property is fully respected or at least protected. There is dispute about the label, of course, mostly because its definition is often a precondition of having either a favorable or unfavorable view of the system. Capitalism is also the political economy that's most hospitable to commerce and business. In economics, for example, the social science that studies commerce and business, capitalism is the default system · in terms of which commerce and business are to be understood. Any departures from that system are treated as impediments to commerce and business and are in need of justification.[1]

By itself, capitalism is an *economic* arrangement of an organized human community or polity. Often, however, entire societies are called capitalist, mainly to stress their thriving commerce and industry and the legal infrastructure that make these possible. But more rigorously understood, capitalism presupposes but is not itself a type of legal order governed by the rule of law in which the principle of private property rights plays a central role. Such a system of laws is usually grounded on *classical liberal* ideals in political thinking. These ideals may incorporate positivism, utilitarianism, natural rights theory, and/or individualism, as well as notions about the merits of laissez-faire (no government interference in commerce), the "invisible hand" (as a principle of spontaneous social organization), prudence and industriousness (as significant virtues), the price system as distinct from central planning (for registering supply and demand), and so on.

Put differently, "capitalism" refers to that feature of a human community whereby citizens are understood to have the basic right to make their own decisions concerning what they will do with their labor and property. Thus, capitalism includes freedom of trade and contract, free movement of labor, and protection of property rights against both criminal and official intrusiveness.

The concept "freedom" plays a central role in the understanding of capitalism. There are two prominent ways the nature of freedom is conceived as it pertains to human relationships. The one that fits with capitalism is *negative* freedom, namely, the condition of everyone in society not being ruled by others with respect to the use and disposal of themselves and what belongs to them. Citizens are free, in this sense, when no one else has authority over them that they have not granted of their own volition. In short, in capitalism one enjoys negative freedom, which amounts to being free *from* others' intrusiveness. In the U.S. political tradition, government is charged with the primary if not the sole task of securing the rights to such negative freedom—to life, liberty, and the pursuit of happiness.

The other meaning of "freedom" is that citizens have their goals and purposes supported by others, via their government, so as to prosper. Under this conception of freedom, one is free to progress, advance, develop, or flourish only when one is enabled to do so by the efforts of capable others. Government is charged with the task of arranging the securement of such freedom via taxation and wealth redistribution.

In international political discussions, the concept "capitalist" is used very loosely, so that such diverse types of societies such as Italy, New Zealand, the United States, Sweden, and France are all considered capitalist. Clearly, however, no country in our times is completely capitalist, nor has there ever been one. Of course, this is true of all other political economic systems, which are more or less faithfully approximated in various societies.

No country, accordingly, enjoys a condition of economic laissez-faire in which government stays out of people's commercial transactions except when conflicting claims over various valued items are advanced and the dispute needs to be resolved in line with the due process of law. But many Western-type societies protect a good deal of free trade, even if they also regulate most of it as well.[2] Still, just as those countries are called "democratic" if there is substantial suffrage—even though many citizens may be prevented from voting—if there exists substantial free trade and private ownership of the major means of production (labor, capital, intellectual creations, etc.), the country is usually designated as capitalist.

Of course, there are somewhat different versions of substantially capitalist countries; Japan, for example, enjoys a great deal of free trade. Yet, corporations are not free to pursue profit as the managers choose but must serve various social goals. They are required, for example, to heed the welfare of stakeholders—those whose lives are influenced by the decisions of corporate managers even if they lack any proprietary rights—for example, shares—in the company.

A similar situation applies in Germany, where many corporations are legally required to provide extensive benefits to employees and often may not even lay them off, even when this would be economically prudent. This is sometimes referred to as the "third way," a type of compromise between capitalism and socialism, the completely free and the completely planned economy.[3]

The most common reason among political theorists and economists for supporting capitalism is the system's strong support of wealth creation.[4] Such theorists also credit capitalism with other worthwhile traits, such as encouragement of progress, political liberty, innovation, and so on.

Those who defend the system for its utilitarian virtues—its propensity to encourage the production of wealth—are distinct from others who champion the system—or the broader framework within which it exists (what F. A. von Hayek called *The Constitution of Liberty*[5])—because they consider it morally and politically just.[6]

The first group of supporters argues that a free market or capitalist economic system is of great public benefit, even though this depends on private or even social vice, such as greed, ambition, and exploitation. As Bernard Mandeville, the author of *The Fable of the Bees*, puts it, this system produces "private vice, public benefit."[7] Many moral theorists see nothing virtuous in efforts to improve one's own life. Some believe, however, that enhancing the overall wealth of a human community is a worthwhile goal and also worth the price of a substantial measure of vice.

Those who stress the moral or normative merits of capitalism say the system rewards hard work, ingenuity, industry, entrepreneurship, and personal or individual responsibility, and this is all to the good. This alone makes the system morally preferable to alternatives. They also maintain that capitalism is a morally preferable system because it makes possible the exercise of personal choice and responsibility, something that would be obliterated in noncapitalist, collectivist systems or economic organizations. The point isn't that in capitalism everyone gets to choose the morality he/she likes, but that the right thing to do, whatever that really is, has to be chosen by a person, that one isn't forced by others to just behave in certain ways deemed to be proper.[8]

The most influential critic of capitalism is the nineteenth-century German thinker and social activist Karl Marx. He did not oppose capitalism, but he argued that it occupies only a specific period of humanity's development. Capitalism, as Marx saw it, is the adolescent period of humanity, as it were. Socialism is the young adulthood, while communism is full maturity. Marx believed that supporters are wrong to assume that the system has universal relevance and validity. Instead, Marx held, the system must be accepted as a temporary fact of the life of humanity—two hundred or perhaps four hundred years long.

In response, capitalism's defenders have argued that economic liberty is best suited to human beings because human nature is reasonably stable over time. Human beings, in turn, tend always to be motivated by self-interest or they will always want to be rewarded for their work and will not likely develop into creatures who are loyal primarily to humanity or society, never mind their self-interest.

Others have responded to Marx by claiming that not only is his position untenable, but that it is also morally despicable. The vision of human life Marx champions cuts directly against what is best about human beings, namely, their individuality, uniqueness, and resulting multifaceted creativity, that is, their often single-minded vision. Capitalism accords more with the idea of human excellence exemplified by the great artists, scientists, and industrialists of the world, not the vision exemplified by members of a stagnant commune.

Capitalism is an economic organization based on some very limited rules or principles. People are at liberty to do anything except intrude on the sovereignty of other human beings and what they own. As such, it is a system said to be well suited to human nature, whereby one may embark on various tasks and do well or badly at them but avoid intruding on others. This is best done when one's own sphere of authority—one's private property rights—is clearly identifiable.

With the 1989 collapse of the centrally planned economy of the Soviet Union, the debate about the ultimate merits of capitalism has heated up once again. It had been somewhat lukewarm earlier because of the dominance and apparent success of the welfare state. But that system began to falter from the malaise of stagflation, that is, both inflation and recession at the same time. Such East European scholars as Janos Kornai have argued in favor of moving toward a full-fledged free market system,[9] instead of attempting to institute the welfare state, mainly because they believed that the latter is only possible, at least for a while, in robust economies that can support the redistribution of wealth. But Kornai argued that the East European countries—indeed, all those with serious economic deficiencies—require robust economic activity, something the welfare state tends to stifle.

Others have urged that a "third way" be found, such as communitarianism or market socialism. They argue that capitalism is too harsh a system to be fully adopted in any decent society, echoing what earlier critics said about the system (e.g., John Maynard Keynes in The End of Laissez-Faire[10]). Indeed, one such warning comes from Robert Kuttner, himself the author of a recent book (coincidentally?) entitled The End of Laissez-Faire.[11] In all of these criticisms, despite protestations to the contrary, the conception of capitalism the critics embrace differs little from Marx's. What differs are the proposed solutions, which are closer to the pre-Marxist utopian socialist solutions.

Marx had argued, in his *Das Kapital*[12] and other works, that although unavoidable, capitalism leads to the alienation of the members of its community, not to mention the exploitation of the working class. In the end, this will also be the immediate cause of its necessary demise, namely, workers' disenchantment. Marx also argued that capitalism, as all societies prior to socialism and communism, is essentially a class system, so that the working and the capitalist classes are locked in an irresolvable conflict that will result in fundamental change, namely, a revolution (either peaceful or violent) leading to a socialist system.

The more recent critics wish to forge some kind of hybrid between capitalism and socialism. But the welfare state is just that hybrid and it is suffering from the inconsistencies that such systems wish to live with but that also haunts them. Trying to preserve both negative and positive liberty is futile. The disorder of allotting a portion of one to some and a portion of the other to others tends to slow everything down. By only partially protecting private property, for example, the welfare state or market socialism or communitarianism instills major uncertainties into people's lives, some of whom set property aside only to find it confiscated for some public cause just when they wish to make it useful for themselves and possibly others. In such a system, it is the state, rather than individual property owners, that has the final say.

Those who champion capitalism have different answers to Marx and the welfare statists. Mainly, they argue that although capitalism permits some harshness of treatment, such harshness is neither inherent in nor unique to capitalism. Nor need economic and social classes be rigidly formed—people travel from one economic level to the other more often than the critics imagine and certainly more so under capitalism than its alternatives. Exploitation is really just a way to meet the needs of differently positioned members of the community—some need certain goods and services more at one time than others, some have too much, some lack even elementary survival resources, but it is still best to leave things to the marketplace of free trade.

Capitalist theorists also note that most critics of capitalism demean wealth. Indeed, they virtually attack the pursuit of human well-being itself and, especially, luxury anytime there are needy people left anywhere on Earth, as well as, more recently, if any portion of nature is overrun by human beings (as if they were not natural creatures). But, the champions of capitalism argue, this stems from utopian thinking and has the consequence of begrudging anyone a measure of welfare, since some people will always be poor some of the time and nature will continue to be transformed by people.

Yet, the capitalist advocate need not be seen as reckless toward the environment. Indeed, arguably the strict and consistent institution of the principle of private property rights—through, for example, privatization and prohibition of dumping waste into other private as well as public realms—may solve the environmental problems we face better than any central planning champions of the environment tend to propose.[13]

Finally, critics of capitalism do not credit owners of wealth with any moral virtues—not even for their industry and prudence (often denying that these are virtues at all). This, its champions maintain, is a grave and indeed tragic mistake. We all depend on the wealth created by our fellow human beings, even as we try to produce wealth ourselves. Despite this, the activity is rarely appreciated, leaving business with very bad press, indeed.

In order to be effective navigators of our lives, we require what Robert Nozick, a philosopher at Harvard University, calls "moral space."[14] We need some sphere of exclusive jurisdiction, sovereign power, and a certain measure of autonomy. Thus, for some of the most crucial decisions of our lives, other people must ask permission to participate. We have a veto power—the only way that our moral worth can be developed and recognized by others as indeed our worth.

If we do not act in some measures as independent, sovereign agents, then we are like conscripted members of committees, in every decision we make; every bad or good decision is really the forced labor of a group, and no one is responsible.

Then the rapist is not responsible; nor the architect, Mozart, Beethoven, Albert Schweitzer, Mother Teresa, or even Osama bin Laden! They are all simply products of some large or small committee: a tribe, a clan, a community, or a society. And the committee itself is but a product of forces over which no one has control, responsibility, or accountability.

If one denies this measure of individual initiative and this social requirement of moral space, of a sphere of protected private jurisdiction, then no one can be held responsible, admired, or faulted for anything. Despite the widespread view that no one is responsible, there is also the widespread view that, for example, whoever creates pollution or waste should clean it up, or at least pay for it.

To the extent that individualism and the economics of capitalism are rejected, we have what we would call the moral tragedy of the commons: the inability to distinguish between those who are deserving and those who are not deserving, fundamentally, of moral recognition or praise. If everyone is a victim, then there is no room for either culprits or heroes. The institution of private property rights is a concrete, legally implementable manifestation of this concept of moral space.

The first issue of politics is or should be: Are we going to be able to act as moral agents in a social context? Though we are surrounded by countless others, is there going to be some place where we are sovereign judges? The principle of private property—which assigns to me those things that are justly and naturally mine, to you those things that are yours, from a watch to stocks and bonds, to business firms, to novels or computer programs—defines the arena where we are responsible. Here, other people may enter only at our discretion and with our consent. If that place is not secured for us, then our moral agency is not secure and we do not operate as independent, sovereign, and moral agents. Then we are mere subjects of the will of others who have taken power over us, be that a king, a tribal chief, a democratic assembly, or a central committee of a ruling political party.

If other people have legal authority to coerce us to use our private property and if they can impose their rule on us, then our moral responsibility is seriously diminished. For example, consider how environmental problems arise in any society. They arise, in part, because many firms utilize the commons without being fully accountable for how they behave there. It's the politicians who give them permission; it's the judges who rule in favor of a certain public ground being utilizable by the people! Firms get blamed all the time, but the firms cannot justly regard themselves to be guilty because they don't know how much of that public ground they really own and are responsible for. How much of it is at their disposal to rule, to navigate, and to manage? They just say: "Well, they tell me I can throw my soot into Lake Erie. I will do so," because the law says they are doing what everyone has the right to do, namely, take advantage of certain entitlements. The same with people who lobby for public funds for the arts, sciences, education, business, or whatnot. They all regard the public realm—for example, the treasury of their governments—as for their special use.

Most people who criticize firms don't realize that managers of firms are convinced that their activities are perfectly honorable and when they utilize the public realm, the legal system has said, "Yes, it's available for you to use." So they don't, indeed, cannot see, themselves as exploiters and defilers. They see themselves as responsible people, having utilized whatever resources are legitimately available to them to advance a goal that they pursue as a matter of their professional duty. This is the goal of maximizing the profits of their stockholders, who include pensioners, teachers, nurses, and thousands or millions of people who trusted them with the responsibility of giving them a return on investment.

Similarly for all those who utilize government funds for their various projects (which, of course, they tend to characterize as "being in the public interest"). They all have causes they believe in and want to promote. If the public coffers are there for them to use, they believe it is their right and responsibility to do so. This then leads to more and more people using the resources regardless of which portion if any should go to their cause. That is something no one can tell. Thus, the tragedy of the commons!

From this perspective, one can see that blaming business or any other segment of society seeking public resources—including regions of the wilds publicly owned and managed by government—is quite unjust. It's the system that makes it possible; a system that has socialized a great deal of resources and made it impossible to distinguish between what is one person's realm of operations and what is someone else's. Just compare Disneyland to a public beach and the picture becomes clear. Or consider one's private budget, which when exhausted, is immediately evident, in contrast with utilizing public support!

On the public beach, many people thoughtlessly litter and often leave without cleaning up. Meanwhile, Disneyland stays cleaned up. Why? Because it's privately owned and people know how to take care of that, or at least have a greater propensity to do so.

This is one function of private property rights, to enable people to operate their lives with the sense that they alone are responsible for it. It also allows others to notice when someone intrudes or takes advantage without permission. So, one very important and systemic element of the morality of capitalism is that it enables people to be moral agents.

Capitalism has experienced widespread disrespect in part because throughout human history there has been a powerful intellectual tradition of *otherworldliness*. In the Bible, Jesus decries wealth acquisition when he asks, rhetorically, "For what shall it profit a man, if he shall gain the whole world, and lose his own soul?" And, again, the Bible states that sooner will a camel go through the eye of the needle than the rich man enter the kingdom of heaven. Socrates, Plato, and even Aristotle tended to denigrate wealth production, regarding trade and commerce as lowly and base. Throughout much of Western history, taking interest (i.e., earnings from lending money) was deemed usurious, hoarding, miserly, and avaricious. Marx's criticism was different not in the standards he employed to judge the system but by his claim that it is a necessary evil soon to be superseded evil and nothing more.

Some supporters of the system argue that this view is untrue to the facts of human nature and has misled us about the moral merits of commerce and business and, thus, of capitalism itself as a vital human institution. Because of its challenge of some central ideas of the past, it is arguable that capitalism is far more radical than even communism. The commune has always existed, in its relatively small versions, and it has much in common with the prominent social organization of primitive times, namely, tribalism (both as idealized and as actually manifest).

Capitalism, however, rests in large part on the belief that human beings are essentially or by nature sovereign individuals and a society's laws must value individuals above all else. Contrast this with Marx's conservative view that "The human essence is the true collectivity of man."[15] Most historians of ideas admit that whether the importance of human individuality should have been recognized in earlier times, it certainly was not much heeded until the modern age. Even in our time it is more often that groups—ethnic, religious, racial, sexual, national, cultural, and so on—are taken to have greater significance than individuals. The latter are constantly asked to make sacrifices for the former. In capitalism, however, the individual—for example, as the sovereign citizen or the consumer—is king. Undoubtedly, a capitalist system does not give prime place to economic equality among people, something that group thinking seems to favor since in groups all are deemed to be entitled to a fair share.

Capitalism's champions take it as more reasonable that people may differ in their abilities, talents, and willingness pertaining to economic achievement. So what is crucial is that they should be *equally unimpeded by the aggressiveness of others*—whether criminals or bureaucrats—in their access to the marketplace or, indeed, to any other place in a human community whenever they gain permission to enter or reach satisfactory terms of agreement. From this, it is proposed that they will not only benefit in the long run, collectively, but will have their individuality as human beings with dignity and choice, more respected than in alternative systems.

Capitalism tends to be favored most by academic economists, even more so than by members of the commercial community (who often do not understand and may even wish to subvert the system). They are unique in the academic world and are often met with severe criticism from outside their field.[16]

The most prominent academic economists who champion capitalism are known as members of the neoclassical or Chicago School. Another that stands foursquare behind capitalism is the Austrian School.[17] Others include the well-known Public Choice and the law and economics theorists. With certain variations in their approach, all these believe that capitalism is well suited to people living in communities, mainly because any other system places obstacles before the natural inclination of human beings to advance their own lot and thus improve the world.

But is that enough? An economic organization of society needs to appeal to what people believe is just and proper; it may not offend moral sensibilities. Unless supporters of capitalism reconcile their vision of economic life with the demands most people make for their society to conform to a sound view of justice, they will not succeed. Despite the demise of centrally planned socialism and the great deal of skepticism about socialism of any kind, capitalism is by no means the hands-down winner in the race for the hearts and minds of people in the world regarding the kind of community they ought to support.

Notes

1. Even in welfare states or mixed economies, the provisions making them such are dealt with as departures from the default system of commerce and business.

2. The extent of such regulation in the United States alone, thus the divergence from pure capitalism, is chronicled in Jonathan R. T. Hughes, *The Governmental Habit*, 2d ed. (Princeton, NJ: Princeton University Press, 1991).

3. Some economists note that one reason for the high unemployment rates of countries that practice the "third way" is that to start a business is extremely difficult and those who attempt it take on enormous costs independently of whether what they do is purchased by consumers.

4. See Adam Smith, *Inquiry into the Nature and Causes of the Wealth of Nations* (New York: Modern Library Edition, 1927); Milton Friedman, *Capitalism and Freedom* (Chicago: University of Chicago Press, 1961); F. A. von Hayek, *The Road to Serfdom* (Chicago: University of Chicago Press, 1944).

5. F. A. von Hayek, *The Constitution of Liberty* (Chicago: University of Chicago Press, 1960).

6. For example, see Ayn Rand, *Capitalism: The Unknown Ideal* (New York: New American Library, 1966); John Hospers, *Libertarianism* (Los Angeles: Nash, 1970); Robert Nozick, *Anarchy, State, and Utopia* (New York: Basic, 1974).

7. Bernard Mandeville, *The Fable of the Bees* (Indianapolis, IN: Liberty Classics, 1988).

8. The point here is that some argue that morality is subjective and capitalism makes possible doing what one subjectively feels one ought to do. But while this is possible, if there is an objectively right way for one to act, the action is morally worthwhile only if it is chosen. And in a capitalist society, because one enjoys substantial sovereignty and autonomy, one has the right to choose to do the right thing or, of course, to choose not to do it. So there is a risk, admittedly, but without choice the very possibility of moral conduct is eliminated.

9. See Janos Kornai, *The Road to the Free Economy* (New York: Norton, 1990).

10. John Maynard Keynes, *The End of Laissez-Faire* (London: L. and Virginia Woolf, 1926).

11. Robert Kuttner, *The End of Laissez-Faire* (New York: Knopf, 1991).

12. Karl Marx, *Das Kapital* (New York: International, 1967).

13. In this connection, see the works of such free market environmentalists as John Baden, Richard Stroup, Fred Singer, and Tibor R. Machan.

14. Nozick, *Anarchy, State, and Utopia*, 79.

15. Karl Marx, "On the Jewish Question."

16. For example, see Amitai Etzioni, *The Moral Dimension* (New York: Free Press, 1988); Kenneth Lux, *Adam Smith's Mistake* (Boston: Shambhala, 1990); Andrew Bard Schmookler, *The Illusion of Choice* (Albany: SUNY Press, 1993).

17. For a collection of nontechnical essays by such thinkers and others who favor capitalism, see Lawrence S. Stepelevich, ed., *The Capitalist Reader* (New Rochelle, NY: Arlington House, 1977).

Alienated Labour

Karl Marx

We shall begin from a *contemporary* economic fact. The worker becomes poorer the more wealth he produces and the more his production increases in power and extent. The worker becomes an ever cheaper commodity the more goods he creates. The *devaluation* of the human world increases in direct relation with the *increase in value* of the world of things. Labour does not only create goods; it also produces itself and the worker as a *commodity*, and indeed in the same proportion as it produces goods. . . .

All these consequences follow from the fact that the worker is related to the *product of his labour* as to an *alien* object. For it is clear on this presupposition that the more the worker expends himself in work the more powerful becomes the world of objects which he creates in face of himself, the poorer he becomes in his inner life, and the less he belongs to himself. It is just the same as in religion. The more of himself man attributes to God the less he has left in himself. The worker puts his life into the object, and his life then belongs no longer to himself but to the object. The greater his activity, therefore, the less he possesses. What is embodied in the product of his labour is no longer his own. The greater this product is, therefore, the more he is diminished. The *alienation* of the worker in his product means not only that his labour becomes an object, assumes an *external* existence, but that it exists independently, *outside himself*, and alien to him, and that it stands opposed to him as an autonomous power. The life which he has given to the object sets itself against him as an alien and hostile force.

. . . The worker becomes a slave of the object; first, in that he receives an *object of work*, i.e. receives *work*, and secondly, in that he receives *means of subsistence*. Thus the object enables him to exist, first as a *worker* and secondly as a *physical subject*. The culmination of this enslavement is that he can only maintain himself as a *physical subject* so far as he is a *worker*, and that it is only as a *physical subject* that he is a worker. . . .

What constitutes the alienation of labour? First, that the work is *external* to the worker, and that it is not part of his nature; and that, consequently, he does not fulfill himself in his work but denies himself, has a feeling of misery rather than well-being, does not develop freely his mental and physical energies but is physically exhausted and mentally debased. The worker, therefore, feels himself at home only during his leisure time, whereas at work he feels homeless. His work is not voluntary but imposed, *forced labour*. It is not the satisfaction of a need, but only a *means* for satisfying other needs. Its alien character is clearly shown by the fact that as soon as there is no physical or other compulsion it is avoided like the plague. External labour, labour in which man alienates himself, is a labour of self-sacrifice, of mortification. Finally, the external character of work for the worker is shown by the fact that it is not his own work but work for someone else, that in work he does not belong to himself but to another person. . . .

We arrive at the result that man (the worker) feels himself to be freely active only in his animal functions—eating, drinking, and procreating, or at most also in his dwelling and in personal adornment—while in his human functions he is reduced to an animal. The animal becomes human and the human becomes animal.

Eating, drinking, and procreating are of course also genuine human functions. But abstractly considered, apart from the environment of human activities, and turned into final and sole ends, they are animal functions.

We have now considered the act of alienation of practical human activity, labour, from two aspects: (1) the relationship of the worker to the *product of labour* as an alien object which dominates him. This relationship is at the same time the relationship to the sensuous external world, to natural objects, as an alien and hostile world; (2) the relationship of labour to the *act of production* within *labour*. This is the relationship of the worker to his own activity as something alien and not belonging to him, activity as suffering (passivity), strength as powerlessness, creation as emasculation, the *personal* physical and mental energy of the worker, his personal life (for what is life but activity?), as an activity which is directed against himself, independent of him and not belonging to him. This is *self-alienation* as against the above-mentioned alienation of the *thing*.

We have now to infer a third characteristic of *alienated labour* from the two we have considered.

Man is a species-being not only in the sense that he makes the community (his own as well as those of other things) his object both practically and theoretically, but also (and this is simply another expression for the same thing) in the sense that he treats himself as the present, living species, as a *universal* and consequently free being.[1]

Species-life, for man as for animals, has its physical basis in the fact that man (like animals) lives from inorganic nature, and since man is more universal than an animal so the range of inorganic nature from which he lives is more universal. . . . The universality of man appears in practice in the universality which makes the whole of nature into his inorganic body: (1) as a direct means of life; and equally (2) as the material object and instrument of his life activity. Nature is the inorganic body of man; that is to say nature, excluding the human body itself. To say that man *lives* from nature means that nature is his *body* with which he must remain in a continuous interchange in order not to die. The statement that the physical and mental life of man, and nature, are interdependent means simply that nature is interdependent with itself, for man is a part of nature.

Since alienated labour: (1) alienates nature from man; and (2) alienates man from himself, from his own active function, his life activity; so it alienates him from the species. It makes *species-life* into a means of individual life. In the first place it alienates species-life and individual life, and secondly, it turns the latter, as an abstraction, into the purpose of the former, also in its abstract and alienated form.

For labour, *life activity,* *productive life*, now appear to man only as *means* for the satisfaction of a need, the need to maintain his physical existence. Productive life is, however, species-life. It is life creating life. In the type of life activity resides the whole character of a species, its species-character; and free, conscious activity is the species-character of human beings. Life itself appears only as a *means of life*.

The animal is one with its life activity. It does not distinguish the activity from itself. It is *its activity*. But man makes his life activity itself an object of his will and consciousness. He has a conscious life activity. It is not a determination with which he is completely identified. Conscious life activity distinguishes man from the life activity of animals. Only for this reason is he a species-being. Or rather, he is only a self-conscious being, i.e., for his own life is an object for him, because he is a species-being. Only for this reason is his activity free activity. Alienated labour reverses the relationship, in that man because he is a self-conscious being makes his life activity, his *being*, only a means for his *existence*.

The practical construction of an *objective world*, the *manipulation* of inorganic nature, is the confirmation of man as a conscious species-being, i.e., a being who treats the species as his own being or himself as a species-being. . . .

It is just in his work upon the objective world that man really proves himself as a *species-being*. This production is his active species-life. By means of it nature appears as *his* work and his reality. The object of labour is, therefore, the *objectification of man's species-life:* for he no longer reproduces himself merely intellectually, as in consciousness, but actively and in a real sense, and he sees his own reflection in a world which he has constructed. While, therefore, alienated labour takes away the object of production from man, it also takes away his *species-life*, his real objectivity as a species-being, and changes his advantage over animals into a disadvantage in so far as his inorganic body, nature, is taken from him.

Just as alienated labour transforms free and self-directed activity into a means, so it transforms the species-life of man into a means of physical existence.

Consciousness, which man has from his species, is transformed through alienation so that species-life becomes only a means for him. (3) Thus alienated labour turns the *species-life of man*, and also nature as his mental species-property, into an *alien* being and into a *means* for his *individual existence*. It alienates from man his own body, external nature, his mental life and his *human* life. (4) A direct consequence of the alienation of man from the product of his labour, from his life activity and from his species-life, is that *man is alienated* from other *men*. When man confronts himself he also confronts *other* men. What is true of man's relationship to his work, to the product of his work and to himself, is also true of his relationship to other men, to their labour and to the objects of their labour.

In general, the statement that man is alienated from his species-life means that each man is alienated from others, and that each of the others is likewise alienated from human life.

Human alienation, and above all the relation of man to himself, is first realized and expressed in the relationship between each man and other men. Thus in the relationship of alienated labour every man regards other men according to the standards and relationships in which he finds himself placed as a worker.

We began with an economic fact, the alienation of the worker and his production. We have expressed this fact in conceptual terms as *alienated labour*, and in analysing the concept we have merely analysed an economic fact. . . .

The *alien* being to whom labour and the product of labour belong, to whose service labour is devoted, and to whose enjoyment the product of labour goes, can only be *man* himself. If the product of labour does not belong to the worker, but confronts him as an alien power, this can only be because it belongs to *a man other than the worker.* . . .

Thus, through alienated labour the worker creates the relation of another man, who does not work and is outside the work process, to this labour. The relation of the workers to work also produces the relation of the capitalist (or whatever one likes to call the lord of labour) to work. *Private property* is, therefore, the product, the necessary result, of *alienated labour*, of the external relation of the worker to nature and to himself.

Private property is thus derived from the analysis of the concept of *alienated labor;* that is, alienated man, alienated labour, alienated life, and estranged man.

We have, of course, derived the concept of *alienated labour* (*alienated life*) from political economy, from the analysis of the *movement of private property*. But the analysis of this concept shows that although private property appears to be the basis and cause of alienated labour, it is rather a consequence of the latter, just as the gods are *fundamentally* not the cause but the product of confusion of human reason. At a later stage, however, there is a reciprocal influence.

Only in the final state of the development of private property is its secret revealed, namely, that it is on one hand the *product* of alienated labour, and on the other hand the *means* by which labour is alienated, *the realization of this alienation.* . . .

Just as *private property* is only the sensuous expression of the fact that man is at the same time an *objective* fact for himself and becomes an alien and non-human object for himself; just as his manifestation of life is also his alienation of life and his self-realization a loss of reality, the emergence of an *alien* reality; so the positive supersession of private property, i.e., the *sensuous* appropriation of the human essence and of human life, of objective man and of human *creations*, by and for man, should not be taken only in the sense of *immediate*, exclusive *enjoyment*, or only in the sense of *possession* or *having*. Man appropriates his manifold being in an all-inclusive way, and thus as a whole man. All his *human* relations to the world—seeing, hearing, smelling, tasting, touching, thinking, observing, feeling, desiring, acting, loving—in short, all the organs of his individuality, like the organs which are directly communal in form, are in their objective action (their *action in relation to the object*) the appropriation of this object, the appropriation of human reality. The way in which they react to the object is the confirmation of *human reality*. It is human effectiveness and human *suffering*, for suffering humanly considered is an enjoyment of the self for man.

Private property has made us so stupid and partial that an object is only *ours* when we have it, when it exists for us as capital or when it is directly eaten, drunk, worn, inhabited, etc., in short, *utilized* in some way. But private property itself only conceives these various forms of possession as *means of life,* and the life for which they serve as means is the life of *private property*— labour and creation of capital.

The supersession of private property is, therefore, the complete *emancipation* of all the human qualities and senses. It is such an emancipation because these qualities and senses have become *human,* from the subjective as well as the objective point of view. The eye has become a *human* eye when its *object* has become a *human,* social object, created by man and destined for him. The senses have, therefore, become directly theoreticians in practice. They relate themselves to the thing for the sake of the thing, but the thing itself is an *objective human* relation to itself and to man, and vice versa. Need and enjoyment have thus lost their *egoistic* character and nature has lost its mere *utility* by the fact that its utilization has become *human* utilization. . . .

Note

1. In this passage Marx reproduces Feuerbach's argument in *Das Wesen des Christentums.*

Distributive Justice

Joel Feinberg

The term "distributive justice" traditionally applied to burdens and benefits directly distributed by political authorities, such as appointed offices, welfare doles, taxes, and military conscription, but it has now come to apply also to goods and evils of a nonpolitical kind that can be distributed by private citizens to other private citizens. In fact, in most recent literature, the term is reserved for *economic* distributions, particularly the justice of differences in economic income between classes, and of various schemes of taxation which discriminate in different ways between classes. Further, the phrase can refer not only to acts of distributing but also to de factor states of affairs, such as *the fact that* at present "the five percent at the top get 20 percent [of our national wealth] while the 20 percent at the bottom get about five percent.[1] There is, of course, an ambiguity in the meaning of "distribution." The word may refer to the *process* of distributing, or the *product* of some process of distributing, and either or both of these can be appraised as just or unjust. In addition, a "distribution" can be understood to be a "product" which is *not* the result of any deliberate distributing process, but simply a state of affairs whose production has been too complicated to summarize or to ascribe to any definite group of persons as their deliberate doing. The present "distribution" of American wealth is just such a state of affairs.

Are the 5 percent of Americans "at the top" really different from the 20 percent "at the bottom" in any respect that would justicize the difference between their incomes? It is doubtful that there is any characteristic—relevant or irrelevant—common and peculiar to all members of either group. *Some* injustices, therefore, must surely exist. Perhaps there are some traits, however, that are more of less characteristic of the members of the privileged group, that make the current arrangements at least approximately just. What could (or should) those traits be? The answer will state a standard of relevance and a principle of material justice for questions of economic distributions, at least in relatively affluent societies like that of the United States.

At this point there appears to be no appeal possible except to *basic attitudes*, but even at this level we should avoid premature pessimism about the possibility of rational agreement. Some answers to our question have been generally discredited, and if we can see why those answers are inadequate, we might discover some important clues to the properties any adequate answer must possess. Even philosophical adversaries with strongly opposed initial attitudes may hope to come to eventual agreement if they share *some* relevant beliefs and standards and a common commitment to consistency. Let us consider why we all agree (that is the author's assumption) in rejecting the view that differences in race, sex, IQ, or social "rank" are the grounds of just differences in wealth or income. Part of the answer seems obvious. People cannot by their own voluntary choices determine what skin color, sex, or IQ they shall have, or which hereditary caste they shall enter. To make such properties the basis of discrimination between individuals in the distribution of social benefits would be "to treat people differently in ways that profoundly affect their lives because of differences for which they have no responsibility."[2] Differences in a given respect are *relevant* for the aims of distributive justice, then, only if they are differences for which their possessors can be held responsible; properties can be the grounds of just discrimination between persons only if those persons had a *fair opportunity* to acquire or avoid them. Having rejected a number of material principles that clearly fail to satisfy the "fair opportunity" requirement, we are still left with as many as five candidates for our acceptance. (It is in theory open to us to accept two or more of these five as valid principles, there being no a priori necessity that the list be reduced to one.) These are: (1) the principle of perfect equality; (2) the principle[s] of need; (3) the principles of merit and achievement; (4) the principle of contribution (or due return); (5) the principle of effort (or labor). I shall discuss each of these briefly.

(i) Equality

The principle of perfect equality obviously has a place in any adequate social ethic. Every human being is equally a human being, and . . . that minimal qualification entitles all human beings equally to certain absolute human rights: positive rights to noneconomic "goods" that by their very natures cannot be in short supply, negative rights not to be treated in cruel or inhuman ways, and negative rights not to be exploited or degraded even in "humane" ways. It is quite another thing, however, to make the minimal qualification of humanity the ground for an absolutely equal distribution of a country's *material wealth* among its citizens. A strict equalitarian could argue that he is merely applying Aristotle's formula of proportionate equality (presumably accepted by all parties to the dispute) with a criterion of relevance borrowed from the human rights theorists. Thus, distributive justice is accomplished between *A* and *B* when the following ratio is satisfied:

$$\frac{A's \text{ share of } P}{B's \text{ share of } P} = \frac{A's \text{ possession of } Q}{B's \text{ possession of } Q}$$

Where *P* stands for economic goods, *Q* must stand simply for "humanity" or "a human nature," and since every human being possesses *that Q* equally, it follows that all should also share a society's economic wealth (the *P* in question) equally.

The trouble with this argument is that its major premise is no less disputable than its conclusion. The standard of relevance it borrows from other contexts where it seems very little short of self-evident, seems controversial, at best, when applied to purely economic contexts. It seems evident to most of us that merely being human entitles *everyone*—bad men as well as good, lazy as well as industrious, inept as well as skilled—to a fair trial if charged with a crime, to equal protection of the law, to equal consideration of his interests by makers of national policy, to be spared torture or other cruel and inhuman treatment, and to be permanently ineligible for the status of chattel slave. Adding a right to an equal share of the economic pie, however, is to add a benefit of a wholly different order, one whose presence on the list of goods for which mere humanity is the sole qualifying condition is not likely to win wide assent without further argument.

It is far more plausible to posit a human right to the satisfaction of (better: to an opportunity to satisfy) one's *basic* economic needs, that is, to enough food and medicine to remain healthy, to minimal clothing, housing, and so on. As Hume pointed out,[3] even these rights cannot exist under conditions of extreme scarcity. Where there is not enough to go around, it cannot be true that everyone has a right to an equal share.[4] But wherever there is moderate abundance or better—wherever a society produces more than enough to satisfy the *basic needs of everyone*—there it seems more plausible to say that mere possession of basic human needs qualifies a person for the opportunity to satisfy them. It would be a rare and calloused sense of justice that would not be offended by an affluent society, with a large annual agricultural surplus and a great abundance of manufactured goods, which permitted some of its citizens to die of starvation, exposure, or easily curable disease. It would certainly be *unfair* for a nation to produce more than it needs and not permit some of its citizens enough to satisfy their basic biological requirements. Strict equalitarianism, then, is a perfectly plausible material principle of distributive justice when confined to affluent societies and basic biological needs, but it loses plausibility when applied to division of the "surplus" left over after basic needs are met. To be sure, the greater the degree of affluence, the higher the level at which we might draw the line between "basic needs" and merely "wanted" benefits, and insofar as social institutions create "artificial needs," it is only fair that society provide all with the opportunity to satisfy them.[5] But once the line has been drawn between what is needed to live a minimally decent life by the realistic standards of a given time and place and what is only added "gravy," it is far from evident that justice still insists upon absolutely equal shares of the total. And it is evident that justice does *not* require strict equality wherever there is reason to think that unequal distribution causally determines greater production and is therefore in the interests of everyone, even those who receive the relatively smaller shares.

Still, there is no way to *refute* the strict equalitarian who requires exactly equal shares for everyone whenever that can be arranged without discouraging total productivity to the point where everyone loses. No one would insist upon equal distributions that would diminish the size of the total pie and thus leave smaller slices for *everyone*; that would be opposed to reason. John Rawls makes this condition part of his "rational principle" of justice: "Inequalities are arbitrary unless it is reasonable to expect that they will work out to everyone's advantage. . . .[6] We are left then with a version of strict equalitarianism that is by no means evidently true and yet is impossible to refute. That is the theory that purports to apply not only to basic needs but to the total wealth of a society, and allows departures from strict equality when, *but only when*, they will work out to everyone's advantage. Although I am not persuaded by this theory, I think that any adequate material principle will have to attach great importance to keeping differences in wealth within reasonable limits, even after all basic needs have been met. One way of doing this would be to raise the standards for a "basic need" as total wealth goes up, so that differences between the richest and poorest citizens (even when there is no real "poverty") are kept within moderate limits.

(ii) Need

The principle of need is subject to various interpretations, but in most of its forms it is not an independent principle at all, but only a way of mediating the application of the principle of equality. It can, therefore, be grouped with the principle of perfect equality as a member of the equalitarian family and contrasted with the principles of merit, achievement, contribution, and effort, which are all members of the nonequalitarian family. Consider some differences in "needs" as they bear on distributions. Doe is a bachelor with no dependents; Roe has a wife and six children. Roe must satisfy the needs of eight persons out of his paycheck, whereas Doe need satisfy the needs of only one. To give Roe and Doe equal pay would be to treat Doe's interests substantially *more* generously than those of anyone in the Roe family. Similarly, if a small private group is distributing food to its members (say a shipwrecked crew waiting rescue on a desert island), it would not be fair to give precisely the same quantity to a one hundred pounder as to a two hundred pounder, for that might be giving one person all he needs and the other only a fraction of what he needs—a difference in treatment not supported by any relevant difference between them. In short, to distribute goods in proportion to basic needs is not really to depart from a standard of equality, but rather to bring those with some greater initial burden or deficit up to the same level as their fellows.

The concept of a "need" is extremely elastic. In a general sense, to say that S needs X is to say simply that if he doesn't have X he will be harmed. A "basic need" would then be for an X in whose absence a person would be harmed in some crucial and fundamental way, such as suffering injury, malnutrition, illness, madness, or premature death. Thus we all have a basic need for foodstuffs of a certain quantity and variety, fuel to heat our dwellings, a roof over our heads, clothing to keep us warm, and so on. In a different but related sense of need, to say that S needs X is to say that without X he cannot achieve some specific purpose or perform some specific function. If they are to do their work, carpenters need tools, merchants need capital and customers, authors need paper and publishers. Some helpful goods are not strictly needed in this sense: an author with pencil and paper does not really need a typewriter to write a book, but he may need it to write a book speedily, efficiently, and conveniently. We sometimes come to rely upon "merely helpful but unneeded goods" to such a degree that we develop a strong habitual dependence on them, in which case (as it is often said) we have a "psychological" as opposed to a material need for them. If we don't possess that for which we have a strong psychological need, we may be unable to be happy, in which case a merely psychological need for a functional instrument may become a genuine need in the first sense distinguished above, namely, something whose absence is harmful to us. (Cutting across the distinction between material and psychological needs is that between "natural" and "artificial" needs, the former being those that can be expected to develop in any normal person, the latter being those that are manufactured or contrived, and somehow implanted in, or imposed upon, a person.) The more abundant a society's material goods, the higher the level at which we are required (by the force of psychological needs) to fix the distinction between "necessities" and "luxuries"; what *everyone* in a given society regards as "necessary" tends to become an actual, basic need.

(iii) Merit and Achievement

The remaining three candidates for material principles of distributive justice belong to the nonequalitarian family. These three principles would each distribute goods in accordance, not with need, but with *desert*; since persons obviously differ in their deserts, economic goods would be distributed unequally. The three principles differ from one another in their conceptions of the relevant *bases of desert* for economic distributions. The first is the principle of *merit*. Unlike the other principles in the nonequalitarian family, this one focuses not on what a person has *done* to deserve his allotment, but rather on what kind of person he is—what characteristics he has.

Two different types of characteristic might be considered meritorious in the appropriate sense: skills and virtues. Native skills and inherited aptitudes will not be appropriate desert bases, since they are forms of merit ruled out by the fair opportunity requirement. No one deserves credit or blame for his genetic inheritance, since no one has the opportunity to select his own genes. Acquired skills may seem more plausible candidates at first, but upon scrutiny they are little better. First, all acquired skills depend to a large degree on native skills. Nobody is born knowing how to read, so reading is an acquired skill, but actual differences in reading skill are to a large degree accounted for by genetic differences that are beyond anyone's control. Some of the differences are no doubt caused by differences in motivation afforded different children, but again the early conditions contributing to a child's motivation are also largely beyond his control. We may still have some differences in acquired skills that are to be accounted for solely or primarily by differences in the degree of practice, drill, and perseverance expended by persons with roughly equal opportunities. In respect to these, we can propitiate the requirement of fair opportunity, but only by nullifying the significance of acquired skill as such, for now skill is a relevant basis of desert only to the extent that it is a product of one's own effort. Hence, *effort* becomes the true basis of desert (as claimed by our fifth principle, discussed below), and not simply skill as such.

Those who would propose rewarding personal *virtues* with a larger than average share of the economic pie, and punishing defects of character with a smaller than average share, advocate assigning to the economic system a task normally done (if it is done at all) by noneconomic institutions. What they propose, in effect, is that we use retributive criteria of distributive justice. Our criminal law, for a variety of good reasons, does not purport to punish people for what they are, but only for what they do. A man can be as arrogant, rude, selfish, cruel, insensitive, irresponsible, cowardly, lazy, or disloyal as he wishes; unless he *does* something prohibited by the criminal law, he will not be made to suffer legal punishment. At least one of the legal system's reasons for refusing to penalize character flaws as such would also explain why such defects should not be listed as relevant differences in a material principle of distributive justice. The apparatus for detecting such flaws (a "moral police"?) would be enormously cumbersome and impractical, and its methods so uncertain and fallible that none of us could feel safe in entrusting the determination of our material allotments to it. We could, of course, give roughly equal shares to all except those few who have *outstanding* virtues—gentleness, kindness, courage, diligence, reliability, warmth, charm, considerateness, generosity. Perhaps these are traits that deserve to be rewarded, but it is doubtful that larger economic allotments are the appropriate vehicles of rewarding. As Benn and Peters remind us, "there are some sorts of 'worth' for which rewards in terms of income seem inappropriate. Great courage in battle is recognized by medals, not by increased pay."[7] Indeed, there is something repugnant, as Socrates and the Stoics insisted, in paying a man to be virtuous. Moreover, the rewards would offer a pecuniary motive for certain forms of excellence that require motives of a different kind, and would thus tend to be self-defeating.

The most plausible nonequalitarian theories are those that locate relevance not in meritorious traits and excellences of any kind, but rather in prior doings: not in what one is, but in what one has done. Actions, too, are sometimes called "meritorious," so there is no impropriety in denominating the remaining families of principles in our survey as "meritarian." One type of action-oriented meritarian might cite *achievement* as a relevant desert basis for pecuniary rewards, so that departures from equality in income are to be justicized only by distinguished achievements in science, art, philosophy, music, athletics, and other basic areas of human activity. The attractions and disadvantages of this theory are similar to those of theories which I rejected above that base rewards on skills and virtues. Not all persons have a fair opportunity to achieve great things, and economic rewards seem inappropriate as vehicles for expressing recognition and admiration of noneconomic achievements.

(iv) Contribution or "Due Return"

When the achievements under consideration are themselves contributions to our general economic well-being, the meritarian principle of distributive justice is much more plausible. Often it is conjoined with an economic theory that purports to determine exactly what percentage of our total economic product a given worker or class has produced. Justice, according to this principle, requires that each worker get back exactly that proportion of the national wealth that he has himself created. This sounds very much like a principle of "commutative justice" directing us to *give back* to every worker what is really his own property, that is, the product of his own labor.

The French socialist writer and precursor of Karl Marx, Pierre Joseph Proudhon (1809–1865), is perhaps the classic example of this kind of theorist. In his book, *What Is Property?* (1840), Proudhon rejects the standard socialist slogan. "From each according to his ability, to each according to his needs."[8] in favor of a principle of distributive justice based on contribution, as interpreted by an economic theory that employed a pre-Marxist "theory of surplus value." The famous socialist slogan was not intended, in any case, to express a principle of distributive justice. It was understood to be a rejection of all considerations of "mere" justice for an ethic of human brotherhood. The early socialists thought it unfair, in a way, to give the great contributors to our wealth a disproportionately small share of the product. But in the new socialist society, love of neighbor, community spirit, and absence of avarice would overwhelm such bourgeois notions and put them in their proper (subordinate) place.

Proudhon, on the other hand, based his whole social philosophy not on brotherhood (an ideal he found suitable only for small groups such as families) but on the kind of distributive justice to which even some capitalists gave lip service:

> The key concept was "mutuality" or "reciprocity." "Mutuality, reciprocity exists," he wrote, "when all the workers in an industry, instead of working for an entrepreneur who pays them and keeps their products, work for one another and thus collaborate in the making of a common product whose profits they share among themselves."[9]

Proudhon's celebrated dictum that "property is theft" did not imply that all *possession* of goods is illicit, but rather that the system of rules that permitted the owner of a factory to hire workers and draw profits ("surplus value") from *their* labor robs the workers of what is rightly theirs. "This profit, consisting of a portion of the proceeds of labor that rightfully belonged to the laborer himself, was 'theft.'"[10] The injustice of capitalism, according to Proudhon, consists in the fact that those who create the wealth (through their labor) get only a small part of what they create, whereas those who "exploit" their labor, like voracious parasites, gather in a greatly disproportionate share. The "return of contribution" principle of distributive justice, then, cannot work in a capitalist system, but requires a *fédération mutualiste* of autonomous producer-cooperatives in which those who create wealth by their work share it in proportion to their real contributions.

Other theorists, employing different notions of what produces or "creates" economic wealth, have used the "return of contribution" principle to support quite opposite conclusions. The contribution principle has even been used to justicize quite unequalitarian capitalistic status quos, for it is said that capital as well as labor creates wealth, as do ingenious ideas, inventions, and adventurous risk-taking. The capitalist who provided the money, the inventor who designed a product to be manufactured, the innovator who thought of a new mode of production and marketing, the advertiser who persuaded millions of customers to buy the finished product, the investor who risked his savings on the success of the enterprise—these are the ones, it is said, who did the most to produce the wealth created by a business, not the workers who contributed only their labor, and of course, these are the ones who tend, on the whole, to receive the largest personal incomes.

Without begging any narrow and technical questions of economics, I should express my general skepticism concerning such facile generalizations about the comparative degrees to which various individuals have contributed to our social wealth. Not only are there impossibly difficult problems of measurement involved, there are also conceptual problems that appear beyond all nonarbitrary solution. I refer to the elements of luck and chance, the social factors not attributable to any assignable individuals, and the contributions of population trends, uncreated natural resources, and the efforts of people now dead, which are often central to the explanation of any given increment of social wealth.

The difficulties of separating out causal factors in the production of social wealth might influence the partisan of the "return of contribution" principle in either or both of two ways. He might become very cautious in his application of the principle, requiring that deviations from average shares be restricted to very clear and demonstrable instances of unusually great or small contributions. But the moral that L. T. Hobhouse[11] drew from these difficulties is that *any* individual contribution will be very small relative to the immeasurably great contribution made by political, social, fortuitous, natural, and "inherited" factors. In particular, strict application of the "return of contribution" principle would tend to support a larger claim for the *community* to its own "due return," through taxation and other devices.

In a way, the principle of contribution is not a principle of mere *desert* at all, no matter how applied. As mentioned above, it resembles a principle of commutative justice requiring repayment of debts, return of borrowed items, or compensation for wrongly inflicted damages. If I lend you my car on the understanding that you will take good care of it and soon return it, or if you steal it, or damage it, it will be too *weak* to say that I "deserve" to have my own car, intact, back from you. After all, the car is *mine* or my due, and questions of ownership are not settled by examination of deserts; neither are considerations of ownership and obligation commonly outbalanced by considerations of desert. It is not merely "unfitting" or "inappropriate" that I should not have my own or my due; it is downright *theft* to withhold it from me. So the return of contribution is not merely a matter of merit deserving reward. It is a matter of a maker demanding that which he has created and is thus properly his. The ratio—A's share of X is to B's share of X as A's contribution to X is to B's contribution to X—appears, therefore, to be a very strong and plausible principle of distributive justice, whose main deficiencies, when applied to economic distributions, are of a practical (though severe) kind. If

Hobhouse is right in claiming that there are social factors in even the most pronounced individual contributions to social wealth, then the principle of due return serves as a moral basis in support of taxation and other public claims to private goods. In any case, If A's contribution, though apparently much greater than B's, is nevertheless only the tiniest percentage of the total contribution to X (whatever that may mean and however it is to be determined), it may seem like the meanest quibbling to distinguish very seriously between A and B at all.

(v) Effort

The principle of due return, as a material principle of distributive justice, does have some vulnerability to the fair opportunity requirement. Given unavoidable variations in genetic endowments and material circumstances, different persons cannot have precisely the same opportunities to make contributions to the public weal. Our final candidate for the status of a material principle of distributive justice, the *principle of effort*, does much better in this respect, for it would distribute economic products not in proportion to successful achievement but according to the degree of effort exerted. According to the principle of effort, justice decrees that hard-working executives and hard-working laborers receive precisely the same remuneration (although there may be reasons having nothing to do with justice for paying more to the executives), and that freeloaders be penalized by allotments of proportionately lesser shares of the joint products of everyone's labor. The most persuasive argument for this principle is that it is the closest approximation to the intuitively valid principle of due return that can pass the fair opportunity requirement. It is doubtful, however, that even the principle of effort fully satisfies the requirement of fair opportunity, since those who inherit or acquire certain kinds of handicap may have little opportunity to *acquire the motivation* even to do their best. In any event, the principle of effort does seem to have intuitive cogency giving it at least some weight as a factor determining the justice of distributions.

In very tentative conclusion, it seems that the principle of equality (in the version that rests on needs rather than that which requires "perfect equality") and the principles of contribution and effort (where nonarbitrarily applicable, and only *after* everyone's basic needs have been satisfied) have the most weight as determinants of economic justice, whereas all forms of the principle of merit are implausible in that role. The reason for the priority of basic needs is that, where there is economic abundance, the claim to life itself and to minimally decent conditions are, like other human rights, claims that all men make with perfect equality. As economic production increases, these claims are given ever greater consideration in the form of rising standards for distinguishing basic needs from other wanted goods. But no matter where that line is drawn, when we go beyond it into the realm of economic surplus or "luxuries," nonequalitarian considerations (especially contribution and effort) come increasingly into play.

Notes

1. "T. R. B. from Washington" in *The New Republic*, Vol. CLX, No. 12 (March 22, 1969), p. 4.

2. W. K. Frankena, "Some Beliefs About Justice," *The Lindley Lecture*, Department of Philosophy Pamphlet (Lawrence: University of Kansas, 1966), p. 10.

3. David Hume, *Enquiry Concerning the Principles of Morals* Part III (LaSalle, Ill.: The Open Court Publishing Company, 1947). Originally published in 1777.

4. Except in the "manifesto sense" of "right" discussed on p. 67.

5. This point is well made by Katzner, "An Analysis of the Concept of Justice," pp. 173–203.

6. John Rawls, "Justice as Fairness," *The Philosophical Review*, LXVII (1958), 165.

7. S. I. Bean and R. S. Peters, *Social Principles and the Democratic State* (London: George Allen and Unwin Ltd., 1959), p. 139.

8. Traced to Louis Blanc. For a clear brief exposition of Proudhon's view which contrasts it with that of other early socialists and also that of Karl Marx, see Robert Tucker's "Marx and Distributive Justice," in *Nomos VI: Justice*, ed. C. J. Friedrich and J. W. Chapman (New York: Aldine-Atherton Press, 1963), pp. 306–325.

9. Tucker, "Marx and Distributive Justice," p. 310.

10. Tucker, "Marx and Distributive Justice," p. 311.

11. L. T. Hobhouse, *The Elements of Social Justice* (London: George Allen and Unwin Ltd., 1922). See especially pp. 161–163.

Justice as Fairness

John Rawls

The Main Idea of the Theory of Justice

My aim is to present a conception of justice which generalizes and carries to a higher level of abstraction the familiar *theory of the social contract* as found, say, in Locke, Rousseau, and Kant.[1] In order to do this we are not to think of the original contract as one to enter a particular society or to set up a particular form of government. Rather, the guiding idea is that the principles of justice for the basic structure of society are the object of the original agreement. They are the principles that free and rational persons concerned to further their own interests would accept in an initial position of equality as defining the fundamental terms of their association. These principles are to regulate all further agreements; they specify the kinds of social cooperation that can be entered into and the forms of government that can be established. This way of regarding the principles of justice I shall call justice as fairness.

Thus we are to imagine that those who engage in social cooperation choose together, in one joint act, the principles which are to assign basic rights and duties and to determine the division of social benefits. Men are to decide in advance how they are to regulate their claims against one another and what is to be the foundation charter of their society. Just as each person must decide by rational reflection what constitutes his good, that is, the system of ends which it is rational for him to pursue, so a group of persons must decide once and for all what is to count among them as just and unjust. The choice which rational men would make in this hypothetical situation of equal liberty, assuming for the present that this choice problem has a solution, determines the principles of justice.

In justice as fairness the original position of equality corresponds to the state of nature in the traditional theory of the social contract. This original position is not, of course, thought of as an actual historical state of affairs, much less as a primitive condition of culture. It is understood as a purely hypothetical situation characterized so as to lead to a certain conception of justice.[2] Among the essential features of this situation is that no one knows his place in society, his class position or social status, nor does any one know his fortune in the distribution of natural assets and abilities, his intelligence, strength, and the like. I shall even assume that the parties do not know their conceptions of the good or their special psychological propensities. The principles of justice are chosen behind a veil of ignorance. This ensures that no one is advantaged or disadvantaged in the choice of principles by the outcome of natural chance or the contingency of social circumstances. Since all are similarly situated and no one is able to design principles to favor his particular condition, the principles of justice are the result of a fair agreement or bargain. For given the circumstances of the original position, the symmetry of everyone's relations to each other, this initial situation is fair between individuals as moral persons, that is, as rational beings with their own ends and capable, I shall assume, of a sense of justice. The original position is, one might say, the appropriate initial status quo, and thus the fundamental agreements reached in it are fair. This explains the propriety of the name "justice as fairness": it conveys the idea that the principles of justice are agreed to in an initial situation that is fair. The name does not mean that the concepts of justice and fairness are the same, any more than the phrase "poetry as metaphor" means that the concepts of poetry and metaphor are the same.

Justice as fairness begins, as I have said, with one of the most general of all choices which persons might make together, namely, with the choice of the first principles of a conception of justice which is to regulate all subsequent criticism and reform of institutions. Then, having chosen a conception of justice, we can suppose that they are to choose a constitution and a legislature to enact laws, and so on, all in accordance with the principles of justice initially agreed upon. Our social situation is just if it is such that by this sequence of hypothetical agreements we would have contracted into the general system of rules which defines it. Moreover, assuming that the original position does determine a set of principles (that is, that a particular conception of justice would be chosen), it will then be true that whenever social institutions satisfy these principles those engaged in them can say to one another that they are cooperating on terms to which they would agree if they were free and equal persons whose relations with respect to one another were fair. They could all view their arrangements as meeting the stipulations which they would acknowledge in an initial situation that embodies widely accepted and reasonable constraints on the choice of principles. The general recognition of this fact would provide the basis for a public acceptance of the corresponding principles of justice. No society can, of course, be a scheme of cooperation which men enter voluntarily in a literal sense; each person finds himself placed at birth in some particular position in some particular society, and the nature of this position materially affects his life prospects. Yet a society satisfying the principles of justice as fairness comes as close as a society can to being a voluntary scheme, for it meets the principles which free and equal persons would assent to under circumstances that are fair. In this sense its members are autonomous and the obligations they recognize self-imposed.

One feature of justice as fairness is to think of the parties in the initial situation as rational and mutually disinterested. This does not mean that the parties are egoists, that is, individuals with only certain kinds of interests, say in wealth, prestige, and domination. But they are conceived as not taking an interest in one another's interests. They are to presume that even their spiritual aims may be opposed, in the way that the aims of those of different religions may be opposed. Moreover, the concept of rationality must be interpreted as far as possible in the narrow sense, standard in economic theory, of taking the most effective means to given ends. I shall modify this concept to some extent . . . but one must try to avoid introducing into it any controversial ethical elements. The initial situation must be characterized by stipulations that are widely accepted.

In working out the conception of justice as fairness one main task clearly is to determine which principles of justice would be chosen in the original position. To do this we must describe this situation in some detail and formulate with care the problem of choice which it presents. . . . It may be observed, however, that once the principles of justice are thought of as arising from an original agreement in a situation of equality, it is an open question whether the principle of utility would be acknowledged. Offhand it hardly seems likely that persons who view themselves as equals, entitled to press their claims upon one another, would agree to a principle which may require lesser life prospects for some simply for the sake of a greater sum of advantages enjoyed by others. Since each desires to protect his interests, his capacity to advance his conception of the good, no one has a reason to acquiesce in an enduring loss for himself in order to bring about a greater net balance of satisfaction. In the absence of strong and lasting benevolent impulses, a rational man would not accept a basic structure merely because it maximized the algebraic sum of advantages irrespective of its permanent effects on his own basic rights and interests. Thus it seems that the principle of utility is incompatible with the conception of social cooperation among equals for mutual advantage. It appears to be inconsistent with the idea of reciprocity implicit in the notion of a well-ordered society. Or, at any rate, so I shall argue.

I shall maintain instead that the persons in the initial situation would choose two rather different principles: the first requires equality in the assignment of basic rights and duties, while the second holds that social and economic inequalities, for example inequalities of wealth and authority, are just only if they result in compensating benefits for everyone, and in particular for the least advantaged members of society. These principles rule out justifying institutions on the grounds that the hardships of some are offset by a greater good in the aggregate. It may be expedient but it is not just that some should have less in order that others may prosper. But there is no injustice in the greater benefits earned by a few provided that the situation of persons not so fortunate is thereby improved. The intuitive idea is that since everyone's well-being depends upon a scheme of cooperation without which no one could have a satisfactory life, the division of advantages should be such as to draw forth the willing cooperation of everyone taking part in it, including those less well situated. Yet this can be expected only if reasonable terms are proposed. The two principles mentioned seem to be a fair agreement on the basis of which those better endowed, or more fortunate in their social position, neither of which we can be said to deserve, could expect the willing cooperation of others when some workable scheme is a necessary condition of the welfare of all.[3] Once we decide to look for a conception of justice that nullifies the accidents of natural endowment and the contingencies of social circumstance as counters in quest for political and economic advantage, we are led to these principles. They express the result of leaving aside those aspects of the social world that seem arbitrary from a moral point of view.

The problem of the choice of principles, however, is extremely difficult. I do not expect the answer I shall suggest to be convincing to everyone. It is, therefore, worth noting from the outset that justice as fairness, like other contract views, consists of two parts: (1) an interpretation of the initial situation and of the problem of choice posed there, and (2) a set of principles which, it is argued, would be agreed to. One may accept the first part of the theory (or some variant thereof), but not the other, and conversely. The concept of the initial contractual situation may seem reasonable although the particular principles proposed are rejected. To be sure, I want to maintain that the most appropriate conception of this situation does lead to principles of justice contrary to utilitarianism and perfectionism, and therefore that the contract doctrine provides an alternative to these views. . . .

A final remark. Justice as fairness is not a complete contract theory. For it is clear that the contractarian idea can be extended to the choice of more or less an entire ethical system, that is, to a system including principles for all the virtues and not only for justice. Now for the most part I shall consider only principles of justice and others closely related to them; I make no attempt to discuss the virtues in a systematic way. Obviously if justice as fairness succeeds reasonably well, a next step would be to study the more general view suggested by the name "rightness as fairness." But even this wider theory fails to embrace all moral relationships, since it would seem to include only our relations with other persons and to leave out of account how we are to conduct ourselves toward animals and the rest of nature. I do not contend that the contract notion offers a way to approach these questions which are certainly of the first importance; and I shall have to put them aside. We must recognize the limited scope of justice as fairness and of the general type of view that it exemplifies. How far its conclusions must be revised once these other matters are understood cannot be decided in advance. . . .

Two Principles of Justice

I shall now state in a provisional form the two principles of justice that I believe would be chosen in the original position. In this section I wish to make only the most general comments, and therefore the first formulation of these principles is tentative. As we go on I shall run through several formulations and approximate step by step the final statement to be given much later. I believe that doing this allows the exposition to proceed in a natural way.

The first statement of the two principles reads as follows.

> First: each person is to have an equal right to the most extensive basic liberty compatible with a similar liberty for others.

> Second: social and economic inequalities are to be arranged so that they are both (a) reasonably expected to be to everyone's advantage, and (b) attached to positions and offices open to all. . . .

By way of general comment, these principles primarily apply, as I have said, to the basic structure of society. They are to govern the assignment of rights and duties and to regulate the distribution of social and economic advantages. As their formulation suggests, these principles presuppose that the social structure can be divided into two more or less distinct parts, the first principle applying to the one, the second to the other. They distinguish between those aspects of the social system that define and secure the equal liberties of citizenship and those that specify and establish social and economic inequalities. The basic liberties of citizens are, roughly speaking, political liberty (the right to vote and to be eligible for public office) together with freedom of speech and assembly; liberty of conscience and freedom of thought; freedom of the person along with the right to hold (personal) property; and freedom from arbitrary arrest and seizure as defined by the concept of the rule of law. These liberties are all required to be equal by the first principle, since citizens of a just society are to have the same basic rights.

The second principle applies, in the first approximation, to the distribution of income and wealth and to the design of organizations that make use of differences in authority and responsibility, or chains of command. While the distribution of wealth and income need not be equal, it must be to everyone's advantage, and at the same time, positions of authority and offices of command must be accessible to all. One applies the second principle by holding positions open, and then, subject to this constraint, arranges social and economic inequalities so that everyone benefits.

These principles are to be arranged in a serial order with the first principle prior to the second. This ordering means that a departure from the institutions of equal liberty required by the first principle cannot be justified by, or compensated for, by greater social and economic advantages. The distribution of wealth and income, and the hierarchies of authority, must be consistent with both the liberties of equal citizenship and equality of opportunity.

It is clear that these principles are rather specific in their content, and their acceptance rests on certain assumptions that I must eventually try to explain and justify. A theory of justice depends upon a theory of society in ways that will become evidence as we proceed. For the present, it should be observed that the two principles (and this holds for all formulations) are a special case of a more general conception of justice that can be expressed as follows.

> All social values—liberty and opportunity, income and wealth, and the bases of self-respect—are to be distributed equally unless an unequal distribution of any, or all, of these values is to everyone's advantage.

Injustice, then, is simply inequalities that are not to the benefit of all. Of course, this conception is extremely vague and requires interpretation.

As a first step, suppose that the basic structure of society distributes certain primary goods, that is, things that every rational man is presumed to want. These goods normally have a use whatever a person's rational plan of life. For simplicity, assume that the chief primary goods at the disposition of society are rights and liberties, powers and opportunities, income and wealth. . . . These are the social primary goods. Other primary goods such as health and vigor, intelligence and imagination, are natural goods; although their possession is influenced by the basic structure, they are not so directly under its control. Imagine, then, a hypothetical initial arrangement in which all the social primary goods are equally distributed: everyone has similar rights and duties, and income and wealth are evenly shared. This state of affairs provides a benchmark for judging improvements. If certain inequalities of wealth and organizational powers would make everyone better off than in this hypothetical starting situation, then they accord with the general conception.

Now it is possible, at least theoretically, that by giving up some of their fundamental liberties men are sufficiently compensated by the resulting social and economic gains. The general conception of justice imposes no restrictions on what sort of inequalities are permissible; it only requires that everyone's position be improved. We need not suppose anything so drastic as consenting to a condition of slavery. Imagine instead that men forego certain political rights when the economic returns are significant and their capacity to influence the course of policy by the exercise of these rights would be marginal in any case. It is this kind of exchange which the two principles as stated rule out; being arranged in serial order they do not permit exchanges between basic liberties and economic and social gains. The serial ordering of principles expresses an underlying preference among primary social goods. When this preference is rational so likewise is the choice of these principles in this order.

In developing justice as fairness I shall, for the most part, leave aside the general conception of justice and examine instead the special case of the two principles in serial order. The advantage of this procedure is that from the first the matter of priorities is recognized and an effort made to find principles to deal with it. One is led to attend throughout to the conditions under which the acknowledgment of the absolute weight of liberty with respect to social and economic advantages, as defined by the lexical order of the two principles, would be reasonable. Offhand, this ranking appears extreme and too special a case to be of much interest; but there is more justification for it than would appear at first sight. Or at any rate, so I shall maintain. . . . Furthermore, the distinction between fundamental rights and liberties and economic and social benefits marks a difference among primary social goods that one should try to exploit. It suggests an important division in the social system. Of course, the distinctions drawn and the ordering proposed are bound to be at best only approximations. There are surely circumstances in which they fail. But it is essential to depict clearly the main lines of a reasonable conception of justice; and under many conditions anyway, the two principles in serial order may serve well enough. When necessary we can fall back on the more general conception.

The fact that the two principles apply to institutions has certain consequences. Several points illustrate this. First of all, the rights and liberties referred to by these principles are those which are defined by the public rules of the basic structure. Whether men are free is determined by the fights and duties established by the major institutions of society. Liberty is a certain pattern of social forms. The first principle simply requires that certain sorts of rules, those defining basic liberties, apply to everyone equally and that they allow the most extensive liberty compatible with a like liberty for all. The only reason for circumscribing the rights defining liberty and making men's freedom less extensive than it might otherwise be is that these equal rights as institutionally defined would interfere with one another.

Another thing to bear in mind is that when principles mention persons, or require that everyone gain from an inequality, the reference is to representative persons holding the various social positions, or offices, or whatever, established by the basic structure. Thus in applying the second principle I assume that it is possible to assign an expectation of well-being to representative individuals holding these positions. This expectation indicates their life prospects as viewed from their social station. In general, the expectations of representative persons depend upon the distribution of rights and duties throughout the basic structure. When this changes, expectations change. I assume, then, that expectations are connected: by raising the prospects of the representative man in one position we presumably increase or decrease the prospects of representative men in other positions. Since it applies to institutional forms, the second principle (or rather the first part of it) refers to the expectations of representative individuals. As I shall discuss below, neither principle applies to distributions of particular goods to particular individuals who may be identified by their proper names. The situation where someone is considering how to allocate certain commodities to needy persons who are known to him is not within the scope of the principles. They are meant to regulate basic institutional arrangements. We must not assume that there is much similarity from the standpoint of justice between an administrative allotment of goods to specific persons and the appropriate design of society. Our common sense intuitions for the former may be a poor guide to the latter.

Now the second principle insists that each person benefit from permissible inequalities in the basic structure. This means that it must be reasonable for each relevant representative man defined by this structure, when he views it as a going concern, to prefer his prospects with the inequality to his prospects without it. One is not allowed to justify differences in income or organizational powers on the ground that the disadvantages of those in one position are outweighed by the greater advantages of those in another. Much less can infringements of liberty be counterbalanced in this way. Applied to the basic structure, the principle of utility would have us maximize the sum of expectations of representative men (weighted by the number of persons they represent, on the classical view); and this would permit us to compensate for the losses of some by the gains of others. Instead, the two principles require that everyone benefit from economic and social inequalities. It is obvious, however, that there are indefinitely many ways in which all may be advantaged when the initial arrangement of equality is taken as a benchmark. How then are we to choose among these possibilities? The principles must be specified so that they yield a determinate conclusion. I now turn to this problem. . . .

Notes

1. As the text suggests, I shall regard Locke's *Second Treatise of Government*, Rousseau's *The Social Contract*, and Kant's ethical works beginning with *The Foundations of the Metaphysics of Morals* as definitive of the contract tradition. For all of its greatness, Hobbes's *Leviathan* raises special problems. A general historical survey is provided by J. W. Gough, *The Social Contract*, 2nd ed. (Oxford, The Clarendon Press, 1957), and Otto Gierke, *Natural Law and the Theory of Society*, trans. with an introduction by Ernest Barker (Cambridge, The University Press, 1934). A presentation of the contract view as primarily an ethical theory is to be found in G. R. Grice, *The Grounds of Moral Judgment* (Cambridge, The University Press, 1967). See also § 19, note 30. [The footnotes have been renumbered—Ed.]

2. Kant is clear that the original agreement is hypothetical. See *The Metaphysics of Morals*, pt. I (*Rechtslehre*), especially §§ 47, 52; and pt. II of the essay "Concerning the Common Saying: This May Be True in Theory but It Does Not Apply in Practice," in *Kant's Political Writings*, ed. Hans Reiss and trans. by H. B. Nisbet (Cambridge, The University Press, 1970), pp. 73–87. See Georges Vlachos, *La Pensée politique de Kant* (Paris, Presses Universitaires de France, 1962), pp. 326–335; and J. G. Murphy, *Kant: The Philosophy of Right* (London, Macmillan, 1970), pp. 109–112, 133–136, for a further discussion.

3. For the formulation of this intuitive idea I am indebted to Allan Gibbard.

The Entitlement Theory

Robert Nozick

The minimal state is the most extensive state that can be justified. Any state more extensive violates people's rights. Yet many persons have put forth reasons purporting to justify a more extensive state. It is impossible within the compass of this book to examine all the reasons that have been put forth. Therefore, I shall focus upon those generally acknowledged to be most weighty and influential, to see precisely wherein they fail. In this chapter we consider the claim that a more extensive state is justified, because necessary (or the best instrument) to achieve distributive justice; in the next chapter we shall take up diverse other claims.

The term "distributive justice" is not a neutral one. Hearing the term "distribution," most people presume that some thing or mechanism uses some principle or criterion to give out a supply of things. Into this process of distributing shares some error may have crept. So it is an open question, at least, whether *re*distribution should take place; whether we should do again what has already been done once, though poorly. However, we are not in the position of children who have been given portions of pie by someone who now makes last-minute adjustments to rectify careless cutting. There is no *central* distribution, no person or group entitled to control all the resources, jointly deciding how they are to be doled out. What each person gets, he gets from others who give to him in exchange for something, or as a gift. In a free society, diverse persons control different resources, and new holdings arise out of the voluntary exchanges and actions of persons. There is no more a distributing or distribution of shares than there is a distributing of mates in a society in which persons choose whom they shall marry. The total result is the product of many individual decisions which the different individuals involved are entitled to make. Some uses of the term "distribution," it is true, do not imply a previous distributing appropriately judged by some criteron (for example, "probability distribution"); nevertheless, despite the title of this chapter, it would be best to use a terminology that clearly is neutral. We shall speak of people's holdings; a principle of justice in holdings describes (part of) what justice tells us (requires) about holdings. I shall state first what I take to be the correct view about justice in holdings, and then turn to the discussion of alternate views.

I

The Entitlement Theory

The subject of justice in holdings consists of three major topics. The first is the *original acquisition of holdings,* the appropriation of unheld things.

75

This includes the issues of how unheld things may come to be held, the process, or processes, by which unheld things may come to be held, the things that may come to be held by these processes, the extent of what comes to be held by a particular process, and so on. We shall refer to the complicated truth about this topic, which we shall not formulate here, as the principle of justice in acquisition. The second topic concerns the *transfer of holdings* from one person to another. By what processes may a person transfer holdings to another? How may a person acquire a holding from another who holds it? Under this topic come general descriptions of voluntary exchange, and gift and (on the other hand) fraud, as well as reference to particular conventional details fixed upon in a given society. The complicated truth about this subject (with placeholders for conventional details) we shall call the principle of justice in transfer. (And we shall suppose it also includes principles governing how a person may divest himself of a holding, passing it into an unheld state.)

If the world were wholly just, the following inductive definition would exhaustively cover the subject of justice in holdings.

1. A person who acquires a holding in accordance with the principle of justice in acquisition is entitled to that holding.
2. A person who acquires a holding in accordance with the principle of justice in transfer, from someone else entitled to the holding, is entitled to the holding.
3. No one is entitled to a holding except by (repeated) applications of 1 and 2.

The complete principle of distributive justice would say simply that a distribution is just if everyone is entitled to the holdings they possess under the distribution.

A distribution is just if it arises from another just distribution by legitimate means. The legitimate means of moving from one distribution to another are specified by the principle of justice in transfer. The legitimate first "moves" are specified by the principle of justice in acquisition.[1] Whatever arises from a just situation by just steps is itself just. The means of change specified by the principle of justice in transfer preserve justice. As correct rules of inference are truth-preserving, and any conclusion deduced via repeated application of such rules from only true premises is itself true, so the means of transition from one situation to another specified by the principle of justice in transfer are justice-preserving, and any situation actually arising from repeated transitions in accordance with the principle from a just situation is itself just. The parallel between justice-preserving transformations and truth-preserving transformations illuminates where it fails as well as where it holds. That a conclusion could have been deduced by truth-preserving means from premises that are true suffices to show its truth. That from a just situation a situation *could* have arisen via justice-preserving means does *not* suffice to show its justice. The fact that a thief's victims voluntarily *could* have presented him with gifts does not entitle the thief to his ill-gotten gains. Justice in holdings is historical; it depends upon what actually has happened. We shall return to this point later.

Not all actual situations are generated in accordance with the two principles of justice in holdings: the principle of justice in acquisition and the principle of justice in transfer. Some people steal from others, or defraud them, or enslave them, seizing their product and preventing them from living as they choose, or forcibly exclude others from competing in exchanges. None of these are permissible modes of transition from one situation to another. And some persons acquire holdings by means not sanctioned by the principle of justice in acquisition. The existence of past injustice (previous violations of the first two principles of justice in holdings) raises the third major topic under justice in holdings: the rectification of injustice in holdings. If past injustice has shaped present holdings in various ways, some identifiable and some not, what now, if anything, ought to be done to rectify these injustices? What obligations do the performers of injustice have toward those whose position is worse than it would have been had the injustice not been done? Or, than it would have been had compensation been paid promptly? How, if at all, do things change if the beneficiaries and those made worse off are not the direct parties in the act of injustice, but, for example, their descendants? Is an injustice done to someone whose holding was itself based upon an unrectified injustice? How far back must one go in wiping clean the historical slate of injustices? What may victims of injustice permissibly do in order to rectify the injustices being done to them, including the many injustices done by persons acting through their government? I do not know of a thorough or theoretically sophisticated treatment of such issues. Idealizing greatly, let us suppose theoretical investigation will produce a principle of rectification. This principle uses historical information about previous situations and injustices done in them (as defined by the first two principles of justice and rights against interference), and information about the actual course of events that flowed from these injustices, until the present, and it yields a description (or descriptions) of holdings in the society. The principle of rectification presumably will make use of its best estimate of subjunctive information about what would have occurred (or a probability distribution over what might have occurred, using the expected value) if the injustice had not taken place. If the actual description of holdings turns out not to be one of the descriptions yielded by the principle, then one of the descriptions yielded must be realized.

The general outlines of the theory of justice in holdings are that the holdings of a person are just if he is entitled to them by the principles of justice in acquisition and transfer, or by the principle of rectification of injustice (as specified by the first two principles). If each person's holdings are just, then the total set (distribution) of holdings is just. To turn these general outlines into a specific theory we would have to specify the details of each of the three principles of justice in holdings: the principle of acquisition of holdings, the principle of transfer of holdings, and the principle of rectification of violations of the first two principles. I shall not attempt that task here. . . .

Historical Principles and End-Result Principles

The general outlines of the entitlement theory illuminate the nature and defects of other conceptions of distributive justice. The entitlement theory of justice in distribution is *historical;* whether a distribution is just depends upon how it came about. In contrast, *current time-slice principles* of justice hold that the justice of a distribution is determined by how things are distributed (who has what) as judged by some *structural* principle(s) of just distribution. A utilitarian who judges between any two distributions by seeing which has the greater sum of utility and, if the sums tie, applies some fixed equality criterion to choose the more equal distribution, would hold a current time-slice principle of justice. As would someone who had a fixed schedule of trade-offs between the sum of happiness and equality. According to a current time-slice principle, all that needs to be looked at, in judging the justice of a distribution, is who ends up with what; in comparing any two distributions one need look only at the matrix presenting the distributions. No further information need be fed into a principle of justice. It is a consequence of such principles of justice that any two structurally identical distributions are equally just. (Two distributions are structurally identical if they present the same profile, but perhaps have different persons occupying the particular slots. My having ten and your having five, and my having five and your having ten are structurally identical distributions.) Welfare economics is the theory of current time-slice principles of justice. The subject is conceived as operating on matrices representing only current information about distribution. This, as well as some of the usual conditions (for example, the choice of distribution is invariant under relabeling of columns), guarantees that welfare economics will be a current time-slice theory, with all of its inadequacies.

Most persons do not accept current time-slice principles as constituting the whole story about distributive shares. They think it relevant in assessing the justice of a situation to consider not only the distribution it embodies, but also how that distribution came about. If some persons are in prison for murder or war crimes, we do not say that to assess the justice of the distribution in the society we must look only at what this person has, and that person has, and that person has, . . . at the current time. We think it relevant to ask whether someone did something so that he *deserved* to be punished, deserved to have a lower share. Most will agree to the relevance of further information with regard to punishments and penalties. Consider also desired things. One traditional socialist view is that workers are entitled to the product and full fruits of their labor; they have earned it; a distribution is unjust if it does not give the workers what they are entitled to. Such entitlements are based upon some past history. No socialist holding this view would find it comforting to be told that because the actual distribution *A* happens to coincide structurally with the one he desires *D, A* therefore is no less just than *D;* it differs only in that the "parasitic" owners of capital receive under *A* what the workers are entitled to under *D,* and the workers receive under *A* what the owners are entitled to under *D,* namely very little. This socialist rightly, in my view, holds onto the notions of earning, producing, entitlement, desert, and so forth, and he rejects current time-slice principles that look only to the structure of the resulting set of holdings. (The set of holdings resulting from what? Isn't it implausible that how holdings are produced and come to exist has no effect at all on who should hold what?) His mistake lies in his view of what entitlements arise out of what

78

sorts of productive processes.

We construe the position we discuss too narrowly by speaking of *current* time-slice principles. Nothing is changed if structural principles operate upon a time sequence of current time-slice profiles and, for example, give someone more now to counterbalance the less he has had earlier. A utilitarian or an egalitarian or any mixture of the two over time will inherit the difficulties of his more myopic comrades. He is not helped by the fact that *some* of the information others consider relevant in assessing a distribution is reflected, unrecoverably, in past matrices. Henceforth, we shall refer to such unhistorical principles of distributive justice, including the current time-slice principles, as *end-result principles* or *end-state principles*.

In contrast to end-result principles of justice, *historical principles* of justice hold that past circumstances or actions of people can create differential entitlements or differential deserts to things. An injustice can be worked by moving from one distribution to another structurally identical one, for the second, in profile the same, may violate people's entitlements or deserts; it may not fit the actual history.

———————

How Liberty Upsets Patterns

It is not clear how those holding alternative conceptions of distributive justice can reject the entitlement conception of justice in holdings. For suppose a distribution favored by one of these nonentitlement conceptions is realized. Let us suppose it is your favorite one and let us call this distribution D_1; perhaps everyone has an equal share, perhaps shares vary in accordance with some dimension you treasure. Now suppose that Wilt Chamberlain is greatly in demand by basketball teams, being a great gate attraction. (Also suppose contracts run only for a year, with players being free agents.) He signs the following sort of contract with a team: In each home game, twenty-five cents from the price of each ticket of admission goes to him. (We ignore the question of whether he is "gouging" the owners, letting them look out for themselves.) The season starts, and people cheerfully attend his team's games; they buy their tickets, each time dropping a separate twenty-five cents of their admission price into a special box with Chamberlain's name on it. They are excited about seeing him play; it is worth the total admission price to them. Let us suppose that in one season one million persons attend his home games, and Wilt Chamberlain winds up with $250,000, a much larger sum than the average income and larger even than anyone else has. Is he entitled to this income? Is this new distribution D_2, unjust? If so, why? There is *no* question about whether each of the people was entitled to the control over the resources they held in D_1; because that was the distribution (your favorite) that (for the purposes of argument) we assumed was acceptable. Each of these persons *chose* to give twenty-five cents of their money to Chamberlain. They could have spent it on going to the movies, or on candy bars, or on copies of *Dissent* magazine, or of *Monthly Review*. But they all, at least one million of them, converged on giving it to Wilt Chamberlain in exchange for watching him play basketball. If D_1 was a just distribution, and people voluntarily moved from it to D_2, transferring parts of their shares they were given under D_1 (what was it for if not to do something with?), isn't D_2 also just? If the people were entitled to dispose of the resources to which they were entitled (under D_1), didn't this include their being entitled to give it to, or exchange it with, Wilt Chamberlain? Can anyone else complain on grounds of justice? Each other person already has his legitimate share under D_1. Under D_1, there is nothing that anyone has that anyone else has a claim of justice against. After someone transfers something to Wilt Chamberlain, third parties *still* have their legitimate shares; *their* shares are not changed. By what process could such a transfer among two persons give rise to a legitimate claim of distributive justice on a portion of what was transferred, by a third party who had no claim of justice on any holding of the others *before* the transfer? To cut off objections irrelevant here, we might imagine the exchanges occurring in a socialist society, after hours. After playing whatever basketball he does in his daily work, or doing whatever other daily work he does, Wilt Chamberlain decides to put in *overtime* to earn additional money. (First his work quota is set; he works time over that.) Or imagine it is a skilled juggler people like to see, who puts on shows after hours.

Why might someone work overtime in a society in which it is assumed their needs are satisfied? Perhaps because they care about things other than needs. I like to write in books that I read, and to have easy access to books for browsing at odd hours. It would be very pleasant and convenient to have the resources of Widener Library in my back yard. No society, I assume, will provide such resources close to each person who would like them as part of his regular allotment (under D_1). Thus, persons either must do without some extra things that they want, or be allowed to do something extra to get some of these things. On what basis could the inequalities that would eventuate be forbidden? Notice also that small factories would spring up in a socialist society, unless forbidden. I melt down some of my personal possessions (under D_1) and build a machine out of the material. I offer you, and others, a philosophy lecture once a week in exchange for your cranking the handle on my machine, whose products I exchange for yet other things, and so on. (The raw materials used by the machine are given to me by others who possess them under D_1, in exchange for hearing lectures.) Each person might participate to gain things over and above their allotment under D_1. Some persons even might want to leave their job in socialist industry and work full time in this private sector. I shall say something more about these issues in the next chapter. Here I wish merely to note how private property even in means of production would occur in a socialist society that did not forbid people to use as they wished some of the resources they are given under the socialist distribution D_1. The socialist society would have to forbid capitalist acts between consenting adults.

The general point illustrated by the Wilt Chamberlain example and the example of the entrepreneur in a socialist society is that no end-state principle or distributional patterned principle of justice can be continuously realized without continuous interference with people's lives. Any favored pattern would be transformed into one unfavored by the principle, by people choosing to act in various ways; for example, by people exchanging goods and services with other people, or giving things to other people, things the transferrers are entitled to under the favored distributional pattern. To maintain a pattern one must either continually interfere to stop people from transferring resources as they wish to, or continually (or periodically) interfere to take from some persons resources that others for some reason chose to transfer to them. (But if some time limit is to be set on how long people may keep resources others voluntarily transfer to them, why let them keep these resources for *any* period of time? Why not have immediate confiscation?) It might be objected that all persons voluntarily will choose to refrain from actions which would upset the pattern. This presupposes unrealistically (1) that all will most want to maintain the pattern (are those who don't, to be "reeducated" or forced to undergo "self-criticism"?), (2) that each can gather enough information about his own actions and the ongoing activities of others to discover which of his actions will upset the pattern, and (3) that diverse and far-flung persons can coordinate their actions to dove-tail into the pattern. Compare the manner in which the market is neutral among persons' desires, as it reflects and transmits widely scattered information via prices, and coordinates persons' activities.

It puts things perhaps a bit too strongly to say that every patterned (or end-state) principle is liable to be thwarted by the voluntary actions of the individual parties transferring some of their shares they receive under the principle. For perhaps some *very* weak patterns are not so thwarted. Any distributional pattern with any egalitarian component is overturnable by the voluntary actions of individual persons over time; as is every patterned condition with sufficient content so as actually to have been proposed as presenting the central core of distributive justice. Still, given the possibility that some weak conditions or patterns may not be unstable in this way, it would be better to formulate an explicit description of the kind of interesting and contentful patterns under discussion, and to prove a theorem about their instability. Since the weaker the patterning, the more likely it is that the entitlement system itself satisfies it, a plausible conjecture is that any patterning either is unstable or is satisfied by the entitlement system.

Note

1. Applications of the principle of justice in acquisition may also occur as part of the move from one distribution to another. You may find an unheld thing now and appropriate it. Acquisitions also are to be understood as included when, to simplify, I speak only of transitions by transfers.

Values in Tension:
Ethics Away from Home

Thomas Donaldson

When we leave home and cross our nation's boundaries, moral clarity often blurs. Without a backdrop of shared attitudes, and without familiar laws and judicial procedures that define standards of ethical conduct, certainty is elusive. Should a company invest in a foreign country where civil and political rights are violated? Should a company go along with a host country's discriminatory employment practices? If companies in developed countries shift facilities to developing nations that lack strict environmental and health regulations, or if those companies choose to fill management and other top-level positions in a host nation with people from the home country, whose standards should prevail?

Even the best-informed, best-intentioned executives must rethink their assumptions about business practice in foreign settings. What works in a company's home country can fail in a country with different standards of ethical conduct. Such difficulties are unavoidable for businesspeople who live and work abroad.

But how can managers resolve the problems? What are the principles that can help them work through the maze of cultural differences and establish codes of conduct for globally ethical business practice? How can companies answer the toughest question in global business ethics: What happens when a host country's ethical standards seem lower than the home country's?

Competing Answers

One answer is as old as philosophical discourse. According to cultural relativism, no culture's ethics are better than any other's; therefore there are no international rights and wrongs. If the people of Indonesia tolerate the bribery of their public officials, so what? Their attitude is no better or worse than that of people in Denmark or Singapore who refuse to offer or accept bribes. Likewise, if Belgians fail to find insider trading morally repugnant, who cares? Not enforcing insider-trading laws is no more or less ethical than enforcing such laws.

The cultural relativist's creed—When in Rome, do as the Romans do—is tempting, especially when failing to do as the locals do means forfeiting business opportunities. The inadequacy of cultural relativism, however, becomes apparent when the practices in question are more damaging than petty bribery or insider trading.

In the late 1980s, some European tanneries and pharmaceutical companies were looking for cheap waste-dumping sites. They approached

---

The Culture and Ethics of Software Piracy

Before jumping on the cultural relativism bandwagon, stop and consider the potential economic consequences of a when-in-Rome attitude toward business ethics. Take a look at the current statistics on software piracy: In the United States, pirated software is estimated to be 35% of the total software market, and industry losses are estimated at $2.3 billion per year. The piracy rate is 57% in Germany and 80% in Italy and Japan; the rates in most Asian countries are estimated to be nearly 100%.

There are similar laws against software piracy in those countries. What, then, accounts for the differences? Although a country's level of economic development plays a large part, culture, including ethical attitudes, may be a more crucial factor. The 1995 annual report of the Software Publishers Association connects software piracy directly to culture and attitude. It describes Italy and Hong Kong as having "'first world' per capita incomes, along with 'third world' rates of piracy." When asked whether one should use software without paying for it, most people, including people in Italy and Hong Kong, say no. But people in some countries regard the practice as *less* unethical than people in other countries do. Confucian culture, for example, stresses that individuals should share what they create with society. That may be, in part, what prompts the Chinese and other Asians to view the concept of intellectual property as a means for the West to monopolize its technological superiority.

What happens if ethical attitudes around the world permit large-scale software piracy? Software companies won't want to invest as much in developing new products, because they cannot expect any return on their investment in certain parts of the world. When ethics fail to support technological creativity, there are consequences that go beyond statistics—jobs are lost and livelihoods jeopardized.

Companies must do more than lobby foreign governments for tougher enforcement of piracy laws. They must cooperate with other companies and with local organizations to help citizens understand the consequences of piracy and to encourage the evolution of a different ethic toward the practice.

---

virtually every country on Africa's west coast from Morocco to the Congo. Nigeria agreed to take highly toxic polychlorinated biphenyls. Unprotected local workers, wearing thongs and shorts, unloaded barrels of PCBs and placed them near a residential area. Neither the residents nor the workers knew that the barrels contained toxic waste.

We may denounce governments that permit such abuses, but many countries are unable to police transnational corporations adequately even if they want to. And in many countries, the combination of ineffective enforcement and inadequate regulations leads to behavior by unscrupulous companies that is clearly wrong. A few years ago, for example, a group of investors became interested in restoring the SS *United States*, once a luxurious ocean liner. Before the actual restoration could begin, the ship had to be stripped of its asbestos lining. A bid from a U.S. company, based on U.S. standards for asbestos removal, priced the job at more than $100 million. A company in the Ukranian city of Sevastopol offered to do the work for less than $2 million. In October 1993, the ship was towed to Sevastopol.

A cultural relativist would have no problem with that outcome, but I do. A country has the right to establish its own health and safety regulations, but in the case described above, the standards and the terms of the contract could not possibly have protected workers in Sevastopol from known health risks. Even if the contract met Ukranian standards, ethical businesspeople must object. Cultural relativism is morally blind. There are fundamental values that cross cultures, and companies must uphold them. (For an economic argument against cultural relativism, see the insert "The Culture and Ethics of Software Piracy.")

At the other end of the spectrum from cultural relativism is ethical imperialism, which directs people to do everywhere exactly as they do at home. Again, an understandably appealing approach but one that is clearly inadequate. Consider the large U.S. computer-products company that in 1993 introduced a course on sexual harassment in its Saudi Arabian facility. Under the banner of global consistency, instructors used the same approach to train Saudi Arabian managers that they had used with U.S. managers: the participants were asked to discuss a case in which a manager makes sexually explicit remarks to a new female employee over drinks in a bar. The instructors failed to consider how the exercise would work in a culture with strict conventions governing relationships between men and women. As a result, the training sessions

84

were ludicrous. They baffled and offended the Saudi participants, and the message to avoid coercion and sexual discrimination was lost.

The theory behind ethical imperialism is absolutism, which is based on three problematic principles. Absolutists believe that there is a single list of truths, that they can be expressed only with one set of concepts, and that they call for exactly the same behavior around the world.

The first claim clashes with many people's belief that different cultural traditions must be respected. In some cultures, loyalty to a community—family, organization, or society—is the foundation of all ethical behavior. The Japanese, for example, define business ethics in terms of loyalty to their companies, their business networks, and their nation. Americans place a higher value on liberty than on loyalty; the U.S. tradition of rights emphasizes equality, fairness, and individual freedom. It is hard to conclude that truth lies on one side or the other, but an absolutist would have us select just one.

The second problem with absolutism is the presumption that people must express moral truth using only one set of concepts. For instance, some absolutists insist that the language of basic rights provide the framework for any discussion of ethics. That means, though, that entire cultural traditions must be ignored. The notion of a right evolved with the rise of democracy in post-Renaissance Europe and the United States, but the term is not found in either Confucian or Buddhist traditions. We all learn ethics in the context of our particular cultures, and the power in the principles is deeply tied to the way in which they are expressed. Internationally accepted lists of moral principles, such as the United Nations' Universal Declaration of Human Rights, draw on many cultural and religious traditions. As philosopher Michael Walzer has noted, "There is no Esperanto of global ethics."

The third problem with absolutism is the belief in a global standard of ethical behavior. Context must shape ethical practice. Very low wages, for example, may be considered unethical in rich, advanced countries, but developing nations may be acting ethically if they encourage investment and improve living standards by accepting low wages. Likewise, when people are malnourished or starving, a government may be wise to use more fertilizer in order to improve crop yields, even though that means settling for relatively high levels of thermal water pollution.

When cultures have different standards of ethical behavior—and different ways of handling unethical behavior—a company that takes an absolutist approach may find itself making a disastrous mistake. When a manager at a large U.S. specialty-products company in China caught an employee stealing, she followed the company's practice and turned the employee over to the provincial authorities, who executed him. Managers cannot operate in another culture without being aware of that culture's attitudes toward ethics.

If companies can neither adopt a host country's ethics nor extend the home country's standards, what is the answer? Even the traditional litmus test—What would people think of your actions if they were written up on the front page of the newspaper?—is an unreliable guide, for there is no international consensus on standards of business conduct.

Balancing the Extremes: Three Guiding Principles

Companies must help managers distinguish between practices that are merely different and those that are wrong. For relativists, nothing is sacred and nothing is wrong. For absolutists, many things that are different are wrong. Neither extreme illuminates the real world of business decision making. The answer lies somewhere in between.

When it comes to shaping ethical behavior, companies must be guided by three principles.

- Respect for core human values, which determine the absolute moral threshold for all business activities.
- Respect for local traditions.
- The belief that context matters when deciding what is right and what is wrong.

Consider those principles in action. In Japan, people doing business together often exchange gifts—sometimes expensive ones—in keeping with long-standing Japanese tradition. When U.S. and European companies started doing a lot of business in Japan, many Western businesspeople thought that the practice of gift giving might be wrong rather than simply different. To them, accepting a gift felt like accepting a bribe. As Western companies have become more familiar with Japanese traditions, however, most have come to tolerate the practice and to set different limits on gift giving in Japan than they do elsewhere.

What Do These Values Have in Common?

Non-Western	Western
Kyosei (Japanese): Living and working together for the common good.	Individual liberty
Dharma (Hindu): The fulfillment of inherited duty.	Egalitarianism
Santutthi (Buddhist): The importance of limited desires.	Political participation
Zakat (Muslim): The duty to give alms to the Muslim poor.	Human rights

Respecting differences is a crucial ethical practice. Research shows that management ethics differ among cultures; respecting those differences means recognizing that some cultures have obvious weaknesses—as well as hidden strengths. Managers in Hong Kong, for example, have a higher tolerance for some forms of bribery than their Western counterparts, but they have a much lower tolerance for the failure to acknowledge a subordinate's work. In some parts of the Far East, stealing credit from a subordinate is nearly an unpardonable sin.

People often equate respect for local traditions with cultural relativism. That is incorrect. Some practices are clearly wrong. Union Carbide's tragic experience in Bhopal, India, provides one example. The company's executives seriously underestimated how much on-site management involvement was needed at the Bhopal plant to compensate for the country's poor infrastructure and regulatory capabilities. In the aftermath of the disastrous gas leak, the lesson is clear: companies using sophisticated technology in a developing country must evaluate that country's ability to oversee its safe use. Since the incident at Bhopal, Union Carbide has become a leader in advising companies on using hazardous technologies safely in developing countries.

Some activities are wrong no matter where they take place. But some practices that are unethical in one setting may be acceptable in another. For instance, the chemical EDB, a soil fungicide, is banned for use in the United States. In hot climates, however, it quickly becomes harmless through exposure to intense solar radiation and high soil temperatures. As long as the chemical is monitored, companies may be able to use EDB ethically in certain parts of the world.

Defining the Ethical Threshold: Core Values

Few ethical questions are easy for managers to answer. But there are some hard truths that must guide managers' actions, a set of what I call *core human values*, which define minimum ethical standards for all companies.[1] The right to good health and the right to economic advancement and an improved standard of living are two core human values. Another is what Westerners call the Golden Rule, which is recognizable in every major religious and ethical tradition around the world. In Book 15 of his *Analects*, for instance, Confucius counsels people to maintain reciprocity, or not to do to others what they do not want done to themselves.

Although no single list would satisfy every scholar, I believe it is possible to articulate three core values that incorporate the work of scores of theologians and philosophers around the world. To be broadly relevant, these values must include elements found in both Western and non-Western cultural and religious traditions. Consider the examples of values in the insert "What Do These Values Have in Common?"

At first glance, the values expressed in the two lists seem quite different. Nonetheless, in the spirit of what philosopher John Rawls calls *overlapping consensus*, one can see that the seemingly divergent values converge at key points. Despite important differences between Western and non-Western cultural and religious traditions, both express shared attitudes about what it means to be human. First, individuals must not treat others simply as tools; in other words, they must recognize a person's value as a human being. Next, individuals and communities must treat people in ways that respect people's basic rights. Finally, members of a community must work together to support and improve the institutions on which the community depends. I call those three values *respect for human dignity, respect for basic rights,* and *good citizenship*.

Those values must be the starting point for all companies as they formulate and evaluate standards of ethical conduct at home and abroad. But they are only a starting point. Companies need much more specific guidelines, and the first step to developing those is to translate the core human values into core values for business. What does it mean, for example, for a company to respect human dignity? How can a company be a good citizen?

I believe that companies can respect human dignity by creating and sustaining a corporate culture in which employees, customers, and suppliers are treated not as means to an end but as people whose intrinsic value must be acknowledged, and by producing safe products and services in a safe workplace. Companies can respect basic rights by acting in ways that support and protect the individual rights of employees, customers, and surrounding communities, and by avoiding relationships that violate human beings' rights to health, education, safety, and an adequate standard of living. And companies can be good citizens by supporting essential social institutions, such as the economic system and the education system, and by working with host governments and other organizations to protect the environment.

The core values establish a moral compass for business practice. They can help companies identify practices that are acceptable and those that are intolerable even if the practices are compatible with a host country's norms and laws. Dumping pollutants near people's homes and accepting inadequate standards for handling hazardous materials are two examples of actions that violate core values.

Similarly, if employing children prevents them from receiving a basic education, the practice is intolerable. Lying about product specifications in the act of selling may not affect human lives directly, but it too is intolerable because it violates the trust that is needed to sustain a corporate culture in which customers are respected.

Sometimes it is not a company's actions but those of a supplier or customer that pose problems. Take the case of the Tan family, a large supplier for Levi Strauss. The Tans were allegedly forcing 1,200 Chinese and Filipino women to work 74 hours per week in guarded compounds on the Mariana Islands. In 1992, after repeated warnings to the Tans, Levi Strauss broke off business relations with them.

Creating an Ethical Corporate Culture

The core values for business that I have enumerated can help companies begin to exercise ethical judgment and think about how to operate ethically in foreign cultures, but they are not specific enough to guide managers through actual ethical dilemmas. Levi Strauss relied on a written code of conduct when figuring out how to deal with the Tan family. The company's Global Sourcing and Operating Guidelines, formerly called the Business Partner Terms of Engagement, state that Levi Strauss will "seek to identify and utilize business partners who aspire as individuals and in the conduct of all their businesses to a set of ethical standards not incompatible with our own." Whenever intolerable business situations arise, managers should be guided by precise statements that spell out the behavior and operating practices that the company demands.

Ninety percent of all *Fortune* 500 companies have codes of conduct, and 70% have statements of vision and values. In Europe and the Far East, the percentages are lower but are increasing rapidly. Does that mean that most companies have what they need? Hardly. Even though most large U.S. companies have both statements of values and codes of conduct, many might be better off if they didn't. Too many companies don't do anything with the documents; they simply paste them on the wall to impress employees, customers, suppliers, and the public. As a result, the senior managers who drafted the statements lose credibility by proclaiming values and not living up to them. Companies such as Johnson & Johnson, Levi Strauss, Motorola, Texas Instruments, and Lockheed Martin, however, do a great deal to make the words meaningful. Johnson & Johnson, for example, has become well known for its Credo Challenge sessions, in which managers discuss ethics in the context of their current business problems and are invited to criticize the company's credo and make suggestions for changes. The participants' ideas are passed on to the company's senior managers. Lockheed Martin has created an innovative site on the World Wide Web and on its local network that gives employees, customers, and suppliers access to the company's ethical code and the chance to voice complaints.

Codes of conduct must provide clear direction about ethical behavior when the temptation to behave unethically is strongest. The pronouncement in a code of conduct that bribery is unacceptable is useless unless accompanied by guidelines for gift giving, payments to get goods through customs, and "requests" from intermediaries who are hired to ask for bribes.

Motorola's values are stated very simply as "How we will always act: [with] constant respect for people [and] uncompromising integrity." The company's code of conduct, however, is explicit about actual business practice. With respect to bribery, for example, the code states that the "funds and assets of Motorola shall not be used, directly or indirectly, for illegal payments of any kind." It is unambiguous about what sort of payment is illegal: "the payment of a bribe to a public official or the kickback of funds to an employee of a customer. . . ." The code goes on to prescribe specific procedures for handling commissions to intermediaries, issuing sales invoices, and disclosing confidential information in a sales transaction—all situations in which employees might have an opportunity to accept or offer bribes.

Codes of conduct must be explicit to be useful, but they must also leave room for a manager to use his or her judgment in situations requiring cultural sensitivity. Host-country employees shouldn't be forced to adopt all home-country values and renounce their own. Again, Motorola's code is exemplary. First, it gives clear direction: "Employees of Motorola will respect the laws, customs, and traditions of each country in which they operate, but will, at the same time, engage in no course of conduct which, even if legal, customary, and accepted in any such country, could be deemed to be in violation of the accepted business ethics of Motorola or the laws of the United States relating to business ethics." After laying down such absolutes, Motorola's code then makes clear when individual judgment will be necessary. For example, employees may sometimes accept certain kinds of small gifts "in rare circumstances, where the refusal to accept a gift" would injure Motorola's "legitimate business interests." Under certain circumstances, such gifts "may be accepted so long as the gift inures to the benefit of Motorola" and not "to the benefit of the Motorola employee."

Striking the appropriate balance between providing clear direction and leaving room for individual judgment makes crafting corporate values statements and ethics codes one of the hardest tasks that executives confront. The words are only a start. A company's leaders need to refer often to their organization's credo and code and must themselves be credible, committed, and consistent. If senior managers act as though ethics don't matter, the rest of the company's employees won't think they do, either.

Conflicts of Development and Conflicts of Tradition

Managers living and working abroad who are not prepared to grapple with moral ambiguity and tension should pack their bags and come home. The view that all business practices can be categorized as either ethical or unethical is too simple. As Einstein is reported to have said, "Things should be as simple as possible—but no simpler." Many business practices that are considered unethical in one setting may be ethical in another. Such activities are neither black nor white but exist in what Thomas Dunfee and I have called *moral free space*.[2] In this gray zone, there are no tight prescriptions for a company's behavior. Managers must chart their own courses—as long as they do not violate core human values.

Consider the following example. Some successful Indian companies offer employees the opportunity for one of their children to gain a job with the company once the child has completed a certain level in school. The companies honor this commitment even when other applicants are more qualified than an employee's child. The perk is extremely valuable in a country where jobs are hard to find, and it reflects the Indian culture's belief that the West has gone too far in allowing economic opportunities to break up families. Not surprisingly, the perk is among the most cherished by employees, but in most Western countries, it would be branded unacceptable nepotism. In the United States, for example, the ethical principle of equal opportunity holds that jobs should go to the applicants with the best qualifications. If a U.S. company made such promises to its employees, it would violate regulations established by the Equal Employment Opportunity Commission. Given this difference in ethical attitudes, how should U.S. managers react to Indian nepotism? Should they condemn the Indian companies, refusing to accept them as partners or suppliers until they agree to clean up their act?

Despite the obvious tension between nepotism and principles of equal opportunity, I cannot condemn the practice for Indians. In a country, such as India, that emphasizes clan and family relationships and has catastrophic levels of unemployment, the practice must be viewed in moral free space. The decision to allow a special perk for employees and their children is not necessarily wrong—at least for members of that country.

How can managers discover the limits of moral free space? That is, how can they learn to distinguish a value in tension with their own from one that is intolerable? Helping managers develop good ethical judgment requires companies to be clear about their core values and codes of conduct. But even the most explicit set of guidelines cannot always provide answers. That is especially true in the thorniest ethical dilemmas, in which the host country's ethical standards not only are different but also seem lower than the home country's. Managers must recognize that when countries have different ethical standards, there are two types of conflict that commonly arise. Each type requires its own line of reasoning.

In the first type of conflict, which I call a *conflict of relative development*, ethical standards conflict because of the countries' different levels of economic development. As mentioned before, developing countries may accept wage rates that seem inhumane to more advanced countries in order to attract investment. As economic conditions in a developing country improve, the incidence of that sort of conflict usually decreases. The second type of conflict is a *conflict of cultural tradition*. For example, Saudi Arabia, unlike most other countries, does not allow women to serve as corporate managers. Instead, women may work in only a few professions, such as education and health care. The prohibition stems from strongly held religious and cultural beliefs; any increase in the country's level of economic development, which is already quite high, is not likely to change the rules.

To resolve a conflict of relative development, a manager must ask the following question: Would the practice be acceptable at home if my country were in a similar stage of economic development? Consider the difference between wage and safety standards in the United States and in Angola, where citizens accept lower standards on both counts. If a U.S. oil company is hiring Angolans to work on an offshore Angolan oil rig, can the company pay them lower wages than it pays U.S. workers in the Gulf of Mexico? Reasonable people have to answer yes if the alternative for Angola is the loss of both the foreign investment and the jobs.

Consider, too, differences in regulatory environments. In the 1980s, the government of India fought hard to be able to import Ciba-Geigy's Entero Vioform, a drug known to be enormously effective in fighting dysentery but one that had been banned in the United States because some users experienced side effects. Although dysentery was not a big problem in the United States, in India, poor public sanitation was contributing to epidemic levels of the disease. Was it unethical to make the drug available in India after it had been banned in the United States? On the contrary, rational people should consider it unethical not to do so. Apply our test: Would the United States, at an earlier stage of development, have used this drug despite its side effects? The answer is clearly yes.

But there are many instances when the answer to similar questions is no. Sometimes a host country's standards are inadequate at any level of economic development. If a country's pollution standards are so low that working on an oil rig would considerably increase a person's risk of developing cancer, foreign oil companies must refuse to do business

---

The Problem with Bribery

Bribery is widespread and insidious. Managers in transnational companies routinely confront bribery even though most countries have laws against it. The fact is that officials in many developing countries wink at the practice, and the salaries of local bureaucrats are so low that many consider bribes a form of remuneration. The U.S. Foreign Corrupt Practices Act defines allowable limits on petty bribery in the form of routine payments required to move goods through customs. But demands for bribes often exceed those limits, and there is seldom a good solution.

Bribery disrupts distribution channels when goods languish on docks until local handlers are paid off, and it destroys incentives to compete on quality and cost when purchasing decisions are based on who pays what under the table. Refusing to acquiesce is often tantamount to giving business to unscrupulous companies.

I believe that even routine bribery is intolerable. Bribery undermines market efficiency and predictability, thus ultimately denying people their right to a minimal standard of living. Some degree of ethical commitment—some sense that everyone will play by the rules—is necessary for a sound economy. Without an ability to predict outcomes, who would be willing to invest?

There was a U.S. company whose shipping crates were regularly pilfered by handlers on the docks of Rio de Janeiro. The handlers would take about 10% of the contents of the crates, but the company was never sure which 10% it would be. In a partial solution, the company began sending two crates—the first with 90% of the merchandise, the second with 10%. The handlers learned to take the second crate and leave the first untouched. From the company's perspective, at least knowing which goods it would lose was an improvement.

Bribery does more than destroy predictability; it undermines essential social and economic systems. That truth is not lost on businesspeople in countries where the practice is woven into the social fabric. CEOs in India admit that their companies engage constantly in bribery, and they say that they have considerable disgust for the practice. They blame government policies in part, but Indian executives also know that their country's business practices perpetuate corrupt behavior. Anyone walking the streets of Calcutta, where it is clear that even a dramatic redistribution of wealth would still leave most of India's inhabitants in dire poverty, comes face-to-face with the devastating effects of corruption.

there. Likewise, if the dangerous side effects of a drug treatment outweigh its benefits, managers should not accept health standards that ignore the risks.

When relative economic conditions do not drive tensions, there is a more objective test for resolving ethical problems. Managers should deem a practice permissible only if they can answer no to both of the following questions: Is it possible to conduct business successfully in the host country without undertaking the practice? And is the practice a violation of a core human value? Japanese gift giving is a perfect example of a conflict of cultural tradition. Most experienced businesspeople, Japanese and non-Japanese alike, would agree that doing business in Japan would be virtually impossible without adopting the practice. Does gift giving violate a core human value? I cannot identify one that it violates. As a result, gift giving may be permissible for foreign companies in Japan even if it conflicts with ethical attitudes at home. In fact, that conclusion is widely accepted, even by companies such as Texas Instruments and IBM, which are outspoken against bribery.

Does it follow that all nonmonetary gifts are acceptable or that bribes are generally acceptable in countries where they are common? Not at all. (See the insert "The Problem with Bribery.") What makes the routine practice of gift giving acceptable in Japan are the limits in its scope and intention. When gift giving moves outside those limits, it soon collides with core human values. For example, when Carl Kotchian, president of Lockheed in the 1970s, carried suitcases full of cash to Japanese politicians, he went beyond the norms established by Japanese tradition. That incident galvanized opinion in the United States Congress and helped lead to passage of the Foreign Corrupt Practices Act. Likewise, Roh Tae Woo went beyond the norms established by Korean cultural tradition when he accepted $635.4 million in bribes as president of the Republic of Korea between 1988 and 1993.

Guidelines for Ethical Leadership

Learning to spot intolerable practices and to exercise good judgment when ethical conflicts arise requires practice. Creating a company culture that rewards ethical behavior is essential. The following guidelines for developing a global ethical perspective among managers can help.

Treat corporate values and formal standards of conduct as absolutes.
Whatever ethical standards a company chooses, it cannot waver on its
principles either at home or abroad. Consider what has become part of
company lore at Motorola. Around 1950, a senior executive was negotiat-
ing with officials of a South American government on a $10 million sale
that would have increased the company's annual net profits by nearly
25%. As the negotiations neared completion, however, the executive
walked away from the deal because the officials were asking for $1 mil-
lion for "fees." CEO Robert Galvin not only supported the executive's
decision but also made it clear that Motorola would neither accept the
sale on any terms nor do business with those government officials again.
Retold over the decades, this story demonstrating Galvin's resolve has
helped cement a culture of ethics for thousands of employees at
Motorola.

**Design and implement conditions of engagement for suppliers and
customers.** Will your company do business with any customer or supplier? What if a customer or supplier uses child labor? What if it has strong
links with organized crime? What if it pressures your company to break
a host country's laws? Such issues are best not left for spur-of-the-
moment decisions. Some companies have realized that. Sears, for
instance, has developed a policy of not contracting production to companies that use prison labor or infringe on workers' rights to health and
safety. And BankAmerica has specified as a condition for many of its
loans to developing countries that environmental standards and human
rights must be observed.

**Allow foreign business units to help formulate ethical standards and
interpret ethical issues.** The French pharmaceutical company
Rhône-Poulenc Rorer has allowed foreign subsidiaries to augment lists of
corporate ethical principles with their own suggestions. Texas
Instruments has paid special attention to issues of international business
ethics by creating the Global Business Practices Council, which is made
up of managers from countries in which the company operates. With the
overarching intent to create a "global ethics strategy, locally deployed,"
the council's mandate is to provide ethics education and create local
processes that will help managers in the company's foreign business
units resolve ethical conflicts.

In host countries, support efforts to decrease institutional corruption.
Individual managers will not be able to wipe out corruption in a host

country, no matter how many bribes they turn down. When a host country's tax system, import and export procedures, and procurement practices favor unethical players, companies must take action.

Many companies have begun to participate in reforming host-country institutions. General Electric, for example, has taken a strong stand in India, using the media to make repeated condemnations of bribery in business and government. General Electric and others have found, however, that a single company usually cannot drive out entrenched corruption. Transparency International, an organization based in Germany, has been effective in helping coalitions of companies, government officials, and others work to reform bribery-ridden bureaucracies in Russia, Bangladesh, and elsewhere.

Exercise moral imagination. Using moral imagination means resolving tensions responsibly and creatively. Coca-Cola, for instance, has consistently turned down requests for bribes from Egyptian officials but has managed to gain political support and public trust by sponsoring a project to plant fruit trees. And take the example of Levi Strauss, which discovered in the early 1990s that two of its suppliers in Bangladesh were employing children under the age of 14—a practice that violated the company's principles but was tolerated in Bangladesh. Forcing the suppliers to fire the children would not have ensured that the children received an education, and it would have caused serious hardship for the families depending on the children's wages. In a creative arrangement, the suppliers agreed to pay the children's regular wages while they attended school and to offer each child a job at age 14. Levi Strauss, in turn, agreed to pay the children's tuition and provide books and uniforms. That arrangement allowed Levi Strauss to uphold its principles and provide long-term benefits to its host country.

Many people think of values as soft; to some they are usually unspoken. A South Seas island society uses the word *mokita*, which means, "the truth that everybody knows but nobody speaks." However difficult they are to articulate, values affect how we all behave. In a global business environment, values in tension are the rule rather than the exception. Without a company's commitment, statements of values and codes of ethics end up as empty platitudes that provide managers with no foundation for behaving ethically. Employees need and deserve more, and responsible members of the global business community can set examples for others to follow. The dark consequences of incidents such as Union Carbide's disaster in Bhopal remind us how high the stakes can be.

Notes

1. In other writings, Thomas W. Dunfee and I have used the term *hypernorm* instead of *core human value*.

2. Thomas Donaldson and Thomas W. Dunfee, "Toward a Unified Conception of Business Ethics: Integrative Social Contracts Theory," *Academy of Management Review*, April 1994; and "Integrative Social Contracts Theory: A Communitarian Conception of Economic Ethics," *Economics and Philosophy*, spring 1995.

Part II

Ethical Principles and Moral Theories

Part II: Ethical Principles and Moral Theories

Theoretical principles govern sound thinking about ethics. Good moral reasoning about the problems of business ethics is best accomplished when concerned individuals bring the contextually appropriate principles to bear on moral problems and ethical dilemmas. Reasoned analysis brings clarity and focus to difficult moral problems and helps ethical decision makers choose correctly.

Aristotle's "Virtue Ethics," (Books I and II of his *Nicomachean Ethics*), makes important contributions to business ethics in two ways. First, this work sets forth a philosophical perspective from which one is able to see life whole. Furthermore, it demonstrates how to think about the value of life's various activities and ends. Secondly, Aristotle's work offers insights about the moral worth of individuals based on character.

Aristotle tells us that all human actions aim at some good. But, some aims are subordinate to others. Some aims and actions function as a means to an end. In other words, they are not performed for their own sake. Those things, states, or activities not valued in and for their own sake, but for the sake of their consequences, are said to have **extrinsic** or **instrumental value**. That which is valued for its own sake or in itself, without regard to consequences, is said to have **intrinsic** or **final value**. Aristotle put it this way:

> Now we call that which is in itself worthy of pursuit more final than that which is worthy of pursuit for the sake of something else, and that which is never desirable for the sake of something else more final than the things that are desirable both in themselves and for the sake of that other thing, and therefore we call that final without qualification that which is always desirable in itself and never for the sake of something else.

For Aristotle, the one end that is final without qualification is happiness.

Happiness, Aristotle tells us, is the chief good. It is the "activity of the soul in accordance with complete virtue." The good life or the happy life is achieved by balancing wealth, health, friendship, and knowledge on a foundation of moral excellence.

The key question in virtue ethics is "What traits of character make one a good person?" Vices, such as cowardice, jealousy, envy, greed, gluttony, and spite, are morally undesirable character traits. Through the indulgence of degrading appetites, lack of self-discipline and education, or the habitual practice of degrading or immoral conduct, vices become embedded in the life of a man or woman. Vices render their possessor base and ignoble. The life of the base person is governed by impulse, not reason. As a result, the ignoble person is discontent and anxiety ridden. A person whose character lacks virtue is plagued by inner tension and chaos. The stormy inner life of the vicious individual manifests itself outwardly in deeds that are corrupt, ignoble, and immoral.

Virtues, in contrast to vices, are "human excellences." They include character traits such as honesty, loyalty, courage, wisdom, and temperance. Virtues render the life of their possessor morally, intellectually, and practically superior. Although the virtuous person, like the vicious individual, lives in a world of trouble, the life of the virtuous person is marked by inner strength, contentment, happiness, and purpose.

Aristotle argued that virtue is necessary for honor and true success. Virtue lies in the mean between excess, on one hand, and deficiency, on the other. He stated,

> Virtue is a state of character concerned with choice, lying in a mean, i.e., the mean relative to us, this being determined by a rational principle by which the man of practical wisdom would determine it.

On Aristotle's account we learn that exemplars, those who have cultivated within their lives practical excellence in moral matters, are an essential part of the human context of good ethical decision making.

Historically, two basic types or classifications of moral theories have emerged. **Deontological theories** (Gk. *Deon* = "duty," literally, "that which binds,") hold that individuals have basic duties and obligations. Simply put, there are certain things we must do and certain things we must not do. Right conduct involves knowing and discharging one's basic moral duties. On this view, the consequences of an action are not taken into account in moral decision making. The moral worth of an individual, from a deontological perspective, is tied to the performance of particular kinds of actions and to certain motivations.

In contrast, **teleological theories** (Gk. *Telos* = "end" or "purpose") make right and wrong a function of an action's consequences or outcomes.

Right actions are those whose consequences or intended consequences bring about benefits and wrong actions are those which do not yield beneficial outcomes.

The deontological moral perspective is powerfully expressed in the writings of Immanuel Kant. Kant placed the ground and foundation of morality in the structure of human reason and in the logical form of moral imperatives. Reason, he argued, is a lawgiver and is universal. As such, the moral imperatives handed down by reason will be absolutely binding on all people at all times.

In "Good Will, Duty and the Categorical Imperative," Kant tells us what a person of moral worth does. According to Kant, persons of moral worth act from a good will, one that is "good in itself," and therefore, act only from the motive of doing what is right. Kant's categorical imperative states: **Act only on that maxim whereby thou canst at the same time will that it should become a universal law.**

Rational human beings have the capacity to distinguish right from wrong and free human beings have a choice. Good human beings choose to do what is right simply because *they* know that it is the right thing to do and they respect those things that are good and right.

The teleological theory of utilitarianism was originated by the philosopher Jeremy Bentham. It was refined by Bentham's contemporary, John Stuart Mill. Mill expressed the utilitarian view as follows:

> The creed which accepts as the foundation of morals "utility" or the "greatest happiness principle" holds that actions are right in proportion as they tend to promote happiness; wrong as they tend to promote the reverse of happiness.

Utility is the property of producing pleasure or happiness in a conscious being and, by extension, in a community. Mill wrote about both the quantitative and qualitative aspects of pleasure, not as abstract principles, but, as concrete realities in human life.

An alternative to the rational-cognitive approach to morality is an ethics of care. "As human beings," says Nel Noddings, "we want to care and be cared for. Caring is important in itself." An ethic built on caring is concrete and approaches ethical problems and moral decision making from the perspective of the one caring. In other words, this perspective is rooted in and grows out of the concrete experience of the individual. The ethic of care, does not, in contrast to traditional moral systems, impose abstract moral structures upon human experience.

Noddings contends that an ethics of care is characteristically feminine but, it may be embraced by all humanity.

According to Noddings, "Apprehending the other's reality, feeling what he feels as nearly as possible, is an essential part of caring from the view of the one caring." An ethics of care ideally promotes a reciprocity rooted in felt-reality. In what ways does this approach open up possibilities that would positively transform human relationships and the nature of the workplace? In what ways might the ethics of care complement traditional approaches to ethics?

Ethical egoism is a teleological moral theory that is based on the principle of self-interest. The egoist maintains that **one ought always act in a way that will maximize self-interest**. Ayn Rand's writings present a form of ethical egoism called "objectivism," the philosophy that the pursuit of rational self-interest or attaining one's own happiness is life's proper moral purpose. And in order for an individual to effectively achieve the aims of rational self-interest a social/economic system that guarantees human rights and promotes free-market capitalism is necessary. Rand rejected all versions of collectivism and statism. She favored limited government and would strongly oppose the idea of the welfare state.

In "The Virtue of Selfishness" Ayn Rand makes a compelling case for the ethics of rational self-interest. But, why use the word "selfishness" to denote virtuous activities? Such an identification of virtue and selfishness seems both counter-intuitive and needlessly confusing, especially since Rand's meaning of selfishness really means *concern for one's own self-interests*. According to Rand, popular usage of the word "selfishness" and, by extension, "self-interest," has become synonymous with evil and produces an ethics characterized by cynicism and guilt: ". . . cynicism, because they neither practice nor accept the altruistic morality—guilt, because they dare not reject it." The dominant morality requires one to continually sacrifice self for the benefit of another and, Rand says that there is no greater evil. So, one must rebel because, "To redeem both man and morality, it is the concept of *"selfishness"* that one has to redeem."

In the developing theory of globalization human rights issues occupy center-stage. The long history of rights-based thinking was institutionalized as a part of the Western enlightenment tradition. For the past half-century the theory and language of rights has framed all moral debates in the West. Rights-based structures are characteristic of liberal democratic governments and free-market economies. Rights play a critical role in business ethics.

In "The Concept of a Right," John Boatright clarifies the important notion of rights and other concepts related to rights. In addition, he traces the history of the development of rights-based thinking with particular emphasis on the contributions made by John Locke, John Stuart Mill, and Immanuel Kant. According to Boatright:

> Rights can be understood, therefore, as entitlements. To have rights is to be entitled to act on our own or to be treated by others in certain ways without asking permission of anyone or being dependent on other people's goodwill. Rights entitle us to make claims on other people either to refrain from interfering in what we do to contribute actively to our well-being not as beggars, who can only entreat others to be generous, but as creditors, who can demand what is owed them.

It should be evident from the above description, that rights are extraordinarily powerful concepts.

Boatright also calls attention to important related concepts and distinctions. **Legal rights** are dependent upon a legal system and, in contrast, **moral rights** do not depend on the existence of a moral system. Furthermore, some rights are **specific** in that they involve identifiable individuals. **Specific** or *in personam* rights make up a major part of contract law. Other rights are **general**, or *in rem*, rights. This later group of rights applies generally to all human beings. Finally, all rights presuppose corresponding duties or obligations. An analysis of the relationship of rights and obligations is often called the correlativity thesis.

Although the ethics of rights has been well defined, nevertheless, most of the world's population lives in societies that are not rights-based. Currently, there is considerable debate about the kind and character of morality that will govern international business. Cultural universalists embrace a view of history from the Western enlightenment tradition. According to this view, fundamental truths about what is good and right in human life can be objectively defined. Proponents of this view hold that these truths apply universally to all people independently of place or circumstance. In contrast, cultural particularists argue that morally correct behavior must be viewed contextually as a response to unique circumstances. Some believe that it is impossible to engage in serious "intellectual communication" concerning distinctively different moral discourses.

Daryl Koehn asks "What Can Eastern Philosophy Teach Us about Business Ethics?" Because of the prominence of Asian nations in international affairs, a knowledge of so-called "Asian Values" and Asian ethical systems is critical for Western firms that desire to do business in the lucrative Asian markets. Koehn dismisses much of the rhetoric of "Asian Values" as political positioning. Since Asia covers a vast geographical area and includes a diversity of cultures it is difficult to ascertain a "core" set of values that various Asian cultures share. However, Koehn sees value in a different approach to Eastern ethics. She describes the approach as follows:

> If we take the expression "Eastern ethics" in a more limited sense, however, and think of it as applying to the ethics of particular individuals living within China, or Japan or India, then business can learn something from Eastern ethics.

Koehn draws from individual thinkers such as Confucius and Watsuji Tetsuro to capture some dimensions of the moral thinking of Asian peoples. She explores three basic themes:

1. The meaning of trust
2. Relations for life
3. Ethics beyond rights

In the final article of this section, Iwao Taka looks at the philosophical and religious basis for business ethics in Japan. Certain business practices that are morally acceptable or even obligatory in the Japanese culture are seen as morally questionable according to Western moralities. One example is the Japanese *keiretsu* system that has been criticized in the United States as anticompetitive. But, special treatment is given to keiretsu members because of what Taka calls, the concentric circles view of ethical obligations. A person's obligations are greatest to those close to you and least to those farthest away. In other words, one's ethical duties to family and friends are greater than one's duties to foreigners. This principle is derived from the Confucian maxim that allows "people to treat others in proportion to the intimacy of their relations."

Taka points out the basis for Japanese criticisms of American businesses and also shows the justification for certain criticisms of Japanese practice that has been leveled by the West. Better understanding of the point of view of the other will, hopefully, make business better for all.

from Nicomachean Ethics

Aristotle

Book I

Every art and every inquiry, and similarly every action and pursuit, is thought to aim at some good; and for this reason the good has rightly been declared to be that at which all things aim. But a certain difference is found among ends; some are activities, others are products apart from the activities that produce them. Where there are ends apart from the actions, it is the nature of the products to be better than the activities. Now, as there are many actions, arts, and sciences, their ends also are many; the end of the medical art is health, that of shipbuilding a vessel, that of strategy victory, that of economics wealth. But where such arts fall under a single capacity—as bridle-making and the other arts concerned with the equipment of horses fall under the art of riding, and this and every military action under strategy, in the same way other arts fall under yet others—in all of these the ends of the master arts are to be preferred to all the subordinate ends; for it is for the sake of the former that the latter are pursued. It makes no difference whether the activities themselves are the ends of the actions, or something else apart from the activities, as in the case of the sciences just mentioned.

*　　*　　*

Let us again return to the good we are seeking, and ask what it can be. It seems different in different actions and arts; it is different in medicine, in strategy, and in the other arts likewise. What then is the good of each? Surely that for whose sake everything else is done. In medicine this is health, in strategy victory, in architecture a house, in any other sphere something else, and in every action and pursuit the end; for it is for the sake of this that all men do whatever else they do. Therefore, if there is an end for all that we do, this will be the good achievable by action, and if there are more than one, these will be the goods achievable by action.

So the argument has by a different course reached the same point; but we must try to state this even more clearly. Since there are evidently more than one end, and we choose some of these (e.g. wealth, flutes, and in general instruments) for the sake of something else, clearly not all ends are final ends; but the chief good is evidently something final. Therefore, if there is only one final end, this will be what we are seeking, and if there are more than one, the most final of these will be what we are seeking. Now we call that which is in itself worthy of pursuit more final than that which is worthy of pursuit for the sake of something else, and that which is never desirable for the sake of something else more final than the things that are desirable both in themselves and for the sake of that other thing, and therefore we call final without qualification that which is always desirable in itself and never for the sake of something else.

Now such a thing happiness, above all else, is held to be; for this we choose always for itself and never for the sake of something else, but honour, pleasure, reason, and every virtue we choose indeed for themselves (for if nothing resulted from them we should still choose each of them), but we choose them also for the sake of happiness, judging that by means of them we shall be happy. Happiness, on the other hand, no one chooses for the sake of these, nor, in general, for anything other than itself.

From the point of view of self-sufficiency the same result seems to follow; for the final good is thought to be self-sufficient. Now by self-sufficient we do not mean that which is sufficient for a man by himself, for one who lives a solitary life, but also for parents, children, wife, and in general for his friends and fellow citizens, since man is born for citizenship. But some limit must be set to this; for if we extend our requirement to ancestors and descendants and friends' friends we are in for an infinite series. Let us examine this question, however, on another occasion,[1] the self-sufficient we now define as that which when isolated makes life desirable and lacking in nothing; and such we think happiness to be; and further we think it most desirable of all things, without being counted as one good thing among others—if it were so counted it would clearly be made more desirable by the addition of even the least of goods; for that which is added becomes an excess of goods, and of goods the greater is always more desirable. Happiness, then, is something final and self-sufficient, and is the end of action.

Presumably, however, to say that happiness is the chief good seems a platitude, and a clearer account of what it is is still desired. This might perhaps be given, if we could first ascertain the function of man. For just as for a flute-player, a sculptor, or any artist, and, in general, for all things that have a function or activity, the good and the 'well' is thought to reside in the function, so would it seem to be for man, if he has a function. Have the carpenter, then, and the tanner certain functions or activities, and has man none? Is he born without a function? Or as eye, hand, foot, and in general each of the parts evidently has a function, may one lay it down that man similarly has a function apart from all these? What then can this be? Life seems to be common even to plants, but we are seeking what is peculiar to man. Let us exclude, therefore, the life of nutrition and growth. Next there would be a life of perception, but *it* also seems to be common even to the horse, the ox, and every animal. There remains, then, an active life of the element that has a rational principle; of this, one part has such a principle in the sense of being obedient to one, the other in the sense of possessing one and exercising thought. And, as 'life of the rational element' also has two meanings, we must state that life in the sense of activity is what we mean; for this seems to be the more proper sense of the term. Now if the function of man is an activity of soul which follows or implies a rational principle, and if we say 'a so-and-so' and 'a good so-and-so' have a function which is the same in kind, e.g. a lyre-player and a good lyre-player, and so without qualification in all cases, eminence in respect of goodness being added to the name of the function (for the function of a lyre-player is to play the lyre, and that of a good lyre-player is to do so well): if this is the case, [and we state the function of man to be a certain kind of life, and this to be an activity or actions of the soul implying a rational principle, and the function of a good man to be the good and noble performance of these, and if any action is well performed when it is performed in accordance with the appropriate excellence: if this is the case,] human good turns out to be activity of soul in accordance with virtue, and if there are more than one virtue, in accordance with the best and most complete.

But we must add 'in a complete life'. For one swallow does not make a summer, nor does one day; and so too one day, or a short time, does not make a man blessed and happy.

Let this serve as an outline of the good; for we must presumably first sketch it roughly, and then later fill in the details. But it would seem that any one is capable of carrying on and articulating what has once been well outlined, and that time is a good discoverer or partner in such a work; to which facts the advances of the arts are due; for any one can add what is lacking. And we must also remember what has been said before,[2] and not look for precision in all things alike, but in each class of things such precision as accords with the subject-matter, and so much as is appropriate to the inquiry. For a carpenter and a geometer investigate the right angle in different ways; the former does so in so far as the right angle is useful for his work, while the latter inquires what it is or what sort of thing it is; for he is a spectator of the truth. We must act in the same way, then, in all other matters as well, that our main task may not be subordinated to minor questions. Nor must we demand the cause in all matters alike; it is enough in some cases that the *fact* be well established, as in the case of the first principles; the fact is the primary thing or first principle. Now of first principles we see some by induction, some by perception, some by a certain habituation, and others too in other ways. But each set of principles we must try to investigate in the natural way, and we must take pains to state them definitely, since they have a great influence on what follows. For the beginning is thought to be more than half of the whole, and many of the questions we ask are cleared up by it.

Book II

Next we must consider what virtue is. Since things that are found in the soul are of three kinds—passions, faculties, states of character, virtue must be one of these. By passions I mean appetite, anger, fear, confidence, envy, joy, friendly feeling, hatred, longing, emulation, pity, and in general the feelings that are accompanied by pleasure or pain; by faculties the things in virtue of which we are said to be capable of feeling these, e.g. of becoming angry or being pained or feeling pity; by states of character the things in virtue of which we stand well or badly with reference to the passions, e.g. with reference to anger we stand badly if we feel it violently or too weakly, and well if we feel it moderately; and similarly with reference to the other passions.

Now neither the virtues nor the vices are *passions,* because we are not called good or bad on the ground of our passions, but are so called on the ground of our virtues and our vices, and because we are neither praised nor blamed for our passions (for the man who feels fear or anger is not praised, nor is the man who simply feels anger blamed, but the man who feels it in a certain way), but for our virtues and our vices we *are* praised or blamed.

Again, we feel anger and fear without choice, but the virtues are modes of choice or involve choice. Further, in respect of the passions we are said to be moved, but in respect of the virtues and the vices we are said not to be moved but to be disposed in a particular way.

For these reasons also they are not *faculties;* for we are neither called good nor bad, nor praised nor blamed, for the simple capacity of feeling the passions; again, we have the faculties by nature, but we are not made good or bad by nature; we have spoken of this before.[3]

If, then, the virtues are neither passions nor faculties, all that remains is that they should be *states of character.*

Thus we have stated what virtue is in respect of its genus.

We must, however, not only describe virtue as a state of character, but also say what sort of state it is. We may remark, then, that every virtue or excellence both brings into good condition the thing of which it is the excellence and makes the work of that thing be done well; e.g. the excellence of the eye makes both the eye and its work good; for it is by the excellence of the eye that we see well. Similarly the excellence of the horse makes a horse both good in itself and good at running and at carrying its rider and at awaiting the attack of the enemy. Therefore, if this is true in every case, the virtue of man also will be the state of character which makes a man good and which makes him do his own work well.

How this is to happen we have stated already,[4] but it will be made plain also by the following consideration of the specific nature of virtue. In everything that is continuous and divisible it is possible to take more, less, or an equal amount, and that either in terms of the thing itself or relatively to us; and the equal is an intermediate between excess and defect. By the intermediate in the object I mean that which is equidistant from each of the extremes, which is one and the same for all men; by the intermediate relatively to us that which is neither too much nor too little—and this is not one, nor the same for all. For instance, if ten is many and two is few, six is the intermediate, taken in terms of the object; for it exceeds and is exceeded by an equal amount; this is intermediate according to arithmetical proportion. But the intermediate relatively to us is not to be taken so; if ten pounds are too much for a particular person to eat and two too little, it does not follow that the trainer will order six pounds; for this also is perhaps too much for the person who is to take it, or too little—too little for Milo,[5] too much for the beginner in athletic exer cises. The same is true of running and wrestling. Thus a master of any art avoids excess and defect, but seeks the intermediate and chooses this—the in termediate not in the object but relatively to us.

If it is thus, then, that every art does its work well—by looking to the intermediate and judging its works by this standard (so that we often say of good works of art that it is not possible either to take away or to add anything, implying that excess and defect destroy the goodness of works of art, while the mean preserves it; and good artists, as we say, look to this in their work), and if, further, virtue is more exact and better than any art, as nature also is, then virtue must have the quality of aiming at the intermediate. I mean moral virtue; for it is this that is concerned with passions and actions, and in these there is excess, defect, and the intermediate. For instance, both fear and confidence and appetite and anger and pity and in general pleasure and pain may be felt both too much and too little, and in both cases not well; but to feel them at the right times, with reference to the right objects, towards the right people, with the right motive, and in the right way, is what is both intermediate and best, and this is characteristic of virtue. Similarly with regard to actions also there is excess, defect, and the intermediate. Now virtue is concerned with passions and actions, in which excess is a form of failure, and so is defect, while the intermediate is praised and is a form of success; and being praised and being successful are both characteristics of virtue. Therefore virtue is a kind of mean, since, as we have seen, it aims at what is intermediate.

Again, it is possible to fail in many ways (for evil belongs to the class of the unlimited, as the Pythagoreans conjectured, and good to that of the limited), while to succeed is possible only in one way (for which reason also one is easy and the other difficult—to miss the mark easy, to hit it difficult); for these reasons also, then, excess and defect are characteristic of vice, and the mean of virtue;

For men are good in but one way, but bad in many.

Virtue, then, is a state of character concerned with choice, lying in a mean, i.e. the mean relative to us, this being determined by a rational principle, and by that principle by which the man of practical wisdom would determine it. Now it is a mean between two vices, that which depends on excess and that which depends on defect; and again it is a mean because the vices respectively fall short of or exceed what is right in both passions and actions, while virtue both finds and chooses that which is intermediate. Hence in respect of its substance and the definition which states its essence virtue is a mean, with regard to what is best and right an extreme.

But not every action nor every passion admits of a mean; for some have names that already imply badness, e.g. spite, shamelessness, envy, and in the case of actions adultery, theft, murder; for all of these and suchlike things imply by their names that they are themselves bad, and not the excesses or deficiencies of them. It is not possible, then, ever to be right with regard to them; one must always be wrong. Nor does goodness or badness with regard to such things depend on committing adultery with the right woman, at the right time, and in the right way, but simply to do any of them is to go wrong. It would be equally absurd, then, to expect that in unjust, cowardly, and voluptuous action there should be a mean, an excess, and a deficiency; for at that rate there would be a mean of excess and of deficiency, an excess of excess, and a deficiency of deficiency. But as there is no excess and deficiency of temperance and courage because what is intermediate is in a sense an extreme, so too of the actions we have mentioned there is no mean nor any excess and deficiency, but however they are done they are wrong; for in general there is neither a mean of excess and deficiency, nor excess and deficiency of a mean.

We must, however, not only make this general statement, but also apply it to the individual facts. For among statements about conduct those which are general apply more widely, but those which are particular are more genuine, since conduct has to do with individual cases, and our statements must harmonize with the facts in these cases. We may take these cases from our table. With regard to feelings of fear and confidence courage is the mean; of the people who exceed, he who exceeds in fearlessness has no name (many of the states have no name), while the man who exceeds in confidence is rash, and he who exceeds in fear and falls short in confidence is a coward. With regard to pleasures and pains—not all of them, and not so much with regard to the pains—the mean is temperance, the excess self-indulgence. Persons deficient with regard to the pleasures are not often found; hence such persons also have received no name. But let us call them 'insensible'.

With regard to giving and taking of money the mean is liberality, the excess and the defect prodigality and meanness. In these actions people exceed and fall short in contrary ways; the prodigal exceeds in spending and falls short in taking, while the mean man exceeds in taking and falls short in spending. (At present we are giving a mere outline or summary, and are satisfied with this; later these states will be more exactly determined.[6]) With regard to money there are also other dispositions—a mean, magnificence (for the magnificent man differs from the liberal man; the former deals with large sums, the latter with small ones), an excess, tastelessness and vulgarity, and a deficiency, niggardliness; these differ from the states opposed to liberality, and the mode of their difference will be stated later.[7]

With regard to honour and dishonour the mean is proper pride, the excess is known as a sort of 'empty vanity', and the deficiency is undue humility; and as we said[8] liberality was related to magnificence, differing from it by dealing with small sums, so there is a state similarly related to proper pride, being concerned with small honours while that is concerned with great. For it is possible to desire honour as one ought, and more than one ought, and less, and the man who exceeds in his desires is called ambitious, the man who falls short unambitious, while the intermediate person has no name. The dispositions also are nameless, except that that of the ambitious man is called ambition. Hence the people who are at the extremes lay claim to the middle place; and we ourselves sometimes call the intermediate person ambitious and sometimes unambitious, and sometimes praise the ambitious man and sometimes the unambitious. The reason of our doing this will be stated in what follows;[9] but now let us speak of the remaining states according to the method which has been indicated.

With regard to anger also there is an excess, a deficiency, and a mean. Although they can scarcely be said to have names, yet since we call the intermediate person good-tempered let us call the mean good temper; of the persons at the extremes let the one who exceeds be called irascible, and his vice irascibility, and the man who falls short an inirascible sort of person, and the deficiency inirascibility.

There are also three other means, which have a certain likeness to one another, but differ from one another: for they are all concerned with intercourse in words and actions, but differ in that one is concerned with truth in this sphere, the other two with pleasantness; and of this one kind is exhibited in giving amusement, the other in all the circumstances of life. We must therefore speak of these too, that we may the better see that in all things the mean is praiseworthy, and the extremes neither praiseworthy nor right, but worthy of blame. Now most of these states also have no names, but we must try, as in the other cases, to invent names ourselves so that we may be clear and easy to follow. With regard to truth, then, the intermediate is a truthful sort of person and the mean may be called truthfulness, while the pretence which exaggerates is boastfulness and the person characterized by it a boaster, and that which understates is mock modesty and the person characterized by it mock-modest. With regard to pleasantness in the giving of amusement the intermediate person is ready-witted and the disposition ready wit, the excess is buffoonery and the person characterized by it a buffoon, while the man who falls short is a sort of boor and his state is boorishness. With regard to the remaining kind of pleasantness, that which is exhibited in life in general, the man who is pleasant in the right way is friendly and the mean is friendliness, while the man who exceeds is an obsequious person if he has no end in view, a flatterer if he is aiming at his own advantage, and the man who falls short and is unpleasant in all circumstances is a quarrelsome and surly sort of person.

There are also means in the passions and concerned with the passions; since shame is not a virtue, and yet praise is extended to the modest man. For even in these matters one man is said to be intermediate, and another to exceed, as for instance the bashful man who is ashamed of everything; while he who falls short or is not ashamed of anything at all is shameless, and the intermediate person is modest. Righteous indignation is a mean between envy and spite, and these states are concerned with the pain and pleasures that are felt at the fortunes of our neighbours; the man who is characterized by righteous indignation is pained at undeserved good fortune, the envious man, going beyond him, is pained at all good fortune, and the spiteful man falls so far short of being pained that he even rejoices. But these states there will be an opportunity of describing elsewhere;[10] with regard to justice, since it has not one simple meaning, we shall, after describing the other states, distinguish its two kinds and say how each of them is a mean;[11] and similarly we shall treat also of the rational virtues.[12]

Notes

1. i. 10, 11, ix. 10.
2. 1094^b 11–27.
3. 1103^a 18-^{b} 2.
4. 1104^a 11–27.
5. A famous wrestler.
6. iv. 1.
7. 1122^a 20–9,^{b} 10–18.
8. ll. 17–19.
9. ^{b}11–26, 1125^b 14–18.
10. The reference may be to the whole treatment of the moral virtues in iii. 6-iv. 9, or to the discussion of shame in iv. 9 and an intended corresponding discussion of righteous indignation, or to the discussion of these two states in *Rhet.* ii. 6, 9, 10.
11. 1129^a 26-^{b}1; 1130^{a}14-^{b}5; 1131^b 9–15; Bk vi.
12. 1132^a 24–30; 1133^{b}30–1134^{a}1.

Good Will, Duty, and the Categorical Imperative

Immanuel Kant

OTHING can possibly be conceived in the world, or even out of it, which can be called good without qualification, except a *good will.* Intelligence, wit, judgment, and other *talents* of the mind, however they may be named, or courage, resolution, perseverance, as qualities of temperament, are undoubtedly good and desirable in many respects; but these gifts of nature may also become extremely bad and mischievous if the will which is to make use of them, and which, therefore, constitutes what is called *character,* is not good. It is the same with the *gifts of fortune.* Power, riches, honor, even health, and the general well-being and contentment with one's condition which is called *happiness,* inspire pride, and often presumption, if there is not a good will to correct the influence of these on the mind, and with this also to rectify the whole principle of acting, and adapt it to its end. The sight of a being who is not adorned with a single feature of a pure and good will, enjoying unbroken prosperity, can never give pleasure to an impartial rational spectator. Thus a good will appears to constitute the indispensable condition even of being worthy of happiness.

There are even some qualities which are of service to this good will itself, and may facilitate its action, yet which have no intrinsic unconditional value, but always presuppose a good will, and this qualifies the esteem that we justly have for them, and does not permit us to regard them as absolutely good. Moderation in the affections and passions, self-control, and calm deliberation are not only good in many respects, but even seem to constitute part of the intrinsic worth of the person; but they are far from deserving to be called good without qualification, although they have been so unconditionally praised by the ancients. For without the principles of a good will, they may become extremely bad; and the coolness of a villain not only makes him far more dangerous, but also directly makes him more abominable in our eyes than he would have been without it.

A good will is good not because of what it performs or effects, not by its aptness for the attainment of some proposed end, but simply by virtue of the volition—that is, it is good in itself, and considered by itself is to be esteemed much higher than all that can be brought about by it in favor of any inclination, hay, even of the sum-total of all inclinations. Even if it should happen that, owing to special disfavor of fortune, or the niggardly provision of a stepmotherly nature, this will should wholly lack power to accomplish its purpose, if with its greatest efforts it should yet achieve nothing, and there should remain only the good will (not, to be sure, a mere wish, but the summoning of all means in our power), then, like a jewel, it would still shine by its own light, as a thing which has its whole value in itself. Its usefulness or fruitlessness can neither add to nor take away anything from this value. It would be, as it were, only the setting to enable us to handle it the more conveniently in common commerce, or to attract to it the attention of those who are not yet connoisseurs, but not to recommend it to true connoisseurs, or to determine its value....

Everything in nature works according to laws. Rational beings alone have the faculty of acting according *to the conception* of laws, that is according to principles, *i.e.* have a *will.* Since the deduction of actions from principles requires *reason,* the will is nothing but practical reason. If reason infallibly determines the will, then the actions of such a being which are recognized as objectively necessary are subjectively necessary also, *i.e.* the will is a faculty to choose *that only* which reason independent of inclination recognizes as practically necessary, *i.e.* as good. But if reason of itself does not sufficiently determine the will, if the latter is subject also to subjective conditions (particular impulses) which do not always coincide with the objective conditions; in a word, if the will does not in *itself* completely accord with reason (which is actually the case with men), then the actions which objectively are recognized as necessary are subjectively contingent, and the determination of such a will according to objective laws is *obligation,* that is to say, the relation of the objective laws to a will that is not thoroughly good is conceived as the determination of the will of a rational being by principles of reason, but which the will from its nature does not of necessity follow.

The conception of an objective principle, in so far as it is obligatory for a will, is called a command (of reason), and the formula of the command is called an Imperative....

Now all *imperatives* command either *hypothetically* or *categorically.* The former represent the practical necessity of a possible action as means to something else that is willed (or at least which one might possibly will). The categorical imperative would be that which represented an action as necessary of itself without reference to another end, *i.e.* as objectively necessary.

Since every practical law represents a possible action as good, and on this account, for a subject who is practically determinable by reason, necessary, all imperatives are formulae determining an action which is necessary according to the principle of a will good in some respects. If now the action is good only as a means to *something else,* then the imperative is *hypothetical;* if it is conceived as good in itself and consequently as being necessarily the principle of a will which of itself conforms to reason, then it is *categorical....*

When I conceive a hypothetical imperative, in general I do not know beforehand what it will contain until I am given the condition. But when I conceive a categorical imperative, I know at once what it contains. For as the imperative contains besides the law only the necessity that the maxims shall conform to this law, while the law contains no conditions restricting it, there remains nothing but the general statement that the maxim of the action should conform to a universal law, and it is this conformity alone that the imperative properly represents as necessary.

There is ... but one categorical imperative, namely, this: *Act only on that maxim whereby thou canst at the same time will that it should become a universal law.*

Now if all imperatives of duty can be deduced from this one imperative as from their principle, then, although it should remain undecided whether what is called duty is not merely a vain notion, yet at least we shall be able to show what we understand by it and what this notion means.

Since the universality of the law according to which effects are produced constitutes what is properly called *nature* in the most general sense (as to form), that is the existence of things so far as it is determined by general laws, the imperative of duty may be expressed thus: *Act as if the maxim of thy action were to become by thy will a universal law of nature.*

We will now enumerate a few duties, adopting the usual division of them into duties to ourselves and to others, and into perfect and imperfect duties.

1. A man reduced to despair by a series of misfortunes feels wearied of life, but is still so far in possession of his reason that he can ask himself whether it would not be contrary to his duty to himself to take his own life. Now he inquires whether the maxim of his action could become a universal law of nature. His maxim is: From self-love I adopt it as a principle to shorten my life when its longer duration is likely to bring more evil than satisfaction. It is asked then simply whether this principle founded on self-love can become a universal law of nature. Now we see at once that a system of nature of which it should be a law to destroy life by means of the very feeling whose special nature it is to impel to the improvement of life would contradict itself, and therefore could not exist as a system of nature; hence that maxim cannot possibly exist as a universal law of nature, and consequently would be wholly inconsistent with the supreme principle of all duty.

2. Another finds himself forced by necessity to borrow money. He knows that he will not be able to repay it, but sees also that nothing will be lent to him, unless he promises stoutly to repay it in a definite time. He desires to make this promise, but he has still so much conscience as to ask himself: Is it not unlawful and inconsistent with duty to get out of a difficulty in this way? Suppose, however, that he resolves to do so, then the maxim of his action would be expressed thus: When I think myself in want of money. I will borrow money and promise to repay it, although I know that I never can do so. Now this principle of self-love or of one's own advantage may perhaps be consistent with my whole future welfare; but the question now is. Is it right? I change then the suggestion of self-love into a universal law, and state the question thus: How would it be if my maxim were a universal law? Then I see at once that it could never hold as a universal law of nature, but would necessarily contradict itself. For supposing it to be a universal law that everyone when he thinks himself in a difficulty should be able to promise whatever he pleases, with the purpose of not keeping his promise, the promise itself would become impossible, as well as the end that one might have in view in it, since no one would consider that anything was promised to him, but would ridicule all such statements as vain pretences.

3. A third finds in himself a talent which with the help of some culture might make him a useful man in many respects. But he finds himself in comfortable circumstances, and prefers to indulge in pleasure rather than to take pains in enlarging and improving his happy natural capacities. He asks, however, whether his maxim of neglect of his natural gifts, besides agreeing with his inclination to indulgence, agrees also with what is called duty. He sees then that a system of nature could indeed subsist with such a universal law although men (like the South Sea islanders) should let their talents rest, and resolve to devote their lives merely to idleness, amusement, and propagation of their species—in a word, to enjoyment; but he cannot possibly *will* that this should be a universal law of nature, or be implanted in us as such by a natural instinct. For, as a rational being, he necessarily wills that his faculties be developed, since they serve him, and have been given him, for all sorts of possible purposes.

4. A fourth, who is in prosperity, while he sees that others have to contend with great wretchedness and that he could help them, thinks: What concern is it of mine? Let everyone be as happy as Heaven pleases, or as he can make himself; I will take nothing from him nor even envy him, only I do not wish to contribute anything to his welfare or to his assistance in distress! Now no doubt if such a mode of thinking were a universal law, the human race might very well subsist, and doubtless even better than in a state in which everyone talks of sympathy and good-will, or even takes care occasionally to put it into practice, but, on the other side, also cheats when he can, betrays the rights of men, or

otherwise violates them. But although it is possible that a universal law of nature might exist in accordance with that maxim, it is impossible to *will* that such a principle should have the universal validity of a law of nature. For a will which resolved this would contradict itself, inasmuch as many cases might occur in which one would have need of the love and sympathy of others, and in which, by such a law of nature, sprung from his own will, he would deprive himself of all hope of the aid he desires....

We have thus established at least this much, that if duty is a conception which is to have any import and real legislative authority for our actions, it can only be expressed in categorical, and not at all in hypothetical imperatives. We have also, which is of great importance, exhibited clearly and definitely for every practical application the content of the categorical imperative, which must contain the principle of all duty if there is such a thing at all. We have not yet, however, advanced so far as to prove *à priori* that there actually is such an imperative, that there is a practical law which commands absolutely of itself, and without any other impulse, and that the following of this law is duty....

Now I say: man and generally any rational being *exists* as an end in himself, *not merely as a means* to be arbitrarily used by this or that will, but in all his actions, whether they concern himself or other rational beings, must be always regarded at the same time as an end. All objects of the inclinations have only a conditional worth; for if the inclinations and the wants founded on them did not exist, then their object would be without value. But the inclinations themselves being sources of want are so far from having an absolute worth for which they should be desired, that, on the contrary, it must be the universal wish of every rational being to be wholly free from them. Thus the worth of any object which is *to be acquired* by our action is always conditional. Beings whose existence depends not on our will but on nature's, have nevertheless, if they are rational beings, only a relative value as means, and are therefore called *things;* rational beings, on the contrary, are called *persons,* because their very nature points them out as ends in themselves, that is as something which must not be used merely as means, and so far therefore restricts freedom of action (and is an object of respect). These, therefore, are not merely subjective ends whose existence has a worth for *us* as an effort of our action, but *objective ends,* that is things whose existence is an end in itself: an end moreover for which no other can be substituted, which they should subserve *merely* as means, for otherwise nothing whatever would possess *absolute worth;* but if all worth were conditioned and therefore contingent, then there would be no supreme practical principle of reason whatever.

If then there is a supreme practical principle or, in respect of the human will, a categorical imperative, it must be one which, being drawn from the conception of that which is necessarily an end for everyone because it is *an end in itself,* constitutes an *objective* principle of will, and can therefore serve as a universal practical law. The foundation of this principle is: *rational nature exists as an end in itself.* Man necessarily conceives his own existence as being so: so far then this is a *subjective* principle of human actions. But every other rational being regards its existence similarly, just on the same rational principle, that holds for me: so that it is at the same time an objective principle, from which as a supreme practical law all laws of the will must be capable of being deduced. Accordingly the practical imperative will be as follows: *So act as to treat humanity, whether in thine own person or in that of any other, in every case as an end withal, never as means only....*

The conception of every rational being as one which must consider itself as giving all the maxims of its will universal laws, so as to judge itself and its actions from this point of view—this conception leads to another which depends on it and is very fruitful, namely, that of a *kingdom of ends.*

By a *kingdom* I understand the union of different rational beings in a system by common laws. Now since it is by laws that ends are determined as regards their universal validity, hence, if we abstract from the personal differences of rational beings, and likewise from all the content of their private ends, we shall be able to conceive all ends combined in a systematic whole (including both rational beings as ends in themselves, and also the special ends which each may propose to himself), that is to say, we can conceive a kingdom of ends, which on the preceding principles is possible.

from Utilitarianism

John Stuart Mill

What Utilitarianism Is

A passing remark is all that needs be given to the ignorant blunder of supposing that those who stand up for utility as the test of right and wrong use the term in that restricted and merely colloquial sense in which utility is opposed to pleasure. An apology is due to the philosophical opponents of utilitarianism for even the momentary appearance of confounding them with anyone capable of so absurd a misconception; which is the more extraordinary, inasmuch as the contrary accusation, of referring everything to pleasure, and that, too, in its grossest form, is another of the common charges against utilitarianism: and, as has been pointedly remarked by an able writer, the same sort of persons, and often the very same persons, denounce the theory "as impracticably dry when the word 'utility' precedes the word 'pleasure,' and as too practically voluptuous when the word 'pleasure' precedes the word 'utility.'" Those who know anything about the matter are aware that every writer, from Epicurus to Bentham, who maintained the theory of utility meant by it, not something to be contradistinguished from pleasure, but pleasure itself, together with exemption from pain; and instead of opposing the useful to the agreeable or the ornamental, have always declared that the useful means these, among other things. Yet the common herd, including the herd of writers, not only in newspapers and periodicals, but in books of weight and pretension, are perpetually falling into this shallow mistake. Having caught up the word "utilitarian," while knowing nothing whatever about it but its sound, they habitually express by it the rejection or the neglect of pleasure in some of its forms: of beauty, of ornament, or of amusement. Nor is the term thus ignorantly misapplied solely in disparagement, but occasionally in compliment, as though it implied superiority to frivolity and the mere pleasures of the moment. And this perverted use is the only one in which the word is popularly known, and the one from which the new generation are acquiring their sole notion of its meaning. Those who introduced the word, but who had for many years discontinued it as a distinctive appellation, may well feel themselves called upon to resume it if by doing so they can hope to contribute anything toward rescuing it from this utter degradation.

The creed which accepts as the foundation of morals "utility" or the "greatest happiness principle" holds that actions are right in proportion as they tend to promote happiness; wrong as they tend to produce the reverse of happiness. By happiness is intended pleasure and the absence of pain; by unhappiness, pain and the privation of pleasure. To give a clear view of the moral standard set up by the theory, much more requires to be said; in particular, what things it includes in the ideas of pain and pleasure, and to what extent this is left an open question. But these supplementary explanations do not affect the theory of life on which this theory of morality is grounded—namely, that pleasure and freedom from pain are the only things desirable as ends; and that all desirable things (which are as numerous in the utilitarian as in any other scheme) are desirable either for pleasure inherent in themselves or as means to the promotion of pleasure and the prevention of pain.

Now such a theory of life excites in many minds, and among them in some of the most estimable in feeling and purpose, inveterate dislike. To suppose that life has (as they express it) no higher end than pleasure—no better and nobler object of desire and pursuit—they designate as utterly mean and groveling, as a doctrine worthy only of swine, to whom the followers of Epicurus were, at a very early period, contemptuously likened; and modern holders of the doctrine are occasionally made the subject of equally polite comparisons by its German, French, and English assailants.

When thus attacked, the Epicureans have always answered that it is not they, but their accusers, who represent human nature in a degrading light, since the accusation supposes human beings to be capable of no pleasures except those of which swine are capable. If this supposition were true, the charge could not be gainsaid, but would then be no longer an imputation; for if the sources of pleasure were precisely the same to human beings and to swine, the rule of life which is good enough for the one would be good enough for the other. The comparison of the Epicurean life to that of beasts is felt as degrading, precisely because a beast's pleasures do not satisfy a human being's conceptions of happiness. Human beings have faculties more elevated than the animal appetites and, when once made conscious of them, do not regard anything as happiness which does not include their gratification. I do not, indeed, consider the Epicureans to have been by any means faultless in drawing out their scheme of consequences from the utilitarian principle.

To do this in any sufficient manner, many Stoic, as well as Christian, elements require to be included. But there is no known Epicurean theory of life which does not assign to the pleasures of the intellect, of the feelings and imagination, and of the moral sentiments a much higher value as pleasures than to those of mere sensation. It must be admitted, however, that utilitarian writers in general have placed the superiority of mental over bodily pleasures chiefly in the greater permanency, safety, uncostliness, etc., of the former—that is, in their circumstantial advantages rather than in their intrinsic nature. And on all these points utilitarians have fully proved their case; but they might have taken the other and, as it may be called, higher ground with entire consistency. It is quite compatible with the principle of utility to recognize the fact that some kinds of pleasure are more desirable and more valuable than others. It would be absurd that, while in estimating all other things quality is considered as well as quantity, the estimation of pleasure should be supposed to depend on quantity alone.

If I am asked what I mean by difference of quality in pleasures, or what makes one pleasure more valuable than another, merely as a pleasure, except its being greater in amount, there is but one possible answer. Of two pleasures, if there be one to which all or almost all who have experience of both give a decided preference, irrespective of any feeling of moral obligation to prefer it, that is the more desirable pleasure. If one of the two is, by those who are competently acquainted with both, placed so far above the other that they prefer it, even though knowing it to be attended with a greater amount of discontent, and would not resign it for any quantity of the other pleasure which their nature is capable of, we are justified in ascribing to the preferred enjoyment a superiority in quality so far outweighing quantity as to render it, in comparison, of small account.

Now it is an unquestionable fact that those who are equally acquainted with and equally capable of appreciating and enjoying both do give a most marked preference to the manner of existence which employs their higher faculties. Few human creatures would consent to be changed into any of the lower animals for a promise of the fullest allowance of a beast's pleasures; no intelligent human being would consent to be a fool, no instructed person would be an ignoramus, no person of feeling and conscience would be selfish and base, even though they should be persuaded that the fool, the dunce, or the rascal is better satisfied with his lot than they are with theirs. They would not resign what they possess more than he for the most complete satisfaction of all the desires which they have in common with him. If they ever fancy they would, it is only in cases of unhappiness so extreme that to escape from it they would exchange their lot for almost any other, however undesirable in their own eyes. A being of higher faculties requires more to make him happy, is capable probably of more acute suffering, and certainly accessible to it at more points, than one of an inferior type; but in spite of these liabilities, he can never really wish to sink into what he feels to be a lower grade of existence. We may give what explanation we please of this unwillingness; we may attribute it to pride, a name which is given indiscriminately to some of the most and to some of the least estimable feelings of which mankind are capable; we may refer it to the love of liberty and personal independence, an appeal to which was with the Stoics one of the most effective means for the inculcation of it; to the love of power or to the love of excitement, both of which do really enter into and contribute to it; but its most appropriate appellation is a sense of dignity, which all human beings possess in one form or other, and in some, though by no means in exact, proportion to their higher faculties, and which is so essential a part of the happiness of those in whom it is strong that nothing which conflicts with it could be otherwise than momentarily an object of desire to them. Whoever supposes that this preference takes place at a sacrifice of happiness—that the superior being, in anything like equal circumstances, is not happier than the inferior—confounds the two very different ideas of happiness and content. It is indisputable that the being whose capacities of enjoyment are low has the greatest chance of having them fully satisfied; and a highly endowed being will always feel that any happiness which he can look for, as the world is constituted, is imperfect. But he can learn to bear its imperfections, if they are at all bearable; and they will not make him envy the being who is indeed unconscious of the imperfections, but only because he feels not at all the good which those imperfections qualify. **It is better to be a human being dissatisfied than a pig satisfied; better to be Socrates dissatisfied than a fool satisfied.** And if the fool, or the pig, are of a different opinion, it is because they only know their own side of the question. The other party to the comparison knows both sides. . . .

I have dwelt on this point as being a necessary part of a perfectly just conception of utility or happiness considered as the directive rule of human conduct. But it is by no means an indispensable condition to the acceptance of the utilitarian standard; for that standard is not the agent's own greatest happiness, but the greatest amount of happiness altogether; and if it may possibly be doubted whether a noble character is always the happier for its nobleness, there can be no doubt that it makes other people happier, and that the world in general is immensely a gainer by it. Utilitarianism, therefore, could only attain its end by the general cultivation of nobleness of character, even if each individual were only benefited by the nobleness of others, and his own, so far as happiness is concerned, were a sheer deduction from the benefit. But the bare enunciation of such an absurdity as this last renders refutation superfluous.

According to the greatest happiness principle, as above explained, the ultimate end, with reference to and for the sake of which all other things are desirable—whether we are considering our own good or that of other people—is an existence exempt as far as possible from pain, and as rich as possible in enjoyments, both in point of quantity and quality; the test of quality and the rule for measuring it against quantity being the preference felt by those who, in their opportunities of experience, to which must be added their habits of self-consciousness and self-observation, are best furnished with the means of comparison. This, being according to the utilitarian opinion the end of human action, is necessarily also the standard of morality, which may accordingly be defined "the rules and precepts for human conduct," by the observance of which an existence such as has been described might be, to the greatest extent possible, secured to all mankind; and not to them only, but, so far as the nature of things admits, to the whole sentient creation. . . .

Of What Sort of Proof the Principle of Utility Is Susceptible

. . . (Q)uestions of ultimate ends do not admit of proof, in the ordinary acceptation of the term. To be incapable of proof by reasoning is common to all first principles, to the first premises of our knowledge, as well as to those of our conduct. But the former, being matters of fact, may be the subject of a direct appeal to the faculties which judge of fact—namely, our senses and our internal consciousness. Can an appeal be made to the same faculties on questions of practical ends? Or by what other faculty is cognizance taken of them?

Questions about ends are, in other words, questions what things are desirable. The utilitarian doctrine is that happiness is desirable, and the only thing desirable, as an end; all other things being only desirable as means to that end. What ought to be required of this doctrine, what conditions is it requisite that the doctrine should fulfill—to make good its claim to be believed?

The only proof capable of being given that an object is visible is that people actually see it. The only proof that a sound is audible is that people hear it; and so of the other sources of our experience. In like manner, I apprehend, the sole evidence it is possible to produce that anything is desirable is that people do actually desire it. If the end which the utilitarian doctrine proposes to itself were not, in theory and in practice, acknowledged to be an end, nothing could ever convince any person that it was so. No reason can be given why the general happiness is desirable, except that each person, so far as he believes it to be attainable, desires his own happiness. This, however, being a fact, we have not only all the proof which the case admits of, but all which it is possible to require, that happiness is a good, that each person's happiness is a good to that person, and the general happiness, therefore, a good to the aggregate of all persons. Happiness has made out its title as *one* of the ends of conduct and, consequently, one of the criteria of morality.

But it has not, by this alone, proved itself to be the sole criterion. To do that, it would seem, by the same rule, necessary to show, not only that people desire happiness, but that they never desire anything else. Now it is palpable that they do desire things which, in common language, are decidedly distinguished from happiness. They desire, for example, virtue and the absence of vice no less really than pleasure and the absence of pain. The desire of virtue is not as universal, but it is as authentic a fact as the desire of happiness. And hence the opponents of the utilitarian standard deem that they have a right to infer that there are other ends of human action besides happiness, and that happiness is not the standard of approbation and disapprobation.

But does the utilitarian doctrine deny that people desire virtue, or maintain that virtue is not a thing to be desired? The very reverse. It maintains not only that virtue is to be desired, but that it is to be desired disinterestedly, for itself. Whatever may be the opinion of utilitarian moralists as to the original conditions by which virtue is made virtue, however they may believe (as they do) that actions and dispositions are only virtuous because they promote another end than virtue, yet this being granted, and it having been decided, from considerations of this description, what is virtuous, they not only place virtue at the very head of the things which are good as means to the ultimate end, but they also recognize as a psychological fact the possibility of its being, to the individual, a good in itself, without looking to any end beyond it; and hold that the mind is not in a right state, not in a state conformable to utility, not in the state most conducive to the general happiness, unless it does love virtue in this manner—

as a thing desirable in itself, even although, in the individual instance, it should not produce those other desirable consequences which it tends to produce, and on account of which it is held to be virtue. This opinion is not, in the smallest degree, a departure from the happiness principle. The ingredients of happiness are very various, and each of them is desirable in itself, and not merely when considered as swelling an aggregate. The principle of utility does not mean that any given pleasure, as music, for instance, or any given exemption from pain, as for example health, is to be looked upon as means to a collective something termed happiness, and to be desired, on that account. They are desired and desirable in and for themselves; besides being means, they are a part of the end. Virtue, according to the utilitarian doctrine, is not naturally and originally part of the end, but it is capable of becoming so; and in those who live it disinterestedly it has become so, and is desired and cherished, not as a means to happiness, but as a part of their happiness.

To illustrate this further, we may remember that virtue is not the only thing originally a means, and which if it were not a means to anything else would be and remain indifferent, but which by association with what it is a means to comes to be desired for itself, and that too with the utmost intensity. What, for example, shall we say of the love of money? There is nothing originally more desirable about money than about any heap of glittering pebbles. Its worth is solely that of the things which it will buy; the desires for other things than itself, which it is a means of gratifying. Yet the love of money is not only one of the strongest moving forces of human life, but money is, in many cases, desired in and for itself; the desire to possess it is often stronger than the desire to use it, and goes on increasing when all the desires which point to ends beyond it, to be compassed by it, are falling off. It may, then, be said truly that money is desired not for the sake of an end, but as part of the end. From being a means to happiness, it has come to be itself a principal ingredient of the individual's conception of happiness. The same may be said of the majority of the great objects of human life: power, for example, or fame, except that to each of these there is a certain amount of immediate pleasure annexed, which has at least the semblance of being naturally inherent in them—a thing which cannot be said of money. Still, however, the strongest natural attraction, both of power and of fame, is the immense aid they give to the attainment of our other wishes; and it is the strong association thus generated between them and all our objects of desire which gives to the direct desire of them the intensity it often assumes, so as in some characters to surpass in strength all other desires. In these cases the means have become a part of the end, and a more important part of it than any of the things which they are means to. What was once desired as an instrument for the attainment of happiness has come to be desired for its own sake. In being desired for its own sake it is, however, desired as *part* of happiness. The person is made, or thinks he would be made, happy by its mere possession; and is made unhappy by failure to obtain it. The desire of it is not a different thing from the desire of happiness any more than the love of music or the desire of health. They are included in happiness. They are some of the elements of which the desire of happiness is made up. Happiness is not an abstract idea but a concrete whole; and these are some of its parts. And the utilitarian standard sanctions and approves their being so. Life would be a poor thing, very ill provided with sources of happiness, if there were not this provision of nature by which things originally indifferent, but conducive to, or otherwise associated with, the satisfaction of our primitive desires, become in themselves sources of pleasure more valuable than the primitive pleasures, both in permanency, in the space of human existence that they are capable of covering, and even in intensity.

Virtue, according to the utilitarian conception, is a good of this description. There was no original desire of it, or motive to it, save its conduciveness to pleasure, and especially to protection from pain. But through the association thus formed it may be felt a good in itself, and desired as such with as great intensity as any other good; and with this difference between it and the love of money, of power, or of fame—that all of these may, and often do, render the individual noxious to the other members of the society to which he belongs, whereas there is nothing which makes him so much a blessing to them as the cultivation of the disinterested love of virtue. And consequently, the utilitarian standard, while it tolerates and approves those other acquired desires, up to the point beyond which they would be more injurious to the general happiness than promotive of it, enjoins and requires the cultivation of the love of virtue up to the greatest strength possible, as being above all things important to the general happiness.

It results from the preceding considerations that there is in reality nothing desired except happiness. Whatever is desired otherwise than as a means to some end beyond itself, and ultimately to happiness, is desired as itself a part of happiness, and is not desired for itself until it has become so. Those who desire virtue for its own sake desire it either because the consciousness of it is a pleasure, or because the consciousness of being without it is a pain, or for both reasons united; as in truth the pleasure and pain seldom exist separately, but almost always together—

the same person feeling pleasure in the degree of virtue attained, and pain in not having attained more. If one of these gave him no pleasure, and the other no pain, he would not love or desire virtue, or would desire it only for the other benefits which it might produce to himself or to persons whom he cared for.

We have now, then, an answer to the question, of what sort of proof the principle of utility is susceptible. If the opinion which I have now stated is psychologically true—if human nature is so constituted as to desire nothing which is not either a part of happiness or a means of happiness—we can have no other proof, and we require no other, that these are the only things desirable. If so, happiness is the sole end of human action, and the promotion of it the test by which to judge of all human conduct; from whence it necessarily follows that it must be the criterion of morality, since a part is included in the whole.

And now to decide whether this is really so, whether mankind do desire nothing for itself but that which is a pleasure to them, or of which the absence is a pain, we have evidently arrived at a question of fact and experience, dependent, like all similar questions, upon evidence. It can only be determined by practiced self-consciousness and self-observation, assisted by observation of others. I believe that these sources of evidence, impartially consulted, will declare that desiring a thing and finding it pleasant, aversion to it and thinking of it as painful, are phenomena entirely inseparable or, rather, two parts of the same phenomenon—in strictness of language, two different modes of naming the same psychological fact; that to think of an object as desirable (unless for the sake of its consequences) and to think of it as pleasant are one and the same thing; and that to desire anything except in proportion as the idea of it is pleasant is a physical and metaphysical impossibility.

So obvious does this appear to me that I expect it will hardly be disputed; and the objection made will be, not that desire can possibly be directed to anything ultimately except pleasure and exemption from pain, but that the will is a different thing from desire; that a person of confirmed virtue or any other person whose purposes are fixed carries out his purposes without any thought of the pleasure he has in contemplating them or expects to derive from their fulfillment, and persists in acting on them, even though these pleasures are much diminished by changes in his character or decay of his passive sensibilities, or are outweighed by the pains which the pursuit of the purposes may bring upon him. All this I fully admit and have stated it elsewhere as positively and emphatically as anyone. Will, the active phenomenon, is a different thing from desire, the state of passive sensibility, and, though originally an offshoot from it, may in time take root and detach itself from the parent stock, so much so that in the case of a habitual purpose, instead of willing the thing because we desire it, we often desire it only because we will it. This, however, is but an instance of that familiar fact, the power of habit, and is nowise confined to the case of virtuous actions. Many indifferent things which men originally did from a motive of some sort they continue to do from habit. Sometimes this is done unconsciously, the consciousness coming only after the action; at other times with conscious volition, but volition which has become habitual and is put in operation by the force of habit, in opposition perhaps to the deliberate preference, as often happens with those who have contracted habits of vicious or hurtful indulgence. Third and last comes the case in which the habitual act of will in the individual instance is not in contradiction to the general intention prevailing at other times, but in fulfillment of it, as in the case of the person of confirmed virtue and of all who pursue deliberately and consistently any determinate end. The distinction between will and desire thus understood is an authentic and highly important psychological fact; but the fact consists solely in this—that will, like all other parts of our constitution, is amenable to habit, and that we may will from habit what we no longer desire for itself, or desire only because we will it. It is not the less true that will, in the beginning, is entirely produced by desire, including in that term the repelling influence of pain as well as the attractive one of pleasure. Let us take into consideration no longer the person who has a confirmed will to do right, but him in whom that virtuous will is still feeble, conquerable by temptation, and not to be fully relied on; by what means can it be strengthened? How can the will to be virtuous, where it does not exist in sufficient force, be implanted or awakened? Only by making the person *desire* virtue—by making him think of it in a pleasurable light, or of its absence in a painful one. It is by associating the doing right with pleasure, or the wrong with pain, or by eliciting and impressing and bringing home to the person's experience the pleasure naturally involved in the one or the pain in the other, that it is possible to call forth that will to be virtuous which, when confirmed, acts without any thought of either pleasure or pain. Will is the child of desire, and passes out of the dominion of its parent only to come under that of habit. That which is the result of habit affords no presumption of being intrinsically good; and there would be no reason for wishing that the purpose of virtue should become independent of pleasure and pain were it not that the influence of the pleasurable and painful associations which prompt to virtue is not sufficiently to be depended on for unerring constancy of action until it has acquired the support of habit. Both in feeling and in conduct, habit is the only thing which imparts certainty; and it is because of the importance to others of being able to rely absolutely on one's feelings and conduct, and to oneself of being able to rely on one's own, that the will to do right ought to be cultivated into this habitual independence. In other words, this state of the will is a means to good, not intrinsically a good; and does not contradict the doctrine that nothing is a good to human beings but in so far as it is either itself pleasurable or a means of attaining pleasure or averting pain.

But if this doctrine be true, the principle of utility is proved. Whether it is so or not, must now be left to the consideration of the thoughtful reader.

An Ethics of Care

Nel Noddings

The main task in this chapter is a preliminary analysis of caring. I want to ask what it means to care and to lay down the lines along which analysis will proceed in chapters two and three [of the author's original work]. It seems obvious in an everyday sense why we should be interested in caring. Everywhere we hear the complaint "Nobody cares!" and our increasing immersion in bureaucratic procedures and regulations leads us to predict that the complaint will continue to be heard. As human beings we want to care and to be cared for. *Caring* is important in itself. It seems necessary, however, to motivate the sort of detailed analysis I propose; that is, it is reasonable in a philosophical context to ask: Why care about caring?

If we were starting out on a traditional investigation of what it means to be moral, we would almost certainly start with a discussion of moral judgment and moral reasoning. This approach has obvious advantages. It gives us something public and tangible to grapple with—the statements that describe our thinking on moral matters. But I shall argue that this is not the only—nor even the best—starting point. Starting the discussion of moral matters with principles, definitions, and demonstrations is rather like starting the solution of a mathematical problem formally. Sometimes we can and do proceed this way, but when the problematic situation is new, baffling, or especially complex, we cannot start this way. We have to operate in an intuitive or receptive mode that is somewhat mysterious, internal, and nonsequential. After the solution has been found by intuitive methods, we may proceed with the construction of a formal demonstration or proof. As the mathematician Gauss put it: "I have got my result but I do not know yet how to get (prove) it."[1]

A difficulty in mathematics teaching is that we too rarely share our fundamental mathematical thinking with our students. We present everything ready-made as it were, as though it springs from our foreheads in formal perfection. The same sort of difficulty arises when we approach the teaching of morality or ethical behavior from a rational-cognitive approach. We fail to share with each other the feelings, the conflicts, the hopes and ideas that influence our eventual choices. We share only the justification for our acts and not what motivates and touches us.

I think we are doubly mistaken when we approach moral matters in this mathematical way. First, of course, we miss sharing the heuristic processes in our ethical thinking just as we miss that sharing when we approach mathematics itself formally. But this difficulty could be remedied pedagogically. We would not have to change our approach to ethics but only to the teaching of ethical behavior or ethical thinking. Second, however, when we approach moral matters through the study of moral reasoning, we are led quite naturally to suppose that ethics is necessarily a subject that must be cast in the language of principle and demonstration. This, I shall argue, is a mistake.

Many persons who live moral lives do not approach moral problems formally. Women, in particular, seem to approach moral problems by placing themselves as nearly as possible in concrete situations and assuming personal responsibility for the choices to be made. They define themselves in terms of *caring* and work their way through moral problems from the position of one-caring.[2] This position or attitude of caring activates a complex structure of memories, feelings, and capacities. Further, the process of moral decision making that is founded on caring requires a process of concretization rather than one of abstraction. An ethic built on caring is, I think, characteristically and essentially feminine—which is not to say, of course, that it cannot be shared by men, any more than we should care to say that traditional moral systems cannot be embraced by women. But an ethic of caring arises, I believe, out of our experience as women, just as the traditional logical approach to ethical problems arises more obviously from masculine experience.

One reason, then, for conducting the comprehensive and appreciative investigation of caring to which we shall now turn is to capture conceptually a feminine—or simply an alternative—approach to matters of morality.

What Does It Mean to Care

Our dictionaries tell us that "care" is a state of mental suffering or of engrossment: to care is to be in a burdened mental state, one of anxiety, fear, or solicitude about something or someone. Alternatively, one cares for something or someone if one has a regard for or inclination toward that something or someone. If I have an inclination toward mathematics, I may willingly spend some time with it, and if I have a regard for you, what you think, feel, and desire will matter to me. And, again, to care may mean to be charged with the protection, welfare, or maintenance of something or someone.

These definitions represent different uses of "care" but, in the deepest human sense, we shall see that elements of each of them are involved in caring. In one sense, I may equate "cares" with "burdens"; I have cares in certain matters (professional, personal, or public) if I have burdens or worries, if I fret over current and projected states of affairs. In another sense, I *care* for someone if I feel a stir of desire or inclination toward him. In a related sense, I *care* for someone if I have regard for his views and interests. In the third sense, I have the care of an elderly relative if I am charged with the responsibility for his physical welfare. But, clearly, in the deep human sense that will occupy us, I cannot claim to care for my relative if my caretaking is perfunctory or grudging.

We see that it will be necessary to give much of our attention to the one-caring in our analysis. Even though we sometimes judge caring from the outside, as third-persons, it is easy to see that the essential elements of caring are located in the relation between the one-caring and the cared-for. In a lovely little book, *On Caring*, Milton Mayeroff describes caring largely through the view of one-caring. He begins by saying: "To care for another person, in the most significant sense, is to help him grow and actualize himself."[3]

I want to approach the problem a bit differently, because I think emphasis on the actualization of the other may lead us to pass too rapidly over the description of what goes on in the one-caring. Further, problems arise in the discussion of reciprocity, and we shall feel a need to examine the role of the cared-for much more closely also. But Mayeroff has given us a significant start by pointing to the importance of constancy, guilt, reciprocation, and the limits of caring. All of these we shall consider in some detail.

Let's start looking at caring from the outside to discover the limitations of that approach. In the ordinary course of events, we expect some action from one who claims to care, even though action is not all we expect. How are we to determine whether Mr. Smith cares for his elderly mother, who is confined to a nursing home? It is not enough, surely, that Mr. Smith should say, "I care." (But the possibility of his saying this will lead us onto another path of analysis shortly. We shall have to examine caring from the inside.) We, as observers, must look for some action, some manifestation in Smith's behavior, that will allow us to agree that he cares. To care, we feel, requires some action in behalf of the cared-for. Thus, if Smith never visits his mother, nor writes to her, nor telephones her, we would be likely to say that, although he is charged formally with her care—he pays for her confinement—he does not really care. We point out that he seems to be lacking in regard, that he is not troubled enough to see for himself how his mother fares. There is no desire for her company, no inclination toward her. But notice that a criterion of action would not be easy to formulate from this case. Smith, after all, does perform some action in behalf of his mother: he pays for her physical maintenance. But we are looking for a qualitatively different sort of action.

Is direct, externally observable action necessary to caring? Can caring be present in the absence of action in behalf of the cared-for? Consider the problem of lovers who cannot marry because they are already committed to satisfactory and honorable marriages. The lover learns that his beloved is ill. All his instincts cry out for his presence at her bedside. Yet, if he fears for the trouble he may bring her, for the recriminations that may spring from his appearance, he may stay away from her. Surely, we would not say in such a case that the lover does not care. He is in a mental state of engrossment, even suffering; he feels the deepest regard and, charged by his love with the duty to protect, he denies his own need in order to spare her one form of pain. Thus, in caring, he chooses not to act directly and tenderly in response to the beloved's immediate physical pain. We see that, when we consider the action component of caring in depth, we shall have to look beyond observable action to acts of commitment, those acts that are seen only by the individual subject performing them.

In the case of the lover whose beloved has fallen ill, we might expect him to express himself when the crisis has passed. But even this might not happen. He might resolve never to contact her again, and his caring could then be known only to him as he renews his resolve again and again. We do not wish to deny that the lover cares, but clearly, something is missing in the relationship: caring is not completed in the cared-for. Or, consider the mother whose son, in young adulthood, leaves home in anger and rebellion. Should she act to bring about reconciliation? Perhaps. Are we sure that she does not care if she fails to act directly to bring him into loving contact with his family? She may, indeed, deliberately abstain from acting in the belief that her son must be allowed to work out his problem alone. Her regard for him may force her into anguished and carefully considered inaction. Like the lover, she may eventually express herself to her son—when the crisis has passed—but then again, she may not. After a period of, say, two years, the relationship may stabilize, and the mother's caring may resume its usual form. Shall we say, then, that she "cares again" and that for two years she "did not care"?

There are still further difficulties in trying to formulate an action criterion for caring. Suppose that I learn about a family in great need, and suppose that I decide to help them. I pay their back rent for them, buy food for them, and supply them with the necessities of life. I do all this cheerfully, willingly spending time with them. Can it be doubted that I care? This sort of case will raise problems also. Suppose both husband and wife in this family want to be independent, or at least have a latent longing in this direction. But my acts tend to suppress the urge toward independence. Am I helping or hindering?[4] Do I care or only seem to care? If it must be said that my relation to the needy family is not, properly, a caring relation, what has gone wrong?

Now, in this brief inspection of caring acts, we have already encountered problems. Others suggest themselves. What of indirect caring, for example? What shall we say about college students who engage in protests for the blacks of South Africa or the "boat people" of Indochina or the Jews of Russia? Under what conditions would we be willing to say that they care? Again, these may be questions that can be answered only by those claiming to care. We need to know, for example, what motivates the protest. Then, as we shall see, there is the recurring problem of "completion." How is the caring conveyed to the cared-for? What sort of meeting can there be between the one-caring and the cared-for?

We are not going to be able to answer all of these questions with certainty. Indeed, this essay is not aiming toward a systematic exposition of criteria for caring. Rather, I must show that such a systematic effort is, so far as the system is its goal, mistaken. We expend the effort as much to show what is not fruitful as what is. It is not my aim to be able to sort cases at the finish: A cares, B does not care, C cares but not about D, etc. If we can understand how complex and intricate, indeed how subjective, caring is, we shall perhaps be better equipped to meet the conflicts and pains it sometimes induces. Then, too, we may come to understand at least in part how it is that, in a country that spends billions on caretaking of various sorts, we hear everywhere the complaint, "Nobody cares."

In spite of the difficulties involved, we shall have to discuss behavioral indicators of caring in some depth, because we will be concerned about problems of entrusting care, of monitoring caretaking and assigning it. When we consider the possibility of institutional caring and what might be meant by the "caring school," we shall need to know what to look for. And so, even though the analysis will move us more and more toward first- and second-person views of caring, we shall examine caring acts and the "third-person" view also. In this initial analysis, we shall return to the third-person view after examining first- and second-person aspects.

So far, we have talked about the action component of caring, and we certainly have not arrived at a determinate set of criteria. Suppose, now, that we consider the engrossment we expect to find in the one-caring. When Mr. Smith, whose "caring" seems to us to be at best perfunctory, says, "I care," what can he mean? Now, clearly we can only guess, because Mr. Smith has to speak for himself on this. But he might mean: (1) I *do* care. I think of my mother often and worry about her. It is an awful burden. (2) I *do* care. I should see her more often, but I have so much to do—a houseful of kids, long working hours, a wife who needs my companionship. . . . (3) I *do* care. I pay the bills, don't I? I have sisters who could provide company. . . .

These suggested meanings do not exhaust Mr. Smith's possibilities, but they give us something to work with. In the first case, we might rightly conclude that Mr. Smith does not care for his mother as much as he does for himself as caretaker. He is burdened with cares, and the focus of his attention has shifted inward to himself and his worries. This, we shall see, is a risk of caring. There exists in all caring situations the risk that the one-caring will be overwhelmed by the responsibilities and duties of the task and that, as a result of being burdened, he or she will cease to care for the other and become instead the object of "caring." Now, here—and throughout our discussion on caring—we must try to avoid equivocation. There are, as we have noted, several common meanings of "to care," but no one of them yields the deep sense for which we are probing. When it is clear that "caring" refers to one of the restricted senses, or when we are not yet sure to what it refers, I shall enclose it in quotes. In the situation where Mr. Smith is *burdened with cares*, he is the object of "caring."

In the third case, also, we might justifiably conclude that Mr. Smith does not care. His interest is in equity. He wants to be credited with caring. By doing something, he hopes to find an acceptable substitute for genuine caring. We see similar behavior in the woman who professes to love animals and whisks every stray to the animal shelter. Most animals, once at the shelter, suffer death. Does one who cares choose swift and merciful death for the object of her care over precarious and perhaps painful life? Well, we might say, it depends. It depends on our caretaking capabilities, on traffic conditions where we live, on the physical condition of the animal. All this is exactly to the point. What we do depends not upon rules, or at least not wholly on rules—not upon a prior determination of what is fair or equitable—but upon a constellation of conditions that is viewed through both the eyes of the one-caring and the eyes of the cared-for. By and large, we do not say with any conviction that a person cares if that person acts routinely according to some fixed rule.

The second case is difficult. This Mr. Smith has a notion that caring involves a commitment of self, but he is finding it difficult to handle the commitments he has already made. He is in conflict over how he should spend himself. Undergoing conflict is another risk of caring, and we shall consider a variety of possible conflicts. Of special interest to us will be the question: When should I attempt to remove conflict, and when should I resolve simply to live with the conflict? Suppose, for example, that I care for both cats and birds. (I must use "care for" at this stage without attempting to justify its use completely.) Having particular cats of my own and *not* having particular birds of my own at the same time are indications of my concern for each. But there are wild birds in my garden, and they are in peril from the cats. I may give the matter considerable thought. I feed the cats well so that they will not hunt out of hunger. I hang small bells on their collars. I keep bird cages ready for victims I am able to rescue. I keep bird baths and feeders inaccessible to the cats. Beyond this, I live with the conflict. Others might have the cats declawed, but I will not do this. Now, the point here is not whether I care more for cats than birds, or whether Ms. Jones (who declaws her cats) cares more for birds than I do. The point lies in trying to discern the kinds of things I must think about when I am in a conflict of caring. When my caring is directed to living things, I must consider their natures, ways of life, needs, and desires. And, although I can never accomplish it entirely, I try to apprehend the reality of the other.

This is the fundamental aspect of caring from the inside. When I look at and think about how I am when I care, I realize that there is invariably this displacement of interest from my own reality to the reality of the other. (Our discussion now will be confined to caring for persons.)

Kierkegaard has said that we apprehend another's reality as *possibility*.[5] To be touched, to have aroused in me something that will disturb my own ethical reality, I must see the other's reality as a possibility for my own. This is not to say that I cannot try to see the other's reality differently. Indeed, I can. I can look at it objectively by collecting factual data; I can look at it historically. If it is heroic, I can come to admire it. But this sort of looking does not touch my own ethical reality; it may even distract me from it. As Kierkegaard put it:

> Ethically speaking there is nothing so conductive to sound sleep as admiration of another person's ethical reality. And again ethically speaking, if there is anything that can stir and rouse a man, it is a possibility ideally requiring itself of a human being.[6]

But I am suggesting that we do not see only the direct possibilities for becoming better than we are when we struggle toward the reality of the other. We also have aroused in us the feeling, "I must do something." When we see the other's reality as a possibility for us, we must act to eliminate the intolerable, to reduce the pain, to fill the need, to actualize the dream. When I am in this sort of relationship with another, when the other's reality becomes a real possibility for me, I care. Whether the caring is sustained, whether it lasts long enough to be conveyed to the other, whether it becomes visible in the world, depends upon my sustaining the relationship or, at least, acting out of concern for my own ethicality as though it were sustained.

In this latter case, one in which something has slipped away from me or eluded me from the start but in which I strive to regain or to attain it, I experience a genuine caring for self. This caring for self, for the *ethical* self, can emerge only from a caring for others. But a sense of my physical self, a knowledge of what gives me pain and pleasure, precedes my caring for others. Otherwise, their realities as possibilities for my own reality would mean nothing to me. When we say of someone, "He cares only for himself," we mean that, in our deepest sense, he does not care at all. He has only a sense of that physical self—of what gives him pain and pleasure. Whatever he sees in others is pre-selected in relation to his own needs and desires. He does not see the reality of the other as a possibility for himself but only as an instance of what he has already determined as self or not-self. Thus, he is ethically both zero and finished. His only "becoming" is a physical becoming. It is clear, of course, that I must say more about what is meant by "ethical reality" and "ethical self," and I shall return to this question.

I need not, however, be a person who cares only for myself in order to behave occasionally as though I care only for myself. Sometimes I behave this way because I have not thought through things carefully enough and because the mode of the times pushes the thoughtless in its own direction. Suppose, for example, that I am a teacher who loves mathematics. I encounter a student who is doing poorly, and I decide to have a talk with him. He tells me that he hates mathematics. *Aha,* I think. *Here is the problem. I must help this poor boy to love mathematics, and then he will do better at it.* What am I doing when I proceed in this way? I am not trying to grasp the reality of the other as a possibility for myself. I have not even asked: *How would it feel to hate mathematics?* Instead, I project my own reality onto my student and say, *You will be just fine if only you learn to love mathematics.* And I have "data" to support me. There is evidence that intrinsic motivation is associated with higher achievement. (Did anyone ever doubt this?) So my student becomes an object of study and manipulation for me. Now, I have deliberately chosen an example that is not often associated with manipulation. Usually, we associate manipulation with trying to get our student to achieve some learning objective that we have devised and set for him. Bringing him to "love mathematics" is seen as a noble aim. And so it is, if it is held out to him as a possibility that he glimpses by observing me and others; but then I shall not be disappointed in him, or in myself, if he remains indifferent to mathematics. It is a possibility that may not be actualized. What matters to me, if I care, is that he find some reason, acceptable in his inner self, for learning the mathematics required of him or that he reject it boldly and honestly. How would it feel to hate mathematics? What reasons could I find for learning it? When I think this way, I refuse to cast about for rewards that might pull him along. He must find his rewards. I do not begin with dazzling performances designed to intrigue him or to change his attitude. I begin, as nearly as I can, with the view from his eyes: Mathematics is bleak, jumbled, scary, boring, boring, boring. . . . What in the world could induce me to engage in it? From that point on, we struggle together with it.

Apprehending the other's reality, feeling what he feels as nearly as possible, is the essential part of caring from the view of the one-caring. For if I take on the other's reality as possibility and begin to feel its reality, I feel, also, that I must act accordingly; that is, I am impelled to act as though in my own behalf, but in behalf of the other. Now, of course, this feeling that I must act may or may not be sustained. I must make a commitment to act. The commitment to act in behalf of the cared-for, a continued interest in his reality throughout the appropriate time span, and the continual renewal of commitment over this span of time are the essential elements of caring from the inner view. Mayeroff speaks of devotion and the promotion of growth in the cared-for. I wish to start with engrossment and motivational displacement. Both concepts will require elaboration.

Problems Arising in the Analysis of One-Caring

As I think about how I feel when I care, about what my frame of mind is, I see that my caring is always characterized by a move away from self. Yet not all instances of caring are alike even from the view of one-caring. Conditions change, and the time spanned by caring varies. While I care for my children throughout our mutual lifetimes, I may care only momentarily for a stranger in need. The intensity varies. I care deeply for those in my inner circles and more lightly for those farther removed from my personal life. Even with those close to me, the intensity of caring varies; it may be calm and steady most of the time and desperately anxious in emergencies.

The acts performed out of caring vary with both situational conditions and type of relationship. It may bother me briefly, as a teacher, to learn that students in general are not doing well with the subject I teach, but I cannot really be said to care for each of the students having difficulty. And if I have not taken up a serious study of the difficulties themselves, I cannot be said to care about the problem qua problem. But if one of my own students is having difficulty, I may experience the engrossment and motivational displacement of caring. Does this caring spring out of the relationship I have formed with the student? Or, is it possible that I cared in some meaningful way before I even met the particular student?

The problems arising here involve time spans, intensity, and certain formal aspects of caring. Later, I shall explore the concept of chains of caring in which certain formal links to known cared-fors bind us to the possibility of caring. The construction of such formal chains places us in a state of readiness to care. Because my future students are related (formally, *as* students) to present, actual students for whom I do care, I am prepared to care for them also.

As we become aware of the problems involving time, intensity, and formal relationships, we may be led to reconsider the requirement of engrossment. We might instead describe caring of different sorts, on different levels and at varying degrees of intensity. Although I understand why several writers have chosen to speak of special kinds of caring appropriate to particular relationships, I shall claim that these efforts obscure the fundamental truth. At bottom, all caring involves engrossment. The engrossment need not be intense nor need it be pervasive in the life of the one-caring, but it must occur. This requirement does not force caring into the model of romantic love, as some critics fear,[7] for our engrossment may be latent for long periods. We may say of caring as Martin Buber says of love, "it endures, but only in the alternation of actuality and latency."[8] The difference that this approach makes is significant. Whatever roles I assume in life, I may be described in constant terms as one-caring. My first and unending obligation is to meet the other as one-caring. Formal constraints may be added to the fundamental requirement, but they do not replace or weaken it. When we discuss pedagogical caring, for example, we shall develop it from the analysis of caring itself and not from the formal requirements of teaching as a profession.[9]

Another problem arises when we consider situations in which we do not naturally care. Responding to my own child crying in the night may require a physical effort, but it does not usually require what might be called an ethical effort. I naturally want to relieve my child's distress. But receiving the other as he feels and trying to do so are qualitatively different modes. In the first, I am already "with" the other. My motivational energies are flowing toward him and, perhaps, toward his ends. In the second, I may dimly or dramatically perceive a reality that is a repugnant possibility for me. Dwelling in it may bring self-revulsion and disgust. Then I must withdraw. I do not "care" for this person. I may hate him, but I need not. If I do something in his behalf—defend his legal rights or confirm a statement he makes—it is because I care about my own ethical self. In caring for my ethical self, I grapple with the question: Must I try to care? When and for whom? A description of the ethical ideal and its construction will be essential in trying to answer these questions.

There are other limitations in caring. Not only are there those for whom I do not naturally care—situations in which engrossment brings revulsion and motivational displacement is unthinkable—but there are, also, many beyond the reach of my caring. I shall reject the notion of universal caring—that is, caring for everyone—on the grounds that it is impossible to actualize and leads us to substitute abstract problem solving and mere talk for genuine caring. Many of us think that it is not only possible to care for everyone but morally obligatory that we should do so. We can, in a sense that will need elaboration, "care about" everyone; that is, we can maintain an internal state of readiness to try to care for whoever crosses our path. But this is different from the caring-for to which we refer when we use the word "caring." If we are thoughtful persons, we know that the

140

difference is great, and we may even deliberately restrict our contacts so that the caring-for of which we are capable does not deteriorate to mere verbal caring-about. I shall not try to maintain this linguistic distinction, because it seems somewhat unnatural, but we should keep in mind the real distinction we are pointing at: in one sense, "caring" refers to an actuality; in the other, it refers to a verbal commitment to the possibility of caring.

We may add both guilt and conflict to our growing list of problems in connection with the analysis of caring. Conflict arises when our engrossment is divided, and several cared-fors demand incompatible decisions from us. Another sort of conflict occurs when what the cared-for wants is not what we think would be best for him, and still another sort arises when we become overburdened and our caring turns into "cares and burdens." Any of these conflicts may induce guilt. Further, we may feel guilty when we fall short of doing what the cared-for wants us to do or when we bring about outcomes we ourselves did not intend to bring about. Conflict and guilt are inescapable risks of caring, and their consideration will suggest an exploration of courage.

The one-caring is, however, not alone in the caring relationship. Sometimes caring turns inward—as for Mr. Smith in his description of worries and burdens—because conditions are intolerable or because the cared-for is singularly difficult. Clearly, we need also to analyze the role of the cared-for.

The Cared-For

We want to examine both the effects of caring on the cared-for and the special contributions that the cared-for makes to the caring relation. The first topic has received far more attention, and we shall start there also. We shall see that for (A, B) to be a caring relation, both A (the one-caring) and B (the cared-for) must contribute appropriately. Something from A must be received, completed, in B. Generally, we characterize this something as an attitude. B looks for something which tells him that A has regard for him, that he is not being treated perfunctorily.

Gabriel Marcel characterizes this attitude in terms of "disposability (disponibilité), the readiness to bestow and spend oneself and make oneself available, and its contrary, indisposability."[10] One who is disposable recognizes that she has a self to invest, to give. She does not identify herself with her objects and possessions. She is present to the cared-for. One who is indisposable, however, comes across even to one physically present as absent, as elsewhere. Marcel says: "When I am with someone who is indisposable, I am conscious of being with someone for whom I do not exist; I am thrown back on myself."[11]

The one-caring, in caring, is *present* in her acts of caring. Even in physical absence, acts at a distance bear the signs of presence: engrossment in the other, regard, desire for the other's well-being. Caring is largely reactive and responsive. Perhaps it is even better characterized as receptive. The one-caring is sufficiently engrossed in the other to listen to him and to take pleasure or pain in what he recounts. Whatever she does for the cared-for is embedded in a relationship that reveals itself as engrossment and in an attitude that warms and comforts the cared-for.

The caring attitude, this quality of disposability, pervades the situational time-space. So far as it is in my control, if we are conversing and if I care, I remain present to you throughout the conversation. Of course, if I care and you do not, then I may put my presence at a distance, thus freeing you to embrace the absence you have chosen. This is the way of dignity in such situations. To be treated as though one does not exist is a threatening experience, and one has to gather up one's self, one's presence, and place it in a safer, more welcome environment. And, of course, it is the way of generosity.

The one cared-for sees the concern, delight, or interest in the eyes of the one-caring and feels her warmth in both verbal and body language. To the cared-for no act in his behalf is quite as important or influential as the attitude of the one-caring. A major act done grudgingly may be accepted graciously on the surface but resented deeply inwardly, whereas a small act performed generously may be accepted nonchalantly but appreciated inwardly. When the attitude of the one-caring bespeaks caring, the cared-for glows, grows stronger, and feels not so much that he has been given something as that something has been added to him. And this "something" may be hard to specify. Indeed, for the one-caring and the cared-for in a relationship of genuine caring, there is no felt need on either part to specify what sort of transformation has taken place.

The intangible something that is added to the cared-for (and often, simultaneously, to the one-caring) will be an important consideration for us when we discuss caring in social institutions and, especially, in schools. It may be that much of what is most valuable in the teaching-learning relationship cannot be specified and certainly not pre-specified. The attitude characteristic of caring comes through in acquaintance. When the student associates with the teacher, feeling free to initiate conversation and to suggest areas of interest, he or she is better able to detect the characteristic attitude even in formal, goal-oriented situations such as lectures. Then a brief contact of eyes may say, "I am still the one interested in you. All of this is of variable importance and significance, but you still matter more." It is no use saying that the teacher who "really cares" wants her students to learn the basic skills which are necessary to a comfortable life; I am not denying that, but the notion is impoverished on both ends. On the one extreme, it is not enough to want one's students to master basic skills. I would not want to choose, but if I had to choose whether my child would be a reader or a loving human being, I would choose the latter with alacrity. On the other extreme, it is by itself too much, for it suggests that I as a caring teacher should be willing to do almost anything to bring my students to mastery of the basic skills. And I am not. Among the intangibles that I would have my students carry away is the feeling that the subject we have struggled with is both fascinating and boring, significant and silly, fraught with meaning and nonsense, challenging and tedious, and that whatever attitude we take toward it, it will not diminish our regard for each other. The student is infinitely more important than the subject.

So far in this discussion of the cared-for, I have emphasized the attitude of the one-caring and how its reception affects the cared-for. But we are interested also in the unique contribution of the cared-for to the relation. In chapter three [of the original book], where we shall discuss the role of the cared-for in some detail, we shall encounter the problem of *reciprocity*. What exactly does the cared-for give to the relation, or does he simply receive? What responsibility does he have for the maintenance of the relation? Can he be blamed for ethical deterioration in the one-caring? How does he contribute to the construction of the ethical ideal in the one-caring?

Aesthetical Caring

I am going to use the expression "aesthetical caring" for caring about things and ideas, and I shall justify that use a bit later. Caring about things or ideas seems to be a qualitatively different form of caring. We do use "care about" and "care for" in relation to objects. We say, "Mr. Smith really cares about his lawn," and "Ms. Brown cares more for her kitchen than for her children." But we cannot mean by these expressions what we have been talking about in connection with caring for persons. We may be engrossed in our lawn or kitchen, but there is no "other" toward whom we move, no other subjective reality to grasp, and there is no second person to whom an attitude is conveyed. Such "caring" may be related to caring for persons other than ourselves and, of course, it is related to the ways in which we care for ourselves, but it may also distract us from caring about persons. We can become too busy "caring" for things to care about people.

We shall encounter challenging anomalies in this area of caring also. Most of us commonly take as pejorative, "He cares only about money;" but we have mixed feelings when we hear, "He cares only about mathematics," or "She cares only about music." In part, we react this way because we feel that a person who cares only about money is likely to hurt others in his pursuit of it, while one who cares only about mathematics is a harmless and, perhaps, admirable person who is denying himself the pleasures of life in his devotion to an esoteric object. But, again, our attitude may be partially conditioned by a traditional respect and regard for the intellectual and, especially, the aesthetic, here interpreted as a sort of passionate involvement with form and nonpersonal content. It will be a special problem for us to ask about the relation between the ethical and the aesthetic and how caring, which we shall take to be the very foundation of the ethical, may be enhanced, distorted, or even diminished by the aesthetic. From the writing of T. E. Lawrence on his Arabian adventures[12] to Kierkegaard's disinterested and skeptical "Mr. A,"[13] we see the loss of the ethical in a highly intellectualized aesthetic. To be always apart in human affairs, a critical and sensitive observer, to remain troubled but uncommitted, to be just so much affected or affected in just such a way, is to lose the ethical in the aesthetic.

And yet we feel, perhaps rightly, that the receptivity characteristic of aesthetic engagement is very like the receptivity of caring. Consciousness assumes a similar mode of being—one that attempts to grasp or to receive a reality rather than to impose it. Mozart spoke of hearing melodies in his head,[14] and the mathematician Gauss was "seized" by mathematics.[15] Similarly, one who cares for another is seized by the other's projects or plight and often "hears" without words having been spoken by the other. Further, the creative artist, in creating, is present to the work of art as it is forming: listening, watching, feeling, contributing. This exchange between artist and work, this sense of an apprehended or received reality that is nevertheless uniquely one's own, was attested to by Mozart when he asked: "Now, how does it happen that, while I am at work, my compositions assume the form or style which characterize Mozart and are not like anybody else's?"[16]

The sense of having something created through one and only incidentally *by* one is reported frequently by artists. In an interview celebrating his eighty-sixth birthday, Joan Miró tried to explain his creativity to questioning interviewers. He said such things as, "The paper has magnetism," "My hand is guided by a magnetic force," "It is like I am drunk." Yet when we discuss creativity in schools our focus is almost invariably on the activity, the manipulation, the freedom. And, similarly, when we talk about caring, our emphasis is again on the action, on what might properly be called the caretaking. But the caring that gives meaning to the caretaking is too often dismissed as "sentiment." In part, our approaches to creativity and caring are induced by the dominating insistency on objective evaluation. How can we emphasize the receptivity that is at the core of both when we have no way of measuring it? Here we may ultimately decide that some things in life, and in education, must be undertaken and sustained by faith and not by objective evaluation.

Even though the receptivity characteristic of artistic creation resembles that of caring, we shall find important differences, and we are by no means convinced that artistic receptivity is correlated (in individual human beings) with the receptivity of caring. After all, we have known artistic monsters (Wagner comes to mind); men who have loved orchids and despised human life (Conan Doyle's fictional "Moriarty"); people such as some in the Nazi high command, who loved music and art and yet performed unbelievable cruelty on humans. And, of course, we are acquainted with those who care passionately for their families, tribes, or nations and tear the heads off enemies with gusto. We do not expect, then, to find a simple formula that will describe what our children should learn to care about in order to care meaningfully for persons. But we shall see, again, the great importance of the cared-for in contributing to caring relations. Perhaps some people find ideas and things more responsive than the humans they have tried to care for.

Finally, in our discussion of education, we shall be interested in aesthetical caring in its own right. Schools and teachers may, if they wish to do so, exercise some control over the nature and responsiveness of the potential "cared-fors" presented to students as subject matter, and there may be reasonable ways in which to give perceptive/creative modes an appropriate place alongside judgmental/evaluative modes.

Caring and Acting

Let's return briefly to the issue of action. Perhaps, with a better notion of what constitutes the first- and second-person aspects of caring, we can now say something more determinate about acts of caring. Our motivation in caring is directed toward the welfare, protection, or enhancement of the cared-for. When we care, we should, ideally, be able to present reasons for our action/inaction which would persuade a reasonable, disinterested observer that we have acted in behalf of the cared-for. This does not mean that all such observers have to agree that they would have behaved exactly as we did in a particular caring situation. They may, on the contrary, see preferred alternatives. They may experience the very conflicts that caused us anxiety and still suggest a different course of action; or they may proceed in a purely rational-objective way and suggest the same or a different course. But, frequently, and especially in the case of inaction, we are not willing to supply reasons to an actual observer; our ideal observer is, and remains, an abstraction. The reasons we would give, those we give to ourselves in honest subjective thinking, should be so well connected to the objective elements of the problem that our course of action clearly either stands a chance of succeeding in behalf of the cared-for, or can have been engaged in only with the hope of effecting something for the cared-for.

Caring involves stepping out of one's own personal frame of reference into the other's. When we care, we consider the other's point of view, his objective needs, and what he expects of us. Our attention, our mental engrossment is on the cared-for, not on ourselves. Our reasons for acting, then, have to do both with the other's wants and desires and with the objective elements of his problematic situation. If the stray cat is healthy and relatively safe, we do not whisk it off to the county shelter; instead, we provide food and water and encourage freedom. Why condemn it to death when it might enjoy a vagabond freedom? If our minds are on ourselves, however—if we have never really left our own a priori frame of reference—our reasons for acting point back at us and not outward to the cared-for. When we want to be thought of as caring, we often act routinely in a way that may easily secure that credit for us.

This gives us, as outsiders to the relation, a way, not infallible to be sure, to judge caretaking for signs of real caring. To care is to act not by fixed rule but by affection and regard. It seems likely, then, that the actions of one-caring will be varied rather than rule-bound; that is, her actions, while predictable in a global sense, will be unpredictable in detail.

Variation is to be expected if the one claiming to care really cares, for her engrossment is in the variable and never fully understood other, in the particular other, in a particular set of circumstances. Rule-bound responses in the name of caring lead us to suspect that the claimant wants most to be credited with caring.

To act as one-caring, then, is to act with special regard for the particular person in a concrete situation. We act not to achieve for ourselves a commendation but to protect or enhance the welfare of the cared-for. Because we are inclined toward the cared-for, we want to act in a way that will please him. But we wish to please him for his sake and not for the promise of his grateful response to our generosity. Even this motivation—to act so that the happiness and pleasure of the cared-for will be enhanced—may not provide a sure external sign of caring. We are sometimes thrown into conflict over what the cared-for wants and what we think would be best for him. As caring parents, for example, we cannot always act in ways which bring immediate reactions of pleasure from our children, and to do so may bespeak a desire, again, to be credited with caring.

The one-caring desires the well-being of the cared-for and acts (or abstains from acting—makes an internal act of commitment) to promote that well-being. She is inclined to the other. An observer, however, cannot see the crucial motive and may misread the attitudinal signs. The observer, then, must judge caring, in part, by the following: First, the action (if there has been one) either brings about a favorable outcome for the cared-for or seems reasonably likely to do so; second, the one-caring displays a characteristic variability in her actions—she acts in a nonrule-bound fashion in behalf of the cared-for.

We shall have to spend some time and effort on the discussion of nonrule-bound, caring behavior. Clearly, I do not intend to advocate arbitrary and capricious behavior, but something more like the inconsistency advocated long ago by Ralph Waldo Emerson,[18] the sort of behavior that is conditioned not by a host of narrow and rigidly defined principles but by a broad and loosely defined ethic that molds itself in situations and has a proper regard for human affections, weaknesses, and anxieties. From such an ethic we do not receive prescriptions as to how we must behave under given conditions, but we are somewhat enlightened as to the kinds of questions we should raise (to ourselves and others) in various kinds of situations and the places we might look for appropriate answers. Such an ethic does not attempt to reduce the need for human judgment with a series of "Thou shalts" and "Thou shalt nots." Rather, it recognizes and calls forth human judgment across a wide range of fact and feeling, and it allows for situations and conditions in which judgment (in the impersonal, logical sense) may properly be put aside in favor of faith and commitment.

We establish funds, or institutions, or agencies in order to provide the caretaking we judge to be necessary. The original impulse is often the one associated with caring. It arises in individuals. But as groups of individuals discuss the perceived needs of another individual or group, the imperative changes from "I must do something" to "Something must be done." This change is accompanied by a shift from the nonrational and subjective to the rational and objective. What should be done? Who should do it? Why should the persons named do it? This sort of thinking is not in itself a mistake; it is needed. But it has buried within it the seed of major error. The danger is that caring, which is essentially nonrational in that it requires a constitutive engrossment and displacement of motivation, may gradually or abruptly be transformed into abstract problem solving. There is, then, a shift of focus from the cared-for to the "problem." Opportunities arise for self-interest, and persons entrusted with caring may lack the necessary engrossment in those to be cared-for. Rules are formulated and the characteristic variation in response to the needs of the cared-for may fade away. Those entrusted with caring may focus on satisfying the formulated requirements for caretaking and fail to be present in their interactions with the cared-for. Thus caring disappears and only its illusion remains.

It is clear, of course, that there is also danger in failing to think objectively and well in caring situations. We quite properly enter a rational-objective mode as we try to decide exactly what we will do in behalf of the cared-for. If I am ill informed, or if I make a mistake, or if I act impetuously, I may hurt rather than help the cared-for. But one may argue, here, that the failure is still at the level of engrossment and motivational displacement. Would I behave so carelessly in my own behalf?

It would seem, then, that one of the greatest dangers to caring may be premature switching to a rational-objective mode. It is not that objective thinking is of no use in problems where caring is required, but it is of limited and particular use, and we shall have to inquire deeply into what we shall call "turning points." If rational-objective thinking is to be put in the service of caring, we must at the right moments turn it away from the abstract toward which it tends and back to the concrete. At times we must suspend it in favor of subjective thinking and reflection, allowing time and space for *seeing* and *feeling*. The rational-objective mode must continually be re-established and redirected from a fresh base of commitment. Otherwise, we find ourselves deeply, perhaps inextricably, enmeshed in procedures that somehow serve only themselves; our thoughts are separated, completely detached, from the original objects of caring.

Now, before turning to a closer look at the one-caring, perhaps we should consider where we are headed through our analysis of caring.

Ethics and Caring

It is generally agreed that ethics is the philosophical study of morality, but we also speak of "professional ethics" and "a personal ethic." When we speak in the second way, we refer to something explicable—a set of rules, an ideal, a constellation of expressions—that guides and justifies our conduct. One can, obviously, behave ethically without engaging in ethics as a philosophical enterprise, and one can even put together an ethic of sorts—that is, a description of what it means to be moral—without seriously questioning what it means to be moral. Such an ethic, it seems to me, may or may not be a guide to moral behavior. It depends, in a fundamental way, on an assessment of the answer to the question: What does it mean to be moral? This question will be central to our investigation. I shall use "ethical" rather than "moral" in most of our discussions but, in doing so, I am assuming that to behave ethically is to behave under the guidance of an acceptable and justifiable account of what it means to be moral. To behave ethically is not to behave in conformity with just any description of morality, and I shall claim that ethical systems are not equivalent simply because they include rules concerning the same matters or categories.

In an argument for the possibility of an objective morality (against relativism), anthropologist Ralph Linton makes two major points that may serve to illuminate the path I am taking. In one argument, he seems to say that ethical relativism is false because it can be shown that all societies lay down rules of some sort for behavior in certain universal categories. All societies, for example, have rules governing sexual behavior. But Linton does not seem to recognize that the content of the rules, and not just their mere existence, is crucial to the discussion of ethicality. He says, for example: ". . . practically all societies recognize adultery as unethical and punish the offenders. The same man who will lend his wife to a friend or brother will be roused to fury if she goes to another man without his permission."[19] But, surely, we would like to know what conception of morality makes adultery "wrong" and the lending of one's wife "right." Just as surely, an ethical system that renders such decisions cannot be equivalent to one that finds adultery acceptable and wife lending unacceptable.

In his second claim, Linton is joined by a substantial number of anthropologists. Stated simply, the claim is that morality is based on common human characteristics and needs and that, hence, an objective morality is possible. That morality is rooted somehow in common human needs, feelings, and cognitions is agreed. But it is not clear to me that we can move easily or swiftly from that agreement to a claim that objective morality is possible. We may be able to describe the moral impulse as it arises in response to particular needs and feelings, and we may be able to describe the relation of thinking and acting in relation to that impulse; but as we tackle these tasks, we may move farther away from a notion of objective morality and closer to the conviction that an irremovable subjective core, a longing for goodness, provides what universality and stability there is in what it means to be moral.

I want to build an ethic on caring, and I shall claim that there is a form of caring natural and accessible to all human beings. Certain feelings, attitudes, and memories will be claimed as universal. But the ethic itself will not embody a set of universalizable moral judgments. Indeed, moral judgment will not be its central concern. It is very common among philosophers to move from the question: What is morality? to the seemingly more manageable question: What is a moral judgment? Fred Feldman, for example, makes this move early on. He suggests:

> Perhaps we can shed some light on the meaning of the noun "morality" by considering the adjective "moral." Proceeding in this way will enable us to deal with a less abstract concept, and we may thereby be more successful. So instead of asking "What is morality?" let us pick one of the most interesting of these uses of the adjective "moral" and ask instead, "What is a moral judgment?"[20]

Now, I am not arguing that this move is completely mistaken or that nothing can be gained through a consideration of moral judgments, but such move is not the only possibility. We might choose another interesting use of the adjective and ask, instead, about the moral impulse or moral attitude. The choice is important. The long-standing emphasis on the study of moral judgments has led to a serious imbalance in moral discussion. In particular, it is well known that many women—perhaps most women—do not approach moral problems as problems of principle, reasoning, and judgment. I shall discuss this problem at length in chapter four [of the original work]. If a substantial segment of humankind approaches moral problems through a consideration of the concrete elements of situations and a regard for themselves as caring, then perhaps an attempt should be made to enlighten the study of morality in this alternative mode. Further, such a study has significant implications, beyond ethics, for education. If moral education, in a double sense, is guided only by the study of moral principles and judgments, not only are women made to feel inferior to men in the moral realm but also education itself may suffer from impoverished and one-sided moral guidance.

So building an ethic on caring seems both reasonable and important. One may well ask, at this point, whether an ethic so constructed will be a form of "situation ethics." It is not, certainly, that form of act-utilitarianism commonly labeled "situation ethics."[21] Its emphasis is not on the consequences of our acts, although these are not, of course, irrelevant. But an ethic of caring locates morality primarily in the pre-act consciousness of the one-caring. Yet it is not a form of agapism. There is no command to love nor, indeed, any God to make the commandment. Further, I shall reject the notion of universal love, finding it unattainable in any but the most abstract sense and thus a source of distraction. While much of what will be developed in the ethic of caring may be found, also, in Christian ethics, there will be major and irreconcilable differences. Human love, human caring, will be quite enough on which to found an ethic.

We must look even more closely at that love and caring.

Notes

1. Gauss's remark is quoted by Morris Kline, *Why Johnny Can't Add* (New York: Vintage Books, 1974), p. 58.

2. See Carol Gilligan, "In a Different Voice: Women's Conception of the Self and of Morality," *Harvard Educational Review* 47 (1977), 481–517. Also, "Woman's Place in Man's Life Cycle," *Harvard Educational Review* 49 (1979), 431– 446. Also, *In a Different Voice* (Cambridge, Mass.: Harvard University Press), 1982.

3. Milton Mayeroff, *On Caring* (New York: Harper and Row, 1971), p. 1.

4. See David Brandon, *Zen in the Art of Helping* (New York: Dell Publishing Co., 1978), chap. 3.

5. Søren Kierkegaard, *Concluding Unscientific Postscript*, trans. David F. Swenson and Walter Lowrie (Princeton: Princeton University Press, 1941).

6. Ibid., p. 322.

7. See Mary Anne Raywid, "Up from Agape: Response to 'Caring' by Nel Noddings," *Journal of Curriculum Theorizing* (1981),152–156.

8. Martin Buber, *I and Thou*, trans. Walter Kaufmann (New York: Charles Scribner's Sons, 1970), p. 69.

9. See Richard E. Hult, Jr., "On Pedagogical Caring," *Educational Theory* 29 (1979), 237–244.

10. See H. J. Blackman, *Six Existentialist Thinkers* (New York: Harper and Row, 1959), p. 80.

11. Ibid., p. 80.

12. T. E. Lawrence, *Seven Pillars of Wisdom* (New York: Garden City Publishing Co., 1938), pp. 549, 562–566.

13. Søren Kierkegaard, *Either/Or, I*, trans. David F. Swenson and Lillian M. Swenson (Princeton: Princeton University Press, 1959).

14. See the account in Jacques Hadamard, *The Psychology of Invention in the Mathematical Field* (New York: Dover Publications, Inc., 1954), pp. 16–17.

15. See E. T. Bell, *Men of Mathematics* (New York: Simon and Schuster, 1965), p. 254.

16. Quoted in Hadamard, *The Psychology of Invention in the Mathematical Field*, pp. 16–17.

17. On NBC's *Prime Time Sunday* (July 8, 1979).

18. Ralph Waldo Emerson, "Self-Reliance," in *Essays, First Series* (Boston and New York: Houghton Mifflin Company, 1903), pp. 45–90.

19. Ralph Linton, "An Anthropologist's Approach to Ethical Principles," in *Understanding Moral Philosophy*, ed. James Rachels (Encino, CA: Dickenson Publishing Company, Inc., 1976), p. 8.

20. Fred Feldman, *Introductory Ethics* (Englewood Cliffs, NJ: Prentice-Hall, Inc., 1978), p. 2.

21. See, for example, Joseph Fletcher, *Situation Ethics* (Philadelphia: The Westminster Press, 1966).

The Virtue of Selfishness

Ayn Rand

The title of this book may evoke the kind of question that I hear once in a while: "Why do you use the word 'selfishness' to denote virtuous qualities of character, when that word antagonizes so many people to whom it does not mean the things you mean?"

To those who ask it, my answer is: "For the reason that makes you afraid of it."

But there are others, who would not ask that question, sensing the moral cowardice it implies, yet who are unable to formulate my actual reason or to identify the profound moral issue involved. It is to them that I will give a more explicit answer.

It is not a mere semantic issue nor a matter of arbitrary choice. The meaning ascribed in popular usage to the word "selfishness" is not merely wrong: it represents a devastating intellectual "package-deal," which is responsible, more than any other single factor, for the arrested moral development of mankind.

In popular usage, the word "selfishness" is a synonym of evil; the image it conjures is of a murderous brute who tramples over piles of corpses to achieve his own ends, who cares for no living being and pursues nothing but the gratification of the mindless whims of any immediate moment.

Yes the exact meaning and dictionary definition of the word "selfishness" is: *concern with one's own interests.*

This concept does *not* include a moral evaluation; it does not tell us whether concern with one's own interests is good or evil; nor does it tell us what constitutes man's actual interests. It is the task of ethics to answer such questions.

The ethics of altruism has created the image of the brute, as its answer, in order to make men accept two inhuman tenets: (a) that any concern with one's own interests is evil, regardless of what these interests might be, and (b) that the brute's activities are *in fact* to one's own interest (which altruism enjoins man to renounce for the sake of his neighbors).

For a view of the nature of altruism, its consequences and the enormity of the moral corruption it perpetrates, I shall refer you to *Atlas Shrugged*— or to any of today's newspaper headlines. What concerns us here is altruism's *default* in the field of ethical theory.

There are two moral questions which altruism lumps together into one "package-deal": (1) What are values? (2) Who should be the beneficiary of values? Altruism substitutes the second for the first; it evades the task of defining a code of moral values, thus leaving man, in fact, without moral guidance.

Altruism declares that any action taken for the benefit of others is good, and any action taken for one's own benefit is evil. Thus the *beneficiary* of an action is the only criterion of moral value—and so long as the beneficiary is anybody other than oneself, anything goes.

Hence the appalling immorality, the chronic injustice, the grotesque double standards, the insoluble conflicts and contradictions that have characterized human relationships and human societies throughout history, under all the variants of the altruist ethics.

Observe the indecency of what passes for moral judgments today. An industrialist who produces a fortune, and a gangster who robs a bank are regarded as equally immoral, since they both sought wealth for their own "selfish" benefit. A young man who gives up his career in order to support his parents and never rises beyond the rank of grocery clerk is regarded as morally superior to the young man who endures an excruciating struggle and achieves his personal ambition. A dictator is regarded as moral, since the unspeakable atrocities he committed were intended to benefit "the people," not himself.

Observe what this beneficiary-criterion of morality does to a man's life. The first thing he learns is that morality is his enemy: he has nothing to gain from it, he can only lose; self-inflicted loss, self-inflicted pain and the gray, debilitating pall of an incomprehensible duty is all that he can expect. He may hope that others might occasionally sacrifice themselves for his benefit, as he grudgingly sacrifices himself for theirs, but he knows that the relationship will bring mutual resentment, not pleasure—and that, morally, their pursuit of values will be like an exchange of unwanted, unchosen

Christmas presents, which neither is morally permitted to buy for himself. Apart from such times as he manages to perform some act of self-sacrifice, he possesses no moral significance: morality takes no cognizance of him and has nothing to say to him for guidance in the crucial issues of his life; it is only his own personal, private, "selfish" life and, as such, it is regarded either as evil or, at best, *amoral.*

Since nature does not provide man with an automatic form of survival, since he has to support his life by his own effort, the doctrine that concern with one's own interests is evil means that man's desire to live is evil—that man's life, as such, is evil. No doctrine could be more evil than that.

Yet that is the meaning of altruism, implicit in such examples as the equation of an industrialist with a robber. There is a fundamental moral difference between a man who sees his self-interest in production and a man who sees it in robbery. The evil of a robber does *not* lie in the fact that he pursues his own interests, but in *what* he regards as to his own interest; *not* in the fact that he pursues his values, but in *what* he chose to value; *not* in the fact that he wants to live, but in the fact that he wants to live on a subhuman level. . . .

If it is true that what I mean by "selfishness" is not what is meant conventionally, then *this* is one of the worst indictments of altruism: it means that altruism *permits no concept* of a self-respecting, self-supporting man—a man who supports his life by his own effort and neither sacrifices himself nor others. It means that altruism permits no view of men except as sacrificial animals and profiteers-on-sacrifice, as victims and parasites—that it permits no concept of a benevolent coexistence among men—that it permits no concept of *justice.*

If you wonder about the reasons behind the ugly mixture of cynicism and guilt in which most men spend their lives, these are the reasons: cynicism, because they neither practice nor accept the altruist morality—guilt, because they dare not reject it.

To rebel against so devastating an evil, one has to rebel against its basic premise. To redeem both man and morality, it is the concept of *"selfishness"* that one has to redeem.

The Concept of a Right

John R. Boatright

THE CONCEPT OF A RIGHT

Rights play an important role in business ethics—and, indeed, in virtually all moral issues. Both employers and employees are commonly regarded as having certain rights. Employers have the right to conduct business as they see fit, to make decisions about hiring and promotion, and to be protected against unfair forms of competition. Employees have the right to organize and engage in collective bargaining and to be protected against discrimination and hazardous working conditions. Consumers and the general public also have rights in such matters as marketing and advertising, product safety, and the protection of the environment.

Beyond business, the debate over abortion, the use of life support systems, access to medical care, and discrimination in housing and education all involve the rights of different parties. Each side in the abortion debate, for example, appeals to a supposed right: the right to life of the fetus or the right of a woman to choose whether to bear a child. There is growing support for the recognition of the right of the terminally ill to choose to die, the right of people to a minimal level of health care, and so on. Many of our constitutional protections in the Bill of Rights arouse controversy. Does the First Amendment right of free speech, for example, protect obscenity or flag-burning?

Rights are also prominent in the Western political tradition and the present-day international order. The Virginia Declaration of Rights (1776), for example, mentions as inherent rights "the enjoyment of life and liberty, with the means of acquiring and possessing property, and pursuing and obtaining happiness and safety." Other important documents that proclaim rights are the French Declaration of the Rights of Man and of Citizens (1787), the Bill of Rights in the American Constitution (1791), and the Universal Declaration of Human Rights of the United Nations (1948). Among the rights included in this latter document are

Article 3 Everyone has the right to life, liberty and security of person.
Article 4 No one shall be held in slavery or servitude. . . .
Article 5 No one shall be subjected to torture or to cruel, inhuman or

degrading treatment or punishment.

Article 9   No one shall be subjected to arbitrary arrest, detention or exile.

The introduction of rights into the discussion of ethical issues is often confusing. First, the term *rights* is used in many different ways, so that the concept of a right and the various kinds of rights must be carefully distinguished. Second, many rights come into conflict. The right of an employee to leave his or her employer and join a competitor conflicts with the legitimate right of employers to protect trade secrets, for example, so that some balancing is required. And the traditional rights of employers in personnel matters are being increasingly challenged by employees who claim a right to privacy in the workplace and a right to due process in the event of discipline or dismissal. Whether employees should have these rights is hotly debated.

Because of the moral significance that we attach to rights, there is a tendency to stretch the concept in ways that dilute its meaning. For example, the rights to receive adequate food, clothing, and medical care, mentioned in the Universal Declaration of Human Rights, are perhaps better described as political goals rather than rights. Often the dispute is not over the existence of the rights in question, such as the right to life or the right of women to control their own childbearing capacities, but over the extent of these rights and their relative weight when they come into conflict. For all these reasons, the claim of a right is frequently the beginning of an ethical debate rather than the end.

The Nature and Value of Rights

In order to understand the nature and value of rights, consider the following case.

In thirty-two years with the Sees Candy Company, Wayne Pugh worked his way up from washing pots and pans to a vice-presidency and membership on the board of directors of one of Sees's major subsidiaries.[16] During the Christmas and Valentine's Day season, his sales in the San Francisco area set new records, and the March issue of the company newsletter contained two pictures of Pugh along with congratulations on his excellent performance. He thought that he was in line for a promotion when he was summoned to the office of the president. Instead, he was handed a letter informing him of his immediate dismissal. He was ordered not to return to his office or to contact any of his former colleagues during working hours. No reason was given for the dismissal except for the cryptic suggestion of the president to "look within himself."

Although being fired is never pleasant, the experience is especially galling when there is no explanation of the reasons and no opportunity to respond. In 1982, the International Labour Organization (ILO) adopted a convention which lists the rights that every nation ought to recognize in the dismissal of employees.[17] Article 4 of the ILO convention states:

> The employment of a worker shall not be terminated unless there is a valid reason for such termination connected with the capacity or conduct of the worker based on the operational requirements of the undertaking, establishment, or service.

Employees are accorded the right in Article 7 to be notified of the charges against them, and Article 8 provides that employees who believe they have been unjustly dismissed have a right to a review by an impartial body.

These rights, which embody the essentials of due process, provided no protection for Wayne Pugh, since the United States cast the only vote against the ILO convention and lags behind virtually all other major industrial countries in implementing its provisions. There is no comprehensive federal legislation covering unjust dismissal, and only a few states have passed laws in this area. The only substantial protection for workers in the private sector is an employment contract that specifies grounds for termination and the procedures to be followed.[18] Still, we can ask whether employees have a moral right to due process.

The concept of a right can be explained by imagining a company that treats employees fairly but does not recognize due process as a right.[19] In this company, employees are dismissed only for good reasons after a thorough and impartial hearing, but there is no contract, statute, or other provision establishing a right of due process for all employees. Something is still missing, since the fair treatment that the employees enjoy results solely from the company's voluntary acceptance of certain personnel policies. If the company were ever to change these policies, then employees dismissed without due process would have no recourse. Contrast this with a company in which due process is established as a right. Employees in this company have something that was lacking in the previous company. They have an independent basis for challenging a decision by the company to dismiss them. They have something to stand on; namely, their rights.

Rights can be understood, therefore, as *entitlements*.[20] To have rights is to be entitled to act on our own or to be treated by others in certain ways without asking permission of anyone or being dependent on other people's goodwill. Rights entitle us to make claims on other people either to refrain from interfering in what we do or to contribute actively to our well-being—not as beggars, who can only entreat others to be generous, but as creditors, who can demand what is owed to them. This explanation of rights in terms of entitlements runs the risk of circularity (after all, what is an entitlement but something we have a right to?), but it is sufficiently illuminating to serve as a beginning of our examination.

Legal and Moral Rights

A distinction needs to be made at the outset between legal rights and moral rights. *Legal rights* are rights that are recognized and enforced as part of a legal system. In the United States, these consist primarily of the rights set forth in the Constitution, including the Bill of Rights, and those created by acts of Congress and state legislatures. Thus, Americans have a constitutional right to freedom from government interference in matters of speech and religion, to protection from unreasonable searches and seizures, and to equal protection of the laws. There are some rights not specifically mentioned in the Constitution that have been held by the Supreme Court to be a part of it. The Court has interpreted the right of free speech, for example, to protect pornography and symbolic "speech" such as flag-burning. The right to due process means that suspects must be advised of their right to counsel and provided with a lawyer if they cannot afford one. Among the rights created by legislative acts are the many rights that business firms have under the Uniform Commercial Code, the right of workers to form a union and to engage in collective bargaining (established by the National Labor Relations Act of 1935), and the rights of consumers under the Consumer Product Safety Act (1972).

Moral rights, by contrast, are rights that do not depend on the existence of a legal system. They are rights that we (morally) *ought* to have, regardless of whether they are explicitly recognized by law. Moral rights derive their force not from being part of a legal system but from more general ethical rules and principles. Thus, people ought to have a right to free speech even if in some countries such a right is not a part of the legal system. Moral rights of this kind provide an ethical justification for some legal rights and a means for ethically evaluating legal systems that lack them. The justification for including the right of free speech in the Constitution, for example, is that it is a moral right, and a legal system that lacks a right of free speech is, in that respect, morally deficient.

Not every moral right is a legal right, of course, and some perhaps ought not to be. The United States has not implemented Article 23 of the Universal Declaration of Human Rights, which holds that everyone has the right to work, on the grounds that the level of employment ought to be left to the workings of the labor market and not legislated. There are other moral rights, such as a right to respect as an equal, that are simply not capable of being secured by law. Although our legal and moral rights overlap considerably, they are conceptually distinct and rest on different foundations.

The Correlativity of Rights and Duties

A widely held analysis of both legal and moral rights is that they are closely correlated with obligations, or duties. Specifically, one person can have a right only if another person has an obligation to perform a certain action. All rights, in other words, presuppose a corresponding obligation, although not all obligations entail a right. This analysis is commonly called the *correlativity thesis*.[21] A simple example of the correlativity thesis is the following: If A has loaned ten dollars to B, then A has a claim on B for the repayment of the loan. But this is to say that B has an obligation or duty to pay A ten dollars. Rights and obligations in this analysis are simply two ways of describing the same normative relation, distinguished only by the use of the active and passive voice.[22]

If the correlativity thesis is correct, then there is nothing mysterious about rights. They are explainable in terms of obligations, and a justification of rights requires nothing more than a theory of obligation. Unfortunately, the analysis does not fit all legal rights. In his classic treatise *Fundamental Legal Conceptions*, Wesley Newcomb Hohfeld holds that rights and duties are correlated in the case of *claim rights*.[23] Rights of this kind, which are exemplified by the case of a loan, are regarded by Hohfeld as rights in the proper sense of the term. But some rights, such as the right to free speech, are *liberty rights*, which do not impose a correlative obligation on others, except not to interfere. Hohfeld also distinguishes rights that are legal *powers*, such as the right to get married or to make a will and the right of police officers to make an arrest, and legal *immunities*, such as the right not to be compelled to testify against ourselves or to be tried twice for the same crime. Using some ingenuity, we might be able to find obligations that correlate with these rights. David Lyons suggests, for example, that the right of free speech imposes an obligation on Congress not to pass laws limiting speech. The power of police officers is correlated with certain rights and duties of motorists, so that the power of an officer does not extend to interfering when motorists are exercising their rights (making a U-turn where permitted, for example) but does include cases where motorists have a duty to obey (for example, an order to stop).[24] Still, the correlation of rights and obligations in the law is not as neat and tidy as the loan example suggests.

Turning now to moral rights, the correlation is also not perfect. First, insofar as moral rights have the diversity of legal rights, so that some moral rights are also liberties, powers, and immunities,[25] then the analysis does not easily fit. Second, if rights are entitlements, then we may be entitled to something without anyone else having an obligation to provide it. Joel Feinberg, who analyzes rights as valid *claims* against others, holds that rights typically involve two elements: a claim *to* something and a claim *against* someone.[26] Thus, in the loan example, A has a

160

claim *to* the ten dollars and a claim *against* B to repay it. H. J. Mc-
Closkey points out, however, that we can have some rights, such as the
rights to education, adequate nutrition, minimal medical care, and decent housing, even though no one else is obligated to provide these
things.[27]

Despite these difficulties, the correlativity thesis is a valuable re-
minder that many (if not all) rights are correlated with obligations, or
duties. If any person has rights, then there are things that other people
ought to do or refrain from doing. Rights are part of the web of moral
relations that bind us together. No one can have a right in isolation.

Some Other Distinctions Between Rights

Some rights are *specific* in that they involve identifiable individuals.
In the loan example, it is A and no one else who has a right to the ten
dollars, and the obligation to repay it rests on B alone. In law, these are
called *in personam* rights. A major source of specific, or *in personam*,
rights is contracts, since these ubiquitous intruments create a set of
mutual rights as well as duties for the individuals who are parties to
them. Other rights are *general*, or *in rem*, rights, since they involve claims
against everyone, or humanity in general. Thus, the right of free speech
belongs to everyone, and the obligation to enforce this right rests with
the whole community. Similarly, a right to education or medical care is a
right that entitles us to make a claim on our common resources. A
major objection to the correlativity thesis can be expressed in this form:
All specific, or *in personam*, rights are closely correlated with obligations,
but some general, or *in rem*, rights are not.[28]

Another common distinction exists between *negative* and *positive*
rights. Generally, negative rights are correlated with obligations on the
part of others to refrain from acting in certain ways; that is, to act
negatively by not interfering with our own freedom of action. Positive
rights, by contrast, impose obligations on other people to provide us
with some good or service and thereby to act positively on our behalf.[29]
The right to property, for example, is largely a negative right, since no
one else is obligated to provide us with property, but everyone has an
obligation not to use or take our property without permission. The
rights mentioned in the Bill of Rights are negative rights insofar as they
serve to limit the extent to which government can encroach on the
sphere of individual liberty. Some of the rights enumerated in the Universal Declaration of Human Rights, however, are positive rights. Article
25 states, for example:

> Everyone has the right to a standard of living adequate for the health and
> well-being of himself and of his family, including food, clothing, housing
> and medical care and necessary social services, and the right to security in

161

the event of unemployment, sickness, disability, widowhood, old age or other lack of livelihood in circumstances beyond his control.

Implementation of these rights requires extensive action by the state to ensure that basic goods, such as food, clothing, and shelter, are available and to provide a range of social services, such as unemployment insurance, workers' compensation, and old age and survivors' benefits. Joel Feinberg notes that, typically, general, or *in rem*, rights are negative, whereas specific, or *in personam*, rights (contract rights, for example) are positive,[30] but the correspondence is very rough, since the positive rights mentioned in the Universal Declaration are mostly *in rem* rights.

Although it is useful for understanding the concept of a right, the distinction between negative and positive rights is not entirely clear, since the underlying distinction between acting and not acting, or between an action and an omission, is often a matter of interpretation.[31] The right of due process, for example, requires employers *not* to fire employees without good reasons and a fair hearing; but it also requires that employers *do* certain things as well, such as notifying employees of the reasons for their dismissal and conducting hearings. Similarly, the rights of employees in matters of occupational health and safety sometimes involve *not* ordering workers to perform their jobs on unsafe equipment or in unsafe areas. But it also involves taking active steps to make the workplace safer by installing guards on equipment or rails on elevated walkways, for example.

The Foundation of Rights

With this examination of the concept of a right now complete, let us turn to the more difficult and controversial matter of the foundation of rights. Are rights fundamental moral categories with their own source of support? Or are rights part of some more general ethical theory, such as utilitarianism or Kantian ethics? We begin by considering the natural rights tradition, which offers a historically influential account of rights separate from these other possible grounds.

NATURAL RIGHTS THEORY

One prominent foundation for rights focuses on what are called *natural* rights or, more recently, *human* rights. Rights of this kind, which are prominent in historical documents such as the Virginia Declaration of Rights, the Declaration of the Rights of Man and of Citizens, and the Universal Declaration of Human Rights, are rights that belong to all persons purely by virtue of their being human.[32] They are characterized by two main features: *universality* and *unconditionality*.

Universality means that they are possessed by *all* persons, without

162

regard for race, sex, nationality, or any specific circumstances of birth or present condition. Unconditionality means that natural or human rights do not depend on any particular practices or institutions in society. The right of U.S. citizens to vote, for example, depends on the specific form of government and the election laws of this country and so cannot be a natural, or human, right. The unconditionality of rights also means that there is nothing we can do to relinquish them or to deprive ourselves or others of them. This feature of natural, or human, rights is what is usually meant by the term "inalienable."[33]

The Theory of John Locke

The idea of natural rights has a long and distinguished history going back to the ancient Greeks, who held that there is a "higher" law which applies to all persons everywhere and serves as a standard for evaluating the laws of states.[34] Both Roman law and the medieval church adopted this idea and developed it into a comprehensive legal theory. Perhaps the most influential natural rights theory, though, is that presented by John Locke (1633–1704) in his famous *Second Treatise of Government* (1690).[35]

Locke, like Thomas Hobbes before him, began with the supposition of a state of nature, which is the condition of human beings in the absence of any government. Their idea is to imagine what life would be like if there were no government, and then to justify the establishment of a political state to remedy the defects of the state of nature. Hobbes's state of nature is devoid of any moral restrictions, with the result that the state of nature is a state of war in which life is "solitary, poor, nasty, brutish, and short." Locke held, on the contrary, that human beings have rights, even in the state of nature, and that the justification for uniting into a state is to protect these rights.

The most important natural right for Locke is the right to property, which he justified in the following way:

> God, who has given the world to men in common, has also given them reason to make use of it to the best advantage of life and convenience. The earth and all that is therein is given to men for the support and comfort of their being. And though all the fruits it naturally produces and beasts it feeds belong to mankind in common. . . ; yet being given for the use of men, there must of necessity be a means to appropriate them some way or other before they can be of any use or at all beneficial to any particular man.

The means by which people are able to take goods out of the common storehouse of nature and make them their own is by the use of labor, which is also a form of property. "Every man has property in his own person," according to Locke, and so "The labor of his body and the work of his hands . . . are properly his."

Locke's theory of natural rights represents a significant advance over the traditional theory in at least two respects. First, it clearly distinguishes between a right as an entitlement and right action, which are run together in Greek and medieval theories. Rights, in particular, are protections against the encroachment of the state in certain spheres of our lives, so that individuals have moral standing as persons independent of their role as citizens. Second, the particular rights listed by Locke, especially the right to property, are precisely those required for the operation of a free market. Thus, Locke's theory is important in the rise of modern capitalism.

Conclusion

Natural rights theory, in its traditional form or the version offered by Locke, fails to provide a wholly satisfactory basis for the full range of rights in our modern society. A number of contemporary philosophers have attempted to resurrect the notion of natural rights with only limited success.[36] This result is no cause for alarm, however, since many philosophers hold that rights are not fundamental but are properly part of a more comprehensive ethical system. So perhaps the foundation we are seeking can be found in one of two major theories; namely, utilitarianism and Kantian ethics.

UTILITY AND RIGHTS

Any attempt to found rights on utility might seem to be doomed from the start, since a standard objection against utilitarianism is that the theory is incapable of accounting for rights. Bentham's hostility to rights is well-known, but his rejection extended only to moral rights as standards separate from a legal system and not to legal rights, for which he thought utilitarianism provided the only possible foundation. In contrast, Mill recognized moral rights as a necessary part of a complete utilitarian theory, and he presented a well-developed account of them. Other utilitarian writers have offered justifications of moral rights as well.[37] Whether utilitarianism is capable of providing a foundation for both moral and legal rights, then, is an open question that needs to be explored and not dismissed out of hand.

The major stumbling block for the utilitarian theory is that rights often serve to protect individual interests against claims based on general welfare. For example, the right of due process entitles employees to a fair hearing *even if more good could be achieved by firing employees without one.* Similarly, the right of free speech protects unpopular and dangerous opinions that society might be better off without. Ronald Dworkin characterizes rights as "trumps" that override otherwise conclusive utili-

164

tarian arguments.[38] Just as a trump card in bridge takes precedence over a card in any other suit, so rights take precedence over considerations of welfare. A government is justified in making a street one way, for example, in order to achieve some overall benefit, despite the inconvenience to some motorists, since no rights are involved. But the right of free speech, Dworkin contends, denies authority for a government to limit people's expression merely on the grounds of general welfare.[39] In Dworkin's view, rights are nonutilitarian by definition.

However, a tough-minded utilitarian such as Bentham can respond by simply denying that rights are "trumps." We have a right to due process and free speech insofar as respecting these rights usually has good consequences, but if more utility can be achieved in certain instances by denying them, then these rights no longer provide us with any protection.

Mill's Theory of Rights

Mill's writings suggest a different kind of response, however.[40] The ultimate test of a system of morality, for Mill as for Bentham, is whether it maximizes utility. But the greatest amount of utility is apt to be achieved, in Mill's view, not by *direct* pursuit—that is, by selecting in each instance the action that has the best outcome—but *indirectly*, by developing practices and institutions that lead people to act in socially beneficial ways. In contemporary terms, Mill was a rule- rather than an act-utilitarian. The main reason for the superiority of the indirect pursuit of utility or rule-utilitarianism is that we do not know all the consequences of our actions, so that attempts to achieve the utilitarian optimum directly, by using act-utilitarian reasoning, occasionally backfire.

Rights facilitate the indirect pursuit of utility in special kinds of situations where (1) substantial considerations of human welfare are at stake, and (2) the connection between right action and the consequences for human welfare are difficult to see and we are strongly tempted to act in the wrong way. When these two features are present, it is especially urgent that people not reason as act-utilitarians but, in fact, suppress any inclination to do so. Since claims of rights have a stronger moral force than mere rules of obligation, people are induced by them to disregard utilitarian considerations and act on the basis of rights—thereby achieving the greatest good from the utilitarian point of view.

The only foundation for rights, Mill insists, is utility. In Chapter 5, "On the Connection Between Justice and Utility," he wrote:

> When we call anything a person's right, we mean that he has a valid claim on Society to protect him in the possession of it, either by the force of law, or by that of education and opinion.

And later:

> To have a right, then, is, I conceive, to have something which society ought to defend me in the possession of. If the objector goes on to ask, why it ought? I can give him no other reason than general utility.

But not all rules supported by the utilitarian principle are rules setting forth rights—only those concerned with justice. The difference between justice and other moral obligations is the existence of a right, which enables us to compel a person in the way that "one exacts a debt."

> Justice implies something which it is not only right to do and wrong not to do, but which some individual person can claim from us as his moral right.

Right claims are distinguished, further, by the importance of the conduct they regulate. According to Mill:

> Justice is a name for certain classes of moral rules, which concern the essentials of human well-being more nearly, and are therefore of more absolute obligation, than any other rules for the guidance of life; and the notion which we have found to be of the essence of the idea of justice, that of a right residing in an individual, implies and testifies to this more binding obligation.

He continued:

> It appears from what has been said, that justice is a name for certain moral requirements, which, regarded collectively, stand higher in the scale of social utility, and are therefore of more paramount obligation, than any other; though particular cases may occur in which some other social duty is so important, as to overrule any one of the general maxims of justice.

Mill on Free Speech

Mill's analysis neatly fits the right of free speech. At first glance, it is difficult to understand how a utilitarian could justify unbridled liberty for inflammatory racist diatribes or sordid pornographic works. The principle of utility would seem to support some restrictions on the expression of socially undesirable views. Mill contends, however, in his famous defense of free speech in Chapter 2 of *On Liberty*, that by denying a right to free speech we run the risk of suppressing the truth along with error, and to suppose that we can distinguish between the two is to make an assumption of infallibility. History is full of examples of the persecution of people holding unpopular opinions, including Socrates, Jesus, and the early Christians. Even the expression of false beliefs ought to be allowed, since by public discussion their falsity is all the more clearly revealed. Mill presented his argument in the form of a dilemma:

> . . . [T]he peculiar evil of silencing the expression of an opinion is, that it is robbing the human race; posterity as well as the existing generation; those who dissent from the opinion, still more than those who hold it. If the opinion is right, they are deprived of the opportunity of exchanging error for truth; if wrong, they lose what is almost as great a benefit, the clearer perception and livelier impression of truth, produced by its collision with error.

Also, the absence of a right of free speech creates an atmosphere in which thinkers are afraid to challenge prevailing orthodoxies and to entertain new and unfamiliar ideas. "The greatest harm done," Mill said, "is to those who are not heretics and whose whole mental development is cramped, and their reason cowed, by the fear of heresy."

The justification for a right to free speech, then, is that once we start restricting people's expression, we lose much of the benefit of the open exchange of ideas. The utilitarian optimum would be to permit only beneficial speech, while suppressing speech that is socially undesirable; but this ideal is unattainable. And since the utility of suppressing unpopular views is often immediate and evident, while the utility of permitting them distant and speculative, there is a great temptation to deny freedom of speech. Giving free speech the status of a right, therefore, serves to keep us from being shortsighted and acting precipitously

Conclusion

Mill's theory provides a plausible utilitarian foundation for rights. In order to justify them, he found it necessary to abandon the direct pursuit of utility in favor of pursuing utility indirectly. That is, Mill held that we should disregard all consequences and consider only rights and the other rules that make up our system of morality.[41] Still, the justification that Mill offers for various rights is very strong, and in subsequent chapters, we will find utilitarian arguments well-represented in the discussion of many different rights. Although the success of these arguments varies, it is certainly wrong to charge that utilitarianism is incapable of accounting for rights.

A KANTIAN FOUNDATION FOR RIGHTS

Kant himself did not give a great deal of attention to rights, but subsequent philosophers in the Kantian tradition have developed a number of justifications based on the concepts of rational agency and respect for persons.

Kant observed that although rights are correlated with duties, they are further distinguished by the fact that we are justified in using coercion to enforce them.[42] He defined a right, accordingly, as a "moral capacity to bind others."[43] This is similar to Mill's description of a right as something that can be exacted from another as a debt. Rights are divided by Kant into innate and acquired. Innate rights are those that belong to everyone "by nature, independently of any juridical act"; that is, any explicit human convention. These are what other writers call natural, or human, rights. Acquired rights, by contrast, depend on some human convention or "juridical act."

Innate rights are founded by Kant on his conception of humans as rational agents; that is, as beings who are capable of acting autonomously. In order to be agents of this kind, it is necessary for us to be free from limitations imposed by the will of others. Complete freedom is impossible, however, since one person can be free only if others are constrained in some way. We are free to speak, for example, only if everyone else is prevented from interfering. Being rational, autonomous agents requires, therefore, that we be justified in placing restrictions on what others can do, which is to say that we have rights.

Our rights must be in accord with universal law, however. That is, we have rights that justify our limiting the freedom of others only to the extent that others have these same rights to limit us. (This is the requirement of universality contained in the first formulation of the categorical imperative.) It follows that there is only one fundamental innate right, according to Kant, and that is the right to be free from the constraint of the will of others insofar as this is compatible with a similar freedom for all. From this fundamental right follow several subsidiary rights, including the right to equal treatment, equality of opportunity, and the ownership of property.

Some contemporary philosophers have also attempted to found rights on the concept of rational agency, or autonomy.[44] Others have proceeded from the Kantian concepts of dignity and respect for persons. The following passage sketches an argument of this kind:

> Rights, we are suggesting, are fundamental moral commodities because they enable us to stand up on our own two feet, "to look others in the eye, and to feel in some fundamental way the equal of anyone. To think of oneself as the holder of rights is not to be unduly but properly proud, to have that minimal self-respect that is necessary to be worthy of the love and esteem of others." Conversely, to lack the concept of oneself as a rights bearer is to be bereft of a significant element of human dignity. Without such a concept, we could not view ourselves as beings entitled to be treated as not simply means but ends as well.[45]

The writers of this passage conclude, "In our view, human or natural rights are those rights that must be acknowledged if human dignity, self-respect, and respect for persons as ends in themselves are to be secure."[46]

Difficulties with the Kantian Foundation

One criticism of the Kantian foundation for rights is that the fundamental right it supports—namely, the right to freedom—is excessively narrow.[47] In particular, Kant argues primarily for negative rights to noninterference and not for positive rights to welfare. Thus, many of the rights in the Universal Declaration of Human Rights—to education, health care, adequate nutrition, housing, and the like—are not supportable in Kant's theory.

A further difficulty is that Kantian theory provides few resources for determining what rights we do have. Without a doubt, slavery and torture are wrong because they violate the minimal conditions for rational action or dignity and respect. But the minimal conditions in other instances are less clear. Exactly how much freedom and well-being must we have to be rational, or autonomous, agents? Kantian rights theorists are often vague on whether rights are minimal conditions for rational action or dignity and respect, or whether they are maximal conditions. If they are minimal conditions, then their theories run the risk of justifying too little. But if rights are maximal conditions, then these theorists are in danger of justifying too much, since full autonomy and human dignity are ideals that go beyond the obligations that can reasonably be imposed on people.

Conclusion

This concludes our discussion of the two major theories of ethics considered in this book, along with the foundation they provide for rights. As theories about the ultimate justification of our moral judgments (that is, about what makes right actions right), they are very different. To the extent that they suggest patterns of moral reasoning, however, they are not wholly incompatible. For example, a utilitarian can also accept the principle of universalizability and even combine it with the principle of utility to form a hybrid ethical system.[48] Utilitarians no less than Kantians consider the principle of respect for persons and the concepts of dignity and autonomy as essential elements of morality, although they offer different reasons for their importance.

Ultimately, the success of any rights theory depends on the arguments it enables us to construct for specific rights. Both utilitarianism and Kant's ethics provide powerful justifications for this important ethical concept. In the course of this book, many arguments about the rights of employees, consumers, the public, and others are developed, using both theories as grounds. Thus, we will have ample opportunity to evaluate both the utilitarian and Kantian foundations for rights. Our treatment of ethical theory would not be complete, however, without a consideration of one remaining concept—namely, justice—which is the subject of the next chapter.

NOTES

1. W. D. ROSS, *The Right and the Good* (Oxford: Oxford University Press, 1930), 21.
2. G. E. MOORE, *Ethics* (Oxford: Oxford University Press, 1912), 77–80.
3. For a thorough examination of the distinction, see H. J. MCCLOSKEY, "Ross and the Concept of Prima Facie Duty," *Australasian Journal of Philosophy*, 41 (1964), 336–45.
4. For a brief survey of eighteenth-century intuitionism, see W. D. HUDSON, *Ethical Intuitionism* (New York: St. Martin's Press, 1967). A classic study of intuitionism is contained in HENRY SIDGWICK, *The Methods of Ethics*, 7th ed. (Chicago: University of Chicago Press, 1907).
5. For a brief account of twentieth-century intuitionism, see MARY WARNOCK, *Ethics since 1900*, 3rd ed. (Oxford: Oxford University Press, 1978), chap. 2.
6. See, for example, W. D. HUDSON, *Modern Moral Philosophy* (Garden City, NY: Anchor Books, 1970), 100–105. A more detailed criticism of intuitionism is presented in J. KEMP, *Reason, Action and Morality* (London: Routledge and Kegan Paul, 1964), chap. 10.
7. As might be expected, there is considerable controversy over the exact interpretation of Kant's principle. A very good starting point for those unfamiliar with the *Foundations* is FRED FELDMAN, *Introductory Ethics* (Englewood Cliffs, NJ: Prentice Hall, 1978), 97–134. Reprinted in CHRISTINA HOFF SOMMERS, ed. *Right and Wrong: Basic Readings in Ethics* (San Diego: Harcourt Brace Jovanovich, 1986), 18–43. A helpful commentary on the *Foundations* is ROBERT PAUL WOLFF, *The Autonomy of Reason* (New York: Harper & Row, 1973). For a full-length study of the categorical imperative, see ONORA NELL, *Acting on Principle: An Essay on Kantian Ethics* (New York: Columbia University Press, 1975).
8. For objections to Kant's examples, see JONATHAN HARRISON, "Kant's Examples of the First Formulation of the Categorical Imperative," *The Philosophical Quarterly*, 7 (1957), 50–62. A response is J. KEMP, "Kant's Examples of the Categorical Imperative," *The Philosophical Quarterly*, 8 (1958), 63–71; and HARRISON replies in "The Categorical Imperative," *The Philosophical Quarterly*, 8 (1958), 360–64. All three articles are reprinted in ROBERT PAUL WOLFF, ed. *Kant: A Collection of Critical Essays* (Garden City, NY: Anchor Books, 1967).
9. This is the position taken by KEMP in "Kant's Examples of the Categorical Imperative." See also KEMP, *Reason, Action and Morality*, 75–91.
10. For a further development of the logical basis for the principle of universalizability, see R. M. HARE, *Freedom and Reason* (Oxford: Oxford University Press, 1963), chap. 2; and *Moral Thinking: Its Levels, Method and Point* (Oxford: Oxford University Press, 1981), chap. 6. This principle is also called

the generalization principle and is closely related to the principle of utilitarian generalization. See MARCUS G. SINGER, *Generalization in Ethics* (New York: Knopf, 1961), chap. 2.

11. For a discussion of the logical force of this question, see COLIN STRANG, "What If Everyone Did That?" *Durham University Journal*, 53 (1960), 5–10. This article is widely reprinted. One source is SOMMERS, *Right and Wrong*, 51–62.

12. For Singer, this is the generalization argument, which utilizes the generalization principle but also requires the support of a utilitarian principle that he calls the principle of consequences. See SINGER, *Generalization in Ethics*, chap. 4.

13. An ambitious attempt to develop the principle of universalizability into a complete ethical theory is ALAN GEWIRTH, *Reason and Morality* (Chicago: University of Chicago Press, 1978).

14. DOUGLAS MCGREGOR, *The Human Side of Enterprise* (New York: McGraw-Hill, 1960).

15. WILLIAM G. OUCHI, *Theory Z: How American Business Can Meet the Japanese Challenge* (Reading, MA: Addison-Wesley, 1981).

16. The material for this case is taken from DAVID L. NYE, "Fire at Will—Careful, Now, Careful," *Across the Board*, 19 (November 1982), 37–40.

17. The full title is "The ILO Convention concerning Termination of Employment at the Initiative of the Employer." Reprinted in *International Labour Conference, Provisional Record of Sixty-Eighth Session*, No. 30A (June 21, 1982).

18. Government employees, but not those in the private sector, are protected not only by substantially more legislation but also by the due process clause of the Fifth Amendment.

19. This method of explaining rights is derived from JOEL FEINBERG, "The Nature and Value of Rights," *The Journal of Value Inquiry*, 4 (1970), 243–57. Reprinted in JOEL FEINBERG, *Rights, Justice, and the Bounds of Liberty* (Princeton: Princeton University Press, 1980), 143–55, and in DAVID LYONS, ed., *Rights* (Belmont, CA: Wadsworth, 1979), 78–91.

20. This term is used in H. J. MCCLOSKEY, "Rights," *The Philosophical Quarterly*, 15 (1965), 115–27, and also in RICHARD A. WASSERSTROM, "Rights, Human Rights, and Racial Discrimination," *The Journal of Philosophy*, 61 (1964), 628–41. This latter article is reprinted in LYONS, *Rights*, 46–57. For a useful survey of different accounts, see REX MARTIN and JAMES W. NICKEL, "Recent Work on the Concept of Rights," *American Philosophical Quarterly*, 17 (1980), 165–80.

21. The correlativity thesis goes back at least as far as Bentham. See DAVID LYONS, "Rights, Claimants, and Beneficiaries, *American Philosophical Quarterly*, 6 (1969), 173–85, reprinted in LYONS, *Rights*, 58–77; and H.L.A. HART, "Bentham on Legal Rights," in A.W.B. SIMPSON, ed., *Oxford Essays in Jurisprudence* (Oxford: Oxford University Press, 1973), 171–203, reprinted in LYONS, *Rights* 125–48, and (under the title "Legal Rights") in H.L.A. HART, *Essays on Bentham: Jurisprudence and Political Theory* (Oxford: Oxford University Press, 1982), 162–93. It is mentioned in JOHN AUSTIN'S *The Province of Jurisprudence Determined* (1832). Early discussions of the thesis are F. H. BRADLEY, *Ethical Studies*, 2nd ed. (Oxford: Oxford University Press, 1927), 207–13; and ROSS, *The Right and the Good*, 48–56. More recent statements

are S. I. BENN and R. S. PETERS, *Social Principles and the Democratic State* (London: George Allen & Unwin, 1959), 101–4; and RICHARD B. BRANDT, *Ethical Theory* (Englewood Cliffs, NJ: Prentice Hall, 1959), 434–41. Two good critical examinations are JOEL FEINBERG, "Duties, Rights, and Claims," *American Philosophical Quarterly*, 3 (1966), 137–44, reprinted in FEINBERG, *Rights, Justice, and the Bounds of Liberty*, 130–55; and DAVID LYONS, "The Correlativity of Rights and Duties," *Noûs*, 4 (1970), 45–55. Lyon's article is criticized in DAVID BRAYBROOKE, "The Firm But Untidy Correlativity of Rights and Obligations," *Canadian Journal of Philosophy*, 1 (1972), 351–63; and MARCUS G. SINGER, "The Basis of Rights and Duties," *Philosophical Studies*, 23 (1972), 48–57. See also ALAN R. WHITE, *Rights* (Oxford: Oxford University Press, 1984), chap. 5.

22. This way of explaining the distinction is due to BRANDT, *Ethical Theory*, 434.
23. WESLEY NEWCOMB HOHFELD, *Fundamental Legal Conceptions* (New Haven: Yale University Press, 1923). For a clear exposition, see ARTHUR L. CORBIN, "Legal Analysis and Terminology," *Yale Law Journal*, 29 (1919), 163–73.
24. LYONS, "The Correlativity of Rights and Duties."
25. This is maintained by CARL WELLMAN, "A New Conception of Human Rights," in E. KAMENKA and A.E.S. TAY, eds., *Human Rights* (New York: St. Martin's Press, 1978), 48–58.
26. JOEL FEINBERG, "The Rights of Animals and Unborn Generations," in *Justice, Rights, and the Bounds of Liberty*, 159.
27. See MCCLOSKEY, "Rights," 118–19.
28. Feinberg avoids this objection by countering that general, or *in rem*, rights which are only claims *to* but not claims *on* are "manifesto" rights, that is, rights that are put forth as desirable social goals but are not sufficiently accepted at the present time to generate specific rights. FEINBERG, "The Nature and Value of Rights," in *Rights, Justice, and the Bounds of Liberty*, 153.
29. Closely related is a distinction between negative and positive liberty. A poor man is free (in a negative sense) to buy a loaf of bread, for example, as long as no one stands in his way, but he is not free (in a positive sense) unless he has the means to buy the bread. Compare these two senses in the case of "fee for service" medical care, which secures free *choice*, and socialized medicine, which provides free *access*. Which system of medical care is more "free"? The classic discussion of this distinction is ISAIAH BERLIN, "Two Concepts of Liberty," in *Four Essays on Liberty* (Oxford: Oxford University Press, 1969), 118–72.
30. JOEL FEINBERG, *Social Philosophy* (Englewood Cliffs, NJ: Prentice Hall, 1973), 59.
31. See JUDITH LICHTENBERG, "The Moral Equivalence of Action and Omission," *Canadian Journal of Philosophy*, supp. vol. 8 (1982), 19–36; and HENRY SHUE, *Basic Rights: Subsistence, Affluence, and U.S. Foreign Policy* (Princeton: Princeton University Press, 1980), 37–40.
32. Among the many works describing natural or human rights are: MAURICE CRANSTON, *What Are Human Rights?* (New York: Basic Books, 1963); B. MAYO, "What Are Human Rights?" in D. D. RAPHAEL, ed., *Political Theory and the Rights of Man* (Bloomington: Indiana University Press, 1967), 68–80; D. D. RAPHAEL, "Human Rights, Old and New," in RAPHAEL, *Political Theory and the Rights of Man*, 54–67; MAURICE CRANSTON, "Human Rights, Real

and Supposed," in RAPHAEL, *Political Theory and the Rights of Man*, 43–53; FEINBERG, *Social Philosophy*, 84–97; and A. I. MELDEN, *Rights and Persons* (Berkeley and Los Angeles: University of California Press, 1977), 166–69.

33. See STUART M. BROWN, Jr., "Inalienable Rights," *The Philosophical Review*, 64 (1955), 192–211; and B. A. RICHARDS, "Inalienable Rights: Recent Criticism and Old Doctrine," *Philosophy and Phenomenological Research*, 29 (1969), 391–404.

34. A good survey of the early history of natural rights is RICHARD TUCK, *Natural Rights Theories: Their Origin and Development* (Cambridge: Cambridge University Press, 1979).

35. Locke's theory of natural rights is the subject of great controversy. Two articles that provide a good introduction are W. VON LEYDEN, "John Locke and Natural Law," *Philosophy*, 21 (1956), 23–35; and WILLIAM J. WAINWRIGHT, "Natural Rights," *American Philosophical Quarterly*, 4 (1967), 79–84. The thesis that Locke was not a natural rights theorist is developed in LEO STRAUSS, *Natural Right and History* (Chicago: University of Chicago Press, 1953). One response is CHARLES H. MONSON, JR., "Locke and His Interpreters," *Political Studies*, 6 (1958), 120–35.

36. For a survey, see TIBOR R. MACHAN, "Some Recent Work in Human Rights Theory," *American Philosophical Quarterly*, 17 (1980), 103–15. Two important articles are MARGARET MACDONALD, "Natural Rights," *Proceedings of the Aristotelian Society* 47 (1947–1948), reprinted in A. I. MELDEN, ed., *Human Rights* (Belmont, CA: Wadsworth, 1970), 40–60; and H.L.A. HART, "Are There Any Natural Rights?" *The Philosophical Review*, 64 (1955), 175–91, also reprinted in MELDEN, *Human Rights*, 61–75.

37. One notable work is L. W. SUMNER, *The Moral Foundation of Rights* (Oxford: Oxford University Press, 1987).

38. RONALD DWORKIN, *Taking Rights Seriously* (Cambridge: Harvard University Press, 1978). See also RONALD DWORKIN, "Rights as Trumps," in JEREMY WALDRON, ed., *Theories of Rights* (Oxford: Oxford University Press, 1984), 153–81. This article is adapted from RONALD DWORKIN, "Is There a Right to Pornography?" *Oxford Journal of Legal Studies*, 1 (1981), 177–212.

39. DWORKIN, *Taking Rights Seriously*, 191.

40. The account that follows is one developed by DAVID LYONS in several articles, most notably "Human Rights and the General Welfare," *Philosophy and Public Affairs*, 6 (1977), 113–29; but see also "Mill's Theory of Morality," *Noûs*, 10 (1976), 101–20; "Mill's Theory of Justice," in A. I. GOLDMAN and J. KIM, eds., *Values and Morals: Essays in Honor of William Frankena, Charles Stevenson, and Richard Brandt* (Dordrecht: Reidel, 1978), 1–20; and "Benevolence and Justice in Mill," in HARLAN B. MILLER and WILLIAM H. WILLIAMS, eds., *The Limits of Utilitarianism* (Minneapolis: University of Minnesota Press, 1982), 42–70. Lyons is doubtful, however, of the account presented in these articles. See "Utility and Rights" in J. ROLAND PENNOCK and JOHN W. CHAPMAN, eds., *Ethics, Economics and the Law*, (New York: New York University Press, 1982), 107–38, reprinted in WALDRON, *Theories of Rights*, 110–36. Criticism of Lyons is contained in ALAN GEWIRTH, "Can Utilitarianism Justify Any Moral Rights?" in PENNOCK and CHAPMAN, *Ethics, Economics and the Law*, 158–93, reprinted in GEWIRTH, *Human Rights* (Chicago: University of Chicago Press, 1982), 143–62.

41. LYONS, "Utility and Rights," 134.
42. An examination of Kant's account of rights, on which the following discussion is largely based, is BRUCE AUNE, *Kant's Theory of Morals* (Princeton: Princeton University Press, 1979), 141–52.
43. IMMANUEL KANT, *The Metaphysical Elements of Justice: Part I of the Metaphysics of Morals*, trans. JOHN LADD (Indianapolis: Bobbs-Merrill, 1965), 37.
44. The fullest account is GEWIRTH, *Reason and Morality*, discussed below. See also GEWIRTH, "The Basis and Content of Human Rights," in J. ROLAND PENNOCK and JOHN W. CHAPMAN, eds., *Human Rights* (New York: New York University Press, 1981), 119–47, reprinted in GEWIRTH, *Human Rights*, 41–67; and DAVID A. J. RICHARDS, "Rights and Autonomy," *Ethics*, 92 (1981), 3–20.
45. NORMAN E. BOWIE and ROBERT L. SIMON, *The Individual and the Political Order: An Introduction to Social and Political Philosophy*, 1st ed. (Englewood Cliffs, NJ: Prentice Hall, 1977), 78. The quoted passage is from FEINBERG, "The Nature and Value of Rights," in *Rights Justice, and the Bounds of Liberty*, 151.
46. BOWIE and SIMON, *The Individual and the Political Order*, 78.
47. See AUNE, *Kant's Theory of Morals*, 151.
48. This is proposed by R. M. HARE in *Moral Thinking*.

What Can Eastern Philosophy Teach Us about Business Ethics?

Daryl Koehn

As Asian markets have grown, there has been a corresponding increase in interest among businesspeople and philosophers in so-called "Asian Values." Knowledge of the values and ethical systems of Asians is touted as necessary if Western businesses are to successfully negotiate the opening of markets in Japan, South Korea and China and to sell their products to the citizens of these countries. *Real politik* has played an important role as well in generating interest in Asian Values. With the increased wealth of these developing countries has come a greater say in international affairs. Westerners now feel compelled to take note of Asians and to understand them as well as possible. Moreover, as Asian markets have become more lucrative, the power of Southeast Asian governments has increased simply by virtue of the fact that they control which businesses get access to their people and on what terms. The power of voice, coupled with this power to regulate access, has gotten the West's attention.

However, although it is now fashionable to allude to Asian Values, it is far from clear what this term means. In the first part of this paper, I argue: 1) that it is dubious whether such values exist other than as a rhetorical category; 2) that we need to consider the ethics of using such a term; and 3) that we are better advised to speak of certain strands of ethical thinking articulated by particular thinkers within specific countries (e.g., Japan, South Korea, China, etc.). In the second part, I take up two such strands—the ethical views of the famous Japanese ethicist Watsuji Tetsuro and of Confucius. I argue that many of their ideas have profound implications for the conduct of business and the way in which we evaluate that conduct.

Part One: The Rhetoric of "Asian Values"

It is questionable whether Asian Values do exist or ever could do so. The term "Asia" refers to an enormous geographical area. China, Japan, India and the rest of the Southeast and East Asian countries fall under the rubric. The former U.S.S.R., too, historically has been considered part of

Asia by Europeans. The same is true of what we now term the Mideast. The Greek historian Herodotus, for example, consistently treats Persia and Phoenicia as Asian empires. As one would expect, given the vastness of Asia, the cultures therein vary tremendously, reflecting just about every world religion—Buddhism (in numerous varieties), Shintoism, Confucianism, Islam, Christianity, etc. While we can carve out a certain region of the globe and label it "Asia," it is very hard to ascertain what values all of these different cultures might share.

Identifying a "core" set of Asian Values is not the only problem. Even if there were some widely shared values within this region, these values would not be static. Asian Values would be just as subject as Western ones to the transforming effect of political and economic factors. The contrast between Western and Asian Values has the unfortunate effect of making it seem as though the two are eternally opposed to each other. For example, one common variant of this distinction opposes Western individualism to Asian collectivism and deference to authority. Yet, as Kawato rightly notes, the West has not always been as committed to individualism as it now is.[1] Europeans in the Middle Ages were much more clannish than they are today. Aristotle argues that the Greek polis evolved out of tribal arrangements in which there was one dominant leader to whom all tribe members deferred.[2] Asia might become more "individualistic" or the West more "tribal" or "group-centered" as the years unfold. No culture is hermetically sealed and, as Midgely argues, to think that a culture is a closed system grossly misunderstands cultures and their evolution, an evolution stimulated and influenced by contact with other cultures.[3] In other words, "Asian Values" might once have been "Western Values" (or vice versa) and could become so again. So, even if there were a core set of distinct Asian Values, it would be simple-minded to treat these values in a completely ahistorical fashion.

Given the exceptionally diverse cultures of that region we in the West name "Asia"; and given the dynamism inherent in cultural values, we have good reason to doubt whether some monolithic static set of Asian Values exists now, ever has, or ever will. That is not to deny that some leaders in some countries in this region routinely invoke Asian Values. But the rhetorical purposes to which this invocation are being put need to be critically evaluated. . . .

The more substantive issue centers on just what the content of these supposedly unique Asian Values are. It is said, for example, that Asians focus more on responsibilities while Westerners are obsessed with rights. While it is true that neither Buddhism nor Confucianism conceptualizes human rights, the fact that they have not been mentioned in the past by these religions does not mean that the idea of rights in no way resonates with the people living in Asia. Confucius' injunction "Let the government not interfere, so that the people may thrive" sounds like a Western liberal value. Buddhism does not appear especially hostile to rights either. Given this religion's focus on human development, the Buddhist might very well accept that there are human rights but then try to connect them with human potentiality and "feelings and consciousness relative to injustice and inequality." One can get some sense of what such a connection might look like in the context of the Tibetan legal system. This legal system recognizes the individual's "right" to a fair trial, and the court employs procedures designed to insure a fair trial. The system differs from that of most Western countries in the way in which it thinks about punishment. In Tibet, the punishment is not designed to "fit the crime" so much as to suit the particular individual being punished. The punishment should be such as to bring the "criminal" to greater insight and a higher level of awareness. . . .

Part Two: Learning from Watsuji Tetsuro and Confucius

At one level, then, "Eastern ethics" has nothing to teach us about business ethics since such ethics may not even exist. If we take the expression "Eastern ethics" in a more limited sense, however, and think of it as applying to the ethics of particular individuals living within China or Japan or India, then business can learn something from Eastern ethics. While there may not be a single ethic of the Japanese or Chinese, individual thinkers such as Confucius and Watsuji Tetsuro have unquestionably both captured and influenced some dimensions of the ways in which their fellow citizens think about what is morally right. In the remainder of this paper, I draw upon these two thinkers to examine three larger themes:

1. The meaning of trust
2. Relations for life
3. Ethics beyond rights

The Meaning of Trust

Since Watsuji speaks at length about trust, I will develop his idea of trust and show how it contrasts with some views dominant within the

Anglo-American tradition. For Watsuji, human social relations are not grounded in trust. Rather trust is based in human being or *ningen sonzai*. Society cannot be the result of a voluntary decision by citizens to come together and to agree to show each other mutual good will. Trust exists because we are all always already related to each other in a variety of ways—as parents of children and children of parents; as spouses, clients, employees, supervisors, subordinates, etc. We move within these relations conforming to expectations we did not form. Even to deny these expectations is indirectly to confirm them. Over time such role expectations change as the result of individual rebellion, but they do not disappear. Another set of role expectations emerges to take the place of the prior set.

Trusting others is nothing other than living and acting within this social matrix. Sometimes people betray us, but betrayals do not destroy trust. There is no betrayal where there is no trust; and trust exists wherever there are human beings—i.e., activities in accordance with relations. In fact, most betrayals are parasitic upon trust. To take Watsuji's example: The pickpocket can operate only as long as people are not excessively guarded when shopping, going to movies or, more generally, moving within the public space. A theft does not destroy this trust. It might make the individual more cautious but that individual will still be trusting in most dimensions of his or her life. Our trust is never the result of some cost-benefit calculation. Nor is it something we repose in another on the strength of evidence. Anyone who is human trusts simply by virtue of being human.

Perhaps only among enemies at war has trust completely ceased to exist. When each side desires to exterminate the other, humanity is not present. Or maybe we should say it is present but in a very attenuated form. For even here there is a relation of sorts—the relation of enemy to enemy. To declare someone an enemy is to say he or she is not a friend. That means, though, that friendship is potentially applicable to the enemy in a way that it is not with respect to inanimate things. We do not go around saying of rocks or a bottle of distilled vinegar, "It is my enemy." So enemies have a relation and maybe even a modicum of trust.

This non-voluntaristic, non-contractarian, non-evidentiary notion of trust has several interesting implications for business practice: For example, trust is not something companies can or should market. Companies already have our trust, a point that gets driven home every time we read how easy the unscrupulous find it to con the rest of us. Instead of seeing themselves as winning our trust by compiling a good record of healthy products and safe working conditions, businesses should understand themselves as striving to be true to the trust they enjoy simply by virtue of being a human institution operating within the social matrix. Being true to this trust should be the guiding intention behind every action, not just an idea that comes into play when it is time to roll out a major marketing campaign or to negotiate with workers. There is no single moment when trust is reposed or withheld. It is always present as part of the structure of humanity. The issue is therefore less one of whether others will trust you than one of whether you will be true to human being.

Truth also takes on a different meaning within this scheme. Trust cannot be built up by speaking the truth—i.e., by making one's words and deeds correspond with the fact of the matter. Truth depends upon trust. A "true" friend is not one who gives us the facts. Rather true friends speak in the way our friendship with them merits. Similarly businesses will not earn our trust by pursuing a strategy of "truth in advertising." Instead businesspeople should speak in accordance with a consciousness of what it means to be a businessperson in society, a businessperson who is already trusted by customers, government officials, suppliers, etc. Truth should not emerge as the result of a strategic calculation but out of the businessperson's strong sense of himself or herself as a human being in that role which is but one among many.

Truth and trust have the same structure wherever they exist. Watsuji would thus agree in spirit with the powerful statement of Aaron Feuerstein, the CEO whose family rebuilt Malden Mills after a devastating fire: "God is one. There is no god of the family, god of the marketplace, god of the temple. God is one and is present everywhere." For Feuerstein, there never was a possibility of not rebuilding the family-owned business. He was a human being in a community of people who had built their lives around the mill. He thus spoke as a true CEO when he rejected out of hand suggestions that he rebuilt because doing so was a shrewd way of making money.

Relations Are for Life

Both Watsuji and Confucius reject the radical, atomistic understanding of human beings. To be human is always already to be in relation—or, more precisely, in a matrix of interrelated highly determinate relations (e.g., parent-child: older-younger sibling; teacher-student: superior-subordinate, etc.). These relations are for life. Certain problems which plague Western thought simply do not arise in this alternative worldview. For example, if the person is an individual and if an individual is identified with the capacity for rational thought, then a comatose person suffering extensive brain damage may not be a person at all within this Western framework. This problem does not arise in a Watsujian or Confucian framework. The comatose daughter does not cease to be the daughter of the mother. She is and forever will be that mother's child. Should she die, she remains the mother's "dead daughter." Nor does the next daughter in line become the eldest daughter upon her sister's death. She, too, remains the second daughter for life.

Since relations are for life, the person of *jen* or humanity does not form new relations lightly. Friendships, for example, require both parties to show good will to each other as long as each is alive. The sense of obligation to the friend may extend beyond death. For example, the friend may feel it is necessary to help the child of a dead friend to get a college education. The Chinese were shocked and offended when Nixon declared himself a friend to China because America and China would each get something out of the relation. This attitude of expediency is utterly foreign to the way the person of *jen* or person with a true heart (*makoto*) thinks about friendship. Showing good will, not getting advantage, is the mark of the true friend.

From the Watsujian and Confucian perspectives, commercial relations are longterm as well. An action or choice is not good simply because it has taken into account the interests of stockholders or many stakeholders. It goes without saying that the effect of one's actions on the larger social matrix of relations must always be considered. It is also necessary for the actor to consider the longterm effect of her actions on relations. Each generation of agents shows such regard; and that accounts for why many commercial relations in Japan and China (Taiwan, Hong Kong, etc.) go back many generations.

Businesses are not, therefore, selling products or marketing their reputation. They are establishing a relation or, in the catchy phrase of one modern author, developing a customer for life. Customers in Japan historically have not been especially price-conscious; they stick with those they know. Habits have changed somewhat as the Japanese travelled abroad and came to see how much more costly some items were in Japan than in America or Europe. Yet customers still expect that those who sell them a product will stand behind that product for years and will prove solicitous in their service to the buyer. Some Japanese realtors will go into a home after the escrow has been closed and get the utilities turned on as part of the after-sales followup. They understand the real relationship begins after the house has been purchased. Manufacturers will continue to buy from suppliers with whom they have done business in the past, even if these suppliers charge more than others. In China, too, people feel beholden to those who have helped them in the past. Favors are not accepted lightly because one will have to reciprocate.

There are numerous problems with such a system. It is difficult to dump a distributor or supplier who fails to do a good job. These longterm relations may limit competition. Newcomers cannot simply buy marketshare by offering loss leaders in a system where customers remain exceptionally loyal to brandnames. On the other hand, there is an important lesson here for both businesspeople and business ethicists—namely, that business transactions do not occur in a void or in some separate discrete "economic" sphere completely cut off from the rest of social life. The habits acquired in one sphere carry over into others. If we want our citizenry to know what it means to be a good parent and a true friend, then we need to think about the form and bases of our economic transactions as well. Encouraging people to respond only to price signals may develop a deeply-rooted worldview in which everything is valued using a standard of expediency alone.

Ethics Beyond Rights

A third important strand common to Watsuji and Confucius is their emphasis on what we owe to each other. It is tempting to say that their systems and, for that matter, the Japanese and Chinese cultures are duty-based while Western cultures are rights-based. This distinction, while nice and tidy, simplifies too much. If the ethics of the Japanese and Chinese have no idea of rights, they equally have no idea of duty. Duties are the correlatives of rights. There cannot be one without the other. Both duties and rights are enforceable claims. Citizens have the right to demand that elected officers fulfill their responsibilities—i.e., the duties of their office. If the officers fail to do so, the citizens have a right to impeach them, sue, vote them out of office, etc. But the duties Watsuji and Confucius are describing are not enforceable. Quite the contrary. As the noted Japanese legal theorist Kawashima Takeyoshi has observed, it is ethically "improper for the other party (beneficiary) of an obligation to demand or claim that the obligated person fulfill his obligation. An obligation is considered valueless, if, although it is fulfilled by the obligated person, he does not fulfill it in addition with a special friendliness or favor toward the other party.

In other words, the actual value of social obligations depends upon the good will and favor of the obligated person, and there is no place for the existence of the notion of right. . . ."

So an obligation does not derive ethical value from the fact that a rational being would make this demand and want to enforce it. Whatever ethical worth it has comes from the agent's perception or intuitive understanding of her place in the whole of human relations. This understanding will lead her to act with *makoto* or a true-heartedness or *jen*—i.e., humanity. Acts of *makoto* or *jen* are ethically good. An act which honored another's "rights" but which was not done voluntarily or in the spirit of *jen* would not be ethically (or politically) good.

This point of view subordinates the law to moral considerations. Mere adherence to a statute (or, for that matter, a principle such as the categorical imperative) cannot be ethically good. Simple conformity does not exhibit *makoto* or *jen*. In addition, always obeying the law will lead one into a mechanical life. Laws by definition are general. They are not necessarily suited to the circumstances of the particular case or the specific relation. They may therefore be hostile to our truehearted efforts to honor the requirements of particular human relations. It is better not to try to legislate too much. What laws do exist should be enforced in a spirit of equity or *jen*.

This more flexible approach can be dangerous. Those who enforce the law are given a tremendous amount of discretion. If the judges are people of *makoto*, then perhaps the decisions will prove just and appropriate. But such people are not always at the helm of the ship of state. If the judge hands down a bad decision, those affected by the decision have traditionally had few, if any, rights to which they can appeal in order to protest the decision.

The approach does have certain strengths, though, that are relevant to business practice. Managers and employees avoid asserting mutually incompatible rights. While there sometimes are strikes in Japan, these strikes usually occur after a settlement has been reached. They last for one day and are intended more as a PR device for making a statement

182

than a mechanism of confrontation designed to force management's hand. (Strikes also occur with some frequency in South Korea, a supposedly Confucian country. This difference may be due to the greater impact the rights-oriented United States has had on the Korean subcontinent where it has maintained a military presence since 1950, a presence on which the South Koreans rely in order to preserve their democracy.)

Parties who are disagreeing are not so likely to get locked into a rigid position. Both sides must consider what it would mean to be true to the employee-manager relation. Doing so will almost certainly involve them in what Richard Nielsen has termed "doubleloop" negotiations. In this form of negotiations, each side does not try to win and to enforce its will. Instead, they put their controlling values—the values behind their position—into play along with their demands. Each side has the opportunity to affect and mold the other sides' values. The opportunity does not guarantee that these controlling values will be refined. But it at least opens the door to this possibility.

Finally, this more flexible approach changes what it means for a business to be socially responsible. In the West, we tend to say, "Business has a right to make a profit, but they must do so in a socially responsible way." This formulation makes it hard to assess social responsibility. How much profit does business have a right to make? And might not the largely unfettered pursuit by private institutions of maximum profit lead to the greatest social good? If so, then it would be better to just let business go its own way without interference by the government or any other social institution. In other words, having granted business the right to make a profit the problem becomes one of fitting business back into society. The Watsujian and Confucian approaches, by contrast, treat business as just one of many institutions thoroughly embedded within the social matrix. It is not entitled to make absolute claims for itself. The question for the businessperson, as for every human being in the society, is: What is the good of the larger whole and how can I behave in such a way as to contribute to that whole? The first responsibility of an agent is to consider the whole. Only after having done so is the agent able to be true to the specific human relation in which he or she is operating.

On this second view, the business ethicist should be less concerned with whether multinational corporations or their local subsidiaries are honoring workers' rights to a safe environment or a living wage and more concerned with the larger questions of what contributions business is making to China or Japan. As Henry Rosemont, a Sinologist, has put it, we should be asking what a person of good will would wish for the Chinese at this point in their moral development (Rosemont). When we ask that question, we are driven to admit that it is not at all clear that the Chinese will be well-served if American and European countries sell them hundreds of thousands of cars. The Chinese already have severe pollution problems and do not have the road infrastructure to support a huge increase in automobile transportation. The loss of life may be huge just as it was in Nigeria when Western automobiles arrived before eye glasses. Focussing on the rights questions obscures these larger questions, questions which require Westerners to look at their own business practices and controlling values more closely instead of demonizing the Chinese or other developing countries in Asia.

Conclusion

Adopting the perspective of Watsuji or Confucius is certainly not a panacea for all that ails the West. However, taking this tradition seriously will help us to identify our own prejudices regarding business practice as well as to learn about some alternative conceptions of key business ideas such as trust. We may not want to accept these ideas but at least we will be in a better position to make an informed argument for why they should be rejected and to understand the criticisms some Chinese or Japanese businesspeople and philosophers may make regarding our own tradition.

Notes

1. Akio Kawato, "Beyond the Myth of Asian Values," first published in *Chuokoron*, (December, 1995) at http://ifrm.glocom.jp/DOC.

2. Aristotle, *Politics*, 1252b.

3. Mary Midgley, *Can't We Make Moral Judgments?* (New York: St. Martin's Press, 1993), pp. 87–96. Many tend to forget that the United States has played an enormous role in shaping modern Japan. "The differences between Japan before and after 1945 are dramatic. In the years of occupation following the war, the U.S.A. refashioned all of Japan's political and social institutions. During the war, for example, Japan was dominated by the military caste. Afterwards, the U.S. written constitution officially defined Japan as a pacifist state." Daniel Nassim, "Shaming the Japanese," in *Living Marxism* 81 (July/August 1995) at www.junius.co.uk/LM/LM81/LM81_Books.html.

Business Ethics: A Japanese View

Iwao Taka

I. Two Normative Environments—Religious Dimension

In order to evaluate the traditional ethical standards of the Japanese business community, it is necessary to describe the Japanese cultural context or background. When it comes to cultural or ethical background, we can classify Japanese conscious and unconscious beliefs into a "religious dimension" and a "social dimension," in that Japanese culture cannot be understood well in terms of only one of the two dimensions. While the former is closely combined with a metaphysical concept or an idea of human salvation, the latter is based on how Japanese observe or conceive their social environment. Stated otherwise, while the former is "ideal-oriented," the latter is "real-oriented."

First, the religious dimension. This dimension supplies a variety of concrete norms of behavior to the Japanese in relation to the ultimate reality. As a consequence, I shall call this dimension the "normative environment."

By this I mean the environment in which most events and things acquire their own meanings pertaining to something beyond the tangible or secular world. Following this definition, there are mainly two influential normative environments in Japan: the "transcendental normative environment" and the "group normative environment."

1. Transcendental Normative Environment

One of the famous Japanese didactic poems says, "Although there are many paths at the foot of a mountain, they all lead us in the direction of the same moon seen at the top of the mountain." This poem gives us an ontological equivalent of "variety equals one." To put it in another way, though there are innumerable phenomena in this tangible world, each individual phenomenon has its own *numen* (soul, spirit, reason-d'être, or spiritual energy), and its numen is ultimately connected with the unique numen of the universe. In Japanese, this ultimate reality is often called "natural life force," "great life force of the universe," *michi* (path of righteousness), *ri* (justice), *ho* (dharma, laws), and the like.

"Transcendentalism" is the philosophy that every phenomenon is an expression of the great life force and is ultimately connected with the numen of the universe. It follows that the environment where various concrete norms come to exist may be called the "transcendental normative environment." What is more, the set of these norms is simply called "transcendental logic."

In this transcendental environment, everyone has an equal personal numen. This idea has been philosophically supported or strengthened by Confucianism and Buddhism. That is to say, in the case of neo-Confucianism, people are assumed to have a microcosm within themselves, and are considered condensed expressions of the universe (macrocosm). Their inner universe is expected to be able to connect with the outer universe.

In the case of Buddhism, every living creature is said to have an equal Buddhahood, a Buddhahood which is very similar with the idea of numen and microcosm. Buddhism has long taught, "Although there are differences among living creatures, there is no difference among human beings. What makes human beings different is only their name."

In addition, however, under the transcendental normative environment, not only individuals but also jobs, positions, organizations, rituals, and other events and things incorporate their own "numina." Needless to say, these numina are also expected to be associated with the numen of the universe.

Deities of Shintoism, Buddhism, and the Japanese new religions, which have long been considered objects of worship, are often called the "great life force of the universe," or regarded as expressions of that force. In this respect, the life force can be sacred and religious. On the other hand, however, many Japanese people have unconsciously accepted this way of thinking without belonging to any specific religious sect. In this case, it is rather secular, non-religious, and atheistic. Whether it is holy or secular, the significant feature of Japan is that this transcendental normative environment has been influential and has been shared by Japanese people.

2. Meaning of Work in the Transcendental Environment

Inasmuch as Japanese people live in such a normative environment, the meaning of work for them becomes unique. That is to say, work is understood to be a self-expression of the great life force. Work is believed to have its own numen so that work is one of the ways to reach something beyond the secular world or the ultimate reality. Accordingly, Japanese people unconsciously and sometimes consciously try to unify themselves with the great life force by concentrating on their own work.

This propensity can be found vividly in the Japanese tendency to view seemingly trivial activities—such as arranging flowers, making tea, practicing martial arts, or studying calligraphy—as ideal ways to complete their personality (or the ideal ways to go beyond the tangible world). Becoming an expert in a field is likely to be thought of as reaching the stage of *kami* (a godlike state). Whatever job people take, if they reach the *kami* stage or even if they make a strong effort to reach it, they will be respected by others.

M. Imai has concluded that whereas Western managers place priority on innovation, Japanese managers and workers put emphasis on *Kaizen* (continuous improvement of products, of ways to work, and of decision-making processes). While innovation can be done intermittently only by a mere handful of elites in a society, *Kaizen* can be carried on continuously by almost every person.

> Technological breakthroughs in the West are generally thought to take a Ph.D., but there are only three Ph.D.s on the engineering staff at one of Japan's most successfully innovative companies—Honda Motor. One is founder Soichiro Honda, whose Ph.D. is an honorary degree, and the other two are no longer active within the company. At Honda, technological improvement does not seem to require a Ph.D.[1]

The transcendental normative environment has contributed to the formation of this Japanese propensity to place emphasis on *Kaizen*. Work has been an important path for Japanese people to reach the numen of the universe. Thus, they dislike skimping on their work, and instead love to improve their products, ways of working, or the decision-making processes. These Japanese attitudes are closely linked with the work ethics in the transcendental normative environment. Kyogoku describes this as follows:

In marked contrast with an occidental behavioral principle of "Pray to God, and work!" at the cloister, in Japan, "Work, that is a prayer!" became a principle. In this context, devotion of one's time and energy to work, concentration on work to such a degree that one is absorbed in the improvement of work without sparing oneself, and perfectionism of "a demon for work," became institutional traditions of Japan.[2]

In this way, the transcendental environment has supplied many hard workers to the Japanese labor market, providing an ethical basis for "diligence." Nonetheless, it has not created extremely individualistic people who pursue only their own short-term interests. Because they have hoped for job security and life security in the secular world, they have subjectively tried to coordinate their behavior so as to keep harmonious relations with others in the group. Within this subjective coordination, and having the long-term perspective in mind, they pursue their own purposes.

3. Group Normative Environment

The second or group normative environment necessarily derives from this transcendental normative environment, insofar as the latter gives special raisons d'être not only to individuals and their work, but also to their groups. As a result of the transcendental environment, every group holds its own numen. The group acquires this *raison d'être*, as long as it guarantees the life of its members and helps them fulfill their potentials.

But once a group acquires its *raison d'être*, it insists upon its survival. An environment in which norms regarding the existence and prosperity of the group appear and affect its members is called the "group normative environment," and the set of the norms in this environment is called "group logic."

In Japan, the typical groups have been: *ie* (family), *mura* (local community), and *kuni* (nation). After World War II, although the influence of *ie* and *kuni* on their members has been radically weakened, one cannot completely ignore their influence. *Mura* has also lost much power over its members, but *kaisha* (business organization) has taken over many functions of *mura*, in addition to some functions of *ie*. These groups are assumed to have their own numen: *ie* holds the souls of one's ancestors, *mura* relates to a *genius loci* (tutelary deity), *kaisha* keeps its corporate tradition (or culture), and *kuni* has Imperial Ancestors' soul. . . .

Groupism and a group-oriented propensity, which have often been pointed out as Japanese characteristics, stem from this group normative environment.

II. The Ethical Dilemma of Living between Two Environments

Japanese often face an ethical dilemma arising from the fact that they live simultaneously in the two different influential normative environments. In the transcendental environment, groups and individuals are regarded as equal numina and equal expressions of the great life force. In the group environment, however, a group (and its representatives) is considered to be superior to its ordinary members, mainly because while the group is expected to be able to connect with the numen of the universe in a direct way, the members are not related to the force in the same way. The only way for the members to connect with the life force is through the activities of their group.

Depending on which normative environment is more relevant in a given context, the group stands either above or on an equal footing with its members. Generally speaking, as long as harmonious human relations within a group can be maintained, discretion is allowed to individuals. In this situation, the transcendental logic is dominant.

But once an individual begins asking for much more discretion than the group can allow, or the group starts requiring of individuals much more selfless devotion than they are willing to give, ethical tension arises between the two environments. In most cases, the members are expected to follow the requirements of the group, justified by the group logic. . . .

The assertion or gesture by a group leader to persuade subordinate members to follow, is called *tatemae* (formal rule). *Tatemae* chiefly arises from the need of the group to adapt itself to its external environment. In order to adjust itself, the group asks its members to accept changes necessary for the group's survival. In this moment, the group insists upon *tatemae*. On the other hand, the assertion or gesture by the members to refuse *tatemae*, is called *honne* (real motive). *Honne* mainly comes from a desire to let the subordinates' numen express itself in a free way.

Usually, a serious confrontation between *tatemae* and *honne* is avoided, because both the leader and subordinates dislike face-to-face discussions

189

or antagonistic relations. Stated otherwise, the members (the leader and the subordinates) tend to give great weight to harmonious relations within the group. Because of this, the leader might change his or her expectation toward the subordinates, or the subordinates might refrain from pursuing their direct self-interest. In either case, the final decision maker is unlikely to identify whose assertion was adopted, or who was right in the decision making, since an emphasis on who was correct or right in the group often disturbs its harmony.

Simply described, this ambiguous decision-making is done in the following way. The group lets the subordinates confirm a priority of group-centeredness, and requires their selfless devotion. This requirement is generally accepted without reserve in the group normative environment. But if the subordinate individuals do not really want to follow the group orders, they "make a wry face," "look displeased," "become sulky," or the like, instead of revealing their opinions clearly. These attitudes are fundamentally different from formal decision-making procedures. In this case, taking efficiency and the harmonious relation of the group into consideration, the group "gives up compelling," "relaxes discipline," or "allows *amae*" of the subordinates.

If the failure to follow the norms endangers the survival of the group, the leader repeatedly asks the members to follow the order. In this case, at first, the leader says, "I really understand your feeling," in order to show that he or she truly sympathizes with the members. And then he or she adds, "This is not for the sake of me, but for the sake of our group." Such persuasion tends to be accepted, because almost everybody implicitly believes that the group has its own numen and the group survival will bring benefits to all of them in the long run. . . .

III. Ethics of Concentric Circles—Social Dimension

Due to human bounded cognitive rationality or cultural heritage, Japanese moral agents, whether individuals or corporations, tend to conceptualize the social environment in a centrifugal order similar to a water ring. Although there are many individuals, groups, and organizations which taken together constitute the overall social environment, the Japanese are likely to categorize them into four concentric circles: family, fellows, Japan, and the world. On the basis of this way of thinking, Japanese people and organizations are likely to attribute different ethics or moral practices to each circle. Let us look at the concentric circles of individuals and of corporations respectively.

• • •

1. The Concentric Circles of Corporations

Just as individuals understand their social environment as concentric circles, so groups such as corporations have a similar tendency to characterize their environment. For the sake of simplicity, I shall classify the corporate environment into four circles: quasi-family, fellows, Japan, and the world.

First, corporations have a quasi-family circle. Of course, though corporations do not have any blood relationships, they might still have closely related business partners. For example, parent, sister, or affiliated companies can be those partners. "Vertical *keiretsu*" (Vertically integrated industrial groups like Toyota, Hitachi, or Matsushita groups) might be a typical example of the quasi-family circle. In this circle we find something similar to the parent-child relationship.

The main corporate members (about 20 to 30 companies in each group) of "horizontal *keiretsu*" (industrial groups such as Mitsubishi, Mitsui, Sumitomo, Dai Ichi Kangyo, Fuyo, and Sanwa groups) might be viewed as quasi-family members. Nonetheless, most of the cross-shareholding corporations in the horizontal *keiretsu* should be placed in the second circle, because their relations are less intimate than commonly understood.

In the second circle, each corporation has its own main bank, fellow traders, distant affiliated firms, employees, steady customers, and the like. If the corporation or its executives belong to some outside associations like *Nihon Jidousha Kogyo Kai* (Japanese Auto Manufacturers Association), *Doyukai* (Japan Association of Corporate Executives), *Keidanren* (Japan Federation of Economic Organizations), etc., the other members of such outside associations might constitute part of the second circle of the corporation. And if the corporation is influential enough to affect Japanese politics or administration, the Japanese governmental agencies or ministries, and political parties might constitute part of this circle.

Recognition within the fellow circle requires that there must be a balance between benefits and debts in the long run. On account of this, if a corporation does not offer enough benefits to counterbalance its debts to others in this circle, the corporation will be expelled from the circle, being criticized for neither understanding nor appreciating the benefits given it

191

by others. On the other hand, if the corporation can successfully balance benefits and debts or keep the balance in the black, it will preferentially receive many favorable opportunities from other companies or interest groups. For these reasons, every corporation worries about the balance sheet of benefits and debts in the fellow circle.

This way of recognizing the business context is closely related to original Confucianism, in that Confucianism allows people to treat others in proportion to the intimacy of their relations. Unlike Christianity, Confucianism does not encourage people to love one another equally. It rather inspires people to love or treat others differentially on the grounds that, if people try to treat everybody equally in a social context, they will often face various conflicts among interests. This does not mean that Confucianism asserts that people should deny love to unacquainted people. The main point of this idea is that, although people have to treat all others as human beings, they should love intensely those with whom they are most intimate; those who cannot love this way cannot love strangers either. I can call this "the differential principle" in Confucianism. Influenced or justified by this differential principle, Japanese corporations also classify their business environment in this way.

In the Japan circle, the fellow circle ethic is substantially replaced by "the principle of free competition." Competitors, unrelated corporations, ordinary stockholders, consumers (for ordinary corporations, the Japanese government constitutes part of this circle) and so forth, all fall within this circle. Yet almost all corporations in this circle know well that the long-term reciprocal ethics is extremely important in constructing and maintaining their business relations, because of their similar cultural background. This point makes the third circle different from the world circle.

In the fourth or world circle, corporations positively follow "the principle of free competition," subject to the judicial system, with less worrying about their traditional reputations. Roughly speaking, the behavioral imperatives for corporations turn out to be producing or supplying high quality and low price products, dominating much more market share and using the law to resolve serious contractual problems.

As in the case of the individuals, the world circle is conceived as a relatively chaotic sphere causing corporate attitudes to become contradictory.

192

On the one hand, Japanese corporations tend to exclude foreign counter-parts that do not understand the extant Japanese business practices, hoping to maintain the normative order of its own business community. Notwithstanding these closing attitudes, on the other hand, they yearn after foreign technologies, know-how, products and services which are expected to help corporations to be successful and competitive in the Japanese and world market. In particular, western technologies have long been objects of admiration for Japanese companies. This tendency vividly shows their global attitudes.

2. Dynamics of the Concentric Circles

Now that I have roughly described the static relations among the concentric circles (of individuals and of corporations), I need to show the dynamic relations among these circles, that is to say, how these circles are interrelated. . . . In order to describe these complicated relations in a parsimonious light, I shall limit my discussion to the relations between the members of an "ideal big Japanese corporation" and its business environment. By a "big Japanese corporation," I mean the "idealized very influential organization" in an industry that places priority on the interests of employees, and holds a long-term strategic perspective. By "operation base" in this context, I mean the place where the members can relax, charge their energy, and develop action programs to be applied to the business environment. Whether the corporation can be such a base or not heavily depends on its members' abilities with respect to human relations: their ability to sympathize or understand other members' feelings, their ability to put themselves in the others' position, their ability to internalize other members' expectations toward them, and the like.

It has been said that in Japanese corporations, many people have such abilities. For instance, E. Hamaguchi has called people with these abilities "the contextuals" in contrast with "the individuals."

> An "individual" is not a simple unit or element of a society, but a positive and subjective member. This so-called "individual-centered model of man" is the typical human model of the western society.

> This model, however, is clearly different from the Japanese model. The Japanese human model is a "being between people" or an internalized being in its relations. This can be called "the contextual" in contrast with the individual.[3]

To be sure, these abilities have also positively contributed to the performance of Japanese corporations. The corporations have not rigidly divided work into pieces and distributed them to each employee so as to clarify the responsibilities each has to take. The corporations have rather let employees work together so that the contextual members make up for the deficiencies of one another allowing the quality of products and efficiency of performance to be surprisingly improved.

On the contrary, the business environment as a "battlefield" is reckoned to be a strenuous sphere, where "the law of the jungle" is the dominant ethical principle. In the market, the principle of free competition replaces the ethics expected in an operation base (quasi-family and fellow circles). What is more, this principle of free competition is justified by the transcendental logic, because, as I have described earlier, in the transcendental environment, work is one of the most important "ways" or "paths" to reach something sacred or the ultimate reality. In this way, "the principle of free competition" in the battlefield and "the transcendental logic" are coincidentally combined to encourage people to work hard, an encouragement which results in survival and the development of the corporation.

Wealth, power, market share, competitive advantage, or other results acquired in this business context become important scales to measure the degree of the members' efforts to proceed on the "path" to the ultimate stage. And based on these scales, contributors are praised within the operation base, namely in a corporation, in an industrial group, or in Japan.

For example, the Japanese government, administrative agencies, or ministries have so far endorsed the efforts of corporations under the present *Tenno* system (the Emperor System of Japan). The decoration and the Order of Precedence at the Imperial Court have been given to corporate executives who have contributed to the development of the Japanese economy.

Theoretically speaking, it is very hard to compare the performance of various corporations in different industries of a nation, simply because each industry has its own scale or own philosophy to measure performance. In the case of Japan, however, the annual decoration and attendance at the Imperial Court plays the role of a unitary ranking scale, applied to every industry as well as nonbusiness-related fields. Since the Japanese mass media makes the annual decoration and attendance public, the Japanese people know well who or which corporations are praiseworthy winners.

3. The Group Environment and the Concentric Circles

Now that I have explained both the group normative environment and the concentric circles of corporations, I should make clear the relationship between the group normative environment and the concentric circles. According to the group logic, each group has its own numen and has different social status. For example, even if the R&D unit of corporation A has its own numen, the status of the unit is lower than that of A itself. The status of A is also lower than that of the leading company B in the same industry. The status of B is lower than that of the Japanese government. But if I observe their relations from the viewpoint of concentric circles, these groups can be members of the same fellow circle of corporation C. Namely, the R&D unit of corporation A, company B, and the government can constitute part of the fellow circle of C. Therefore, even if they are in the same fellow circle, it does not mean that all members have equal status in the group normative environment.

For these reasons, reciprocal relations within the fellow circle are varied according to the members' status in the group normative environment. For instance, because, in most cases, the Japanese government is regarded as a powerful agent in the fellow circle of large corporation C, C makes efforts to maintain its good relations with the government and is likely to depend on the government.

The main reason why *gyosei-shido* (administrative guidance) has so far worked well in Japan comes from this dependent trait of the corporation and from the fact that the administrative agencies or ministries have a very important status in the second circle of the large Japanese corporations.

Each Japanese corporation also maintains relations with the business associations such as *Keidanren* and *Doyukai*. Once an authoritative business association declares *tatemae*, the member corporations make efforts to follow the formal rules, even though they might have some doubts about *tatemae*, simply because those associations hold socially or politically higher status in the group normative environment.

IV. Japanese Recognition of the American Business Community

Because Japanese follow the transcendental logic, group logic, and concentric circles' ethics, their way of observing other business societies might appear to be idiosyncratic. And this idiosyncrasy might bring serious misunderstanding to trading partners such as the United States, European industrialized countries, Asian NIEs, and the other developing countries.

Because of this, I would like to clarify how Japanese conceive the American business community: how the American business community is seen in the eyes of the Japanese business people who adopt the two normative logics and the concentric circles' ethics.

1. Job Discrimination and the Transcendental Logic

First, as noted earlier, in the transcendental normative environment, whatever job people take, they are believed to reach the same goal or the same level of human development. Because of this logic, Japanese are unlikely to evaluate others in terms of their "job" (specialty). They would rather evaluate one another in terms of their "attitudes" toward work.

To be concrete, it is not important for Japanese to maintain the principle of the division of labor. Of importance is the process and the result of work. If people cannot attain goals in the existing framework of the division of labor, they are likely to try other alternatives which have not been clearly defined in the existing framework. This kind of positive attitude toward work is highly appreciated in Japan.

On the contrary, a society such as the United States, where jobs are strictly divided, is perceived as not only inefficient but also discriminatory in Japanese eyes. To be sure, this society might hold a belief that the division of labor makes itself efficient or makes it possible for diverse people to utilize their own abilities. The Japanese business community, however, is likely to assume that people's reluctance to help others' work in the same group is based on job discrimination.

In America, in a large retail shop, for instance, often those who sell a heavy consumer product are reluctant to carry it for the customer. They have a specific person, whose job is just to carry goods, do so. If the person is busy with other goods, the salespeople will ask the customer to wait until the person is finished carrying the other goods.

Similarly, those who manage a large shop typically do not clean up the street in front of their shop. They let a janitor do so. Even if they find garbage there, when the janitor has not come yet, they are likely to wait for the janitor. This kind of attitude of salespeople or managers is regarded as inefficient and discriminatory by Japanese.

2. Employees' Interest and the Group Logic

Second, in the group normative environment, the group is believed to hold its own numen and expected to guarantee the members' life. That is to say, a corporation is thought to exist for its employees rather than for its shareholders.

Because of this logic, the Japanese business community ethically questions American general attitudes toward the company where many accept the ideas that 1) a company is owned by its shareholders, 2) executives should lay off the employees whenever the layoff brings benefits to the shareholders, 3) executives should buy other companies and sell part of their own company whenever such a strategy brings benefits to the shareholders, etc.

Of course, even in Japan, shareholders are legal owners of a company so that the shareholders might use their legal power to change the company in a favorable way for themselves. Therefore, many Japanese corporations have invented a legitimate way to exclude the legal rights of shareholders, i.e. "cross-shareholding." This is the practice in which a corporation allows trusted companies to hold its own shares, and in return the corporation holds their shares. By holding shares of one another and refraining from appealing to the shareholders' rights, they make it possible to manage the companies for the sake of the employees.[4] Because this cross-shareholding is based on mutual acceptance, any attempts to break this corporate consortium from the outside, whether Japense or foreigners, are often stymied by the consortium of the member corporations.

For example, in April 1989, Boone Company, controlled by T. Boone Pickens, bought a 20 percent stake in Koito Manufacturing, Japanese auto parts maker. In 1990, Pickens increased it to 25 percent, becoming Koito's largest single shareholder.[5] But because Pickens asked for seats on Koito's board for himself as well as three Boone Company associates, and requested an increase in Koito's annual dividend, he was labeled as a "greenmailer" in the Japanese business community. As a result, the other consortium members cooperatively protected Koito from the Pickens' attack.[6] . . .

In addition, the layoff of employees and the high salaries of American executives are also regarded as unethical by the Japanese business community. . . . In Japan, when executives face serious difficulties, they first reduce their own benefits, then dividends and other costs, and, after that, employees' salary or wage. If the situation is extremely hard to overcome with these measures, they sell assets and only as a last resort do they lay off workers. Even in this case, the executives often find and offer new job opportunities for those who are laid off, taking care of their family's life.

Because of this, Japanese executives criticize the American business climate in which only salaries of executives keep rising, even while they lay off employees (especially in the 1980s). This criticism is also based on the Japanese group normative logic.

3. Claims against the Japanese Market and the Concentric Circles' Ethics

As I have noted above, because of the framework of concentric circles, especially of the ethics of the fellow circle, foreign corporations often face difficulties entering the Japanese market. Although Japanese admit that the market is very hard to enter, a majority of them believe that it is still possible to accomplish entry.

Even if the Japanese market has many business-related practices such as semi-annual gifts, entertainment, cross-shareholding, "triangular relationship" among business, bureaucracy, and the Liberal Democratic Party, the long-term relationship is formed mainly through a series of business transactions.

That is to say, the most important factor in doing business is whether suppliers can respond to the assemblers' requests for quality, cost, the date of delivery, and the like, or on how producers can respond to the retailers' or wholesalers' expectations. . . .

Foreign corporations might claim that because they are located outside Japan, they cannot enter even the Japan circle. On this claim, the Japanese business community is likely to insist that if they understand the "long-term reciprocal ethics," they can enter the Japan circle; and what is more, might be fellows of Japanese influential corporations. As I have described, what makes the Japan circle different from the world circle is that people in the Japan circle know well the importance of this ethics. In fact, successfully enjoying the Japanese market are foreign corporations such as IBM, Johnson & Johnson, McDonald's, Apple, and General Mills which have understood well this ethics.

In this respect, realistically, the Japanese business community interprets the criticism by the American counterpart of the Japanese market as unfair and unethical. To put it differently, Japanese believe that if foreign corporations understand the long-term ethics, they will easily be real members of the Japanese business community.

V. Ethical Issues of the Japanese Business Community

I have shown how Japanese people conceive the American business society and its business-related practices from the viewpoint of the two normative environments and the concentric circles. Yet this does not mean that the Japanese business community has no ethical problems. On the contrary, there are many issues it has to solve. What are the ethical issues of the Japanese business community? . . .

1. Discrimination and the Transcendental Logic

I will shed light on the organizational issues (opening the Japanese organizations) from the prime value of transcendental logic. The prime value here is "everybody has an equal microcosm." Whether men or women, Japanese or foreigners, hard workers or non-hard workers, everybody has to be treated equally as a person. When I observe the organizational phenomena from the viewpoint of this value, there are at least the following two discriminatory issues.

First, the transcendental logic has worked favorably only for male society. That is, in this normative environment, Japanese women have been expected to actualize their potentials through their household tasks. Those tasks have been regarded as their path toward the goal. Of course, insofar as women voluntarily agree with this thinking, there seems to be no ethical problem. And in fact, a majority of women have accepted this way of living to date. Nonetheless, now that an increasing number of women work at companies and hope to get beyond such chores as making tea to more challenging jobs, the Japanese corporations have no longer been allowed to treat women unequally.

Second, the transcendental normative logic itself has often been used to accuse certain workers of laziness. As far as a worker voluntarily strives to fulfill his or her own potential according to the transcendental logic, this presents no ethical problems. Nevertheless, once a person begins to apply the logic to others and evaluate them in terms of their performance, the transcendental logic easily becomes the basis for severe accusations against certain workers.

For example, even if a man really wants to change his job or company, his relatives, colleagues, or acquaintances are unlikely to let him do so, because they unconsciously believe that any job or any company can lead him to the same high stage of human development, if he makes efforts to reach it. Put in a different way, it is believed that despite the differences between the jobs or companies, he can attain the same purpose in either. On account of this, many Japanese say, "once you have decided and started something by yourself, you should not give up until reaching your goal." This is likely to end up justifying a teaching that "enough is as good as a feast."

If the person does not follow this teaching, thereby refusing overtime or transfers, he will jeopardize his promotion and be alienated from his colleagues and bosses, since he is not regarded as a praiseworthy diligent worker. Even if he is making efforts to fulfill his potential in work-unrelated fields, he is not highly appreciated, simply because what he is doing is not related to the company's work.

Analyzing those practices from the viewpoint of the prime value (everybody has equal microcosm), I cannot help concluding that the Japanese business community should alter its organizational climate.

2. Employees' Dependency and the Group Logic

In the group normative environment, groups are regarded as having a higher status than their individual members. Because the members are inclined to take this hierarchical order for granted, they come to be dependent on the groups. And their groups also come to be dependent on the next higher groups. This dependency of the agents, whether of individuals or groups, brings the following two problems into the Japanese business community. Because of the dependent trait, 1) the individual members of the group refrain from expressing their opinions about ethical issues, and 2) they tend to obey the organizational orders, even if they disagree with them. The first tendency is related to decision making, while the second affects policy implementation. . . .

One of the typical examples which shows this tendency of members to waive their basic rights is *karoshi* (death caused by overwork). In 1991, the Japanese Labor Ministry awarded 33 claims for *karoshi*. Since it is very hard to prove a direct and quantifiable link between overwork and death, this number is not large enough to clarify the actual working condition, but is certainly large enough to show that there is a possibility of turning the group logic into unconditional obedience.

This corporate climate not only jeopardizes the employees' right to life, but also hampers the healthy human development of the individual members. Because of this, the Japanese business community has to alter this group-centered climate into a democratic ground on which the individuals can express their opinions more frankly than before.

3. *Exclusiveness of the Concentric Circles*

The Japanese conceptualization of the social environment in a centrifugal framework is closely connected with Confucianism (the differential principle): It allows people to treat others in proportion to the intimacy of their relationships. As I touched upon before, however, the main point of this principle is not that people should deny love to strangers, but rather that those who cannot love their most intimate relatives intensely are surely incapable of loving strangers. Stated otherwise, even if the way to achieve a goal is to love differentially, the goal itself is to love everybody. Therefore, "to love everybody" should be regarded as the prime value of the concentric circles' ethics.

If I look at the Japanese market (opening the Japanese market) from the viewpoint of this prime value, there appear to be at least the following two issues. 1) The Japanese business community has to make an effort to help foreigners understand the concept of long-term reciprocal ethics. This effort will bring moral agents of the world circle into the Japan circle. 2) The Japanese community has to give business opportunities to as many newcomers as possible. This effort will bring the newcomers into the fellow circles.

The first issue is how to transfer foreign corporations from the world circle to the Japan circle. . . . This "fairness" implies that they treat foreign companies the same as they treat other Japanese firms. To put it differently, the concept of "fairness" encourages the Japanese corporations to apply the same ethical standard to all companies.

Although this is a very important point of "fairness," there is a more crucial problem involved in opening the market. That is how to let newcomers know what the rules are and how the Japanese business community applies the rules. As mentioned before, for the purpose of constructing and maintaining business relationships with a Japanese company (a core company), a foreign firm has to be a fellow of the company. In this fellow circle, every fellow makes efforts to balance benefits and debts with the core company in material and spiritual terms in the long run, since making a long-term balance is the most important ethics. Yet balancing them is too complicated to be attained for the foreign corporation, as long as benefits and debts are rather subjective concepts.

For example, in Japan, if company A trusts the executive of company B and helps B, when B is in the midst of serious financial difficulties then B will give the most preferential trade status to A after overcoming its difficulties. B will rarely change this policy, even if B finishes repaying its monetary debts to A. Moreover, even if A's products are relatively expensive, as long as the price is not extraordinarily unreasonable, B will continue to purchase A's output. If A's products are not sophisticated enough to meet B's standard, B will often help A to improve A's products in various ways.

If A's help is understood only as financial aid, this close relationship between A and B will not appear reasonable. In Japan, in most cases, B is deeply impressed by the fact that A has trusted B (even if B is in serious difficulties) so that B continues to repay its spiritual debts to A as long as possible. Yet if B were to change this policy soon after repaying the borrowed capital to A, and if it began buying the same but cheaper products from company C, not only A but also other corporations which have been aware of this process from the beginning will regard B as an untrustworthy company in their business community.

"Fairness" in a Japanese sense might involve asking foreign companies to follow the former way of doing business. Nonetheless, foreign companies, especially Americans, do not understand "fairness" this way. Their understanding is rather similar to the latter behavior of B: switching from

A to C. This difference of understanding "fairness" between Americans and Japanese undoubtedly causes a series of accusations against each other.

The Japanese business community should not let this happen over and over again. If the community takes the prime value seriously, as the first duty, it has to explain the long-term reciprocal ethics to foreign counterparts in an understandable way. This effort will help the foreigners enter the Japan circle.

But even if they can enter the Japan circle successfully, there still remains another problem. That is how those foreigners, which have been already in the Japan circle, enter the fellow circles of influential Japanese corporations. This is related to the second issue of opening the Japanese market.

Even when foreign companies understand and adopt long-term reciprocal ethics, they might not be able to enter those fellow circles, if they rarely have the chance to show their competitive products or services to the influential corporations. On account of this, as an ethical responsibility, the Japanese corporations should have "access channels" through which every newcomer can equally approach.

To be sure, the "mutual trust" found in the fellow circle should not be blamed for everything. But if the trust-based business relation is tightly combined among a few influential corporations, it tends to exclude newcomers. As long as such a relation is not against the Japanese Antimonopoly Law, it is safe to say that efforts to maintain the relationship are not problematic, because most of the corporations do so according to their free will. Despite that, if I look at the exclusive tendency of a fellow circle like that of the Japanese distribution system, I cannot help saying that the trust-based relation is a critical obstacle for newcomers.

If the Japanese business community follows the prime value (to love everybody) of the concentric circles' ethics, it has to make an effort to remove the obstacles to entry. One of the ideal ways to do so is to give newcomers more competitive bids than before. Of course, it is not obligatory for Japanese corporations to accept every bidder as a fellow after the tender. If a bidder is not qualified as an ideal business partner in terms of its products or services, Japanese corporations do not need to start transactions with the bidder. But as a minimum ethical requirement, Japanese corporations should have access channels through which every newcomer can equally approach them. . . .

Notes

1. M. Imai, *Kaizen* (New York: McGraw-Hill Publishing Company, 1986), p. 34.

2. Kyogoku, *Nihon no Seiji* (Politics of Japan) (Tokyo: Tokyo University Press, 1983) pp. 182–83.

3. E. Hamaguchi, *"Nihon Rashisa" no Saihakken (Rediscovery of Japaneseness)* (Tokyo: Kodansha, 1988), pp. 66–67.

4. This practice was basically formed for a purpose of defending Japanese industries from foreign threats. But at the same time, Japanese people thought this threat might destroy the employee-centered management. T. Tsuruta, *Sengo Nihon no Sangyo Seisaku (Industrial Policies of Post-War Japan)* (Tokyo: Nihon Keizai Shinbunsha, 1982), pp. 121–30.

5. W. C. Kester, *Japanese Takeovers: The Global Contest for Corporate Control* (Cambridge: Harvard Business School Press, 1991), pp. 258–59.

6. *Mainichi Daily News* (May 15, 1990).

Part III

Practical Applications of Business Ethics

Part III: Practical Applications of Business Ethics

Neither custom and tradition nor law is sufficient to ensure good business ethics. Analysis of ethical problems and sound moral reasoning based on theoretical principles is a requirement and prerequisite for good decision making. But, corporate leaders and managers live and work in the practical realm and must deal with the concrete realities and situations of daily life. Because of this practical reality they seek direction and guidance for handling ethical dilemmas. This section on applied ethics offers both character-based and theory-based practical applications for business leaders and managers. It also discusses ways to structure an ethical workplace and to teach ethical decision making.

In "How Ethics Can Improve Business Success," Dean L. Bottorff tells us that ethical challenges will be one of the determining factors of business survival and prosperity in the twenty-first century. Here is what he says about the ethical imperative for business:

> The ethical challenge facing companies today is real and substantial; Unethical conduct is believed to be prevalent at all levels of employment and is perpetuated by managerial counter-norms and dysfunctional corporate cultures. Unethical behavior has been identified as a leading cause of operational inefficiency and poor quality by management experts and subsequently is viewed as a crisis in the West that is undermining competitive strength. Effective management of ethical issues requires that organizations develop internal assurances that their top executives, managers, and employees are prepared and encouraged to deal appropriately with ethical problems in their everyday work lives.

Bottorff offers a short ethics primer and traces the underlying root causes for unethical behavior. Next, he suggests ways by which corporations can appraise and prevent unethical behavior and, at the same time, promote ethical behavior. Finally, Bottorff demonstrates how the ethical challenges are inextricably woven together with other twenty-first century challenges, such as increased quality, employee motivation and management of diverse workforces to name a few. In a world of dynamic change ethics can be used to improve the quality of decisions made throughout a business organization. Corporations that face the ethical challenges squarely will be in the position that the philosopher Plato described over two millennia ago: "To manage in the world that changes . . . from the world that does not."

"Why Are Bad Things Done by Good People?" asks David Stewart. In other words, why do people who care for their children, are kind to coworkers and animals, contribute to charities, etc. act unethically in corporate settings? Stewart offers an existential analysis of this problem that centers on patterns of thought and action that the philosopher Sartre termed "bad faith." Bad faith is a vicious form of self-deception. The traps of self-deception relate directly to a person's lack of self-knowledge. Self-knowledge is the key to avoiding self-deception and is central to living with integrity. Stewart shows how bad faith leads to rationalization and inaction. In addition to bad faith, Stewart holds that abstraction and depersonalization complicate modern corporate lives, blunt our ethical sensitivity, and diminish the value of personal responsibility.

Patrick E. Murphy asks, what is an ethical company? Ongoing reflective thinking about this question will help us envision the kind of moral enterprise we wish to create. How can an ethical corporate culture be created and sustained? What structural approaches encourage ethical decision making? Murphy looks at three workplace approaches to creating ethical corporate structures: corporate credos, corporate ethics programs, and ethical codes. Although there is no single ideal approach to the problems of corporate ethics those managers who have been involved in the approaches that Murphy describes believe that ethics pays off.

Stephen Covey indicates that our current value system is based solely on skill and personality. Behaviors that issue from these values are, on one extreme, harmless and, at the other extreme, manipulative. Business people have been trained in charm, skill, and technique. These values are largely superficial, productive of immediate gain, but essentially void of meaning. One who embraces these values lives life on the surface.

For Covey, character counts. According to Covey:

> Character is made up of those principles and values that give your life direction, meaning and depth. These constitute your inner sense of what's right and wrong based not on laws or rules of conduct but on who you are. They include such traits as integrity, honesty, courage, fairness and generosity—which arise from hard choices we have to make in life.

Covey maintains that character building is the foundation for an ethics of total integrity.

At this point, the reader may detect a pattern in the structure of Part III. Let me make the structure of this final section explicit: First, we considered the "real and substantial" ethical challenges faced by twenty-first century corporations. Next, we looked at the root sources and attitudes that are the underlying causes of unethical behavior and considered ways by which unethical behavior can be prevented and ethical behavior may be promoted. Part of the solution to the ethical challenges facing business is structural. We looked at ways to structure and re-structure corporate culture and discussed how to create corporate ethical structures. But, clearly, external structures alone are not sufficient to insure good business ethics. Character counts! A character-based approach to ethics is the foundation for corporate morality. But, here in Part III, we complement the character-based approach to ethics with a principle-based approach. Principles are essential for moral reasoning, and ethical decision making. Archie B. Carroll presents a model for ethical decision making based on sound ethical principles.

Michael Josephson takes the corporate ethical enterprise one step further by proposing the ongoing teaching of ethical decision making and principled reasoning. In "Teaching Ethical Decision Making and Principled Reasoning," Josephson advocates ongoing ethics education and presents a theory of ethics education. He describes a framework for analyzing ethical problems that can be taught in professional courses and ethical decision making workshops.

Finally, a comprehensive framework of the world's wisdom offers a global context and perspective for assessing international issues in corporate ethics. In "Wisdom from the World's Religions," Dennis P. McCann argues that this wisdom may be gleaned from the world's religions. McCann states:

> The historic move toward a single, globally integrated, market economy provides a new context in which to ask perennial questions about the role of moral and, especially, religious values in business and economic development. Among these questions, the most timely and yet neglected, at least within conventional thinking on business and economics, is this: What role should the world's major religious traditions play in promoting corporate social responsibilities?

McCann looks at the ethics of major traditions from Protestantism in the West to Hinduism and Confucianism in Asia. Since there are serious difficulties involved in resolving international ethical issues within the limitations of a single cultural perspective, McCann's essay will help open up expanded possibilities for alternative responses to important issues of human concern.

How Ethics Can Improve Business Success

Dean L. Bottorff

The survival and prosperity of business organizations into the 21st century will be determined by how well companies face six challenges: international competition, new technologies, increased quality, employee motivation, management of diverse work forces, and ethical behavior. While these topics have been addressed individually throughout the professional literature, little attention is given to how these issues are interrelated. The fact that these issues are not mutually exclusive, and the proposition that quality is heavily dependent on ethical behavior, needs to be addressed in depth if the quality movement and American business organizations are to realize their true potential in the emerging world economy.

This article focuses on:

- The ethical imperative faced and why it is important to business organizations
- The definition of ethics, its historical importance, and its current relevance to managers
- The root causes of unethical behavior and the underlying ethical theories at work
- Suggestions for appraising and preventing unethical behavior and for promoting ethical behavior
- The interrelationship between a company's ethical behavior, quality, and the other four challenges already described
- How to use ethics to improve the quality of decisions throughout a business organization

The Ethical Imperative

The ethical challenge facing companies today is real and substantial; Unethical conduct is believed to be prevalent at all levels of employment and is perpetuated by managerial counter-norms and dysfunctional corporate cultures.[1][2][3][4] Unethical behavior has been identified as a leading cause of operational inefficiency and poor quality by management experts and subsequently is viewed as a crisis in the West that is under-mining competitive strength.[5][6][7] Effective management of ethical issues requires that organizations develop internal assurances that their top executives, managers, and employees are prepared and encouraged to deal appropriately with ethical problems in their everyday work lives.

An Ethics Primer

Ethics is a body of principles or standards of human conduct that govern the behavior of individuals and groups. Ethics is a branch of philosophy and is considered a normative science because it is concerned with the norms of human conduct, as distinguished from formal sciences (such as mathematics and logic) and empirical sciences (such as chemistry and physics). The study of ethics has been at the heart of intellectual thought since the earliest writings by the ancient Greeks, and its ongoing contri-bution to the advancement of knowledge and science continues to make ethics a relevant, if not vital, aspect of management theory.

Throughout the 20th century, the traditional view of ethics has been the following: Either you learned ethics at home when you were growing up, or it is too late. A contrary view, representing a confluence of ancient and modern thought, is emerging to say that ethics can be learned by just about everybody. Plato wrote that ethical virtue was a knowledge that could be learned.[8] He further argued that to know good was to do good, and that one who behaves immorally does so largely out of ignorance. Recent studies have revealed much to the business world on the topic of ethics that agrees more with Plato than with the prevailing 20th-century view. A survey conducted by the marketing profession, reported in a sales management text, found these views on ethics prominent among managers.[9]

- Most managers believe they face ethical problems.
- Most managers believe they and their employees should be more ethical.
- Managers are more ethical with their friends than with acquaintanc-es and strangers.
- Some managers lower their ethical standards to meet job require-ments.
- Most managers are aware of unethical practices in their companies and in their industries.

- Business ethics can be influenced by management and by the company environment.

Roots of Unethical Behavior

Much of the unethical behavior observed in companies can be traced to seven attitudinal categories (along with their underlying ethical theories) that predispose employees and managers to unethical behavior.

1. When companies favor their own interests over the well-being of their customers, employees, or the public (egoism: I am more important than you are. Darwinism: Might makes right. Machiavellianism: Apply different standards for business and personal lives.)
2. When companies reward behaviors that violate ethical standards, such as increasing sales through false advertising and reducing hazardous-waste disposal costs by discharging or dumping illegally (egoism, Darwinism, Machiavellianism)
3. When counter-norms encourage separate standards of behavior at work than at home, such as secrecy and deceit vs. honesty, do whatever it takes vs. follow the rules, use it or lose it vs. being cost-effective, passing the buck vs. taking responsibility, and grandstanding vs. being a team player (Machiavellianism)
4. When individuals are willing to abuse their positions and power to enhance their individual interests, such as taking excessive compensation for themselves off of the top before other stakeholders can receive their fair share of the profits (egoism, Darwinism)
5. When managerial values exist that undermine integrity (egoism and Darwinism)

    - Bottom-line mentality (at others' expense or suboptimization)
    - Exploitive mentality (using people by labeling them or stereotyping them to promote oneself at their expense)
    - Madison Avenue mentality (anything is right if the public can be convinced it is right)
    - Public-relations mentality (being more concerned about appearing ethical than being ethical)

6. When companies and individuals overemphasize short-term gains at the expense of themselves and others in the long run (Bentham's Hedonistic Bad Calculus: rationalizing that a behavior is acceptable strictly by the degree of utility, pleasure, or good received, regardless

of the bad utility inflicted on others). Examples include common rationalizations such as pretending a behavior is not really unethical, excusing the behavior as being in everyone's best interests when it actually is not, assuming the behavior is acceptable because nobody will ever find out, and expecting your superiors to support you if anything should go wrong.

7. When companies and managers believe their knowlege is infallible and thus miscalculate the true risks and subject themselves and others to excessive risks. (Socrates' Nature of Knowledge: Real absolute knowledge is unattainable. The only real absolute knowledge is knowing that one does not really know anything absolutely.)[10] Some examples of unethical applications of this theory are when financial managers invest company funds in high-risk options trading, and when senior executives risk the future of their organizations by not recognizing the need for quality improvement, contingency planning, and long-term planning.

Predisposition toward unethical behavior is believed to arise from the interaction of three root causes: pressure, opportunity, and attitudes.[11] Therefore, the primary objective of an unethical management program should be to address each of these causes in policies and work processes at every level of the company. Similar to managing quality, managing ethical behavior requires the commitment of top management; new policies and processes; continuous improvement; and investments in appraisal, prevention, and promotion.

Ethics Management Model

The following is an example of a management model that any organization can use to improve its ethical behavior.

Step 1: Appraisal. Ethics costing should be performed to measure the cost of poor ethics in the organization.[12] Costs related to the three root causes should be collected and recorded for periodic review. Any costs that arise from ethically questionable decisions should be included and assigned to one or more of the three main causes. Some of these costs could include:

Costs from pressure: Errors, waste, rework, safety-related failure, employee turnover, lost customers, warranties, or any failure cost that occurs because of well-intentioned but ethically poor decisions made under pressure.

Costs from opportunity: Losses from theft, overstated expenses, excessive compensations, lost productivity, or any kind of failure that resulted from deliberate wrongdoing.

Costs from attitudes: Errors, waste, rework, health care, employee turnover, lost customers, warranties, or any failure that resulted from mistaken beliefs in unethical forms of behavior.

Step 2: Prevention. A system of policies and processes need to be matched to each cause for the purpose of prevention.

Causes found to be of greater significance in the appraisal process need to be emphasized in this step. Some examples of prevention matching are:

To address pressure:

- Require that goal setting with employees be realistic. Give employees access to an objective internal process when they find goals or requirements to be unrealistic.
- Require employees' input when company goals and values are chosen so they will share in ownership.
- Require policies to allow for individual diversity, dissent, and the general prevention of excessive group dominance over individuals in decision making.

To address opportunity:

- Require policies that encourage and protect whistleblowers.
- Require the existence of chaplains or ombudsmen who can work confidentially with employees to solve ethical problems internally.

To address attitudes:

- Require that regular ethics training be provided for all employees to develop higher ethical reasoning skills. Develop and reward internal trainers. Recognize ever-increasing training levels and ethical conduct in the workplace.
- Require that performance appraisals take ethical behavior into consideration.
- Encourage open discussion among employees regarding ethical behavior issues.

Step 3: Promotion of good ethical behavior. Perhaps the best prevention effort of all is to continuously promote ethical behavior by developing a climate, culture, or philosophy within which the company can operate ethically. The organization's ethical climate needs to be clear, positive, and set by the top leadership of the company. All company policies and processes should meet each of these standards.

To be clear, the company's ethical philosophy needs to be spelled out and posted.[13] Standardized ethics training should be required of all employees:

- To teach them how to clarify ethical issues
- To encourage them to get all the possible facts before acting
- To encourage them to consider all options before acting
- To show them how to test each action in advance. An action can be tested by asking the following:
- Is it legal? (law-based ethics)
- Is it right? (deontology, or duty-based ethics)
- Is it beneficial for all involved? (utilitarianism)
- How would I feel if my family and the public found out about it? (utilitarianism litmus test detailed calculus)

To be positive, the culture should be about doing what is right, encouraging principled organizational dissent, and rewarding ethical behavior.[14]

To have leadership, the philosophy must be set and adopted at the top of the company.[15] The chief executive officer and all of the managers should act the way they would have others act and make no exceptions for themselves (Kant's categorical imperative: similar to the golden rule).[16]

By addressing root causes of unethical behavior through a program of appraisal, prevention, and promotion, companies can create a superior culture from which they can successfully compete. The challenge of ethical behavior may be listed last among the six business challenges cited, but it is certainly not the least in importance by any means. While the relative importance of each challenge may vary from industry to industry and from time to time, none is entirely unrelated to the others, and some are highly interrelated. Ethical behavior may well be the most interrelated of them all. Ethical behavior is the only one of the six primary business challenges that can create a successful corporate culture. Because an abundance of management research has linked corporate culture to success with each of the six challenges, a significant economic dividend is likely to transfer to any business that learns how to effectively manage ethical behavior.

Quality Depends on Ethical Behavior

Quality not only benefits from ethical behavior, it is dependent on it. The underlying philosophical foundation of quality is one of advancing quality through the advancement of ethical behavior. The concepts of internal and external customers, process improvement, meeting all customer requirements, doing what's best for all customers, and doing it right the first time are new applications of utilitarianism that are significant ethical advancements over egoism, Darwinism, and Machiavellianism. Doing what is right in the first place and doing what is best for all involved, when done at every level of the organization and in every work process, has proven to be the most efficient way of conducting business.

Quality's alleged failure to deliver its promised benefits is more the result of management's lack of understanding of the philosophical relationship between quality and ethics than any shortcoming of quality. Quality does not derive its power from its ability to reduce costs, improve competitiveness, and create customer satisfaction, as many would believe. The field is full of companies that pursued quality for these reasons only to find their pursuit of quality to be unrewarding. Quality obtains its power to reduce costs, improve competitiveness, and create customer satisfaction from its ability to improve ethical behavior within its management processes. It is for this reason that the advancement of quality as a leading management theory will be heavily influenced by the degree to which it can focus upon and improve ethical behavior in organizations.

Companies, managers, and employees will continue to face many challenges in the years ahead. Even the sharpest managers will frequently find it difficult to know what decisions to make.[17] Business issues can become complicated very quickly, and native intelligence alone may not always be sufficient to guide companies in the right directions. In these challenging times, the quality of everyday activities can be improved by relying more on those things that do not change (such as forms of philosophical ethics) than on our senses, selfish interests, and perceptions which can and will deceive us into making bad business decisions.[18]

A Needed Foundation

In a world that is increasingly characterized by rapid changes in competition, technology, consumer demands, and business relationships, companies more than ever need to anchor themselves to a foundation from which they may face these challenges from a position of confidence and strength. By placing needed emphasis on ethical behavior, companies will be in a position to do what Plato advised more than 2,400 years ago:

> To manage in the world that changes . . . from the world that does not.[19]

Notes

1. S. Silverstein, "One in 15 employees in Study Caught Stealing," *Los Angeles Times*, Dec. 2, 1989, p. D-1.

2. Fred R. David, *Strategic Management*, Second Edition (Columbus, OH: Merrill Publishing Co., 1989), p.8.

3. Robert Corley, O. Lee Reed, and Peter Shedd, *The Legal and Regulatory Environment of Business*, Ninth Edition (New York, NY: McGraw-Hill, 1996), pp. 369–394.

4. S. W. Gellerman, "Why Good Managers Make Bad Ethical Choices," *Harvard Business Review*, July–August 1986, pp. 85–90.

5. J. M. Juran and Frank M. Gryna, *Juran's Quality Handbook*, Fourth Edition (New York, NY: McGraw Hill, 1988), pp. 10–18.

6. Ronald R. Sims, "The Challenge of Ethical Behavior in Organizations," *Journal of Business Ethics*, July 1992, pp. 209–213.

7. Donald Zanderer, "Integrity, an Essential Executive Quality," in *Business Ethics 95/96 Annual Editions*, Seventh Edition, John E. Richardson, editor (Guilford, CT: Dushkin Publishing Group, 1996).

8. Jeremy Bentham, "Utility, Pleasure, and the Good," Immanuel Kant: "Learning Moral Rules," and Plato: "The Citizen and the Law," in *Philosophy For a New Generation*, Second Edition, A. K. Bierman and J. A. Gould, editors (New York, NY: MacMillan, 1973), pp. 115–117, 133–137, 319–326.

9. Charles Futrell, *Sales Management*, Third Edition (Fort Worth, TX: Dryden Press, 1994), pp. 581–600.

10. L. F. Stone, "The Trial of Socrates" (Boston, MA: Little Brown & Co., 1988), pp. 39–52.

11. Sims, "The Challenge of Ethical Behavior in Organizations."

12. Jack Campanella and the ASQC Quality Cost of Committee, *Principles of Quality Costs*, Second Edition (Milwaukee, WI: ASQC Quality Press, 1990), pp. 5–17.

13. Taken from the following codes of ethics: ASQC, American Marketing Association, Manufacturer's Agents National Association and Institute of Management Accountants.

14. Comments from A. Mistro, ethics instructor, Robert Morris College, Pittsburgh, PA.

15. Mary Scott and Howard Rotham, *Companies With a Conscience* (New York, NY: Citadel Press, 1994), p. 6.

16. Bierman and Gould, *Philosophy For a New Generation*.

17. Comments from A. Mistro, ethics instructor.

18. Funk & Wagnalls Corp., "Ethics," and "Plato, Theory of Forms, Theory of Ethics," Microsoft Encarta CD-ROM, 1994.

19. Ibid.

Why Bad Things Are Done by Good People

David Stewart

When we open the newspaper and read about a Wall Street dealer who trades on inside information, a milk company executive who rigs a bid, an accountant who falsifies a balance sheet, an operating engineer who approves a faulty product design, we immediately ask ourselves what kind of person would do something like that. If we were to ask these persons about their ethics, their answer would most probably be that they consider themselves ethical, and the chances are high that their associates would agree with them. Most persons who act unethically in a corporate setting care for their children, are kind to their coworkers, contribute to local charities, and don't kick their dogs or cheat on their golf scores. Why do otherwise good people behave unethically in their business affairs or, as the title of this chapter asks, why are bad things done by good people?

BAD BEHAVIOR AND SELF-UNDERSTANDING

Before proceeding, it is important to acknowledge the inherent difficulty in using the term "good" in the context we have set for it here. The ancient Greek philosopher Plato devoted considerable effort to analyzing what the term "good" means, and what at first might seem to be a somewhat easy inquiry is soon revealed to be a major philosophical mystery. Pursuit of the good is the ultimate challenge for all philosophy, according to Plato, and the idea of Good defies complete understanding (hence the use of the capital G to name it). The Good is to knowing what the sun is to seeing, according to one of Plato's more powerful metaphors, and catching a glimpse of the Good is almost akin to a mystical experience. Plato's student Aristotle also considered the concept of the good a pivotal issue for philosophy, but in his own somewhat more worldly approach, Aristotle pointed out that there are many goods, each appropriate to the particular thing on which it is predicated. For human beings, as we saw in Chapter 2, goodness consists in the exercise of our rational faculties and the development of that which is most human in our nature. The good life, by extension, is that manner of life that leads to the achievement of well-being, and well-being or the good life has many facets. There is, however, no sense in which individuals can be said to be living a good life if in some areas they seek to be good but in other areas abandon that quest. It is in the Aristotelian sense that we are using the term "good" here. A good person is one who seeks goodness in all areas of life, and this for Aristotle means a life ruled by reason and guided by moderation.

An Existentialist Analysis

To understand such conduct better, we turn to a philosopher from the twentieth century, Jean-Paul Sartre. One of a group of philosophers loosely grouped as existentialists, Sartre emphasizes the total freedom of the individual. Coupled with such total freedom is total responsibility. In especially vivid language, Sartre says that human beings are "condemned to be free." Most of us experience such freedom, he thought, as a terrible burden, and we devise numerous ways to escape from it. We play roles. We submerge ourselves in a larger group. We put responsibility—and blame—onto someone else; we say "they" made me do it. We treat ourselves as impersonal entities who are merely being swept along by forces over which we have no control.

Sartre refuses to tolerate any of these excuses. He was one of the few thinkers of his era gladly to accept the label of existentialist, and for him *existence* is the particular property of human beings. Things—rocks, trees, manufactured objects—just *are*. They are the sum total of their essential nature and will never be more than this essence. But human

---

A Case in Point . . .

The former number two person at the Pentagon, Paul Thayer, was sentenced to four years in prison and fined $5,000 for lying to the Securities and Exchange Commission in an insider-trading case. He also agreed to pay a $550,000 fine to the SEC to settle a civil suit. The Anheuser-Busch Company, for which he served as director, sued him for giving inside information to friends about the company's plans to acquire a Dallas Company, Campbell Taggart, Inc. The suit alleged that Anheuser-Busch paid $80 million more for Campbell Taggart stock than it should have due to Thayer's activities. At his sentencing, Thayer told the judge, "It is an understatement to say I am sorry and very remorseful for violating the law. I have destroyed a life of achievement. The last two years have been a living nightmare. I don't like myself as much as I used to."

Sources: Chicago Tribune, Apr. 28, 1985, May 9, 1985; FOR, June 10, 1985; FORB Aug. 10, 1987.

beings *exist*. Although in English the terms "to be" and "to exist" do not seem to be widely different, Sartre, following the German philosopher Martin Heidegger, takes the meaning of the term "exist" from its Greek roots, which emphasize the open-endedness of human life. To be human means to be open to possibilities, and—here is the important point—*we choose which of these possibilities we will be*. But, you might say, I do not choose everything. I did not choose to be born, for example. Even here Sartre does not let you off the hook. Your being in the world as an existing individual is a fact with which you have to come to terms. "I am ashamed of being born or I am astonished at it or I rejoice over it, or in attempting to get rid of my life I affirm that I live and I assume this life is bad. Thus in a certain sense I *choose* being born."[1]

Now all this may strike you as merely a lot of wordplay, simply a clever way of talking. But the important point Sartre is insisting on is the total freedom of the individual. To be human is to exist in a field of open possibilities, and we are free to choose among these possibilities. To attempt to get rid of the burden of this freedom by passing responsibility on to someone else (we really can't do this, Sartre argues, but we try anyway) he calls *bad faith*. It is a kind of lying, not to someone else but to ourselves. And here is what makes bad faith so intriguing: the one doing the lying and the one lied to are *one and the same*. If you think about it for a moment, you'll realize that self-deception or bad faith, or whatever you choose to call it, is quite a feat. We know we are lying, but we convince ourselves that we are not.

The threat of bad faith is everywhere. Some instances of bad faith are significant, and some are trivial. An example Sartre gives is taking on a role or playing a part. Sartre's description of this example in the extract reprinted in this chapter is that of a waiter playing a role so completely that his own individuality is subsumed in that of being a waiter. By playing roles, people retreat from freedom. They do not have to confront the morality of their choices if they believe that their actions are forced on them by forces or persons outside of their control. "It's only business," can be one excuse that we use to deflect responsibility away from ourselves and onto others, to the "game" of business, or to expected patterns of behavior that we feel we cannot control. Sartre's response to this is that we are always in control. When we do something that we feel is expected of us but that we know is wrong, we try to escape responsibility by blaming others. This, however, is simply another instance of bad faith.

Patterns of Bad Faith

The opposite of bad faith is good faith, and although Sartre promises many times in his writings to do a comparable analysis of good faith, he never got around to it.[2] The notion of bad faith stands as a warning to us not to retreat from responsibility by patterns of self-deception, for that is what bad faith is. The major task of a course in business ethics should be to make us aware of what these patterns are by looking at behavior in which they emerge. Just as Sartre's example of the waiter shows us patterned behavior that removed the waiter from full awareness of his actions, it is easy to be led into patterns of behavior by slogans that we use to deceive ourselves. Whenever these or similar phrases are being thrown about, you may be encountering examples of bad faith. It is possible that your associates are attempting to excuse their behavior by retreating to patterned behavior. The list of rationalizing slogans given here is not complete—it could be extended by many other examples—but it is sufficient to alert us to the dangers of such ways of thinking.

1 Nobody is going to be hurt. This is perhaps one of the most widely used of all rationalizations. Time and time again persons whose activities are illegal use it to justify themselves. This rationale was appealed to by a person found guilty of misusing stocks placed in his care. His justification was that the money he was going to make would

---

SARTRE ON BAD FAITH

Let us consider this waiter in the cafe. His movement is quick and forward, a little too precise, a little too rapid. He comes toward the patrons with a step a little too quick. He bends forward a little too eagerly; his voice, his eyes express an interest a little too solicitous for the order of the customer. Finally there he returns, trying to imitate in his walk the inflexible stiffness of some kind of automaton while carrying his tray with the recklessness of a tight-rope walker by putting it in a perpetually unstable, perpetually broken equilibrium which he perpetually reestablishes by a light movement of the arm and hand. All his behavior seems to us a game. He applies himself to chaining his movements as if they were mechanisms, the one regulating the other; his gestures and even his voice seem to be mechanisms; he gives himself the quickness and pitiless rapidity of things. He is playing, he is amusing himself. But what is he playing? We need not watch long before we can explain it: he is playing at being a waiter in a cafe.

Source: Jean-Paul Sartre, *Being and Nothingness* (New York: Philosophical Library, 1956), p. 59.

---

benefit those who owned the stocks as well as himself. This, of course, would happen if all went as planned. If the financial scheme for which the stocks were being used went awry, then many people would have been hurt, some disastrously.[3]

2 **We were just trying to keep the industry healthy.** This justification was used by an electric company executive whose firm was implicated in price-fixing activities. The company was one of four dominating the heavy equipment market. The executive was echoing management's concern that, without some kind of agreement among the companies, they would all be ruined by "cutthroat competition."[4] If one accepts the free market, with all its imperfections, as the fairest known way of distributing a society's goods and services, then attempts to manipulate that market unfairly are unethical, no matter how noble the purpose. The executive in question admitted that such rationalizations were attempts to salve his conscience. Another rationalization used to justify price-fixing was, "We were just trying to make a decent return on our stockholders' investment."

3 **This is the way this street (or this business, or this industry) works.** This rationalization came from a person implicated in an insider-trading deal. Like all patterns of bad faith, this one is partially true. The knowledge of business and industry trends is a stock trader's strength, and there is often a fine line between knowledge that is publicly available and that which is limited to a few insiders. Securities trading laws prohibit trading on knowledge that is not publicly available, for such activities would undercut public confidence in the market. The long-term effect of loss of confidence in the market would be harmful to all interests, so using good utilitarian justification, laws are written to prohibit insiders from taking advantage. The laws prohibiting such activities are not precise, again to encourage caution on the part of traders. Clearly, crossing the line, however, is both illegal and unethical; thus a pattern of bad faith like the one described was necessary for the trader to convince himself that his activity was acceptable. There are other variations on this, such as "If you don't think this is common practice, you aren't in the real world."

4 **If I don't do this, somebody else will.** This slogan has taken on something of the status of a classic. Not only does it enable the person contemplating the action to shift responsibility onto someone else, it is also a way of refusing to face the moral dimensions of the action. If an action is truly unethical, it does not matter whether someone else will do it or not. A good way of spotting a fallacious mode of reasoning is to apply the same pattern of thought to a known case of immoral

behavior. Who would say any of the following? "If I don't commit this murder, someone else will." "If I don't rob this store, someone else will."

5 Nobody will ever find out. This one should really be a bell ringer. Whenever you hear this, run for cover immediately. As we saw in Chapter 4, one of Kant's tests for the morality of a principle of action is whether or not it could be made a universal law. Universalizing a principle implies that it become common practice. If it could not— either because universalizing the behavior would be self-contradictory or would find us willing to do different things, depending on which side of the issue we are on—then the action cannot be an ethical one. By saying that our behavior will remain secret, we are admitting that the practice could not become a universalized pattern for action, a dead giveaway of the inherent unethical nature of the contemplated conduct. A less formal test of whether an action is or is not moral would be to ask yourself how it would look reported on the front page of the local newspaper.

6 The prices were fair; we didn't gouge anyone. Said by someone accused of rigging bids to inflate prices artificially, the justification offered was a classic example of the fallacy known as begging the question. Begging the question occurs whenever a person assumes what the argument attempts to prove. The person setting up this defense assumed that the price was fair even though the market had not determined that it was. In a market economy, a fair price is the price a free market establishes. Manipulating the market in order to achieve a different price from what the free market would have generated cannot therefore determine a fair price. The individual in this case presumed to know what a fair price was and then offered the product to the marketplace at that price.

7 In other countries this practice would not be illegal. To repeat a point made earlier, these patterns of bad faith would not work if they were totally untrue. It is entirely true that laws differ from country to country. Some of these differences reflect dissimilar cultural patterns. Other differences may be due to the fact that the country in question has not made certain kinds of unethical behavior illegal. Just because a country's laws do not prohibit a given activity is no guarantee at all that the behavior is ethically acceptable. If a business practice is illegal in a given country, the presumption is that it is unethical to engage in that activity. There is, of course, justification for civil disobedience, but that is not the practice usually being defended by this pattern of bad faith. The converse of this statement, however, is not true. Just because the laws of a country do not prohibit an activity does not mean that it is ethical to engage in that activity. For example, some U.S. pharmaceutical companies have been criticized as acting unethically when they sold drugs that were banned in the United States in third-world countries.

8 **We were following the spirit, not the letter, of the law.** This slogan is particularly deceptive because it seems so high-minded. Its power consists in its ability to convince us that we really are acting from higher motives rather than base ones. The spirit/letter distinction is a good one, but when applied in a legitimate sense, the people invoking the principle do not usually benefit by the action being defended. When we appeal to this formula to bestow a benefit upon ourselves, we are likely to be engaging in self-deception.

9 **They have plenty of money; they can afford it.** This excuse is the pettiest of them all. Used by people contemplating some kind of fraud, it is self-justification based on resentment. Unpacked, the argument goes something like this: they have plenty of money (probably gained unethically), so when I cheat them I am only giving them a taste of their own medicine. This is a favorite of those who rig government bids or send inflated estimates for auto repair jobs to insurance companies. No one would accept the attempt to justify a burglary by saying the victims had plenty of money and the robber did not really take much.

10 The market is not free, so there is no reason for us to act as though it is. A favorite of insider traders and price fixers, this rationalization appeals to the belief that nothing in this world is perfect. A perfectly free market is a philosophical ideal, and like all such ideals cannot be fully realized in an imperfect world. It is also the case that social policy restrains the market in many ways for the sake of the common good (regulated utilities, licensing requirements for entry into a profession, government subsidies for selected industries, and so forth). When social policy restrains the freedom of the market, it does so for the sake of a common good; when an individual attempts to restrain the market, it is usually for the sake of private benefit. Thus the two cases are not parallel at all, and this slogan is just another example of self-deception.

As a collection of rationalizing slogans that hide examples of bad faith, this list is far from complete, but it is a good starting point. Here are some questions to ask yourself to discover possible patterns of bad faith: Am I willing to take full responsibility for my action, or am I pushing this responsibility off on someone else? Do I attempt to justify my action by appealing to a role I am expected to play—a role as employee, manager, a player in the business "game," a justification that keeps me from having to face up to the fact that it is *my* action, not that of someone else? Is my action something that I would be willing to have known publicly, or would I prefer that it remain secret?

The Power of Abstraction

Part of the power of the kind of self-deception we have been analyzing is that it puts distance between us and the action we are performing. This strategy allows us to avoid thinking about the fact that we are freely choosing to act in this way, whether we admit it or not. Another distancing technique that is at the root of many of our ethical difficulties is that of *abstraction*. The power of abstraction, according to another twentieth-century existential thinker, Gabriel Marcel, is at the root of war, for "it is only through organized lying that we can hope to make war acceptable to those who must wage or suffer it."[5] The practice of business is different from waging war, although sometimes the metaphors used in business discourse are warlike: "we've got a real battle on our hands facing up to foreign competition," or "our market share is under attack," or "we're going to introduce this product with a blitz campaign." Marcel's point, though, is just as applicable to business activity as to any other human endeavor in which we deal with people. The more we remove ourselves from having to regard other persons as human beings like ourselves, the more we will be willing to do outrageous things to them. To kill other persons, even in wartime, requires that we think of them as an abstraction—the enemy, the fascists, the gooks, or whatever. Notice how abstractions enter into the vocabulary of business and how different it is to think of customers as persons or merely as an impersonal market. Here is one way of listing an ascending hierarchy of abstractions: clients, customers, consumers, the market. Similarly we can speak of the work force as associates, staff, employees, workers, labor.

In the Honda automobile plant at Marysville, Ohio, and in the Toyota plant at Georgetown, Kentucky, the term "associates" is used to refer to those working in the plants. A *New York Times* article highlighting the production techniques at the Georgetown plant reported, "'Here it's more like a family,' said Diana Hobbs, 40 years old, of rural Hardin County, Kentucky, who assembles brakes. 'Supervisors listen to you and everyone works together.'"[6] Critics of these industrial plants say that such talk is just a clever way of undermining employee resolve to unionize. The point is, however, the more abstract the terminology we use in referring to a group of persons, the more willing we will be to act unethically toward them.

The sense of powerlessness many people feel in large corporate structures is another example of the power of abstraction. The less control people have over their lives, the less responsibility they feel for their actions. In spite of Sartre's claim that we are totally free and therefore totally responsible, people who perceive themselves as powerless have a diminished sense of accountability. As one contemporary writer in business ethics put it, "Employees of large-scale organizations follow bureaucratic rules that link their activities together to achieve corporate outcomes of which the employee may not even be aware. The engineers in one department may build a component with certain weaknesses, for example, not knowing that another department plans to use that component in a product that these weaknesses will render dangerous. Or employees may feel pressured to conform to company rules with whose corporate outcomes they may not agree but which they feel they are not in a position to change."[7]

Bureaucracy and Depersonalization

Closely associated with the notion of abstraction that Gabriel Marcel describes with such power is depersonalization, the loss of both a sense of authority and responsibility. Depersonalization is a hazard for any organization but especially so for a bureaucracy. A bureaucracy, according to the dictionary definition, is administration through bureaus and departments. Yet the term has ceased to be merely descriptive and has taken on a negative, pejorative connotation. This is due to the tendency of bureaucratic types of organization to reduce the individual's sense of worth and power, a tendency toward *depersonalization,* to use Marcel's term.

In no uncertain terms Marcel says, "Bureaucracy is evil, and it is essentially a metaphysical evil."[8] "Metaphysical" in this context means it is fundamentally evil. This may seem to be a harsh judgment, but it is one that Marcel was driven to by the events he witnessed in Europe during the middle of the century in which faceless bureaucrats unleashed unspeakable horrors on the world and justified their actions by saying they were just following orders or that they were powerless to resist because they were just cogs in a machine. "Has, in fact, the employee who is a tiny cog in a great administrative machine normally the sense of serving a cause, a suprapersonal principle?" Marcel asks. "The answer to this question," he says, "can only be a negative one. Apart from some exceptional cases . . . we cannot seriously maintain that such an employee has a consciousness of serving, in the precise and noble sense of the word: by that I mean above all that he can

---

GABRIEL MARCEL ON ABSTRACTION

There are a number of urgently relevant observations that force themselves on us here. The most important of them seems to me to be the following: as soon as people (*people,* that is to say, the State or a political party or a faction or a religious sect, or what it may be) claim of me that I commit myself to a warlike action against other human beings, . . . it is very necessary that I lose all awareness of the individual reality of the being whom I may be led to destroy. In order to transform him into a mere impersonal target, it is absolutely necessary to convert him into an abstraction: *the* Communist, *the* Anti-Fascist, *the* Fascist, and so on. . . . It is from this point of view that we ought to consider the sinister use that has been made of the ideas of "the masses" in the modern world. "The masses"—this seems to me the most typical, the most significant example of an abstraction which remains an abstraction even after it has become real: has become real, I mean, in the pragmatic sense of becoming a force, a power. Such realized abstractions are in some sense preordained for the purposes of war: that is to say, quite simply, for the purposes of human inter-destructiveness.

Source: Gabriel Marcel, *Man Against Mass Society* (Chicago: Henry Regnery, 1962), pp. 157–159.

hardly know what the honour of serving is."[9] The answer to this problem, as Marcel sees it, is to infuse an administrative organization with values, with ethical principles. "The real problem is that of knowing to what degree an administrative machine can be informed with spiritual values; and it is very hard not to feel very pessimistic when dealing with this problem."[10]

This pessimism is shared by others. In his article "Moral Mazes," which is another "best-seller" from *Harvard Business Review*, Robert Jackall describes how bureaucracy erodes moral values. It "breaks apart substance from appearances, action from responsibility," he says. And "because moral choices are inextricably tied to personal fates, bureaucracy erodes internal and even external standards of morality, not only in matters of individual success and failure but also in all the issues that managers face in their daily work." Pessimism occurs as the result of the particular pressures posed by bureaucracy. Jackall's description of this process can be read as an explanation of the process of depersonalization that Marcel deplores. The problem with a bureaucracy, as Jackall sees it, is that "what matters in the bureaucratic world is not what a person is but how closely his many personae mesh with the organizational ideal; not his willingness to stand by his actions but his agility in avoiding blame; not what he believes or says but how well he has mastered the ideologies that serve his corporation; not what he stands for but whom he stands with in the labyrinths of his organization."[11]

Business leaders are beginning to see the wisdom of Marcel's concerns and the need to counteract the depersonalization that is an occupational hazard of modern corporate life. The reasons? A discovery of the close relation between ethical corporate behavior and the bottom line. To be successful in a global environment, corporations must compete for the long term, building on relations of trust and responsibility. As a *Fortune* magazine feature on ethics observed, "Successful enterprises are inevitably based on a network of trust binding management, employees, shareholders, lenders, suppliers, and customers—akin to the network that Japanese calls keiretsu. When companies slip into shoddy practices, these crucial relationships start to deteriorate."[12] Echoing this thought is Daniel M. Galbreath, chairman and chief executive office of the Galbreath Company, a Columbus, Ohio, development firm, who insists that good ethics are important to his company. "We have to be beyond reproach," for "without our name or without our word, we're just another developer fighting to survive."[13]

ENCOURAGING MORAL BEHAVIOR

If tendencies toward bad faith, abstraction, and depersonalization are hazards of modern corporate life, then counteracting these pressures becomes imperative for those managing business enterprises. There is no rigid formula for how to do it, but here are some strategies that seem to pay off.

Make Employees Moral Guardians

If employees feel depersonalized by their position in an organization, businesses can counteract this sense of powerlessness by empowering associates to take responsibility for their company's moral values. Some businesses set up special offices—ombudsmen, ethics officers, ethics advisory committees—to receive employee reports of possible ethical problems in the organization.[14] The advertising firm N. W. Ayer, based in New York but with offices all over the world, encourages its staff to help the company maintain its high standards. It continually screens its television advertisements in specially designed rooms and distributes comment cards on which employees can note any problems they perceive with the advertisements. A committee is then required to deal with each comment. *Fortune* reports that "more and more companies are appointing full-time ethics officers, generally on the corporate vice-presidential level, who report directly to the chairman of an ethics committee of top officers. One of the most effective tools these ethics specialists employ is a hot line through which workers on all levels can register complaints or ask about questionable behavior."[15]

Reward Ethical Behavior

Stanley C. Pace, chairman of the board and CEO of General Dynamics Corporation, reports that his company responded to criticisms about Defense Department procurement procedures by establishing an elaborate in-house system of moral accountability. All employees are responsible for ensuring that the company's ethical standards are followed. One way the company encourages this sense of employee responsibility is by rewarding ethical behavior. According to Pace, "General Dynamics provides continuing counsel on company rules and regulations to any employee who seeks it and recognizes employees who make an exemplary effort to implement and uphold the standards."[16]

Establish Role Models

When Salomon Brothers was rocked by allegations of trying to manipulate the Treasury securities market, the company sent a message of commitment to reform to the government and the financial community by the appointment, even though temporary, of Warren E. Buffett as chief executive officer. Buffett, a midwesterner, according to the *New York Daily News*, "buys suits off the rack and has a modest home in Omaha, Nebraska," and is described as "a very ethical man, often putting the interest of his clients above his own personal gains."[17] A company's values are reflected in its culture, and its role models may include the founders of the firm whose exemplary conduct still guides the company's attitudes. Leon L. Bean's personal example of giving refunds to customers who purchased his boots stands as an icon in the company's culture and its advertisements. *Fortune* quoted one manager whose advice is, "Senior management has got to find a way to create heroes, people who serve the company's competitive values—and also its social and ethical values."[18]

Good people will be less tempted to do bad things when companies encourage them to feel responsible for their actions. It requires work and attention, from the CEO to the packer on the loading dock, but it can be done, as an increasing number of companies are discovering.

NOTES

1 Jean-Paul Sartre, *Being and Nothingness* (New York: Philosophical Library, 1956), p. 556.
2 The posthumously published writings of Jean-Paul Sartre, *Notebooks for an Ethics*, trans. David Pellauer (Chicago: University of Chicago Press, 1992), deal with some of the problems of bad faith that were first described in *Being and Nothingness*.
3 This is an actual experience related by one of my students to a class in business ethics. In his settlement with the SEC, he was prevented from continuing his career as an equities salesman.
4 This example is from Manuel G. Velasquez, *Business Ethics: Concepts and Cases,* 3rd ed. (Englewood Cliffs, NJ: Prentice-Hall, 1992), pp. 204–205.
5 Gabriel Marcel, *Man Against Mass Society* (Chicago: Henry Regnery, 1962), p. 154.
6 NYT, May 5, 1992.
7 Velasquez, *Business Ethics*, p. 43.
8 Marcel, *Man Against Mass Society*, p. 200.

9 Ibid., p. 202.

10 Ibid., p. 204.

11 Robert Jackall, "Moral Mazes: Bureaucracy and Managerial Work," *Ethics in Practice: Managing the Moral Corporation,* eds. Kenneth R. Andrews and Donald K. David (Boston: Harvard Business School Press, 1989), pp. 182–183.

12 Kenneth Labich, "The New Crisis in Business Ethics," *Fortune,* Apr. 20, 1992.

13 CD, Mar. 18, 1992.

14 BW, Sept. 23, 1991, p. 65.

15 FORT, Apr. 20, 1992, p. 176.

16 Stanley C. Pace, "The CEO's Page: The Business of Ethics," *Graduating Engineer,* Mar. 1989, p. 47.

17 *New York Daily News,* Aug. 17, 1991.

18 FORT, Apr. 20, 1992, p. 176.

Creating Ethical Corporate Structures

Patrick E. Murphy

What is an ethical company? This question is not easy to answer. For the most part, ethical problems occur because corporate managers and their subordinates are *too* devoted to the organization. In their loyalty to the company or zest to gain recognition, people sometimes ignore or overstep ethical boundaries. For example, some sales managers believe that the only way to meet ambitious sales goals is to have the sales reps "buy" business with lavish entertaining and gift giving. This overzealousness is the key source of ethical problems in most business firms.

Employees are looking for guidance in dealing with ethical problems. This guidance may come from the CEO, upper management, or immediate supervisors.[1] We know that ethical business practices stem from an ethical corporate culture. Key questions are, How can this culture be created and sustained? What structural approaches encourage ethical decision making? If the goal is to make the company ethical, managers must introduce structural components that will enhance ethical sensitivity.

In this paper, I examine three promising and workable approaches to infusing ethical principles into businesses:

- corporate credos that define and give direction to corporate values;
- ethics programs where companywide efforts focus on ethical issues; and
- ethical codes that provide specific guidance to employees in functional business areas.

Below I review the virtues and limitations of each and provide examples of companies that successfully employ these approaches.

Corporate Credos

A corporate credo delineates a company's ethical responsibility to its stakeholders; it is probably the most general approach to managing corporate ethics. The credo is a succinct statement of the values permeating

Table 1
The Credo of Security Pacific Corporation

Commitment to Customer

The first commitment is to provide our customers with quality products and services which are innovative and technologically responsive to their current requirements, at appropriate prices. To perform these tasks with integrity requires that we maintain confidentiality and protect customer privacy, promote customer satisfaction, and serve customer needs. We strive to serve qualified customers and industries which are socially responsible according to broadly accepted community and company standards.

Commitment to Employee

The second commitment is to establish an environment for our employees which promotes professional growth, encourages each person to achieve his or her highest potential, and promotes individual creativity and responsibility. Security Pacific acknowledges our responsibility to employees, including providing for open and honest communication, stated expectations, fair and timely assessment of performance and equitable compensation which rewards employee contributions to company objectives within a framework of equal opportunity and affirmative action.

Commitment of Employee to Security Pacific

The third commitment is that of the employee to Security Pacific. As employees, we strive to understand and adhere to the Corporation's policies and objectives, act in a professional manner, and give our best effort to improve Security Pacific. We recognize the trust and confidence placed in us by our customers and community and act with integrity and honesty in all situations to preserve that trust and confidence. We act responsibly to avoid conflicts of interest and other situations which are potentially harmful to the Corporation.

Commitment of Employee to Employee

The fourth commitment is that of employees to their fellow employees. We must be committed to promote a climate of mutual respect, integrity, and professional relationships, characterized by open and honest communication within and across all levels of the organization. Such a climate will promote attainment of the Corporation's goals and objectives, while leaving room for individual initiative within a competitive environment.

Commitment to Communities

The fifth commitment is that of Security Pacific to the communities which we serve. We must constantly strive to improve the quality of life through our support of community organizations and projects, through encouraging service to the community by employees, and by promoting participation in community services. By the appropriate use of our resources, we work to support or further advance the interests of the community, particularly in times of crisis or social need. The Corporation and its employees are committed to complying fully with each community's laws and regulations.

Commitment to Stockholder

The sixth commitment of Security Pacific is to its stockholders. We will strive to provide consistent growth and a superior rate of return on their investment, to maintain a position and reputation as a leading financial institution, to protect stockholder investments, and to provide full and timely information. Achievement of these goals for Security Pacific is dependent upon the successful development of the five previous sets of relationships.

the firm. The experiences of Security Pacific Corporation (a Los Angeles-based national bank that devised a credo in 1987) and of Johnson & Johnson illustrate the credo approach.

Security Pacific's central document is not an ethical code per se; rather, it is six missionlike commitments to customers, employees, communities, and stockholders. The credo's objective is "to seek a set of principles and beliefs which might provide guidance and direction to our work" (see Table 1).

More than 70 high-level managers participated in formulating a first draft of the commitments. During this process, senior managers shared and analyzed examples of ethical dilemmas they had faced in balancing corporate and constituent obligations. An outside consultant, hired to manage the process, helped to draft the language. Ultimately more than 250 employees, from all levels of the bank, participated in the credo formulation process via a series of discussion groups.

Once the commitments were in final form, management reached a consensus on how to communicate these guiding principles to the Security Pacific organization. Credo coordinators developed and disseminated a leader's guide to be used at staff meetings introducing the credo; it contained instructions on the meeting's format and on showing a videotape that explained the credo and the process by which it was developed. At the meetings, managers invited reactions by posing these questions: What are your initial feelings about what you have just read? Are there any specific commitments you would like to discuss? How will the credo affect your daily work? Employees were thus encouraged to react to the credo and to consider its long-run implications.

Security Pacific's credo was recently cited as a model effort, and it serves internally both as a standard for judging existing programs and as a justification for new activities.[2] For example, the "commitment to communities" formed the basis for a program specifically designed to serve low-income constituents in the area. However, this credo should not be considered the definitive approach to ethics management. First, the credo could be interpreted simply as an organizational mission statement, not as a document about ethics. Indeed, the examples supporting the credo and the videotape itself do stress what might just be called good business practice, without particular reference to ethical policies. And second, the credo has not been in place long enough for its impact to be fully assessed.

Table 2
Johnson & Johnson Credo

We believe our first responsibility is to the doctors, nurses, and patients, to mothers and all others who use our products and services. In meeting their needs everything we do must be of high quality. We must constantly strive to reduce our costs in order to maintain reasonable prices. Customers' orders must be serviced promptly and accurately. Our suppliers and distributors must have an opportunity to make a fair profit.

We are responsible to our employees, the men and women who work with us throughout the world. Everyone must be considered as an individual. We must respect their dignity and recognize their merit. They must have a sense of security in their jobs. Compensation must be fair and adequate and working conditions clean, orderly, and safe. Employees must feel free to make suggestions and complaints. There must be equal opportunity for employment, development, and advancement for those qualified. We must provide competent management, and their actions must be just and ethical.

We are responsible to the communities in which we live and work and to the world community as well. We must be good citizens —support good works and charities and bear our fair share of taxes. We must encourage civic improvements and better health and education. We must maintain in good order the property we are privileged to use, protecting the environment and natural resources.

Our final responsibility is to our stockholders. Business must make a sound profit. We must experiment with new ideas. Research must be carried on, innovative programs developed and mistakes paid for. New equipment must be purchased, new facilities provided, and new products launched. Reserves must be created to provide for adverse times. When we operate according to these principles, the stockholders should realize a fair return.

Any discussion of corporate credos would be incomplete without reference to Johnson & Johnson, whose credo is shown in Table 2. This document focuses on responsibilities to consumers, employees, communities, and stockholders. (The current J&J president, David Clare, explains that responsibility to the stockholder is listed last because "if we do the other jobs properly, the stockholder will always be served.") The first version of this credo, instituted in 1945, was revised in 1947. Between 1975 and 1978, chairman James Burke held a series of meetings with J&J's 1,200 top managers; they were encouraged to "challenge" the credo. What emerged from the meetings was that the document in fact functioned as it was intended to function; a slightly reworded but substantially unchanged credo was introduced in 1979.

Over the last two years, the company has begun to survey all employees about how well the company meets its responsibilities to the four principal constituencies. The survey asks employees from all fifty-three countries where J&J operates questions about every line in the credo. An office devoted to the credo survey tabulates the results, which are confidential.

(Department and division managers receive only information pertaining to their units and composite numbers for the entire firm.) The interaction at meetings devoted to discussing these findings is reportedly very good.

Does J&J's credo work? Top management feels strongly that it does. The credo is often mentioned as an important contributing factor in the company's exemplary handling of the Tylenol crises several years ago. It would appear that the firm's commitment to the credo makes ethical business practice its highest priority. One might question whether the credo is adequate to deal with the multitude of ethical problems facing a multinational firm; possibly additional ethical guidelines could serve as reinforcement, especially in dealing with international business issues.

When should a company use a corporate credo to guide its ethical policies? They work best in firms with a cohesive corporate culture, where a spirit of frequent and unguarded communication exists. Generally, small, tightly knit companies find that a credo is sufficient. Among large firms, Johnson & Johnson is an exception. J&J managers consciously use the credo as an ethical guidepost; they find that the corporate culture reinforces the credo.

When is a credo insufficient? This approach does not offer enough guidance for most multinational companies facing complex ethical questions in different societies, for firms that have merged recently and are having trouble grafting disparate cultures, and for companies operating in industries with chronic ethical problems. A credo is like the Ten Commandments. Both set forth good general principles, but many people need the Bible, religious teachings, and guidelines provided by organized religion, as well. Similarly, many companies find that they need to offer more concrete guidance on ethical issues.

Ethics Programs

Ethics programs provide more specific direction for dealing with potential ethical problems than general credos do. Two companies—Chemical Bank and Dow Corning—serve as examples. Although the thrust of the two programs is different, they both illustrate the usefulness of this approach.

Chemical Bank, the nation's fourth largest bank, has an extensive ethics education program. All new employees attend an orientation session at which they read and sign off on Chemical's code of ethics. (This has been in existence for thirty years and was last revised in May 1987.) The training program features a videotaped message from the chairman emphasizing the bank's values and ethical standards. A second and more unusual aspect of the program provides in-depth training in ethical decision making for vice presidents.[3]

The "Decision Making and Corporate Values" course is a two-day seminar that occurs away from the bank. Its purpose, according to a bank official, is "to encourage Chemical's employees to weigh the ethical or value dimensions of the decisions they make and to provide them with the analytic tools to do that." This program began in 1983; more than 250 vice presidents have completed the course thus far. Each meeting is limited to twenty to twenty-five senior vice presidents from a cross-section of departments; this size makes for a seminar-like atmosphere. The bank instituted the program in response to the pressures associated with deregulation, technology, and increasing competition.

The chairman always introduces the seminar by highlighting his personal commitment to the program. Most of the two days is spent discussing case studies. The fictitious cases were developed following interviews with various Chemical managers who described ethically charged situations. The cases are really short stories about loan approval, branch closings, foreign loans, insider trading, and other issues.[4] They do not have "solutions" as such; instead, they pose questions for discussion, such as, Do you believe the individual violated the bank's code? Or, What should X do?

Program evaluations have yielded positive results. Participants said they later encountered dilemmas similar to the cases, and that they had developed a thinking process in the seminar that helped them work through other problems. This program, while it is exemplary, only reaches a small percentage of Chemical's 30,000 employees. Ideally, such a program would be disseminated more widely and would become more than a one-time event.

Dow Corning has a longstanding—and very different—ethics program. Its general code has been revised four times since its inception in 1976 and includes a seven-point values statement. The company started using face-to-face "ethical audits" at its plants worldwide more than a decade ago. The number of participants in these four-to-six-hour audits ranges from five to forty. Auditors meet with the manager in charge the evening before to ascertain the most pressing issues. The actual questions come from relevant sections in the corporate code and are adjusted for the audit location. At sales offices, for example, the auditors concentrate on issues such as kickbacks, unusual requests from customers, and special pricing terms; at manufacturing plants, conservation and environmental issues receive more attention. An ethical audit might include the following questions.

- Are there any examples of business that Dow Corning has lost because of our refusal to provide "gifts" or other incentives to government officials at our customers' facilities?
- Do any of our employees have ownership or financial interest in any of our distributors?
- Have our sales representatives been able to undertake business conduct discussions with distributors in a way that actually strengthens our ties with them?
- Has Dow Corning been forced to terminate any distributors because of their business conduct practices?
- Do you believe that our distributors are in regular contact with their competitors? If so, why?
- Which specific Dow Corning policies conflict with local practices?

John Swanson, manager of Corporate Internal and Management Communications, heads this effort; he believes the audit approach makes it "virtually impossible for employees to consciously make an unethical decision." According to Swanson, twenty to twenty-three meetings occur every year. The Business Conduct Committee members, who act as session leaders, then prepare a report for the Audit Committee of the board. He stresses the fact that there are no shortcuts to implementing this program——it requires time and extensive interaction with the people involved. Recently the audit was expanded; it now examines internal as well as external activities. (One audit found that some salespeople believed manufacturing personnel needed to be more honest when developing production schedules.) One might ask whether the commitment to ethics is constant over time or peaks during the audit sessions; Dow Corning may want to conduct surprise audits, or develop other monitoring mechanisms or a more detailed code.

When should a company consider developing an ethics program? Such programs are often appropriate when firms have far-flung operations that need periodic guidance, as is the case at Dow Corning. This type of program can deal specifically with international ethical issues and with peculiarities at various plant locations. Second, an ethics program is useful when managers confront similar ethical problems on a regular basis, as Chemical Bank executives do. Third, these programs are useful in organizations that use outside consultants or advertising agencies. If an independent contractor does not subscribe to a corporate credo, the firm may want to use an ethical audit or checklist to heighten the outside agency's sensitivity to ethical issues.

When do ethics programs come up lacking? If they are too issue centered, ethics programs may miss other, equally important problems. (Dow's program, for example, depends on the questions raised by the audit.) In addition, the scope of the program may limit its impact to only certain parts of the organization (e.g., Chemical Bank). Managers who want to permanently inculcate ethical considerations may be concerned that such programs are not perceived by some employees as being long term or ongoing. If the credo can be compared with the Ten Commandments, then ethics programs can be likened to weekly church services. Both can be uplifting, but once the session (service) is over, individuals may believe they can go back to business as usual.

Tailored Corporate Codes

Codes of conduct, or ethical codes, are another structural mechanism companies use to signal their commitment to ethical principles. Ninety percent of Fortune 500 firms, and almost half of all other firms, have ethical codes. According to a recent survey, this mechanism is perceived as the most effective way to encourage ethical business behavior.[5] Codes commonly address issues such as conflict of interest, competitors, privacy, gift giving and receiving, and political contributions. However, many observers continue to believe that codes are really public relations documents, or motherhood and apple pie statements; these critics claim that codes belittle employees and fail to address practical managerial issues.[6]

Simply developing a code is not enough. It must be tailored to the firm's functional areas (e.g., marketing, finance, personnel) or to the major line of business in which the firm operates. The rationale for tailored codes is simple. Functional areas or divisions have differing cultures and needs. A consumer products division, for example, has a relatively distant relationship with customers, because it relies heavily on advertising to sell its products. A division producing industrial products, on the other hand, has fewer customers and uses a personal, sales-oriented approach. A code needs to reflect these differences. Unfortunately, very few ethics codes do so.

Several companies have exemplary codes tailored to functional or major business areas. I describe two of these below—the St. Paul Companies (specializing in commercial and personal insurance and related products) and International Business Machines (IBM).

The St. Paul Companies revised their extensive corporate code, entitled "In Good Conscience," in 1986. All new employees get introduced to the code when they join the company, and management devotes biannual meetings to discussing the code's impact on day-to-day activities. In each of the five sections, the code offers specific guidance and examples for employees to follow. The statements below illustrate the kinds of issues, and the level of specificity, contained in the code.

- Insider Information. For example, if you know that the company is about to announce a rise in quarterly profits, or anything else that would affect the price of the company's stock, you cannot buy or sell the stock until the announcement has been made and published.
- Gifts and Entertainment. An inexpensive ballpoint pen, or an appointment diary, is a common gift and generally acceptable. But liquor, lavish entertainment, clothing, or travel should not be accepted.
- Contact with Legislators. If you are contacted by legislators on matters relating to the St. Paul, you should refer them to your governmental affairs or law department.

The "Employee Related Issues" section of the code is the most detailed; it directly addresses the company's relationship to the individual, and vice versa. This section spells out what employees can expect in terms of compensation (it should be based on job performance and administered fairly), advancement (promotion is from within, where possible), assistance (this consists of training, job experience, or counseling) and communications (there should be regular feedback; concerns can be expressed without fear of recrimination). It also articulates the St. Paul Companies' expectation of employees regarding speaking up (when you know something that could be a problem), avoiding certain actions (where the public's confidence could be weakened), and charting your career course.

The company also delineates employee privacy issues. The code outlines how work-related information needed for hiring and promotion is collected. (Only information needed to make the particular decision is gathered; it is collected from the applicant/employee where possible. Polygraphs are not used.) The St. Paul informs employees about what types of information are maintained. Finally, information in an individual's file is open to the employee's review.

The code covers other important personnel issues in depth, as well. It touches on equal opportunity by mentioning discrimination laws, but the emphasis is on the company recognition of past discrimination and its commitments to "make an affirmative effort to address this situation in all of its programs and practices." Data acquired from the St. Paul supports this point. Between 1981 and 1986, hiring and promotion increased 60 percent for minorities in supervisory positions and 49 percent for women in management—even though overall employment rose only about 3 percent during this time. In addition, the code informs employees that the company will reimburse all documented business expenses. And it covers nepotism by stating that officers' and directors' relatives will not be hired; other employees' relatives can be employed, so long as they are placed in different departments.

Being an ethical company requires providing clear guidelines for employees. The St. Paul Companies' extensive discussion of personnel policies does just that. Employees may strongly disapprove of certain policies, but they are fully informed. The termination policy, for example, states that employment is voluntary and that individuals are free to resign at any time; the company, too, can terminate employees "at any time, with or without cause." Some people may consider that policy unfair or punitive, but at least the rules of the game are clear. One limitation of the code is that all sections are not uniformly strong. For example, the marketing section is only one paragraph long and contains few specifics.

The second illustration is of a code tailored to the company's major line of business. IBM's "Business Conduct Guidelines" were instituted in the 1960s and revised most recently In 1983. New employees receive a copy and certify annually that they abide by the code. It has four parts; the most extensive section is entitled "Conducting IBM's Business." Since IBM is, at its core, a marketing and sales organization, this section pertains primarily to these issues.

Six subsections detail the type of activities IBM expects of its sales representatives. First, "Some General Standards" include the following directives, with commentaries: do not make misrepresentations to anyone, do not take advantage of IBM's size, treat everyone fairly (do not extend preferential treatment), and do not practice reciprocal dealing. Second,

"Fairness in the Field" pertains to disparagement (sell IBM products on their merits, not by disparaging competitors' products or services). In addition, it prohibits premature disclosure of product information and of selling if a competitor already has a signed order. Third, "Relations with Other Organizations" cautions employees about firms that have multiple relationships with IBM (deal with only one relationship at a time, and do not collaborate with these firms).

The fourth and fifth sections address "Acquiring and Using Information for or about Others." The code spells out the limits to acquiring information (industrial espionage is wrong) and to using information (adverse information should not be retained). Employees must determine the confidentiality of information gathered from others. The final section outlines IBM's policy on "Bribes, Gifts, and Entertainment." The company allows customary business amenities but prohibits giving presents that are intended to "unduly influence" or "obligate" the recipient, as well as receiving gifts worth more than a nominal amount.

One might contend that it is easy for a large, profitable company like IBM to have an exemplary code. On the other hand, one could also argue that a real reason for the company's continued success is that its sales representatives do subscribe to these principles. Is this a perfect code? No. The gifts area could use more specificity and, even though the company spends millions of dollars a year on advertising, that subject is not addressed in any section of the code. Further, IBM's legal department administers the code, which may mean that problems are resolved more by legal than ethical interpretation.

When should a company use a tailored code of ethics? If a company has one dominant functional unit (like IBM), or if there is diversity among functional areas, divisions, or subsidiaries, then a tailored code might be advisable. It allows the firm to promulgate specific and appropriate standards. Tailored codes are especially useful to complex organizations because they represent permanent guidelines for managers and employees to consult.

When should they be avoided? If a firm's leaders believe specific guidelines may be too restrictive for their employees, then a tailored code is an unsatisfactory choice. Codes are not necessary in most small firms or in ones where a culture includes firmly entrenched ethical policies. If a credo is similar to the Ten Commandments, and programs are similar to religious services, then tailored credos can be considered similar to the

Bible or to other formal religious teachings. They provide the most guidance, but many people do not take the time to read or reflect on them.

Conclusion

My research on ethics in management suggests several conclusions that the corporate manager may wish to keep in mind.

- **There Is No Single Ideal Approach to Corporate Ethics.** I would recommend that a small firm start with a credo, but that a larger firm consider a program or a tailored code. It is also possible to integrate these programs and produce a hybrid: in dealing with insider trading, for example, a firm could develop a training program, then follow it up with a strongly enforced tailored code.[7]
- **Top Management Must Be Committed.** Senior managers must champion the highest ethical postures for their companies, as James Burke of J&J does. This commitment was evident in all the companies described here; it came through loud and clear in the CEOs' letters, reports, and public statements.
- **Developing a Structure Is Not Sufficient by Itself.** The structure will not be useful unless it is supported by institutionalized managerial processes. The credo meetings at Security Pacific and the seminars at Chemical Bank are examples of processes that support structures.
- **Raising the Ethical Consciousness of an Organization Is Not Easy.** All the companies mentioned here have spent countless hours—and substantial amounts of money—developing, discussing, revising, and communicating the ethical principles of the firm. And in fact there are no guarantees that it will work. McDonnell Douglas has an extensive ethics program, but some of its executives were implicated in a recent defense contractor scandal.

In conclusion, let me add that managers in firms with active ethics structures—credos, programs, and tailored codes—are genuinely enthusiastic about them. They believe that ethics pay off. Their conviction should provide others with an encouraging example.

Notes

The author would like to thank Bernard Avishai, Gene Laczniak, Michael Mokwa, Lee Tavis, and Oliver Williams, C.S.C., for their helpful comments on an earlier version of this article.

1. P. E. Murphy and M. G. Dunn, "Corporate Culture and Marketing Management Ethics" (Notre Dame, IN: University of Notre Dame, working paper, 1988).

2. R. E. Berenbeim, *Corporate Ethics* (New York: The Conference Board, research report no. 900, 1987), pp. 15, 20–22.

3. A more detailed discussion of Chemical's comprehensive program, and of Johnson & Johnson's, appears in *Corporate Ethics: A Prime Business Asset* (New York: Business Roundtable, February 1988).

4. One of the case studies appears in "Would You Blow Whistle on Wayward Colleague?" *American Banker*, 17 June 1988, p. 16.

5. Touche Ross, *Ethics in American Business* (New York: Touche Ross & Co., January 1988).

6. Berenbeim (1987), p. 17.

7. G. L. Tidwell, "Here's a Tip—Know the Rules of Insider Trading," *Sloan Management Review*, Summer 1987, pp. 93–99.

Why Character Counts

Stephen R. Covey

SOME TIME AGO I was asked to consult for a bank that was having a problem with employee morale. "I don't know what's wrong," bemoaned their young president. Bright and charismatic, he'd risen through the ranks only to see his institution faltering. Productivity and profits were down. He blamed his employees. "No matter what incentives I provide," he said, "they won't shake off this gloom and doom."

He was right. The atmosphere seemed poisoned with suspicion and lack of trust. For two months I ran workshops, but nothing helped. I was stumped.

"How can anyone trust what's happening here?" was a typical refrain of employee. But no one would tell me the source of this distrust.

Finally, in more casual conversation, the truth emerged. The boss, who was married, was having an affair with an employee. And everyone knew it.

It was obvious now that the company's poor performance was caused by his conduct. But the greatest damage this man was doing was to himself. He was thinking only of his own gratification, disregarding long-term consequences. Moreover, he had violated a sacred trust with his wife.

In a word, his failing was one of *character*.

What Really Matters

Today it is out of vogue to speak in terms of character. But there is no more essential aspect of any person.

Character is made up of those principles and values that give your life direction, meaning and depth. These constitute your inner sense of what's right and wrong based not on laws or rules of conduct but on *who you are*. They include such traits as integrity, honesty, courage, fairness and generosity—which arise from the hard choices we have to make in life. So wrong is simply in doing wrong, not in getting caught.

Yet, some people wonder if our inner values matter anymore. After all, hasn't our noted bank executive succeeded in every visible way, despite his transgressions?

This question demonstrates a quandary of our modern life. Many have come to believe that the only things we need for success are talent, energy and personality. But history has taught us that over the long haul, who we are is more important than who we appear to be.

During the nation's first century and a half, almost everything in the literature of success and self-help focused on what could be called the character ethic. Such eminent figures as Benjamin Franklin and Thomas Jefferson made clear their belief that we can only experience true success and happiness by making character the bedrock of our lives.

After we moved into the industrial age and after World War I, the basic view of success shifted to what we could call the personality ethic. Success became more a function of charm, skills and techniques that, at least on the surface, lubricate the process of human interaction. Rather than struggle with thorny issues of right and wrong, we turned to making things run smoothly.

Some of that philosophy expressed itself with harmless but superficial maxims such as "smiling wins more friends than frowning." Other ideas were clearly manipulative or even deceptive—faking interest in others' hobbies so they will like you, for instance.

With a value system based solely on skill and personality, we find heroes in athletes, musicians and in powerful business executives. But despite the admiration we feel for these achievers, we shouldn't necessarily look upon them as role models. While skill is certainly needed for success, it can never guarantee happiness and fulfillment. These come from developing character.

From the Inside Out

You can begin to build character at any age. The key is learning how to look within—to work *inside out*.

With the inside-out approach, private victories precede public victories. These private victories are simply promises you make to yourself and others and then keep. They don't have to be profound or life-altering, like a career change. They can be as mundane as a commitment to exercise every day.

A promise like this may sound inconsequential, but it represents the hard choices we face in everyday life. The first step toward building character is to tackle a hard choice, commit to change and stay with it.

Day by day, as you make and keep increasingly challenging promises, you will be making deposits in your "character account." What begins as great effort will eventually become habit.

And as you get into the habit of building character in the smaller areas of your life, your ability to develop character strength in more important spheres will grow.

Private victories therefore lead to our larger public victories. For instance, to gain more latitude in your job, you must first be a more responsible employee. To create a happy marriage, first be the kind of person who generates love, generosity, dependability and trust.

There's no more essential ingredient for character growth than trust. Whether it's trust we earn from colleagues or a spouse, it is built slowly over time in an infinite variety of circumstances.

One of the most commonly overlooked ways to build trust is to be loyal to those who are not present. Suppose you and I were criticizing our boss behind his back. What will happen if you and I later have a falling out? You know my nature—I'll bad-mouth you. You've seen me do it.

Now suppose you were to start criticizing the boss and I suggest we go to him and explore how things might be improved. You'd likely assume that I'd act with equal respect if someone were to criticize you.

Start at Home

Another way to build character is to admit your mistakes. Character is revealed in how we handle things that go wrong.

Years ago I had to choose someone to organize a huge meeting. I gave an untested employee a chance, and he bombed it big time. "It was all my fault," he told me. "But if you give me another chance, you have no idea how far I'll go to make the next one succeed."

He displayed such courage in admitting his failure that I did give him another chance. And I've never regretted it. He performed so superbly that my estimation of his character was higher than if he'd done it right the first time.

The best opportunities to build character, however, are within our families, where we are constantly tested—and most vulnerable to lapses. True character begins at home.

Often we sense that we can get away with things around those who know us best, who will love us regardless of our conduct. This can end up subverting our character and our relationships. How often have we heard of someone who is a gem of an employee but treats his or her spouse like a piece of the woodwork?

Perhaps even more common is the following scenario: At one seminar, after I'd spoken on the importance of demonstrating character within the family, a man came up and said, "I like what you're saying, but my wife and I just don't have the same feelings for each other that we used to. I guess we don't love each other anymore. What can I do?"

"Love her," I replied.

He looked puzzled. "How do you love when you don't feel love?"

"My friend," I responded, "love is a verb. The *feeling* of love is the fruit of love. So love your wife. You did it once, you can do it again. Listen. Empathize.

Appreciate. It's your choice. Are you willing to do that?"

Of course, I was asking this man if he was willing to search within himself for the character required to make his marriage work. All our relationships follow the contours of life; they have ups and downs. This is why our families provide a critical measure of our character—and the opportunity, again and again, to nurture it.

WHAT BECAME of the bank president who was involved sexually with an employee? When I confided to him what I knew of his affair and the effect it was having on his staff, he ran his fingers through his hair. "I don't know where to begin," he said.

"Is it over?"

He looked me squarely in the eye.

"Yes. Absolutely."

"Then begin by talking with your wife," I answered.

He told his wife, who forgave him. Then he called a meeting of his staff and addressed their morale problem. "I have found the cause of the problem," he said. "It is me. I am asking you to give me another chance."

It took time, but eventually employee morale—a sense of openness, optimism and trust—improved. In the end, however, the executive was doing himself the greatest favor. He was finding his own path to character.

Ethics of Total Integrity

Stephen R. Covey

I THINK THAT THE SO-CALLED "ETHICS movement" of the past few years has taken many organizations down a wrong path. Many leaders confuse ethical with legal issues, or they take a departmental or compartmental approach rather than an integrated and organic approach to ethics.

With an organic approach, an executive naturally sees everything through an ethical lens; consequently, everything is integrated, not seen in different frames.

Also, with an organic approach, a person can be sincere. The Latin word *sincera* literally means *sine* (without) and *cera* (wax)..."without wax." That is to say, without cosmetics, without putting on a face, without relying on personality, public relations, and appearances—or what *seems* to be. The personality ethic is all about *what seems to be*.

Wrestling with issues of integrity, Shakespeare's Hamlet says, "To be or not to be, that is the question." He ponders, "What a piece of work is man!" He counsels, "Suit the action to the word, the word to the action." And he reasons, "What is a man if his chief good and market of his time be but to sleep and feed? He that made us with such large discourse, gave us not that capability and godlike reason to fust in us unused." To his mother, the Queen, Hamlet responds, "Seems, madam? Nay, it is; I know not 'seems.' "

For executives who have lost integrity, *seems* is all they know. They live and work in a world of *seeming to be* something they are not. They worry more about how others see them than about who they are.

They are actors, who wear wax to cover up covert operations or maintain image.

When I was working in the state of North Carolina recently, I was given a shirt imprinted with the state motto in Latin, *Esse quam videri*, meaning *To be rather than to seem*.

This should be the motto of every executive. Unfortunately, "seeming to be" often substitutes for real integrity. It's "seeming" as opposed to "being." It's neither integral nor integrated, but rather part of a compartment or department.

Three Generations

So, how do you arrive at integrity?

I see integrity as the child of two primary character traits: the mother of humility and the father of courage.

First Generation: the Mother of Humility. The mother of humility means that you realize that over time principles or natural laws ultimately govern, not social values or personal whims and desires. The prideful, arrogant approach is to claim, "I am in control" and "I am in charge of my destiny." That theme, so common in much of the success literature in recent decades, is a product of the social value system. And, our social values may not be based on rock-solid principles but on the shifting sands of ego and opinion. The president of an international communications firm once told me, "Stephen, our company is value-driven."

I said, "Every company is value-driven. The question is this: are the values based on timeless principles, which ultimately control anyway."

He said, "I think so." He showed me their value statement. It included many ideals, including the following: "We are committed to the practice of all praiseworthy values that enhance the worth of individuals and strengthen our communities."

When I asked him about his core values, he mentioned: *honesty, quality, service, profitability, sensitivity, sincerity, and high ethical and moral standards.*

I said, "There's certainly nothing wrong with this set of corporate values, as they are closely aligned with enduring principles. However, what matters most is how you integrate them into your daily operations."

I was trying to teach what every employee already knows: *an emphasis on high ethical and moral standards is best made not simply with words on a poster in the corporate office but with the attitudes and actions of people at all levels.*

This humble business leader well understood the importance of walking the talk—and making sure that the talk, the corporate value system, is based on principles. He realized that we are not in control, that natural laws and principles control, and that the attitude of humility is, in a sense, the mother of all virtues, because all of them come through that spirit of submission.

The Father of Courage. The father of all virtues is courage, because courage is the quality of every quality at its highest testing point. Eventually every value gets tested. Whether or not we will align our values, our lives, and our habits with those principles is the big question. Again, "to be or not to be" is the big question.

In other words, will we really do it? We may be humble, but are we courageous? Will we, in fact, swim upstream against very powerful social values and also against the internal habituated tendencies of our own nature? Will the "chief good and market of our time" be but to sleep and feed? Or will we put our "infinite faculty, admirable form, and godlike reason" to good use? We won't if we lack the courage to act upon our core beliefs. In fact, our principle-centered initiatives will likely be rolled over and flattened by the latest wave of trendy social values.

Second Generation: the Child of Integrity. When you have both humility and courage, you naturally produce the "second generation" child of integrity. Integrity means that your life is integrated around principles and that your security comes from within, not from without. It also means, as my friend suggested, maintaining "the highest levels of honesty and credibility in all relationships."

You won't have the child of integrity if you lack the mother of humility, or if you have the humility but lack the courage to act on your conviction. Instead, you will have duplicity, hypocrisy, and the personality ethic. False integrity means that your security still lies outside yourself—in the degree to which you are accepted from the outside, and to the degree to which you compare or compete favorably with others.

Third Generation: The Fruits of Integrity. The third generation are the many fruits or children of integrity.

• One child of integrity is *wisdom*. If your security comes from within, you simply have better judgment. You're not in an overreactive state; you don't dichotomize; you don't catastrophize; you're not extreme; you have better overall life balance. With wisdom, you see things in correct perspective and proportion; you don't overreact or underreact. You "suit the action to the word, the word to the action."

• A second child of integrity is the *abundance mentality*. When you get your security from within, you are not in a constant state of comparison from without. Therefore, you can have an abundance mind-set toward life. You see life as an ever-enlarging circle of resources, almost like a cornucopia of resources that get larger and larger. As Hamlet says, "There is nothing either good or bad but thinking makes it so."

• A third child of integrity is *synergy*. You can come up with better ideas, transformational thinking and a spirit of win-win partnering when your security is not a function of how people treat you, or of how you compare with others. You can express your ideas with courage and consideration with the intent of finding the best possible alternative, not simply to please or appease others.

• Another sweet fruit of personal and organizational integrity is *relationships of trust with all stakeholders*. Obviously, trust increases when you create high credibility based on trustworthiness. You simply can't have integral relationships without genuine personal integrity; likewise, corporate relationships with stakeholders will suffer with breaches of ethics. Many bottom-line business benefits—including competitiveness, flexibility, responsiveness, quality, economic value-added, and customer service—depend on relationships of trust.

Corporate Ethics Programs

With so much riding on integrity and ethics, why are breaches in ethics, both individual and corporate, all too common? Is it partly because well intentioned university ethics courses and organizational ethics programs don't work?

Over the past 15 years, we've seen a heavy emphasis on ethics, as the ethical dimension has been introduced everywhere from MBA programs to government to small business to major corporations.

Organizations spend lots of money on ethics programs. Sadly, according to one recently retired ethics director, "*Some executives are concerned primarily with public image and perceptions. In fact, the ethics program is often started as a response to public outcry or internal inquiry. Ethics directors serve as a point of contact for whistleblowers and for unempowered and uninformed individuals who don't know how else to get a problem resolved. When executives justify the means by the ends, people pick up the signals. They note who is hired, promoted, and rewarded—and why. They see who gets away with murder and who condones inappropriate behavior. Having an ethics program may make people more sensitive to such issues as sexual harassment or sexist language, but they rarely stop or even slow the avalanche of unethical behavior. In fact, the program may just drive unethical behavior further underground, making people even more devious.*"

This is a fundamentally flawed approach, because it's not about humility—accepting principles, aligning with those principles, submitting to them, and obeying them. It's more about pride. As universities and corporations add classes or offices on ethics, people begin to see issues through that departmental frame of reference, rather than having their perspectives governed by a central frame of reference, the lens of integrity.

The ethics dilemma is analogous to the quality dilemma. We can't inspect in or manage in quality; rather we must design and build it in from the beginning. Likewise, we can't inspect in ethics. Rather, we must build in an ethical frame of reference, through integrated partnering with all stake holders. When everybody accepts personal responsibility to behave in ethical ways, you then hardly even have to think about it, because ethical behavior is your nature, not some artificial department.

When leaders are open and exact in

their observance of ethical codes, they inspire others to do the same. One leader, when stepping down as president of a large university, was commended by the chairman of the board: "A few reach the pinnacle of professional or social or financial success through devious, even evil means. Others may be more virtuous but still show a lack of sensitivity to loved ones, friends, and colleagues as they climb to the top. Those who combine honor, integrity, devotion, and sensitivity to family and friends are rare indeed."

Too often ethics is separate from the reality of the organization. Professional ethicists may huddle and talk, but most of their practice is reactive in response to people not walking their talk, feeling that the only wrong is in getting caught. They may handle a complaint to allay a lawsuit, but they are not preventative or integrative.

As long as there is great disparity and little integration between the corporate ethical stance and individual behavior, the individual will feel no obligation to live by corporate ethical codes.

Your vision, mission, ethics and value statements will be even more valuable if you don't rush the creative process, announce the result, and then ignore or dismiss the document as some meaningless formal exercise. As you involve people in the creation of code and as you review it regularly with them, you build in cultural humility (the acceptance of a value system based on principles) and courage (taking on traditional structures and systems which are contrary to those principles, and aligning your personal style with those structures and systems).

The ethics statement becomes a constitution when it becomes the center from which everything else flows. Then you don't have this "seeming to be" in various areas. In organizations of integrity, ethics is not just another department. The organization serves as a second family. For example, many people who work for Ritz Carlton actually look forward to going to work because they find more harmony, acceptance, integrity, and sense of identity there than they can find even within their own family. People are humble because they know that natural laws and governing principles are in control—not people, programs, and politics. They not only believe in timeless principles, but they have the courage to act on them.

Principles of Business Ethics: Their Role in Decision Making and an Initial Consensus

Archie B. Carroll

> Our principles are the springs of our actions; our actions, the springs of our happiness or misery. Too much care, therefore, cannot be taken in forming our principles.
>
> —*Skelton*

One clear conclusion that has emerged from society's and businesses' preoccupation with business ethics over the last decade is that managers at all levels need help in making ethical decisions in the workplace. It has long been established that decision making is at the heart of management. Managers need to make many decisions in their everyday working lives in which reside questions of right or wrong, fairness, justice, or, as some business ethicists say, the allocation of harms and benefits.

There are dozens of workplace issues in which ethical questions are now coming to the forefront. A recent survey conducted by Ronald Berenbeim, for The Conference Board, identified seven key issues on which at least 80 percent of his 300 respondents agreed represented ethical issues in business today. These seven issues comprised employee conflicts of interest, inappropriate gifts to corporate personnel, sexual harassment, unauthorised payments, affirmative action, employee privacy, and environmental issues.[1]

The purpose of the current discussion is to describe briefly how principles of business ethics are used in a decision-making process, and to report on a survey that was conducted among a group of managers and prospective managers. The survey was designed to present the respondents with a number of alternative business ethical principles, and then to ascertain the usefulness or power of these principles to the respondents. The respondents then ranked the principles in terms of usefulness to them in their work. Finally, we describe the consensus that seems to emerge from the findings of the study.

The Principles Approach

There are several different ways in which managers may go about improving the ethics of their decision making. One popular approach, which we shall call The Principles Approach, is based upon the idea that managers need to compare their proposed actions, decisions or behaviours with certain principles of ethics. This raises the question of *what* is a principle of business ethics and *how* might it be applied?

Figure 1: A Process of Ethical Decision Making

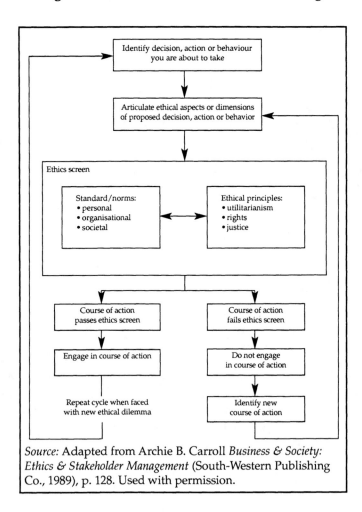

Source: Adapted from Archie B. Carroll *Business & Society: Ethics & Stakeholder Management* (South-Western Publishing Co., 1989), p. 128. Used with permission.

Figure 2: Ranking Ethical Principles

Below are listed 11 different ethical principles that may be used in business decision making. Rank them in terms of how powerful or useful they would be for you.

	Principle	Name of Principle*
1.	You should not adopt principles of action unless they can, without inconsistency, be adopted by everyone else.	Categorical Imperative
2.	Individuals should act to further their self-interests so long as they do not violate the law.	Conventionalist Ethic
3.	Do unto others as you would have them do unto you.	Golden Rule
4.	If it feels good, do it.	Hedonistic Ethic
5.	If you are comfortable with an action or decision after asking yourself whether you would mind if all your associates, friends, and family were aware of it, then you should act or decide.	Disclosure Rule
6.	You do what your "gut feeling" tells you to do.	Intuition Ethic
7.	If the end justifies the means, then you should act.	Means-Ends Ethic
8.	You should take whatever advantage you are strong enough and powerful enough to take without respect for ordinary social conventions and laws.	Might-Equals-Right Ethic
9.	This is an age of large-scale organisations—be loyal to the organisation.	Organisation Ethic
10.	You should do only that which can be explained before a committee of your professional peers.	Professional Ethic
11.	You should follow the principle of "the greatest good for the greatest number."	Utilitarian Principle

* The names of these principles were not included on the survey sheet. They are supplied here just for purposes of explanation.

Figure 3: Ethical Principles Ranked According to Value by Practising Managers. *N=88*

1. The Golden Rule

   Do unto others as you would have them do unto you.

2. Disclosure Rule

   If you are comfortable with an action or decision after asking yourself whether you would mind if all your associations, friends, and family were aware of it, then you should act or decide.

3. The Intuition Ethic

   You do what your "gut feeling" tells you to do.

4. The Categorical Imperative

   You should not adopt principles of action unless they can, without inconsistency, be adopted by everyone else.

(tie) 5. The Professional Ethic

   You should do only that which can be explained before a committee of your professional peers.

(tie) 6. The Utilitarian Principle

   You should follow the principle of "the greatest good for the greatest number."

A principle of business ethics is a guideline or rule which, if applied when you are faced with an ethical dilemma, will assist you in making an ethical decision. Examples of principles which have been articulated and discussed by business philosophers and ethicists include the utilitarian principle, the justice principle and the rights principle. These principles, along with others, have been described in detail elsewhere; and our purpose here is not to add to that body of thought.[2]

In addition to a comparison of personal or corporate behaviour with an ethical principle is the notion of standards or norms of acceptability. These norms might be personal, organisational or societal in terms of their origin. The process of ethical decision making entails, therefore, a consideration of (1) the action, behaviour or decision being considered, (2) standards or norms against which a comparison might be made, and (3) a principle of business ethics which provides guidance as to what is most important in the decision being made: e.g. utilitarianism, justice, rights. Often, decision making is made based upon comparisons of (1) and (2) or (1) and (3).

Such a principles approach might yield a process of ethical decision making similar to that shown in Figure 1. Note here that the term "ethics screen" is used to imply a filtering process wherein actions, behaviors or decisions are compared with standards or norms, and ethical principles or guides with decision making. The proposed decision, action or behaviour then "passes" or "fails" the ethics screen, and results in the course of action being deemed acceptable or unacceptable.

The Survey

The purpose of the survey described here was to see if prospective managers (senior level business students) and actual practising managers would reach any kind of consensus on what principles of business ethics they found useful. On separate occasions, the two groups were presented with the same set of descriptions of ethical principles which were adapted from earlier work by T. K. Das and Steiner and Steiner.[3] Thirty-four business students and 88 middle managers ranked the prin-

Figure 4: Ranking of Ethical Principles by Three Groups

Principle	Managers $n=88$	SE Students $n=34$	SW Students $n=265$
Golden Rule	1	1	1
Disclosure Rule	2	2	2
Intuition Ethic	3	5	6
Categorical Imperative	4	6	8
Professional Ethic	5(tie)	4	7
Utilitarian Ethic	5(tie)	3	3
Proportionality Ethic	*	*	4
Organisation Ethic	*	*	5

* Not on Managers or SE survey

ciples presented in Figure 2. The eleven principles listed were extracted from 14 principles studied earlier by Das.

Figure 3 presents the ethical principles that were considered most important by the 88 managers. Included in the ranking is a brief statement as to what each means. These are reported here first because they come from actual practising managers and must therefore be deemed most credible.

Figure 4 summarises the ranking done by the managers, along with the ranking done by a sample of business students from a large Southeastern university. Also included is the ranking which was done in the T. K. Das study among a large group of Southwestern business students. The researcher regrets that the surveys of managers and Southeastern students did not include all of the principles listed by Das, but most of them (11 out of 14) were on the survey and this provides some useful comparisons.

Some Consensus Emerges

Several interesting findings emerge from these three surveys. Most notable is the fact that there is consensus among the three groups on the Golden Rule and the Disclosure Rule as the top two ranking ethical principles among those considered. Further, the Intuition Ethic and Categorical Imperative were ranked third and fourth by the managerial group and drew strong support from both student groups. Likewise the Professional Ethic and Utilitarian Ethic, which tied for fifth by the Managers, were strongly supported by the SE student group and partially supported by the SW group. The SW group placed two principles in the fourth and fifth position which were not on the survey of the other two groups.

It is worth noting that the *Golden Rule*—"Do unto others [as] you would have them do unto you"—is a fairly straightforward, easy to understand principle. Further, it guides the individual decision maker to behaviour, actions or decisions which he or she should be able to assess as acceptable or not based upon some direct comparisons with what he or she would consider ethical or fair. There is nothing esoteric about this. All it requires—and this is sometimes seen by some as difficult—is that the decision maker affords others the same kind and degree of consideration that he or she would think is right in similar personal circumstances.

The Golden Rule is among the oldest of the principles of living.

The Golden Rule simply argues that, if you want to be treated fairly, treat others fairly; if you want to be told the truth, tell others the truth; if you want your privacy protected, respect the privacy of others. The key is impartiality. According to this principle we are not to make an exception of ourselves. In essence, then, the Golden Rule personalises business relations and brings the ideal of fairness into business deliberations.[4]

Perhaps the reason the Golden Rule is so popular is that it is rooted in history and is among the oldest of the principles of living. Further, it is universal in the sense that it requires no specific religious beliefs or faith. Almost since time began, religious leaders and philosophers have advocated the Golden Rule in one form or another. The following is illustrative:[5]

— The Hindu *Mahabharata* professes: "Men gifted with intelligence and purified souls should always treat others as they themselves wish to be treated."
— Confucius summed up the rules of life as follows: "What you do not want done to yourself, do not do to others."
— In the *Bible* Jesus taught in the book of Matthew: "So in every thing, do to others what you would have them do to you."
— Rabbi Hillel, when asked by a supplicant to be taught the Law, answered: "What thou thyself hatest, do not to thy neighbour. That is the whole Law. The rest is commentary. Go and learn it."

It is easy to see, therefore, why Martin Luther could say that the Golden Rule is part of the "natural law," because it is a moral rule which anyone can recognise without any particular religious teaching. That this thousands-of-years-old wisdom should surface as the number one ethical principle is indeed suggestive of the enduring understanding of how humanity should treat humanity. Some things just never change, it is said.

Intuition is the immediate thought we have before rational thought or inference.

The *Disclosure Rule*, which could be seen as complementary to the Golden Rule, moves the focus of attention to how others whose opinions you respect would regard your decision, action or behaviour. According to the Disclosure Rule, you are probably on a sound ethical footing if you are still comfortable with a proposed action or decision after asking yourself whether you would mind if all your associates, friends, and family were aware of it. The concept of public exposure is a powerful tool; and, though it does not provide ironclad assurance that you are acting ethically, it does provide some strong indication of how the action is likely to be viewed.

The third-ranked principle by the managers studied was the *Intuition Ethic*. Whereas the previous two principles required some degree of rational thought about how the decision maker would like to be treated and how others might regard the proposed action, the intuition ethic is driven by one's quick and ready insight. Intuition, sometimes thought of as "gut feeling," is the immediate thought we have before engaging in rational thought or inference.

A person should not adopt principles unless they can be adopted by everyone else.

Intuition is probably the result of an endowment of moral consciousness we each have, combined with experience and wisdom gained over time. It is a kind of awareness that might be the sum total of all that the decision maker is or has experienced. It is very possible that the intuition ethic might yield an evaluation of a proposed action that embodies considerations of the Golden Rule and the Disclosure Rule as well as other principles. Managers are often driven to make quick decisions, and it is tempting to believe that they go on their own "gut feeling" when time does not permit a more careful assessment based upon other principles or guidelines.

Technically, Immanuel Kant stated the *Categorical Imperative* as follows: "Act only according to that maxim by which you can at the same time will that it should become a universal law." Stated in another way, this principle argues that a person should not adopt principles of action or behaviour unless they can, without inconsistency, be adopted by everyone else. This principle is useful in terms of the manager searching for universal guidelines of consistency, but it really does not provide pointed guidance in a decision making situation. In a sense the categorical imperative is an abstract guideline that could be imposed upon other, more useful, principles.

The *Professional Ethic* holds that you should do only that which can be explained before a committee of your professional peers. In a sense this is a more restricted version of the disclosure rule and, though useful, is not as rigorous because of the possibility that those in similar areas of work might be more understanding of ethical lapses than the general public. In other words, you could more easily find someone in your own profession or line of work to agree with your proposed action than perhaps among your friends or family who are not immediately familiar with the constraints you are up against.

Finally the *Utilitarian Principle*, which argues for the greatest good for the greatest number, is idealistic, somewhat abstract, but quite difficult to apply. How is one ever able to determine what decision or course of action reflects the greatest good for the greatest number? This principle is extremely attractive on first thought, but is very difficult to apply and use.

Summing Up

There are a number of useful ethical principles around should managers *wish* to use them. First, managers must *wish* to use them. All the principles in existence will not suffice if the individual leader or decision maker is not interested in being ethical. An underlying assumption to the use of the ethical principles is, then, that the manager wishes to do the right thing.

A process of ethical decision making was presented, and this entailed the manager subjecting his or her proposed action to an ethics screen composed of an assortment of ethical principles and standards of acceptability. The process should help the manager to think through or "model" what the decision making process should look like when ethical considerations are included. There is no guarantee that the ethics screen will filter out all proposed actions that may be poorly formulated. It does, however, add a measure of ethical process to decision making. It requires the manager to "think ethically" when making decisions.

Finally, a small set of ethical principles rose to the surface as most valuable when considered by a group of practising managers and soon-to-be-managers. The three principles which were ranked highest were quite straightforward and easily understood—treat others as you want to be treated, do only what you would feel comfortable with if those whom you care most about knew it, and follow your intuition. We should add in closing, however, that the modern concern for principles of ethical decision making that are neatly wrapped in a ready-to-use package cannot really be met. Though we desire to have such precision and closure, with no loose ends or puzzling leftovers, we simply cannot identify or agree upon rules, slogans, proverbs or principles that will eliminate all thought and deep introspection.

There are ethical principles that managers can agree upon as useful for management decision making. The real challenge seems to be in their use. As Herman Nelson once said ". . . it is in the application of principles which anyone can understand that management proves itself good or bad." This quite certainly applies here. As so often is the case with successful managers or organisations, the acid test is with implementation.

Notes

1. Berenbeim, R. E., *Corporate Ethics*, The Conference Board, New York, 1987, p. 3.

2. De George, R. T., *Business Ethics*, 2nd Ed., Macmillan, New York, 1986.

3. Steiner, G. A. and Steiner, J. F., *Business, Government and Society: A Managerial Perspective*, Random House, New York, 1980, pp. 383–9; Das, T. K., "Ethical Preferences among Business Students: A Comparative Study of Fourteen Ethical Principles," *Southern Management Association Proceedings*, 13–16 November, 1985, pp. 11–12.

4. Barry, V., *Moral Issues in Business*, Wadsworth, Belmont, California, 1979, pp. 50–51.

5. Shinn, R. L., *The Sermon on the Mount*, United Church Press, Philadelphia, 1962, pp. 76–7.

6. *The Forbes Scrapbook of Thoughts on the Business of Life*, Forbes, New York, 1976, p. 356.

Teaching Ethical Decision Making and Principled Reasoning

Michael Josephson

The ethical quality of our society is determined by the separate actions of public officials and their staffs, employers and their employees, parents and their children, teachers and their students, professionals and their clients, individuals and their friends. Each of us is almost always in one or more of these roles and our decisions are important. They are important on an individual level because they establish and define our ethical character. They are important on a social level because they produce significant direct consequences and, indirectly, help to set the moral tone of all social interactions.

Every day we face situations which test our ethical consciousness and commitment. Sometimes, the ethical implications of our decisions are apparent. Our consciences are awake and active, warning us to be good. In such cases, we know we will be held accountable for our conduct and we do not tell big lies, steal or break important promises.

Most of our decisions, however, are more mundane. They deal with our basic personal and occupational relationships and activities and there are no sirens causing us to view the choice as an ethical one. We rely heavily on habits, common sense and our perceptions of custom (i.e., what we think is generally considered acceptable by those engaged in similar activities). The dominant consideration is expediency—accomplishing our tasks, getting what we want, with as little hassle as possible.

Most of us do pretty well in dealing with the big and obvious ethical decisions. We tend to judge ourselves, and would like others to judge us by, these self-conscious choices which usually display our virtue. Unfortunately, we are more likely to be judged, and tripped up, by the way we handle the hundreds of ethical "sleepers" that cumulatively shape our reputations.

In recent years we have witnessed a growing concern about the way people are behaving. In fact, the proliferation of well-publicized examples of dishonesty, hypocrisy, cheating and greed has created some alarm about the state of personal ethics. If these incidents are indicative of a trend, there is much reason for concern because they reflect a level of selfishness, shortsightedness and insensitivity that could undermine the moral fabric of our society.

Ethics Education

In response to this new awareness, there has been a revived interest in ethics education. The pendulum of social conscience seems to be swinging the other way and there is a call for a return to traditional moral values and value-centered education. It has become clear to many that "value clarification," "situational ethics," and "ethical relativism" do not provide the inspiration, motivation or training to generate either the good will or discipline that are essential to moral conduct. Moreover, most academic courses which teach *about* ethics do not seem to engage students on a level that is likely to affect their behavior. The goal of the reformers is to find a way to increase ethical conduct.

We know that ethics are "learned" or "developed," yet many are not sure if ethics can be "taught." We do know that attitudes and character traits are not conveyed in the same way we convey other forms of knowledge (i.e., ethics is not something that can be taught like history or geography). Basic moral education occurs during the process of growing up. We learn from parents, teachers, religious leaders, coaches, employers, friends and others and, as a result, most of us reach adulthood with our character essentially formed and with a basic understanding of, and fundamental respect for, ethical values.

But, the presumptive values adopted in our youth are not immutably etched in our character. We know that values are constantly shuffled and prioritized, for better and for worse, in response to life experiences. Thus, youthful idealism is tested as we are emancipated into a world where important and binding decisions must be made. Only then do we discover what we are really willing to do to get and hold a job and be successful in a competitive society. By the same process, the blind competitiveness and materialism of young adulthood will later be challenged by life-changing experiences (e.g., illness, parenthood, divorce, death of a loved one) or the simple fact of maturation, causing one to reflect on the meaning of life (sometimes inducing a "mid-life crisis").

The point, and it has enormous significance for ethics educators, is that the formation, refinement and modification of a person's operational value system—the attitudes and beliefs that motivate conduct—are an ongoing process which continues throughout one's adult life. It is never too late.

Approaches To Ethics Education

One approach to conduct-oriented ethics education deals directly with the development of character and the inculcation and reinforcement of basic moral values such as honesty, caring, fairness and accountability. This approach has potential in the education of children and adolescents, but it is not likely to be effective in dealing with young adults and mature professionals.

The second approach focuses on the development of qualities beyond character—qualities that can be developed or enhanced even in adults. Ethical behavior is the result of ethical decisions, and ethical decision making requires: 1) *ethical commitment*—the personal resolve to act ethically, to do the right thing; 2) *ethical consciousness*—the ability to perceive the ethical implications of a situation; 3) *ethical competency*—the ability to engage in sound moral reasoning and develop practical problem solving strategies.

The purpose of this article is to present a theory of ethics education and to describe a framework for analyzing ethical problems which can be taught in college, postgraduate professional courses, and ethical decision making workshops.

Setting Reasonable Goals

> I am only one, but still I am one. I cannot do everything, but I can do something. And, because I cannot do everything, I will not refuse to do what I can.
>
> —*Edwin Hale*

> Those who believe they can do something are probably right, and so are those who believe they can't.
>
> —*Unknown*

It is important to recognize the limitations of ethics education. Many people will simply not respond to appeals to conscience or moral principle.

Many people are unwilling, or at a particular point in their lives, unready, to examine the ethical quality of their conduct and change their priorities. Thus, the most appropriate target for ethics programs is not bad and selfish people who knowingly do wrong, but the vast majority of decent people who are already disposed to act with propriety but who, because of lack of insight, rigorous moral reasoning or practical problem solving ability, lose sight of their ethical aspirations and make wrong decisions.

The importance and value of ethics education does not depend on the eradication of all misconduct. If just some of the people act more ethically just some of the time, the effort is worthwhile.

Defining Terms

In order to avoid the semantic quicksand that often engulfs discussions about ethics, it is necessary to define the essential terms and concepts involved.

Ethics refers to a system or code of conduct based on moral duties and obligations which indicate how we should behave; it deals with the ability to distinguish right from wrong and the commitment to do what is right.

Morals refers to what is good and right in character and conduct. The term is essentially interchangeable with ethics, though in common usage, "morality" often implies particular dogmatic views of propriety, especially as to sexual and religious matters. Since the term "ethics" does not carry these same connotations, it is more neutral.

Personal ethics refers to an individual's operational code of ethics based on personal values and beliefs as to what is right or good.

Values are core beliefs which guide or motivate attitudes and actions. Many values have nothing to do with ethics.

Ethical values are beliefs (e.g., honesty and fairness) which are inherently concerned with what is intrinsically good or right and the way one should act.

Nonethical values are ethically neutral values (e.g., wealth, security, comfort, prestige and approval). They are not necessarily inconsistent with ethical values, but often there is a conflict.

Ethical principles are standards or rules describing the kind of behavior an ethical person should and should not engage in. For example, the value of honesty translates into principles demanding truthfulness and candor and forbidding deception and cheating.

Ethical Norms

What is morality in any given time or place? It is what the majority then and there happen to like and immorality is what they dislike.

—*Alfred North Whitehead*

The so-called new morality is too often the old immorality condoned.

—*Lord Shawcross*

In matters of principle stand like a rock; in matters of taste swim with the current.

—*Thomas Jefferson*

It is critical to effective ethics education to overcome the cynicism of ethical relativism—the view that ethics is just a matter of opinion and personal belief as in politics or religion. Though debatable beliefs regarding sexual matters and religion often do travel under the passport of morality, there are ethical norms that transcend cultures and time.

While ethics educators must be aware that sermonizing and moralizing about particular ethical principles are not generally effective—after all, "No one likes to be 'should' upon" (a wonderful phrase from *How Can I Help?* by Ram Dass and Paul Gorman, Knopf 1985)—it is not constructive to be so value neutral that everyone is allowed to think that ethics is simply a matter of personal opinion and that one person's answer is necessarily as good as that of another's.

In fact, the study of history, philosophy and religion reveal a strong consensus as to certain universal and timeless values essential to the ethical life: 1) *Honesty,* 2) *Integrity,* 3) *Promise-Keeping,* 4) *Fidelity,* 5) *Fairness,* 6) *Caring for Others,* 7) *Respect for Others,* 8) *Responsible Citizenship,* 9) *Pursuit of Excellence,* and 10) *Accountability.*

These ten core values yield a series of *principles,* do's and don'ts, which delineate right and wrong in general terms and, therefore, provide a guide to behavior. Individuals may want to edit or augment the list, but we have found it to be a valuable tool in examining the ethical implications of a situation and providing solid reference points for ethical problem solving.

Ethical Principles

Honesty. Be truthful, sincere, forthright, straightforward, frank, candid; do not cheat, steal, lie, deceive, or act deviously.

Integrity. Be principled, honorable, upright, courageous and act on convictions; do not be two-faced, or unscrupulous or adopt an end-justifies-the-means philosophy that ignores principle.

Promise-Keeping. Be worthy of trust, keep promises, fulfill commitments, abide by the spirit as well as the letter of an agreement; do not interpret agreements in a technical or legalistic manner in order to rationalize noncompliance or create excuses for breaking commitments.

Fidelity. Be faithful and loyal to family, friends, employers, and country; do not use or disclose information learned in confidence; in a professional context, safeguard the ability to make independent professional judgments by scrupulously avoiding undue influences and conflicts of interest.

Fairness. Be fair and open-minded, be willing to admit error and, where appropriate, change positions and beliefs, demonstrate a commitment to justice, the equal treatment of individuals, and tolerance for diversity, do not overreach or take undue advantage of another's mistakes or adversities.

Caring for Others. Be caring, kind and compassionate; share, be giving, serve others; help those in need and avoid harming others.

Respect for Others. Demonstrate respect for human dignity, privacy, and the right to self- determination of all people; be courteous, prompt, and decent; provide others with the information they need to make informed decisions about their own lives; do not patronize, embarrass or demean.

Responsible Citizenship. Obey just laws (if a law is unjust, openly protest it); exercise all democratic rights and privileges responsibly by participation (voting and expressing informed views), social consciousness and public service; when in a position of leadership or authority, openly respect and honor democratic processes of decision making, avoid unnecessary secrecy or concealment of information, and assure that others have the information needed to make intelligent choices and exercise their rights.

Pursuit of Excellence. Pursue excellence in all matters; in meeting personal and professional responsibilities, be diligent, reliable, industrious, and committed; perform all tasks to the best of your ability, develop and maintain a high degree of competence, be well informed and well prepared; do not be content with mediocrity but do not seek to win "at any cost."

Accountability. Be accountable, accept responsibility for decisions and the foreseeable consequences of actions and inactions, and for setting an example for others. Parents, teachers, employers, many professionals and public officials have a special obligation to lead by example, to safeguard and advance the integrity and reputation of their families, companies, professions and the government; avoid even the appearance of impropriety and take whatever actions are necessary to correct or prevent inappropriate conduct of others.

The first question in ethical decision making is: "Which ethical principles are involved in the decision?" Considering the above list is an excellent way to isolate the relevant issues involved.

Ethical Theories

Though we run the risk of alienating many philosophy-oriented ethicists, in the Institute's programs we have not found it particularly useful to dwell on ethical theories. Our time with audiences is limited and most want to get immediately to the heart of ethical problem solving.

In fact, we present a variation of philosopher W. D. Ross' notion that there are certain *prima facie obligations* which impose ethical duties that can be avoided only in order to perform superior ethical duties—a kind of compromise between Kant's strict duty theory and John Stuart Mill's utilitarianism. Thus, implicit in our analysis of practical decision making situations is the principle that ethical duties are real, important and binding, and that they can be overborne only by other ethical duties.

The Golden Rule. On the other hand, we have found it helpful to emphasize the Golden Rule: "Do unto others as you would have them do unto

269

you; and love thy neighbor as thyself" Most of the ethical principles list-ed above can be derived from these simple statements.

This approach to ethical decision making is surprisingly effective. In many cases, simply by asking, "How would I want to be treated in this situation?" the ethical response becomes clear. We do not want to be lied to or deceived, so we should not lie to or deceive others. We want people to keep their promises and treat us fairly, so we should keep our promis-es and treat others fairly.

The major problem with the Golden Rule is that in complex cases, where a decision is likely to affect different people in different ways, a more sophisticated method of sorting out ethical responsibilities is necessary.

Stakeholder Analysis. To deal with these complex situations, we advo-cate an analytical tool developed in the corporate responsibility litera-ture. Since a decision is often likely to affect an entire network of people with differing interests, it is necessary to carefully sort out the interests by determining, in a systematic way, which people have a stake in the deci-sion. Thus, a threshold question in analyzing a problem is: "Who are the stakeholders and how is the decision likely to affect them?" This method does not solve the problem, but it helps the decision maker see all the eth-ical implications of conduct and reduces the likelihood of inadvertent harm.

Ethical Behavior

Would the boy you were be proud of the man you are?

—Laurence Peter

The trouble with the rat race is that even if you win, you're still a rat.

—Lily Tomlin

Ethics education works best when it builds upon our positive inclina-tions. Most people want to be ethical; they want to be worthy of the respect and admiration of others and they want to be proud of them-selves and what they do for a living. Self-esteem and self-respect depend on the private assessment of our own character. Very few people can accept the fact that they are less ethical than others. In fact, most people believe that they are more ethical.

Because of the importance of this positive self-image, many people will alter their conduct if they discover it is inconsistent with their espoused values. Thus, it is important to discuss candidly the common misconceptions and normal excuses, rationalization, and temptations which impede ethical conduct. Although some level of confrontation may be necessary to cut through natural defenses, it is critical to avoid an adversary atmosphere which will merely produce resistance. The most successful methods present participants with the opportunity to discuss pertinent and specific problems with peers and help them to clarify their ethical aspirations, engage in moral reflection, and enhance their ethical issue-spotting, reasoning and problem-solving abilities.

Common Misconceptions

Ethics Are Only Concerned with Misconduct. Most discussions about ethics focus on misconduct and improprieties—the negative dimension of ethics. But, as is apparent from our list of ethical principles, an equally important dimension of ethics focuses on positive actions, doing the right thing, on producing good, helping and caring, rather than on avoiding wrongdoing. Under this affirmative perspective, ethical principles are not merely burdens and limitations; they are also guidelines for the constructive role a person of virtue can play in society.

If It's Legal, It's Ethical. Law abidingness is an aspect of responsible citizenship and an ethical principle especially important in a democracy. We should not, however, confuse ethics with legality. Laws and written codes of ethics are minimalist in nature—they only establish the lines of consensus impropriety.

Ethics requires more of a person than technical compliance with rules. Everything that is lawful is not, *ipso facto*, ethical. Thus, the fact that certain conduct escapes the label of illegality, including the fact that a person has been formally acquitted of a criminal charge, does not, in itself, provide moral exoneration.

People we regard as ethical do not measure their conduct in terms of minimal standards of virtue. They do not walk the line, nor consistently resort to legalistic rationales to circumvent legitimate standards of behavior or the spirit of their agreements. Ethical persons consciously advance ethical principles by choosing to do more than they have to and less than they have a right to do.

The ethical person may, however, occasionally choose to openly violate a law believed to be unjust. The ethical value of lawfulness can be overborne by other conscience driven values. Thus, civil disobedience, the open and deliberate refusal to abide by certain laws, has a long and honorable history. The thing that makes such lawbreaking ethically justifiable is the integrity of the violator and the courage of convictions shown by the willingness to publicly challenge the law and bear the consequences. On the other hand, it is not ethical to break a law one disagrees with in the hope of not being found out. The kind of covert lawlessness that characterized the darker side of the Iran-Contra scandal does not qualify as civil disobedience.

There Is a Single Right Answer. An ethical decision maker does not proceed on the assumption that there is a single "right" answer to all ethical dilemmas. In most situations, there are a number of ethical responses. The first task is to distinguish ethical from unethical responses; the second, is to choose the best response from the ethically appropriate ones. Although there may be several ethical responses to a situation, all are not equal. Some are more ethical than others, and some are more consistent with an individual's personal goals and value system than others.

Excuses, Rationalizations and Temptations

It is important to try to understand why people tend to act unethically. An easy answer is that they are just plain bad. This is simply not so. The truth is that a great deal of improper conduct is committed by fundamentally decent people who believe in and are committed to ethical values. There are three major reasons that ethically concerned persons fail to conform to their own moral principles: 1) *unawareness and insensitivity*, 2) *selfishness*, consisting of self-indulgence, self-protection, and self-righteousness, and 3) *defective reasoning*.

Unawareness and Insensitivity

At the turn of the century, a Russian noblewoman attended an opera and wept out of compassion at the death of a poor peasant. She was still weeping when she left the opera house and found that her footman had frozen to death while waiting for her as he was instructed to do. She became angry, cursing his ignorance and her inconvenience, making no connection between her compassion and her conduct.

Moral blindness, the failure to perceive all the ethical implications of conduct, is a major source of impropriety. In some cases, this blindness results from the operation of subconscious defense mechanisms which protect the psyche from having to cope with the fact that many of the things we do and want to do are not consistent with our ethical beliefs. Elaborate and internally persuasive excuses and rationalizations are used to fool our consciences. Among the most potent are:

- Everyone does it.
- To get along, go along.
- They don't understand.
- I can't do anyone any good if I lose my job.
- I have no time for ethical subtleties.
- Ethics is a luxury I can't afford right now.
- It's not my job/worry/problem.

> You can't learn too soon that the most useful thing about principle is that it can always be sacrificed to expediency.
>
> —*Somerset Maugham*

> Senators who go down in defeat in defense of a single principle will not be on hand to fight for that or any other principle in the future.
>
> —*John F. Kennedy*

A common context for this ethical self-deception is occupational behavior. Most occupations develop the "insider syndrome" which rationalizes ethically dubious conduct and immunizes the occupation from the criticism of outsiders on the grounds that the critics simply don't understand the necessities and values that insiders take for granted.

Insider rationales are particularly effective at making expediency a new ethical principle which overrides integrity, honesty and accountability in order to achieve the "greater good" (i.e., the end justifies the means). For example, politicians are viewed as frequently relying on insider rationales to justify various forms of deception, the leaking of confidential information, and cynical manipulation of campaign financing and outside income rules. Journalists are thought to justify the use of stolen documents, invasions of privacy, and arrogant and offensive interviewing behavior—all based upon vague notions of the public's right to know, though the public regularly denounces such press tactics.

Selfishness. Implicit in all ethical theories is the notion of caring for and respecting others. In many cases, this requires us to forego personal benefits or bear personal burdens; some level of self-sacrifice is essential to consistent ethical conduct. Thus, selfishness continually assaults the conscience with temptations and rationalizations.

The natural inclination to selfishness has been amplified by certain self-actualizing philosophies coming out of the 1960s and 1970s which either advocated or were misinterpreted to condone selfishness. In the 1980s these philosophies seemed to spawn a generation of greedy people whose dominant values stress materialism.

Although there are many who proudly proclaim their individualistic "everyone for himself/herself" creed, most do not. Most still believe in the primacy of traditional values such as integrity, loyalty, giving, and sharing, but they are influenced by their environment and the ample supply of excuses and justifications developed to defend the new faith. Selfishness comes in three major forms: 1) self-indulgence, 2) self-protection, and 3) self-righteousness.

Self-Indulgence. Perhaps the most common and easily identifiable source of unethical conduct is self-indulgence. Although few people are as open as Ivan Boesky was when he publicly asserted that "greed is good," many people lie, break commitments, violate or evade laws, and fail to demonstrate caring, compassion and charity in order to advance narrow personal interests. They often cover-up the selfish motive with noble sounding sentiments, e.g., "I'm doing it for my family"; "I'm creating (or protecting) jobs"; "If the business doesn't survive it will be worse for everyone"; "It's in the interests of all the shareholders (or the public)"; and, "My constituency needs me."

Self-Protection. The instinct for self-protection often generates lying, deception and cover-ups, including big and little lies (e.g., "I knew nothing about this"; "The check is in the mail"; "Tell him I'm not in"), concealment, blameshifting, and even document destruction. These actions frequently result from a fear of, or unwillingness to accept, the consequences of prior behavior. The temptation to sacrifice ethical principles is particularly great when it is believed that the consequences will be unfair or disproportionate—an easy thing to believe when you are the one to suffer the consequences.

Self-Righteousness. A particularly troublesome type of selfishness results from a form of arrogance arising from self-righteousness. For example, Colonel Oliver North demonstrated a type of integrity when he decided to "go above the law" by shredding documents, lying and deceiving, and withholding vital information to advance his strong personal convictions. The ethical problem arises, however, from the fact that he knew that his beliefs were at variance with honest good faith beliefs of others who had at least an equal right to participate in the decision making process. His conduct denied these people the ability to exercise personal autonomy and deprived them of the ability to carry out their constitutional responsibilities. He did not openly disagree with the Congressional mandates and statutes; instead, he sought to privately nullify them by ignoring them. To accomplish his goals he violated ethical principles of honesty, promise-keeping, respect for others, and responsible democratic citizenship.

Defective Reasoning. In addition to sorting out the various values involved and those stakeholders affected, a substantial amount of factual analysis and prediction of consequences is necessary to ethical decision making. This requires sophisticated reasoning skills; defects in reasoning or mistakes in evaluation can result in decisions which are inconsistent with ethical principles. We find two common errors: people consistently overestimate the costs of doing the right thing, and underestimate the cost of failing to do the right thing.

Principled reasoning directs the decision maker to recognize where information is incomplete, uncertain or ambiguous, and to make reasonable efforts to get additional information and clarify the ambiguities! After evaluating the facts, the next step is to predict, with as much certainty as is reasonably possible, the likely consequences of contemplated conduct on all those affected by a decision (i.e., stakeholders).

Another defective reasoning problem, related to the selfishness issues, emanates from the fact that unethical conduct normally yields short-run benefits which, when looked at through the distorted lens of self-interest, seem to outweigh the *possibility* of long-range harms which may flow from unethical conduct. Often, it is easier to lie, deceive, conceal or disregard commitments than to confront a problem head on and accept the costs inherent in honesty and integrity.

The fact is that an ethical person must often sacrifice short-term benefits to achieve long-term advantages. He or she must also be prepared to sacrifice physical or material gains for abstract intangibles such as self-esteem, the respect of others, reputation and a clear conscience. An ethical person must be able to distinguish between short-term and long-term benefits and costs.

Ethical Decision Making

Ethical decision making refers to a process of choosing (i.e., principled reasoning) which systematically considers and evaluates alternate courses of conduct in terms of the list of ethical principles. It does not proceed on the assumption that there is a single "right" answer to most problems. To the contrary, it recognizes that though some responses would be unethical, in most situations there are a number of ethical ways of dealing with a situation.

The first task of ethical decision making is to distinguish ethical from unethical responses; the second is to choose the best response from the ethically appropriate ones. Although there may be several ethical responses to a situation, all are not equal.

Making the distinctions necessary is much more difficult and complex than is normally thought because, in so many real world situations, there are a multitude of competing interests and values, and crucial facts are unknown or ambiguous. Since our actions are likely to benefit some at the expense of others, ethical decision makers also attempt to foresee the likely consequences of their actions.

We cannot solve all problems by resorting to some mechanistic formula, but we can be more effective if we have a structure. A process which systematically takes into account the ethical principles involved in a decision tends to prevent inadvertent unethical conduct and allows us to consciously choose which values to advance—to determine whom to aid and whom to harm.

When one is in the trenches, it is difficult, if not impossible, to analyze problems fully and objectively. While most people do not want more rules telling them what to do, they do want assistance in perceiving the ethical implications of their decisions and in developing realistic, morally-centered approaches for resolving ethical dilemmas. . . .

In the "real world" there are many shades of gray, even in routine decision making. Most of these decisions are made in the context of economic, professional, and social pressures which compete with ethical goals and conceal or confuse the moral issues. We must, therefore, be ever vigilant to use principled reasoning in the pursuit of ethical decision making. The essential skills *can* be taught to adults; their subsequent behavior *can* be more ethical. It may not always be simple to do, but, then again, ethics truly are "easier said than done."

Corporate Social Responsibility: Wisdom from the World's Religions

Dennis P. McCann

The historic move toward a single, globally integrated, market economy provides a new context in which to ask perennial questions about the role of moral and, especially, religious values in business and economic development. Among these questions, the most timely and yet neglected, at least within conventional thinking on business and economics, is this: What role should the world's major religious traditions play in promoting corporate social responsibility? What follows is meant to open this question for general discussion, beyond the professional concerns of theologians, religious ethicists, and specialists in the sociology of religion. It will outline in broad strokes how the relationship between religious values and economic and social organization is generally understood in the field of religious studies and why a general knowledge of comparative religious ethics may provide a useful orientation to corporate social responsibility.

Corporate social responsibility is not a prominent concept in either the literature of comparative religious ethics or of inquiries into business ethics that are in interdisciplinary dialogue with this field. This does not necessarily mean that businesses not under the sway of Western religious and moral values do not exercise corporate social responsibility. Nor does it mean that U.S.-based firms must abandon their commitments to corporate social responsibility to remain competitive in the global economy. The evidence I will present warrants neither conclusion. Instead, it suggests that the ways in which business corporations exercise corporate responsibility are a function of long-term trends that may be as diverse as the cultural histories in which they are embedded. The wisdom of the world's religions thus points out the folly of assuming that there is any single model of economic development, modernization, organizational behavior, or business ethics. Some of the non-Western religious traditions, in fact, may be more effective in promoting corporate social responsibility than we have been recently in the post-Christian West. If the so-called "good corporation" is dead, an autopsy may show that its death has less to do with the pressures of global competition than it does with our own increasingly dysfunctional values.

Laboring in the Shadow of Max Weber

The most accessible place to begin a general discussion of the relationship between religious values and economic and social organization is still Michael Novak's *The Spirit of Democratic Capitalism* (1982). Novak argued convincingly that a certain range of religious values within the history of Christianity was, in fact, creative of the "spirit" of democratic capitalism. Novak's purpose was not analytical—he meant to rally support for democratic capitalism at a time when many intellectuals, including most major theologians and Christian ethicists, had grown skeptical of it during the wearying later stages of the Cold War. Novak's audience, for the most part, did not need to be convinced of the significance of "spirit" because their question, as well as his own, was primarily theological—they were seeking to determine which social system, capitalism or socialism, was more compatible with the moral imperatives and religious world view of classical Christianity. He and they simply presupposed that religious and moral values created social systems and were not, as Marxist and other ideologies would have it, a mere reflection of economic and social arrangements based on other strategic imperatives.

It is to this basic presupposition I must turn to determine the role of the world's religious traditions in shaping the global economy, and not simply those of classical Christianity. Here, Novak rightly appreciates Max Weber's seminal work, *The Protestant Ethic and the Spirit of Capitalism* (1920), for clarifying the relationship between religious values and economic development. But he dissents from Weber's gloomy assessment of capitalism's diminishing prospects and implicitly challenges his assumption that only a specifically Protestant version of the Christian world view and ethos is capable of sustaining a capitalist model of economic development. The theological dimensions of Novak's argument are couched in the traditions of Roman Catholic thought that, in his view, provide a more useful explication of the metaphysics, as it were, of economic development, by showing how capitalist enterprise plays a role in fulfilling humanity's destiny in the Divine Life of the Holy Trinity.

Novak's Catholic celebration of the spirit of capitalism is itself a reflection of the success of American Catholics who have achieved an impressive degree of upward social mobility, especially in the post-New Deal period when capitalism became as democratic as it ever has been in this country. American Catholics became successful capitalists without transferring their religious allegiance to Protestantism. To the extent that Weber argued for an exclusive connection between the Protestant ethic and capitalism, his thesis has been refuted by the social history of American Catholicism. On the other hand, Weber was at least partly right about the historically creative role of the Protestant ethic. For the history of American Catholicism, as well as Novak's own theology, demonstrate that the dominant Protestant ethic did provide a template for social change that unleashed transformative energies within the immigrant Catholic communities that had access to it. The church in the United States transformed itself in response to the challenges of the Protestant social environment, thereby creating both a Catholic work ethic, under the aegis of "devotional Catholicism," and a complementary sense of social responsibility, faithful to the traditions of Catholic social teaching. I must insist, however, that this historic process of acculturation cannot be understood as simply tailoring religious values to fit new economic opportunities. Weber's general defense of the significance of religious values is supported by the broad contours of American Catholic social history which continues to have a transformative impact on the institutions of democratic capitalism.

My purpose is not to rehearse this argument, which is implicit in my discussion of the American Catholic bishops' economic pastoral letter, *New Experiment in Democracy: The Challenge for American Catholicism* (1987). Instead, using this relatively familiar example, I want to launch out into the unfamiliar territory occupied by the world's major religious traditions to see whether something similar to the American Catholic experience with capitalism has been under way in non-Western cultures, with similarly momentous consequences for the global economy. Here, too, one immediately encounters the eminence of Max Weber who was not content to study religion in the narrow confines of European history. Faced with the unprecedented expansion of European hegemony throughout the world that the nineteenth century had witnessed, Weber did similar ground-breaking studies on the religions of China and India. It is not surprising that, given their decadent circumstances at the time of his studies, Weber concluded that the traditional cultures of Asia and their distinctive religious world views were incapable of generating the spirit necessary for capitalist development. If South and East Asia were to develop economically, they would do so to the extent that they would abandon their inherited religious and moral values and adopt the so-called "universal ethic" characteristic of liberal Protestantism.

In reality, at least one Asian nation was already busily refuting Weber's assessment even before it went to print. I refer, of course, to Japan, whose distinct path toward modernization had begun with the Meiji restoration in 1868. By the time Weber was contemplating the fate of East Asia, Japan had selectively opened itself to European models of politics, economics, science, and technology, while adapting its religious traditions to the challenges of an urban industrial society. The success of this new model of Asian development was publicly ratified by Japan's astonishing military victories, first against China and then in 1904 against Russia, the first European state to be defeated by a non-Western power in, perhaps, half a millennium.

The history of Japan's economic development—and, increasingly, that of the rest of South and East Asia—challenges Weber's thesis in a way that is strikingly similar to what I infer from the social history of American Catholicism. The Protestant ethic (and its secular surrogates) is not the only religious and moral foundation capable of supporting capitalist economic development. Modernizing religious traditions such as those of the Japanese and of American Catholics appear to be just as effective in generating an appropriate spirit for capitalism. So Weber is wrong, if he meant to assert any ethical monopoly for liberal Protestantism. On the other hand, Japanese history tends to confirm that Weber is right about the creative role of religious values in economic and social organization, for the history of modern Japan cannot be understood apart from the history of its attempt to modernize its own religious and moral traditions.

Those concerned with business ethics in a global economy ought to be challenged profoundly by the twentieth century's unexpectedly diverse patterns of modernization and economic development. Recent history suggests that business ethics in a global economy can and ought to be religiously pluralistic and grounded in a hermeneutical perspective that takes the world's religious traditions seriously as living witnesses to the moral aspirations of humanity. Business executives who expect to make a significant contribution to the development of a global economy would be well advised to familiarize themselves with the history of religions, and business schools that are serious about business ethics ought to make comparative religious ethics a constitutive part of the core curriculum for the M.B.A. or at least, for M.B.A.s with concentration in international business. But it is not sufficient merely to preach a sermon on this topic. Such proposals require supporting evidence, and the more disruptive the changes proposed, the more compelling the evidence ought to be. In what follows, I hope to present enough evidence to encourage further study of these questions.

The Business Ethics of Classical Hinduism

Throughout the world, the dawn of civilization is generally marked by prayer. Skeptics may dismiss the pervasiveness of religion in antiquity as so much superstition, soon to be dispelled by further advances in science and technology. A more discerning view, however, is possible: Just what do the prayers that have been preserved tell us about the everyday concerns of our ancestors? Here is an ancient prayer that, I, for one, found very surprising. It is from the *Atharva Veda* (The Book of Spells and Incantations), one of the four *samhitas* (hymnbooks) containing the most ancient strands of Hindu tradition. This hymn speaks to our purposes, for it is dedicated to "Success in Trading":

> I stir and animate the merchant Indra: may he approach and be our guide and leader.
> Chasing ill-will, wild beast, and highway robber, may he who hath the power give me riches.
> The many paths which Gods are wont to travel, the paths which go between the earth and heaven,
> May they rejoice with me in milk and fatness that I may make rich profit by my purchase.
> With fuel, Agni! and with butter, longing, mine offering I present for strength and conquest;
> With prayer, so far as I have strength adoring—this holy hymn to gain a hundred treasures.
> Pardon this stubbornness of ours, O Agni, the distant pathway which our feet have trodden.
> Propitious unto us be sale and barter, may interchange of merchandise enrich me.
> Accept, ye twain, accordant, this libation! Prosperous be our ventures and incomings.
> The wealth wherewith I carry on my traffic, seeking, ye Gods! wealth with the wealth I offer,
> May this grow more for me, not less: O Agni, through sacrifice chase those who hinder profit!
>
> *(Atharva Veda*, III:15 in Embree, 1972: 38–39)

The hymn is as noteworthy for what it says as for what it does not say. Not only are Indra (the Aryan sky warrior-king, like the Greek Zeus, the guarantor of the moral order) and Agni (the god of fire, who, among other things, is active in making ritual acts of sacrifice propitious)—two of the most important deities in the Vedic pantheon—invoked on behalf of money-making, but money-making, or commercial-exchange relations generally, clearly is regarded as morally legitimate and ennobling.

Noticeably absent from the hymn is any sense that business is a morally unworthy occupation. This lack of moral ambivalence ought to strike us as surprising if we compare it with the rather different attitude projected in the classical period of Western civilization. Aristotle's *Politics*, for example, enshrines the antibusiness bias of the Hellenistic aristocracy in terms of the natural law. His economics, based as it is on the *oikos* or aristocratic household, offers a theory of property, defined first in relationship to the *oikos* and not with reference to exchange relations in the marketplace. Understood primarily as a means of maintaining the household, property or wealth thus has a fixed or natural limit. Ironically, Aristotle is able to reconcile such a limit by legitimating both slavery and warfare as natural ways of acquiring property. Economics, or household management, thus generally is focused on developing the skills necessary to secure and preserve the *padrone*'s rule over his slaves, women, and children.

Our focus, however, must remain on the way in which Aristotle contends that such natural limits preclude making one's living by commercial exchange:

> There are two sorts of wealth-getting, as I have said; one is part of household management [i.e., agriculture], the other is retail trade: the former is necessary and honorable, while that which consists in exchange is justly censured; for it is unnatural, and a mode by which men gain from one another. The most hated sort, and with the greatest reason, is usury, which makes a gain out of money itself, and not from the natural object of it. For money was intended to be used in exchange, but not to increase at interest. And this term interest, which means the birth of money from money, is applied to the breeding of money because the offspring resembles the parent. That is why of all modes of getting wealth this is the most unnatural.
>
> (Aristotle, 1984: 1997)

Aristotle's dim view of exchange relations, tied as it is to his understanding of natural law, was to survive the passing of the Hellenistic civilization in which it was formulated. More than the teachings of Jesus of Nazareth, Aristotle has shaped the moral skepticism about commerce that is characteristic of Christian social ethics to this day. (Cf. McCann 1994, 1989)

Commerce in ancient India labored under no such similar prejudice, but that does not mean that the Vedas contain teachings that are a functional substitute for Weber's modernizing Protestant ethic. The texts yield a picture that is far more complex, one in which economic activity is embedded in a larger scheme of human and cosmic purposes. The ideal moral order upheld by classical Hinduism consists of a series of interrelated quaternities, the most basic of which are the four *varnas*, commonly known as the caste system. Already in the *Rig Veda*, the earliest of the Vedic hymnbooks, there is the famous *Purusha-sukta* ("The Primeval Sacrifice") in which a sacred Person, "Thousand-headed Purusha," is ritually dismembered in order to create the cosmos. Here is part of that hymn:

> When they divided Purusha, in how many different portions did they arrange him? What became of his mouth, what of his two arms? What were his two thighs and his two feet called?
> His mouth became the *brahmin*; his two arms were made into the *rajanya*; his two thighs the *vaishyas*; from his two feet the *shudra* was born.

The moon was born from the mind, from the eye the sun was born; from the mouth Indra and Agni, from the breath (*prana*) the wind (*vaya*) was born.

(*Rig Veda* 10.90, in deBary, 1958: 14–15)

The ideal division of labor symbolized by the four *varnas*—here designated as *brahmin, rajanya, vaishyas,* and *shudra*—is just as intrinsic to the cosmic order as are the passages of the sun and moon. The *brahmin* are the religious hierarchy, the *rajanya*—usually referred to as *kshatriya*—are the warrior aristocracy, and the *vaishya* are the householders, those who produce wealth, *including* the merchants. The *shudra*, of course, are those who do the dirty work.

Each of these ideal *varnas* has its own distinctive set of caste duties. While there are nine duties that are "eternal" and morally oblige members of "all four orders [equally]"—"the suppression of wrath, truthfulness of speech, justice, forgiveness, begetting one's children on one's own wedded wives, purity of conduct, avoidance of quarrel, simplicity, and maintenance of dependents" (*Mahabharata* XII:60, in Embree, 1972: 80)—the basic sense of how one fits into the cosmic order of things is tied less to this universal ethic than it is to one's distinctive caste duties. Here are those of the *vaishya*. Notice how this discourse knows no moral distinction between commerce and animal husbandry of the sort that Aristotle decreed:

> I shall now tell thee, O Yudhishthira, what the eternal duties of the Vaishya are. A Vaishya should make gifts, study the Vedas, perform sacrifices, and acquire wealth by fair means. With proper attention he should also protect and rear all [domestic] animals as a sire protecting his sons. Anything else that he will do will be regarded as improper for him. . . . I shall tell thee what the Vaishya's profession is and how he is to earn the means of his sustenance. If he keeps [for others] six kine, he may take the milk of one cow as his remuneration; and if he keeps [for others] a hundred kine, he may take a single pair as such fee. If he trades with others' wealth, he may take a seventh part of the profits [as his share]. A seventh also is his share in the profits arising from the trade in horns, but he should take a sixteenth if the trade be in hooves. If he engages in cultivation with seeds supplied by others, he may take a seventh part of the yield. This should be his annual remuneration. A Vaishya should never desire that he should not tend cattle. If a Vaishya desires to tend cattle, no one else should be employed in that task.
>
> (*Mahabharata* XII: 60, in Embree, 1972: 82)

Though cattle are regarded as the primary form of wealth, and the householder's expertise in animal husbandry is understood as the primary means of creating wealth, the Vaishya's duties will lead him inevitably into the commercial activities that usually are seen as the exclusive prerogative of his *varna* as such.

The exceptional circumstances in which members of the other high castes, *brahman* and *kshatriya*, are permitted to engage in commerce tend to confirm my thesis that business ethics in the Hindu tradition is role- and institution-specific and not, as in Weber's Protestant ethic, a reflection of universal moral imperatives. Here is a text that suggests how important the distinction of roles is, not just for understanding business ethics, but for appreciating the very nature of the ideal moral order. Keep in mind that the hierarchical ordering of the *varnas*, in Vedic theory at least, reflects the natural ordering of the various parts of the Purusha's cosmic body:

> Among the several occupations the most commendable are, teaching the Veda for a Brahmana, protecting the people for a Kshatriya, and trade for a Vaishya.
>
> But a Brahmana, unable to subsist by his peculiar occupations just mentioned, may live according to the law applicable to Kshatriyas; for the latter is next to him in rank.
>
> If it be asked, "How shall it be, if he cannot maintain himself by either of these occupations?" the answer is, he may adopt a Vaishya's mode of life, employing himself in agriculture and rearing cattle.
>
> But he who, through a want of means of subsistence, gives up the strictness with respect to his duties, may sell, in order to increase his wealth, the commodities sold by Vaishyas, making however the following exceptions.
>
> He must avoid selling condiments of all sorts, cooked food and sesamum, stones, salt, cattle, and human beings,
>
> All dyed cloth, as well as cloth made of hemp, or flax, or wool, even though they be not dyed, fruit, roots, and medical herbs;
>
> Water, weapons, poison, meat, Soma, and perfumes of all kinds, fresh milk, honey, sour milk, clarified butter, oil, wax, sugar, Kusa-grass;
>
> All beasts of the forest, animals with fangs or tusks, birds, spirituous liquor, indigo, lac, and all one-hoofed beasts.
>
> (*Manu Smriti* X: 80–100, in Embree, 1972: 94)

The extraordinary detail in this list of exceptions suggests two things: (1) that modern India's initial preference for an extraordinarily complicated system of commercial regulations seems to go back a long way; (2) that the specific items in which non-*vaishyas* are forbidden to trade are not prohibited because they are universally immoral as, say, we might regard trafficking in illegal drugs. Castes higher than *vaishya* cannot trade in these items—even if they are forced to abandon their caste duties and go into business—because illegitimate contact with them may incur a penalty for ritual impurity.

The four *varnas*, however, merely scratch the surface of Hindu business ethics. Each of the three higher castes, which alone participate fully in the religious life of classical Hinduism, exhibits an ideal pattern of occupations—the four *ashramas*—that define still further the moral order distinctive of each stage of life. The four *ashramas*—student, householder, retiree, and homeless wanderer or *sannyasin*—spell out how the various stages in life participate in the common pursuit of the four normative goals of human existence. The four goals—*dharma* (the pursuit of virtue or preservation of the moral order), *artha* (wealth), *kama* (sensual pleasure), and *moksha* (ultimate liberation)—suggest that the ultimate meaning of life consists in overcoming *samsara*, the wheel or, if you will, the treadmill of rebirths. This lofty, but bleak account describes the human predicament as a potentially infinite series of lifetimes, in which each person struggles to liberate him- or herself from this world by achieving nirvana. Nirvana should not be confused with the Heaven longed for by orthodox Christians; nirvana is the cessation of *samsara*, the void in which there is no further necessity of rebirth. *Moksha*, the ultimate goal, means finally overcoming the world as we know it. The higher castes are closer to this goal; they are reborn to their higher status precisely because of the degree of success they have had previously in living the *dharmas* assigned to them.

I find this to be an astonishingly powerful religious vision. But we cannot pause here to contemplate its varied ethical implications. Since our focus is on religious resources for business ethics, we must confine ourselves to the penultimate goals, especially *artha* and *kama*, the pursuit of wealth and pleasure, and their overriding significance in the *dharma* specific to the householder stage in life. The Hindu householder, like the Hellenistic *padrone*, presides over an extended family and its dependents. No question: this is also the template of traditional patriarchy. But the patriarchal household, like it or not, was the central economic institution in this society. Upon the householder devolves the responsibilities of management, which are inevitably a mixture of religious, familial, and business duties. Social responsibility, including whatever care the destitute were likely to receive from their neighbors, was incumbent upon the householder who possessed the means of helping others precisely because he was skilled at creating and preserving wealth.

The following text suggests the ideal of selflessness proper to the stage in life devoted to *artha* and *kama*:

A householder should perform every day a Smriti rite. . . . He should
  perform a Vedic rite on the sacred fires. . . .
Offering the food oblation, offerings with the proper utterance,
  performance of Vedic sacrifices, study of the sacred texts, and honoring
  guests—these constitute the five great daily sacrifices dedicated
  respectively to the spirits, the manes, the gods, the Brahman, and men.

He should offer the food oblation to the spirits (by throwing it in the air) out of the remnant of the food offered to the gods. He should also cast food on the ground for dogs, untouchables, and crows.

Food, as also water, should be offered by the householder to the manes and men day after day. He should continuously carry on his study. He should never cook for himself only.

Children, married daughters living in the father's house, old relatives, pregnant women, sick persons, and girls, as also guests and servants—only after having fed these should the householder and his wife eat the food that has remained. . . .

Having risen before dawn the householder should ponder over what is good for the Self. He should not, as far as possible, neglect his duties in respect of the three ends of man, namely, virtue, material gain, and pleasure, at their proper times.

Learning, religious performances, age, family relations, and wealth—on account of these and in the order mentioned are men honored in society. By means of these, if possessed in profusion, even a shudra deserves respect in old age.

(*Yajnavalkya Smriti*, I:97–116; in Embree, 1972: 87–88)

Clearly, the pursuit of wealth traditionally enjoined upon the Hindu householder is anything but a pretext for possessive individualism.

I have suggested that classical Hinduism's role of specific ethics of *dharma* may be a more promising point of departure for business ethics than the classical Western heritage enshrined in the texts of Hellenistic philosophers like Aristotle. Not that Hindu *dharma* is morally superior to Greek *arete* (or virtue ethics), but that in our Western penchant for ethical universalizability, we—or at least some of Aristotle's disciples, notably the influential philosopher Alasdair MacIntyre—have tended to decontextualize Aristotle's comments on money-making as if they were meant, not as prudent advice to future *padrones*, but as an eternally valid judgment on the ethical merits of careers in business as such. Aristotle can be read plausibly either way; the Hindu tradition, however, suffers from no such equivocation. A virtuous life in business is not only *not* an oxymoron, it is the specific way in which *vaishyas* fulfill their religious duties and, by implication, their moral duties to the rest of society, beginning with their own dependents.

Such a perspective, however, is still a far cry from the Weberian version of the Protestant work ethic. The ultimate goal of life, seeking the *moksha* that overcomes *samsara*, clearly suggests the otherworldly asceticism that Weber regarded as a barrier to capitalist development. But the penultimate goals in life—*dharma, artha*, and *kama*—are also given their due, and in a manner that strikes me as more encouraging to business than comparable traditions in the classical antiquity of the West. Why, then, did not the spirit of capitalism first emerge in India?

One could cite India's long history of colonial oppression, to be sure, beginning with the Moghul Empire and, later, the hegemony of the British East India Company, and culminating in the British Raj that reserved to itself control over modern India's economy.

Weber, however, was less impressed by the political history than by the typical patterns of Hindu social organization. He felt that modern capitalism required a degree of impersonalism in business relationships that could be sustained only on the basis of a universal ethic that, in a biblical sense, was no respecter of persons. Business was best kept separate from family affairs; favoritism based on kinship or other forms of social dependency necessarily would inhibit successful economic performance. The Protestant ethic, in his view, provided the key to capitalist development, not simply because of its fresh perspective on worldly affairs but because it encouraged covenantal forms of association that, in principle, were open to strangers. Business enterprises could be hived off from the patriarchal household and managed on the basis of impersonal, contractual agreements, a universal framework of commercial law that embodied, at least in part, the covenantal moral imperatives of Protestant Christianity.

Weber, therefore, remained pessimistic about the future of modern capitalism in Asia because he could find nothing in the traditional cultures of India and China equivalent to the Protestant ethic. Nevertheless, modern capitalism, as we have seen, has found a home in Asia and has become successful enough to be globally competitive, not just as a major exporter of manufactured goods but as an alternative model to our customary thinking about economics and business management. What Weber regarded as most likely to retard capitalist development in Asia, namely, the various cultures' primary commitment to business organization based on kinship and other forms of social dependency, now strikes many observers as the secret to Asian economic success. We turn, then, to East Asia where the religious significance of kinship is as well documented as the successful economic performance of its corporations. Is there a connection between the two?

Capitalism and East Asian Family Values

East Asia's extraordinary record of economic growth is not news and has not been news for the past quarter of a century. What such growth means for the global economy, and how it is reshaping the prospects for U.S. economic development are important strategic questions whose answers will determine, as they are already determining, the parameters for future discussion of corporate social responsibility. My immediate concern, however, is with the religious dimensions of the East Asian challenge. To what extent is East Asia's success based on cultural factors that, inevitably, are religiously rooted? How do religious values continue to shape the meaning of economic activity in this region and the forms of business organization in which it is carried out?

Empirical inquiry into the nature of an "East Asian Development Model" tend to presuppose the so-called post-Confucian hypothesis. This theory explores a possible link between the powerful and pervasive influence of Confucianism upon what has been characterized as East Asia's Sinitic civilization and the region's distinctive patterns of modernization and economic development. The Confucian influence is particularly apparent in Japan and the newly industrializing countries (NIC), heretofore restricted to the "four little tigers," South Korea, Taiwan, Hong Kong, and Singapore but now also including much of coastal China, Viet-Nam, Malaysia, Indonesia, and Thailand. The hypothesis asserts that a modernized form of Confucianism—what Robert M. Bellah aptly called "bourgeois Confucianism" (Berger 1990, 7)—is as important for understanding the distinctive success of the East Asian development model as is the recent political and economic history of the region. If the hypothesis is confirmed, it will tend to reinforce the argument made so far regarding Weber's views of capitalism and religious values, but it will also show how modernizing inherited religious traditions, rather than abandoning them entirely, can actually work to enhance a nation's prospects for economic development.

There are few direct affinities linking classical Hinduism with Confucianism, but both religious perspectives tend to legitimate the household as the central economic and social unit in society. The bedrock of Chinese cultural tradition is emphatically this-worldly and apparently knows nothing of the otherworldly concerns governing classical Hinduism's pursuit of *moksha*. Sacred powers, gods, and goddesses, including the living spirits of dead ancestors, exert a powerful influence upon this world. They are as real, and just as unpredictable, as we are. Religious practice therefore seeks to establish a mutually beneficial accommodation between the sacred and the profane, a harmonious balance of power that is thought to reflect the will of Heaven (*T'ien*), the ultimate—though hardly personal—embodiment of the cosmic order itself (*Tao*).

The moral emphasis in Confucianism is unmistakable. The core of ethical concern is expressed in the concept of *hsiao* or filiality, which is the ideal governing the nucleus of social relationships in the Chinese household. *Hsiao* is to be realized in all five of these relationships: children to their parents; subjects to their ruler; wife to husband; younger brother to older brother; younger friend to older friend. Each of these, obviously, is hierarchical, involving a subordinate and a superior; yet each also involves mutual obligations and mutual respect.

Indeed, the whole of social ethics can be understood as a "rectification of names," insofar as each of these relationships carries its own objective standards. To achieve right relationship one must recognize what is at stake in the name given it. The *hsiao* that a subject owes his ruler, for example, is implicit in what it means to be subject and what it means to be ruler.

Confucian ethics thus emphasizes the thread of continuity linking the reciprocities operative in the five basic relationships. The Chinese nation as a whole was the Emperor's extended family, and the patterns of mutual obligation characteristic of the relationships of children to their parents were expected to set the moral tone for imperial government. The following text suggests the universal scope of *hsiao*:

> The Master said: "Formerly the illustrious kings governed the empire by filiality. They did not dare neglect the ministers of small countries—to say nothing of their own dukes, marquises, earls, counts, and barons! Thus, they gained the readiness of all the countries to serve their former kings. The rulers did not dare insult the widows and the widowers—to say nothing of officials and ordinary citizens! Thus, they gained the grateful love of all the people in the service of their former princes. The heads of families did not dare mistreat their servants and concubines—to say nothing of their wives and children! Thus they gained the readiness of the people to serve their parents. Accordingly, while living, parents enjoyed all prosperity; after their death, sacrifices were offered to their spirits. In this way the world was kept in peace and harmony; calamities did not arise, nor disorders occur. Such was the world government by filiality of the former kings."
>
> The Odes say:
> "They gave an example of virtuous conduct
> And all the nations submitted themselves."
>
> (*Hsiao Ching*: VIII; in Camenisch, 1991: 174–175)

Thus, in the Sinitic civilization, political ethics—at least as an ideal—tend to conform to the norms embodied in the household or extended family. Just the opposite tendency seems to be apparent in our own society, where the ethical expectations governing family life in our post-Christian society seem increasingly dependent upon our continuing experiment with political democracy and human rights.

Asian family values, as commonly discussed in analyses of East Asia's strategic strengths in the global economy, are the pervasive and enduring heritage of the Confucian ethic of *hsiao*. To be sure, modern Japanese business corporations are not simply an extension of the premodern Sinitic household. But the link between the two has been documented in various studies, and that link is highly suggestive of the ways in which modernizing religious traditions are economically significant. One such study is Koichi Shinohara's "Religion and Economic Development in Japan: An Exploration Focusing on the Institution of *Ie*" (Shinohara 1983, 167–178). *Ie*, like its Chinese cognate, *jia*, refers to house or household, in a sense roughly equivalent to the classical Greek, *oikos*, the Latin, *domus*, and the Spanish, *casa*. As Shinohara asserts, "*ie* is best understood as the basic unit of communal life and consists of all those who live under one roof and eat meals prepared in the same kitchen" (1983: 168). He opts here for a broad definition, in order not to restrict the *ie* to blood kinship as such. Adoptions are common within the traditional *ie*. To preserve continuity within the household, it is customary for a widow to remain within her former husband's *ie*, in order to raise the children there. Typically, the *ie* is internally differentiated, as subordinate branches of the family (*bunke*) can be established in relation to the main branch (*honke*), whose head (*kacho*) retains substantial control of the entire household's property. Though the *ie* developed historically in the premodern period and is clearly documented in the mid-Tokugawa period (eighteenth century C.E.), its survival in modern Japan until after World War II is admirably conveyed in Tanizaki's splendid novel, *The Makioka Sisters* (1957).

The religious and moral values embedded in the premodern *ie* came to dominate modern Japanese business practices by a process of cultural diffusion. Shinohara argues that the internal differentiation of *honke* and *bunke* within the *ie*, and its distinctive approach to household property, provided the model for the prewar Japanese enterprise groups known as *zaibatsu*. The *ie* structure, in other words, always was an economic unit; the major change was from a village-oriented agricultural system to an urban industrial economy. As the power of the traditional households declined, Japanese industries increasingly took up, first, the social functions of the *ie* and, later, its distinctive pattern of religious and moral values (1983: 174). It is little wonder, then, as Hamabata has shown (1990), that in many Japanese firms there is an extraordinary degree of continuity linking religious, familial, and business concerns. Religious rites are exercised and social responsibilities discharged, quite naturally, within the firm itself, to a degree that defies modern Western assumptions about the boundaries separating the sacred from the secular. Policies considered typical of Japanese corporations, e.g., lifetime employment, wage distribution based on seniority, management by consensus, and an egalitarian atmosphere within the firm, are shown by Shinohara to be expressions of the enduring influence of the *ie* as a template for Japanese social organization.

Shinohara helpfully concludes his analysis with a parting shot at Max Weber. From a Weberian perspective, because the modern Japanese corporation reflects the social logic of the traditional *ie*, it ought not to succeed—at least, not when measured against any rigorous standard of economic performance. It lacks the impersonalism characteristic of a company of strangers whose relationships are primarily contractual; it will be debilitated by nepotism, Weber would have predicted, and typically will pursue policies that are economically irrational. Japan's impressive economic success may, however, suggest—as it does to James Fallows in his recent book, *Looking at the Sun: The Rise of the New East Asian Economic and Political System* (1994)—that our own assumptions about what is and is not economically rational are arbitrary and at least as derivative from inherited religious and moral norms as any alternative system. Fallows makes a distinction between an autonomous and a "culturally embedded" economy which, within the limits of neoclassical theory, is a contradiction in terms. Japan's economy is culturally embedded in the sense that it is organized to fulfill certain "noneconomic" purposes, the chief of which is national security, broadly understood. Its corporations, as we have seen, are not only a reflection of Asian family values, but an effective instrument for preserving them. This system may be economically irrational; but why does it perform so well in the global economy?

Shinohara's essay responds most effectively to Weber's fears about nepotism. He shows that, even in its premodern reality, the *ie* was geared to successful economic performance. The custom of adoption allowed the *kacho* to designate an heir, either when he lacked a son (*yoshi*) of his own or when his heir already had shown signs of being grossly incompetent. The household's collective future, including its accumulated property, was not to be frittered away by someone who showed no inclination to live by the ethic of *hsiao*—known in Japanese as *ko*. As Shinohara comments, managing the affairs of the *ie* involved "a significant level of economic rationalism" (1983: 172). Though the social responsibilities of kinship were exercised through the *ie*, family ties were not allowed to threaten the *ie*'s own survival. Such an approach to economic performance is seen clearly in Japanese firms, where a manager is not likely to be fired for his failures, but he is also not likely to be given anything else of much importance to do. Clearly, there are ways to keep most people productive, even in a system guaranteeing lifetime employment. Tenured professors should have little difficulty imagining how this is done!

Reinventing the Good Corporation

This brief sketch of some of the resources for business ethics to be discovered in the religious and moral traditions of South and East Asia, among other things, ought to provide enough distance to highlight the irony involved in the alleged death of the "good [U.S.] corporation." If the good corporation is dead, it is not because the competition has killed it but because we have allowed it to die for lack of imagination about the nature of the challenge we face in the global economy. The challenge is not about which nation can make the most microchips or which can protect more of its strategic industries, but about whose traditional values are deep and resilient enough to capitalize on the positive benefits of modernization while resisting its corrosive effects on our humanity.

The good corporation, it turns out, was not simply a strategy for outflanking the labor unions or an expression of the largesse that flowed from the United States' fleeting dominance over the global economy after World War II. The good corporation, whether we knew it or not, was also an expression of certain cultural values in which, apparently, many Americans no longer have the collective will to believe. The irony, of course, is that the good corporation is being dismantled in the name of economic exigency, as if the rigors of competition with, especially, the East Asian system were forcing us to revoke the economic securities that once afforded "good jobs" for the majority of U.S. workers. But as the data I have surveyed suggest, the competition that is beating us is characterized by its own model of the good corporation. It is hard not to think of the Asian challenge in terms of Western cultural decline, religious apathy, and moral confusion.

I have no quick fixes to offer for reviving the good corporation in the United States. I do, however, suggest a conclusion. The good corporation will not be revived by redoubling our efforts to remake this society according to the rigorous axioms of neoclassical economics. Even in business circles, those who once hailed the promise of superior competitiveness through reengineering are now bemoaning the "anorexic corporation" that is too weak, in terms of the accumulated experience and skills embodied in its personnel, to respond to new opportunities. Anyone with a lick of common sense could have predicted the likelihood of this outcome, but those business strategists addicted to the formalisms of neoclassical economics are not known for their common sense. There is an alternative, of course; but taking it seriously would mean dispelling the illusion that economics is a value-neutral science, universally valid without reference to any historical or cultural context. The challenge afforded by our East Asian competitors might lead us to rediscover the cultural embeddedness of our own ways of thinking about economics and business, and the enduring roots of our thinking in Western religious traditions. It might inspire us to cultivate those roots anew, so that we might learn once again what we mean to each other, what we owe to each other, as members of a company of strangers. Whether we like it or not, the original template for the good corporation remains biblical and covenantal. We can revive the good corporation, and make it competitive once again, only if we learn how to use that template effectively.

Bibliography

Aristotle. *The Complete Works of Aristotle: The Revised Oxford Translation,* vol. 2. Jonathan Barnes, ed. Princeton: Princeton University Press, 1984.

Beeman, William O. "Patterns of Religion and Economic Development in Iran from the Qajar Era to the Islamic Revolution of 1978–79," in James Finn, ed., *Global Economics and Religion*. New Brunswick: Transaction Books, 1983: 73–103.

Berger, Peter. *The Capitalist Revolution: Fifty Propositions about Prosperity, Equality, and Liberty*. New York: Basic Books, 1986.

Berger, Peter, and Hsin-Huang Michael Hsiao, eds. *In Search of an East Asian Development Model*. New Brunswick: Transaction Publishers, 1988.

Buultjens, Ralph. "India: Values, Visions, and Economic Development," in James Finn, ed., *Global Economics and Religion*. New Brunswick: Transaction Books, 1983: 17–34.

Camenisch, Paul F. "Chinese Religion: Introduction and Readings," in John Dominic Crossan, ed., *Religious Worlds in Comparative Perspective* (Department of Religious Studies, DePaul University, Chicago). Dubuque, Iowa: Kendall/Hunt Publishing Company, 1991: 141–202.

Camenisch, Paul, and Dennis McCann. "Christian Religious Traditions," in Clarence C. Walton, ed., *Enriching Business Ethics*. New York: Plenum Press, 1990: 63–84.

Carmody, Denise Lardner, and John Tully Carmody. *How to Live Well: Ethics in the World Religions*. Belmont, California: Wadsworth Publishing Company, 1988.

de Bary, Wm. Theodore, ed. *Sources of Indian Tradition*, vol. 1. New York: Columbia University Press, 1958.

Dolan, Jay P. *The American Catholic Experience: A History from Colonial Times to the Present*. Garden City, New York: Doubleday, 1985.

———. *Catholic Revivalism: The American Experience, 1830–1900*. Notre Dame: University of Notre Dame Press, 1978.

Embree, Ainslie T., ed. *The Hindu Tradition: Readings in Oriental Thought*. New York: Random House/Vintage Books, 1972.

Fallows, James. *Looking at the Sun: The Rise of the New East Asian Economic and Political System*. New York: Pantheon Books, 1994.

Frankel, Francine R. "Religio-Cultural Values, Political Gradualism, and Economic Development in India," in James Finn, ed., *Global Economics and Religion*. New Brunswick: Transaction Books, 1983: 35–66.

Hamabata, Matthews Masayuki. *Crested Kimono: Power and Love in the Japanese Business Family*. Ithaca, NY: Cornell University Press, 1990.

Leahy, John T., and Aminah Beverly McCloud. "Islam: Introduction and Readings," in John Dominic Crossan, ed., *Religious Worlds in Comparative Perspective* (Department of Religious Studies, DePaul University, Chicago). Dubuque, Iowa: Kendall/Hunt Publishing Company, 1991: 437–512.

McCann, Dennis P., *New Experiment in Democracy: The Challenge for American Catholicism*. Kansas City, Mo.: Sheed and Ward, 1987.

———. "Accursed Internationalism of Finance: Coping with the Resources of Catholic Social Teaching," in Oliver F. Williams, Frank K. Reilly, and John W. Houck, eds., *Ethics and the Investment Industry.* Savage, Md.: Rowman and Littlefield, 1989: 127–147.

———. "Hinduism: Introduction and Readings," in John Dominic Crossan, ed., *Religious Worlds in Comparative Perspective* (Department of Religious Studies, DePaul University, Chicago). Dubuque, Iowa: Kendall/Hunt Publishing Company, 1991: 13–68.

———. "Toward a Theology of the Corporation: A Second Chance for Catholic Social Teaching," in Oliver F. Williams and John W. Houck, eds., *Catholic Social Thought and the New World Order.* Notre Dame: University of Notre Dame Press, 1993: 329–350.

———. "The World's Parliament of Religion, Then and Now: From Social Gospel to Multiculturalism," in Harlan Beckley, ed., *The Annual of the Society of Christian Ethics,* 1993: 291–296.

———. "Doing Business with the Historical Jesus," in Jeffrey Carlson and Robert A. Ludwig, eds., *Jesus and Faith: A Conversation on the Work of John Dominic Crossan.* Maryknoll, N.Y.: Orbis Books, 1994: 132–141.

Napier, Ron. "Interrelationships of the Economic and Social Systems in Japan," in James Finn, ed., *Global Economics and Religion.* New Brunswick: Transaction Books, 1983: 179–194.

Novak, Michael. *The Spirit of Democratic Capitalism.* New York: Simon and Schuster, 1982.

O'Brien, David J., and Thomas A. Shannon, eds. *Catholic Social Thought: The Documentary Heritage.* Maryknoll, N.Y.: Orbis Books, 1992.

Read, Kay Almere. "Buddhism: Introduction and Readings," in John Dominic Crossan, ed., *Religious Worlds in Comparative Perspective* (Department of Religious Studies, DePaul University, Chicago). Dubuque, Iowa: Kendall/Hunt Publishing Company, 1991: 69–139.

Shinohara, Koichi. "Religion and Economic Development in Japan: An Exploration Focusing on the Institution of *Ie,*" in James Finn, ed., *Global Economics and Religion.* New Brunswick: Transaction Books, 1983: 167–178.

Stackhouse, Max. *Creeds, Society, and Human Rights: A Study in Three Cultures.* Grand Rapids, Mich.: Eerdmans Publishing Co., 1984.

———. "The Hindu Ethic and the Ethos of Development: Some Western Views," *Religion and Society,* vol. 20 (December 1973): 5–28.

Strain, Charles R. "Japanese Religion: Introduction and Readings," in John Dominic Crossan, ed., *Religious Worlds in Comparative Perspective* (Department of Religious Studies, DePaul University, Chicago). Dubuque, Iowa: Kendall/Hunt Publishing Company, 1991: 203–279.

Tanizaki, Junichiro. *The Makioka Sisters (Sasame Yuki).* Translated by Edward G. Seidensticker. New York: Alfred A. Knopf, 1957.

Weber, Max. *The Protestant Ethic and the Spirit of Capitalism.* Translated and edited by Talcott Parsons. New York: Charles Scribner's Sons, 1958.

———. *The Religion of China: Confucianism and Taoism.* Translated and edited by Hans H. Gerth. New York: The Free Press, 1951.

———. *The Religion of India: The Sociology of Hinduism and Buddhism.* Translated and edited by Hans H. Gerth and Don Martindale. New York: The Free Press, 1958.

Appendix I

Thinking Ethically
A Framework for Moral Decision Making

Thinking Ethically
A Framework for Moral Decision Making

Manuel Velasquez, Claire André,
Thomas Shanks, S. J., and Michael J. Meyer

Moral issues greet us each morning in the newspaper, confront us in the memos on our desks, nag us from our children's soccer fields, and bid us good night on the evening news. We are bombarded daily with questions about the justice of our foreign policy, the morality of medical technologies that can prolong our lives, the rights of the homeless, the fairness of our children's teachers to the diverse students in their classrooms.

Dealing with these moral issues is often perplexing. How, exactly, should we think through an ethical issue? What questions should we ask? What factors should we consider?

The first step in analyzing moral issues is obvious but not always easy: Get the facts. Some moral issues create controversies simply because we do not bother to check the facts. This first step, although obvious, is also among the most important and the most frequently overlooked.

But having the facts is not enough. Facts by themselves only tell us what *is*; they do not tell us what *ought* to be. In addition to getting the facts, resolving an ethical issue also requires an appeal to values. Philosophers have developed five different approaches to values to deal with moral issues.

The Utilitarian Approach

Utilitarianism was conceived in the 19th century by Jeremy Bentham and John Stuart Mill to help legislators determine which laws were morally best. Both Bentham and Mill suggested that ethical actions are those that provide the greatest balance of good over evil.

To analyze an issue using the utilitarian approach, we first identify the various courses of action available to us. Second, we ask who will be affected by each action and what benefits or harms will be derived from each. And third, we choose the action that will produce the greatest benefits and the least harm. The ethical action is the one that provides the greatest good for the greatest number.

The Rights Approach

The second important approach to ethics has its roots in the philosophy of the 18th-century thinker Immanuel Kant and others like him, who focused on the individual's right to choose for herself or himself. According to these philosophers, what makes human beings different from mere things is that people have dignity based on their ability to choose freely what they will do with their lives, and they have a fundamental moral right to have these choices respected. People are not objects to be manipulated; it is a violation of human dignity to use people in ways they do not freely choose.

Of course, many different, but related, rights exist besides this basic one. These other rights (an incomplete list below) can be thought of as different aspects of the basic right to be treated as we choose.

- The right to the truth: We have a right to be told the truth and to be informed about matters that significantly affect our choices.
- The right of privacy: We have the right to do, believe, and say whatever we choose in our personal lives so long as we do not violate the rights of others.
- The right not to be injured: We have the right not to be harmed or injured unless we freely and knowingly do something to deserve punishment or we freely and knowingly choose to risk such injuries.
- The right to what is agreed: We have a right to what has been promised by those with whom we have freely entered into a contract or agreement.

In deciding whether an action is moral or immoral using this second approach, then, we must ask, Does the action respect the moral rights of everyone? Actions are wrong to the extent that they violate the rights of individuals; the more serious the violation, the more wrongful the action.

The Fairness or Justice Approach

The fairness or justice approach to ethics has its roots in the teachings of the ancient Greek philosopher Aristotle, who said that "equals should be treated equally and unequals unequally." The basic moral question in this approach is: How fair is an action? Does it treat everyone in the same way, or does it show favoritism and discrimination?

Favoritism gives benefits to some people without a justifiable reason for singling them out; discrimination imposes burdens on people who are no different from those on whom burdens are not imposed. Both favoritism and discrimination are unjust and wrong.

The Common-Good Approach

This approach to ethics presents a vision of society as a community whose members are joined in the shared pursuit of values and goals they hold in common. This community comprises individuals whose own good is inextricably bound to the good of the whole.

The common good is a notion that originated more than 2,000 years ago in the writings of Plato, Aristotle, and Cicero. More recently, contemporary ethicist John Rawls defined the common good as "certain general conditions that are . . . equally to everyone's advantage."

In this approach, we focus on ensuring that the social policies, social systems, institutions, and environments on which we depend are beneficial to all. Examples of goods common to all include affordable health care, effective public safety, peace among nations, a just legal system, and an unpolluted environment.

Appeals to the common good urge us to view ourselves as members of the same community, reflecting on broad questions concerning the kind of society we want to become and how we are to achieve that society. While respecting and valuing the freedom of individuals to pursue their own goals, the common-good approach challenges us also to recognize and further those goals we share in common.

The Virtue Approach

The virtue approach to ethics assumes that there are certain ideals toward which we should strive, which provide for the full development of our humanity. These ideals are discovered through thoughtful reflection on what kind of people we have the potential to become.

Virtues are attitudes or character traits that enable us to be and to act in ways that develop our highest potential. They enable us to pursue the ideals we have adopted.

Honesty, courage, compassion, generosity, fidelity, integrity, fairness, self-control, and prudence are all examples of virtues.

Virtues are like habits; that is, once acquired, they become characteristic of a person. Moreover, a person who has developed virtues will be naturally disposed to act in ways consistent with moral principles. The virtuous person is the ethical person.

In dealing with an ethical problem using the virtue approach, we might ask, What kind of person should I be? What will promote the development of character within myself and my community?

Ethical Problem Solving

These five approaches suggest that once we have ascertained the facts, we should ask ourselves five questions when trying to resolve a moral issue:

- What benefits and what harms will each course of action produce, and which alternative will lead to the best overall consequences?
- What moral rights do the affected parties have, and which course of action best respects those rights?
- Which course of action treats everyone the same, except where there is a morally justifiable reason not to, and does not show favoritism or discrimination?
- Which course of action advances the common good?
- Which course of action develops moral virtues?

This method, of course, does not provide an automatic solution to moral problems. It is not meant to. The method is merely meant to help identify most of the important ethical considerations. In the end, we must deliberate on moral issues for ourselves, keeping a careful eye on both the facts and on the ethical considerations involved.

For Further Reading

Frankena, William. *Ethics*, 2nd ed. (Englewood Cliffs, N.J.: Prentice Hall, 1973).

Halberstam, Joshua. *Everyday Ethics: Inspired Solutions to Real Life Dilemmas* (New York: Penguin Books, 1993).

Martin, Michael. *Everyday Morality* (Belmont, Calif: Wadsworth, 1995).

Rachels, James. *The Elements of Moral Philosophy*, 2nd ed. (New York: McGraw-Hill, 1993).

Velasquez, Manuel. *Business Ethics: Concepts and Cases*, 3rd ed. (Englewood Cliffs, N.J.: Prentice Hall, 1992) 2–110.

Appendix II
Moral Development

Moral Development:
A Review of the Theory

Lawrence Kohlberg and Richard H. Hersh

Whether we like it or not schooling is a moral enterprise. Values issues abound in the content and process of teaching. The interaction of adults and students within a social organization called a school results in human conflict no less so than does such interaction in social organizations labeled "families." Yet moral education has been viewed as the exclusive province of the family and/or church. Disregarded or misunderstood has been the nature of the school as an important moral education institution. Because schools have not been viewed as legitimate institutions of moral education, society has avoided concepts of morality and ethics in evaluating the effects of these institutions on the social development of children and adolescents. Terms like "socialization" or "acculturation" or "citizenship" have been used to refer to the moral impact on students. Such terms ignore the problem of the standard or principle of value implied by such terms. We must face the issue of choice as to whether the outcome of the growth and education process is the creation of a storm trooper, a Buddhist monk or a civil rights activist. All are equally "socialized" in terms of their social group. To consider "socialization" or the "acquisition of values" as moral education, is to consider the moral principles children are developing (or are not developing). It is also to consider the adequacy of these principles in the light of an examined concept of the good and right (the province of moral philosophy) and in the light of knowledge of the moral processes of human development (which is the province of psychology).

We are concerned with the traditional prohibition of schools from teaching values or "morality" normally felt to be the province of the home and church. In keeping family, church, and school separate, however, educators have assumed naively that schools have been harbors of value neutrality. The result has been a moral education curriculum which has lurked beneath the surface in schools, hidden as it were from both educators and the public. This "hidden curriculum"[1] with its emphasis on obedience to authority ("stay in your seat, make no noise, get a hallway pass"; and the feeling of "prison" espoused by so many students), implies many underlying moral assumptions and values, which may be quite different from what educators would admit as their conscious system of morality. Schools have been preaching a "bag of virtues" approach—the teaching of a particular set of values which are peculiar to this culture or to a particular subculture, and which are by nature relativistic and not necessarily more adequate than any other set of values. But the teaching of particular virtues has been proven to be ineffective. We wish to go beyond this approach to moral education and instead to conceptualize and facilitate moral development in a cognitive-developmental sense—toward an increased sense of moral autonomy and a more adequate conception of justice.

Moral development, as initially defined by Piaget[2] and then refined and researched by Kohlberg,[3] does not simply represent an increasing knowledge of cultural values usually leading to ethical relativity. Rather, it represents the transformations that occur in a person's *form* or structure of thought. The content of values varies from culture to culture; hence the study of cultural values cannot tell us how a person interacts with his social environment, or how a person goes about solving problems related to his/her social world. This requires the analysis of developing structures of moral judgment, which are found to be universal in a developmental sequence across cultures.[4]

In analyzing the responses of longitudinal and cross-cultural subjects to hypothetical moral dilemmas it has been demonstrated that moral reasoning develops over time through a series of six stages. The concept of stages of cognitive development refers to the structure of one's reasoning and implies the following characteristics:

1. Stages are "structured wholes," or organized systems of thought. This means individuals are consistent in their level of moral judgment.
2. Stages form an invariant sequence. Under all conditions except extreme trauma, movement is always forward, never backward. Individuals never skip stages, and movement is always to the next stage up. This is true of all cultures.
3. Stages are "hierarchical integrations." Thinking at a higher stage includes or comprehends within it lower stage thinking. There is a tendency to function at or prefer the highest stage available.

The stages of moral development are defined by the following characteristics:

Definition of Moral Stages

I. Preconventional Level

At this level, the child is responsive to cultural rules and labels of good and bad, right or wrong, but interprets these labels either in terms of the physical or the hedonistic consequences of action (punishment, reward, exchange of favors) or in terms of the physical power of those who enunciate the rules and labels. The level is divided into the following two stages:

Stage1: The punishment-and-obedience orientation. The physical consequences of action determine its goodness or badness, regardless of the human meaning or value of these consequences. Avoidance of punishment and unquestioning deference to power are valued in their own right, not in terms of respect for an underlying moral order supported by punishment and authority (the latter being Stage 4).

Stage 2: The instrumental-relativist orientation. Right action consists of that which instrumentally satisfies one's own needs and occasionally the needs of others. Human relations are viewed in terms like those of the marketplace. Elements of fairness, of reciprocity, and of equal sharing are present, but they are always interpreted in a physical, pragmatic way. Reciprocity is a matter of "you scratch my back and I'll scratch yours," not of loyalty, gratitude, or justice.

II. Conventional Level

At this level, maintaining the expectations of the individual's family, group, or nation is perceived as valuable in its own right, regardless of immediate and obvious consequences. The attitude is not only one of *conformity* to personal expectations and social order, but of loyalty to it, of actively *maintaining*, supporting, and justifying the order, and of identifying with the persons or group involved in it. At this level there are the following two stages:

Stage 3: The interpersonal concordance or "good boy—nice girl" orientation. Good behavior is that which pleases or helps others and is approved by them. There is much conformity to stereotypical images of what is majority or "natural" behavior. Behavior is frequently judged by intention —"he means well" becomes important for the first time. One earns approval by being "nice."

Stage 4: The "law and order" orientation. There is orientation toward authority, fixed rules, and the maintenance of the social order. Right behavior consists of doing one's duty, showing respect for authority, and maintaining the given social order for its own sake.

III. Postconventional, Autonomous, or Principled Level

At this level, there is a clear effort to define moral values and principles that have validity and application apart from the authority of the groups or persons holding these principles and apart from the individual's own identification with these groups. This level also has two stages:

Stage 5: The social-contract, legalistic orientation, generally with utilitarian overtones. Right action tends to be defined in terms of general individual rights and standards which have been critically examined and agreed upon by the whole society. There is a clear awareness of the relativism of personal values and opinions and a corresponding emphasis upon procedural rules for reaching consensus. Aside from what is constitutionally and democratically agreed upon, the right is a matter of personal "values" and "opinion." The result is an emphasis upon the "legal point of view," but with an emphasis upon the possibility of changing law in terms of rational considerations of social utility (rather than freezing it in terms of Stage 4 "law and order"). Outside the legal realm, free agreement and contract is the binding element of obligation. This is the "official" morality of the American government and constitution.

Stage 6: The universal-ethical-principle orientation. Right is defined by the decision of conscience in accord with self-chosen *ethical principles* appealing to logical comprehensiveness, universality, and consistency. These principles are abstract and ethical (The Golden Rule, the categorical imperative); they are not concrete moral rules like the Ten Commandments. At heart, these are universal principles of *justice*, of the *reciprocity* and *equality* of human *rights*, and of respect for the dignity of human beings as *individual persons*.[5]

Given that people have the psychological capacity to progress to higher (and therefore more adequate) stages of moral reasoning, the aim of education ought to be the personal development of students toward more complex ways of reasoning. This philosophical argument is based on the earlier contributions of John Dewey:

> The aim of education is growth or development, both intellectual and moral. Ethical and psychological principles can aid the school in the greatest of all constructions—the building of a free and powerful character. Only knowledge of the order and connection of stages in psychological development can insure this. Education is the work of supplying the conditions which will enable the psychological functions to mature in the freest and fullest manner.[6]

Like Piaget, Dewey's idea of development does not reflect an increase in the *content* of thinking (e.g., cultural values) but instead, a qualitative transformation in the *form* of the child's thought or action. This distinction has been elaborated elsewhere:

> What we examine in our work has to do with form rather than content. We are not describing or classifying what people think is right or wrong in situations of moral conflict, for example, whether draft-evading exiles should be given amnesty or thrown in prison if and when they return to this country, or even changes in what individuals think as they grow older. Nor are we assuming that we can specify a certain behavioral response as necessarily "moral" (in the descriptive or category sense, as distinguished from non-moral), for example "cheating," and then discuss moral-development in terms of the frequency with which individuals engage in this behavior as they grow older, perhaps in different kinds of situations ranging from spelling tests to income tax. As distinguished from either of these two avenues of research that might be said to be dealing with moral content, our work focuses on the cognitive structure which underlie such content and give it its claim to the category "moral," where "structure" refers to "the general characteristics of shape, pattern or organization of response rather than to the rate of intensity of response or its pairing with particular stimuli," and "cognitive structure" refers to "rules for processing information or for connecting experienced events." From our point of view it is not any artificially specified set of responses, or degree of intensity of such responses, which characterizes morality as an area of study. Rather, it is the cognitive moral structurings, or the organized systems of assumptions and rules about the nature of moral-conflict situations which give such situations their meaning, that constitute the objects of our developmental study.[7]

Based on this crucial difference between form and content, the aim of moral education should be to stimulate people's thinking ability over time in ways which will enable them to use more adequate and complex reasoning patterns to solve moral problems. The principle central to the development of stages of moral judgment, and hence to proposals for moral education, is that of *justice*. Justice, the primary regard for the value and equality of all human beings and for reciprocity in human relations, is a basic and universal standard. Using justice as the organizing principle for moral education meets the following criteria: It guarantees freedom of belief; it employs a philosophically justifiable concept of morality, and it is based on the psychological facts of human development. The stages may be seen as representing increasingly adequate conceptions of justice and as reflecting an expanding capacity for empathy, for taking the role of the other. And in the end the two are the same thing because the most just solution is the one which takes into account the positions or rights of all the individuals involved. The expansion of empathy thus, in turn, leads to an expansion of points of view and this expansion defines the three levels of moral judgment into which the six stages subdivide.

At the first or preconventional level the individual sees moral dilemmas in terms of the individual needs of the people involved. Situations of moral conflict are seen as situations in which needs collide and are resolved either in terms of who has the most power in the situation (Stage 1) or in terms of simple individual responsibility for one's own welfare (Stage 2) except where bound by simple market-place notions of reciprocity.

These formulations are perfectly consonant with the child's experience. For a young child power is perhaps the most salient characteristic of his social world (Stage 1) and as he learns to see conflicts between conformity to power and individual interests, he shifts to a notion of right as serving individual interests. However, as the child becomes increasingly involved in mutual relationships and sees himself as a sharing and participating member of groups, he sees the individual point of view toward morality as inadequate to deal with the kinds of moral conflicts which confront him. He has then two choices: he can hold on to his preconventional philosophy and simplify experience, or he can expand his philosophy so that it can take into account the expanding complexity of his experience.

The second two stages of moral development are termed "conventional" in that moral conflicts are now seen and resolved in group or social terms rather than in individual terms. Right or justice is seen to reside in interpersonal social relationships (Stage 3) or in the community (Stage 4). At the conventional levels there is an appeal to authority but the authority derives its right to define the good not from greater power as at Stage 1, but from its social sharedness and legitimacy.

However, if society defines the right and the good, what is one to think when one recognizes that different societies choose differently in what they label as good and bad, right and wrong? Eskimos think it is right to leave old people out in the snow to die. When abortions were illegal in this country, they were legal in Sweden. With the increasing exposure of everyone to how others live, there is a greater recognition of the fact that our way is only one among many.

If one cannot simply equate the right with the societal and the legal, then what is one to do? We have found that adolescents may go through a period of ethical relativism during which they question the premises of any moral system. If there are many ways to live, who can presume to say which is best? Perhaps everyone should do as he or she chooses.

The way out of this moral relativism or moral nihilism lies through the perception that underneath the rules of any given society lie moral principles and universal moral rights, and the validity of any moral choice rests on the principles that choice embodies. Such moral principles are universal in their application and constitute a viable standard against which the particular laws or conventions of any society can and should be judged. When obedience to laws violates moral principles or rights, it is right to violate such laws.

At the last two stages, then, choice is based on the principles that supersede convention, just as previously the claims of society or convention were seen as the grounds for adjudicating differences between individuals. This, then, is the sequence of moral development.

What spurs progress from one stage to another and why do some individuals reach the principled stages while others do not? Moral judgment, while primarily a rational operation, is influenced by affective factors such as the ability to empathize and the capacity for guilt. But moral situations are defined cognitively by the judging individual in social interactions. It is this interaction with one's environment which determines development of moral reasoning.

Social interaction requires the assumption of a variety of roles and the entering into a variety of reciprocal relationships. Such relationships demand that one take others' perspectives (role- taking). It is this reworking of one's role-taking experiences into successively more complex and adequate forms of justice which is called moral development. Thus moral development results from the dialogue between the person's cognitive structure and the complexity presented by environment. This interactionist definition of moral development demands an environment which will facilitate dialogue between the self and others. The more one encounters situations of moral conflict that are not adequately resolved by one's present reasoning structure, the more likely one is to develop more complex ways of thinking about and resolving such conflicts.

What can teachers and schools do to stimulate moral development? The teacher must help the student to consider genuine moral conflicts, think about the reasoning he uses in solving such conflicts, see inconsistencies and inadequacies in his way of thinking and find ways of resolving them. Classroom moral discussion are one example of how the cognitive-developmental approach can be applied in the school. Much of the moral development research in schools has focused on moral discussions as the vehicle for stimulating cognitive conflict. But such discussions, if too often used, will become pedantic. The classroom discussion approach should be part of a broader, more enduring involvement of students in the social and moral functioning of the school. Rather than attempting to inculcate a predetermined and unquestioned set of values, teachers should challenge students with the moral issues faced by the school community as problems to be solved, not merely situations in which rules are mechanically applied. One must create a "just community."

At present, the schools themselves are not especially moral institutions. Institutional relationships tend to be based more on authority than on ideas of justice. Adults are often less interested in discovering *how* children are thinking than in telling them *what* to think. The school atmosphere is generally a blend of Stage 1, punishment morality, and Stage 4, "law and order," which fails to impress or stimulate children involved in their own Stage 2 or Stage 3 moral philosophies. Children and adults stop communicating with one another, horizons are narrowed and development is stunted. If schools wish to foster morality, they will have to provide an atmosphere in which interpersonal issues are settled on the basis of principle rather than power. They will have to take moral questions seriously and provide food for thought instead of conventional "right answers."

We do not claim that the theory of cognitive moral development is sufficient to the task of moral education. . . . There are three major areas in which the cognitive developmental approach to moral education is incomplete: 1) the stress placed on form rather than content 2) the focus on concepts of rights and duties rather than issues of the good 3) the emphasis on moral judgment rather than behavior.

We have previously mentioned the distinction between form and content. That we have chosen to delineate the form or structure of moral judgments does not deny the importance of the moral content of school curriculum. That textbooks and other curricula materials have reflected and perhaps reinforced racism, sexism and ethnocentrisms is to be decried. It is imperative that the content of curriculum for moral education be constructed so as to avoid unfair characterizations of others as well as promote opportunities for structural development. The integration of curriculum content is exemplified by articles in this issue by Lickona, Bramble and Garrod, and the Ladenburgs. Additional work in this content dimension is required if educators wish to incorporate the cognitive developmental approach to moral education in the curriculum.

We have stressed in this "theory" the concern for what is right, what is just or fair. To ask "what is right?" or "what ought I do in this situation?" presumes that notions of what is "good" are in conflict. But,

> We are not describing how men formulate different conceptions of the good, the good life, intrinsic value, or purpose. Nor are we discussing how men develop certain kinds of character traits and learn to recognize these traits in judgments of approbation and disapprobation. Instead, we are concentrating on that aspect of morality that is brought to the fore by problematic situations of conflicting claims, whether the conflict is between individuals, groups, societies, or institutions, and whether the source of the conflict lies in incompatible claims based on conceptions of the good, beliefs about human purpose, or character assessments. In short, we intend the term "moral" to be understood in the restricted sense of referring to situations which call for judgments involving denotological concepts such as right and wrong, duty and obligation, having a right, fairness, etc., although such judgments may (or may not) involve either or both of the other two basic concepts or their derivatives.[8]

This is not to say that questions of "good" are less important or need not to be asked. Rather it is an acknowledgement that the cognitive developmental approach is limited in scope and requires that attention be paid to such issues in the development of any moral education program.

The relationship between moral judgment and moral behavior is not fully defined. That is, moral judgment is a necessary but not sufficient condition for moral action. Other variables come into play such as emotion, and a general sense of will, purpose or ego strength. Moral judgment is the only distinctive *moral* factor in moral behavior but not the only factor in such behavior. Educators who are looking for answers as to how to "get children to behave" often meaning to rid themselves of discipline problems will not find *the* answer in one theory. We hypothesize that behavior when informed by mature moral judgment is influenced by the level of moral development.[9] Further research in this crucial area is needed.

Cognitive developmental moral education is rooted in a substantial empirical and philosophical base. The theory is complex and as suggested above insufficient to the task claimed by "moral education." Within limits, however, the theory has informing power for the practitioner. Resourceful practice is required both to validate and inform the theory.

Notes

1. P. Jackson, *Life in the Classrooms* (New York: Holt, Rinehart & Winston, 1968).

2. J. Piaget, *The Moral Judgment of the Child* (1932) (New York: Free Press, 1965).

3. L. Kohlberg. *Stages of Moral Development as a Basis for Moral Education*, in C. Beck and E. Sullivan (eds.), *Moral Education* (Toronto: University of Toronto Press, 1970).

4. L. Kohlberg, "Moral Stages and Moralization: The Cognitive Developmental Approach," In T. Lickona (ed.), *Moral Development and Behavior: Theory, Research, and Social Issues* (New York: Holt, Rinehart & Winston, 1976).

5. L. Kohlberg, "From Is to Ought," in T. Mischel (ed.), *Cognitive Development and Epistemology* (New York: Academic Press, 1971), pp. 164–165.

6. J. Dewey, "What Psychology Can Do for the Teacher," In R. Archambault (ed.), *John Dewey on Education: Selected Writings* (New York: Random House, 1964), p. 207.

7. D. Boyd and L. Kohlberg, "The Is-Ought Problem: A Developmental Perspective," *Zygon*, 1973, 8, 360–361.

8. Ibid., p. 360.

9. The relationship between moral judgment and moral behavior is more fully discussed in: Kohlberg, 1976 "Moral Stages," L. Kohlberg, "Stage and Sequence: The Cognitive Developmental Approach to Socialization," in D. A. Goslin (ed.) *Handbook of Socialization Theory and Research*, vol. I (New York: Russell Sage Foundation, 1964), pp. 383–432.

Moral Orientation and Moral Development

Carol Gilligan

When one looks at an ambiguous figure like the drawing that can be seen as a young or old woman, or the image of the vase and the faces, one initially sees it in only one way. Yet even after seeing it in both ways, one way often seems more compelling. This phenomenon reflects the laws of perceptual organization that favor certain modes of visual grouping. But it also suggests a tendency to view reality as unequivocal and thus to argue that there is one right or better way of seeing.

The experiments of the Gestalt psychologists on perceptual organization provide a series of demonstrations that the same proximal pattern can be organized in different ways so that, for example, the same figure can be seen as a square or a diamond, depending on its orientation in relation to a surrounding frame. Subsequent studies show that the context influencing which of two possible organizations will be chosen may depend not only on the features of the array presented but also on the perceiver's past experience or expectation. Thus, a birdwatcher and a rabbit-keeper are likely to see the duck-rabbit figure in different ways; yet this difference does not imply that one way is better or a higher form of perceptual organization. It does, however, call attention to the fact that the rabbit-keeper, perceiving the rabbit, may not see the ambiguity of the figure until someone points out that it can also be seen as a duck.

This paper presents a similar phenomenon with respect to moral judgment, describing two moral perspectives that organize thinking in different ways. The analogy to ambiguous figure perception arises from the observation that although people are aware of both perspectives, they tend to adopt one or the other in defining and resolving moral conflict. Since moral judgments organize thinking about choice in difficult situations, the adoption of a single perspective may facilitate clarity of decision. But the wish for clarity may also imply a compelling human need for resolution or closure, especially in the face of decisions that give rise to discomfort or unease. Thus, the search for clarity in seeing may blend with a search for justification, encouraging the position that there is one right or better way to think about moral problems. This question, which

315

has been the subject of intense theological and philosophical debate, becomes of interest to the psychologist not only because of its psychological dimensions—the tendency to focus on one perspective and the wish for justification—but also because one moral perspective currently dominates psychological thinking and is embedded in the most widely used measure for assessing the maturity of moral reasoning.

In describing an alternative standpoint, I will reconstruct the account of moral development around two moral perspectives, grounded in different dimensions of relationship that give rise to moral concern. The justice perspective, often equated with moral reasoning, is recast as one way of seeing moral problems and a care perspective is brought forward as an alternate vision or frame. The distinction between justice and care as alternative perspectives or moral orientations is based empirically on the observation that a shift in the focus of attention from concerns about justice to concerns about care changes the definition of what constitutes a moral problem, and leads the same situation to be seen in different ways. Theoretically, the distinction between justice and care cuts across the familiar divisions between thinking and feeling, egoism and altruism, theoretical and practical reasoning. It calls attention to the fact that all human relationships, public and private, can be characterized *both* in terms of equality and in terms of attachment, and that both inequality and detachment constitute grounds for moral concern. Since everyone is vulnerable both to oppression and to abandonment, two moral visions— one of justice and one of care—recur in human experience. The moral injunctions, not to act unfairly toward others, and not to turn away from someone in need, capture these different concerns.

The conception of the moral domain as comprised of at least two moral orientations raises new questions about observed differences in moral judgment and the disagreements to which they give rise. Key to this revision is the distinction between differences in developmental stage (more or less adequate positions within a single orientation) and differences in orientation (alternative perspectives or frameworks). The findings reported in this paper of an association between moral orientation and gender speak directly to the continuing controversy over sex differences in moral reasoning. In doing so, however, they also offer an empirical explanation for why previous thinking about moral development has been organized largely within the justice framework.

My research on moral orientation derives from an observation made in the course of studying the relationship between moral judgment and action. Two studies, one of college students describing their experiences of moral conflict and choice, and one of pregnant women who were considering abortion, shifted the focus of attention from the ways people reason about hypothetical dilemmas to the ways people construct moral conflicts and choices in their lives. This change in approach made it possible to see what experiences people define in moral terms, and to explore the relationship between the understanding of moral problems and the reasoning strategies used and the actions taken in attempting to resolve them. In this context, I observed that women, especially when speaking about their own experiences of moral conflict and choice, often define moral problems in a way that eludes the categories of moral theory and is at odds with the assumptions that shape psychological thinking about morality and about the self.[1] This discovery, that a different voice often guides the moral judgments and the actions of women, called attention to a major design problem in previous moral judgment research: namely, the use of all-male samples as the empirical basis for theory construction.

The selection of an all-male sample as the basis for generalizations that are applied to both males and females is logically inconsistent. As a research strategy, the decision to begin with a single-sex sample is inherently problematic, since the categories of analysis will tend to be defined on the basis of the initial data gathered and subsequent studies will tend to be restricted to these categories. Piaget's work on the moral judgment of the child illustrates these problems since he defined the evolution of children's consciousness and practice of rules on the basis of his study of boys playing marbles, and then undertook a study of girls to assess the generality of his findings. Observing a series of differences both in the structure of girls' games and "in the actual mentality of little girls," he deemed these differences not of interest because "it was not this contrast which we proposed to study." Girls, Piaget found, "rather complicated our interrogatory in relation to what we know about boys," since the changes in their conception of rules, although following the same sequence observed in boys, did not stand in the same relation to social experience. Nevertheless, he concluded that "in spite of these differences in the structure of the game and apparently in the players' mentality, we find the same process at work as in the evolution of the game of marbles."[2]

Thus, girls were of interest insofar as they were similar to boys and confirmed the generality of Piaget's findings. The differences noted, which included a greater tolerance, a greater tendency toward innovation in solving conflicts, a greater willingness to make exceptions to rules, and a lesser concern with legal elaboration, were not seen as germane to "the psychology of rules," and therefore were regarded as insignificant for the study of children's moral judgment. Given the confusion that currently surrounds the discussion of sex differences in moral judgment, it is important to emphasize that the differences observed by Piaget did not pertain to girls' understanding of rules *per se* or to the development of the idea of justice in their thinking, but rather to the way girls structured their games and their approach to conflict resolution—that is, to their use rather than their understanding of the logic of rules and justice.

Kohlberg, in his research on moral development, did not encounter these problems since he equated moral development with the development of justice reasoning and initially used an all-male sample as the basis for theory and test construction. In response to his critics, Kohlberg has recently modified his claims, renaming his test a measure of "justice reasoning" rather than of "moral maturity" and acknowledging the presence of a care perspective in people's moral thinking.[3] But the widespread use of Kohlberg's measure as a measure of moral development together with his own continuing tendency to equate justice reasoning with moral judgment leaves the problem of orientation differences unsolved. More specifically, Kohlberg's efforts to assimilate thinking about care to the six-stage developmental sequence he derived and refined by analyzing changes in justice reasoning (relying centrally on his all-male longitudinal sample), underscores the continuing importance of the points raised in this paper concerning (1) the distinction between differences in developmental stage within a single orientation and differences in orientation, and (2) the fact that the moral thinking of girls and women was not examined in establishing either the meaning or the measurement of moral judgment within contemporary psychology.

An analysis of the language and logic of men's and women's moral reasoning about a range of hypothetical and real dilemmas underlies the distinction elaborated in this paper between a justice and a care perspective. The empirical association of care reasoning with women suggests that discrepancies observed between moral theory and the moral judgments of girls and women may reflect a shift in perspective, a change in moral orientation. Like the figure-ground shift in ambiguous figure perception, justice and care as moral perspectives are not opposites or mirror-images of one another, with justice uncaring and care unjust. Instead, these perspectives denote different ways of organizing the basic elements of moral judgment: self, others, and the relationship between them. With the shift in perspective from justice to care, the organizing dimension of relationship changes from inequality/equality to attachment/detachment, reorganizing thoughts, feelings and language so that words connoting relationship like "dependence" or "responsibility" or even moral terms such as "fairness" and "care" take on different meanings. To organize relationships in terms of attachment rather than in terms of equality changes the way human connection is imagined, so that the images or metaphors of relationship shift from hierarchy or balance to network or web. In addition, each organizing framework leads to a different way of imagining the self as a moral agent.

From a justice perspective, the self as moral agent stands as the figure against a ground of social relationships, judging the conflicting claims of self and others against a standard of equality or equal respect (the Categorical Imperative, the Golden Rule). From a care perspective, the relationship becomes the figure, defining self and others. Within the context of relationship, the self as a moral agent perceives and responds to the perception of need. The shift in moral perspective is manifest by a change in the moral question from "What is just?" to "How to respond?"

For example, adolescents asked to describe a moral dilemma often speak about peer or family pressure in which case the moral question becomes how to maintain moral principles or standards and resist the influence of one's parents or friends. "I have a right to my religious opinions," one teenager explains, referring to a religious difference with his parents. Yet, he adds, "I respect their views." The same dilemma, however, is also construed by adolescents as a problem of attachment, in which case the moral question becomes: how to respond both to oneself and to one's friends or one's parents, how to maintain or strengthen connection in the face of differences in belief. "I understand their fear of my new religious ideas," one teenager explains, referring to her religious disagreement with her parents, "but they really ought to listen to me and try to understand my beliefs."

One can see these two statements as two versions of essentially the same thing. Both teenagers present self-justifying arguments about religious disagreement; both address the claims of self and of others in a way that honors both. Yet each frames the problem in different terms, and the use of moral language points to different concerns. The first speaker casts the problem in terms of individual rights that must be respected within the relationship. In other words, the figure of the considering is the self looking on the disagreeing selves in relationship, and the aim is to get the other selves to acknowledge the right to disagree. In the case of the second speaker, figure and ground shift. The relationship becomes the figure of the considering, and relationships are seen to require listening and efforts at understanding differences in belief. Rather than the right to disagree, the speaker focuses on caring to hear and to be heard. Attention shifts from the grounds for agreement (rights and respect) to the grounds for understanding (listening and speaking, hearing and being heard). This shift is marked by a change in moral language from the stating of separate claims to rights and respect ("I have a right . . . I respect their views.") to the activities of relationship—the injunction to listen and try to understand ("I understand . . . they ought to listen . . . and try to understand."). The metaphor of moral voice itself carries the terms of the care perspective and reveals how the language chosen for moral theory is not orientation neutral.

The language of the public abortion debate, for example, reveals a justice perspective. Whether the abortion dilemma is cast as a conflict of rights or in terms of respect for human life, the claims of the fetus and of the pregnant woman are balanced or placed in opposition. The morality of abortion decisions thus construed hinges on the scholastic or metaphysical question as to whether the fetus is a life or a person, and whether its claims take precedence over those of the pregnant woman. Framed as a problem of care, the dilemma posed by abortion shifts. The connection between the fetus and the pregnant woman becomes the focus of attention and the question becomes whether it is responsible or irresponsible, caring or careless, to extend or to end this connection. In this construction, the abortion dilemma arises because there is no way not to act, and no way of acting that does not alter the connection between self and others. To ask what actions constitute care or are more caring directs attention to the parameters of connection and the costs of detachment, which become subjects of moral concern.

Finally, two medical students, each reporting a decision not to turn in someone who has violated the school rules against drinking, cast their decision in different terms. One student constructs the decision as an act of mercy, a decision to override justice in light of the fact that the violator has shown "the proper degrees of contrition." In addition, this student raises the question as to whether or not the alcohol policy is just, i.e., whether the school has the right to prohibit drinking. The other student explains the decision not to turn in a proctor who was drinking on the basis that turning him in is not a good way to respond to this problem, since it would dissolve the relationship between them and thus cut off an avenue for help. In addition, this student raises the question as to whether the proctor sees his drinking as a problem.

This example points to an important distinction, between care as understood or construed within a justice framework and care as a framework or a perspective on moral decision. Within a justice construction, care becomes the mercy that tempers justice; or connotes the special obligations or supererogatory duties that arise in personal relationships; or signifies altruism freely chosen—a decision to modulate the strict demands of justice by considering equity or showing forgiveness; or characterizes a choice to sacrifice the claims of the self. All of these interpretations of care leave the basic assumptions of a justice framework intact: the division between the self and others, the logic of reciprocity or equal respect.

As a moral perspective, care is less well elaborated, and there is no ready vocabulary in moral theory to describe its terms. As a framework for moral decision, care is grounded in the assumption that self and other are interdependent, an assumption reflected in a view of action as responsive and, therefore, as arising in relationship rather than the view of action as emanating from within the self and, therefore, "self governed." Seen as responsive, the self is by definition connected to others, responding to perceptions, interpreting events, and governed by the organizing tendencies of human interaction and human language. Within this framework, detachment, whether from self or from others, is morally problematic, since it breeds moral blindness or indifference—a failure to discern or respond to need. The question of what responses constitute care and what responses lead to hurt draws attention to the fact that one's own terms may differ from those of others. Justice in this context becomes understood as respect for people in their own terms.

The medical student's decision not to turn in the proctor for drinking reflects a judgment that turning him in is not the best way to respond to the drinking problem, itself seen as a sign of detachment or lack of concern. Caring for the proctor thus raises the question of what actions are most likely to ameliorate this problem, a decision that leads to the question of what are the proctor's terms.

The shift in organizing perspective here is marked by the fact that the first student does not consider the terms of the other as potentially different but instead assumes one set of terms. Thus the student alone becomes the arbiter of what is *the* proper degree of contrition. The second student, in turn, does not attend to the question of whether the alcohol policy itself is just or fair. Thus each student discusses an aspect of the problem that the other does not mention.

These examples are intended to illustrate two cross-cutting perspectives that do not negate one another but focus attention on different dimensions of the situation, creating a sense of ambiguity around the question of what is the problem to be solved. Systematic research on moral orientation as a dimension of moral judgment and action initially addressed three questions: (1) Do people articulate concerns about justice and concerns about care in discussing a moral dilemma? (2) Do people tend to focus their attention on one set of concerns and minimally represent the other? and (3) Is there an association between moral orientation and gender? Evidence from studies that included a common set of questions about actual experiences of moral conflict and matched samples of males and females provides affirmative answers to all three questions.

When asked to describe a moral conflict they had faced, 55 out of 80 (69 percent) educationally advantaged North American adolescents and adults raised considerations of both justice and care. Two-thirds (54 out of 80) however, focused their attention on one set of concerns, with focus defined as 75 percent or more of the considerations raised pertaining either to justice or to care. Thus the person who presented, say, two care considerations in discussing a moral conflict was more likely to give a third, fourth, and fifth than to balance care and justice concerns—a finding consonant with the assumption that justice and care constitute organizing frameworks for moral decision. The men and the women involved in this study (high school students, college students, medical students, and adult professionals) were equally likely to demonstrate the focus phenomenon (two-thirds of both sexes fell into the outlying focus categories). There were, however, sex differences in the direction of focus. With one exception, all of the men who focused, focused on justice. The women divided, with roughly one third focusing on justice and one third on care.[4]

These findings clarify the different voice phenomenon and its implications for moral theory and for women. First, it is notable that if women were eliminated from the research sample, care focus in moral reasoning would virtually disappear. Although care focus was by no means characteristic of all women, it was almost exclusively a female phenomenon in this sample of educationally advantaged North Americans. Second, the fact that the women were advantaged means that the focus on care cannot readily be attributed to educational deficit or occupational disadvantage—the explanation Kohlberg and others have given for findings of lower levels of justice reasoning in women.[5] Instead, the focus on care in women's moral reasoning draws attention to the limitations of a justice-focused moral theory and highlights the presence of care concerns in the moral thinking of both women and men. In this light, the Care/Justice group composed of one third of the women and one third of the men becomes of particular interest, pointing to the need for further research that attends to the way people organize justice and care in relation to one another—whether, for example, people alternate perspectives, like seeing the rabbit and the duck in the rabbit-duck figure, or integrate the two perspectives in a way that resolves or sustains ambiguity.

Third, if the moral domain is comprised of at least two moral orientations, the focus phenomenon suggests that people have a tendency to lose sight of one moral perspective in arriving at moral decision—a liability equally shared by both sexes. The present findings further suggest that men and women tend to lose sight of different perspectives. The most striking result is the virtual absence of care-focus reasoning among the men. Since the men raised concerns about care in discussing moral conflicts and thus presented care concerns as morally relevant, a question is why they did not elaborate these concerns to a greater extent.

In summary, it becomes clear why attention to women's moral thinking led to the identification of a different voice and raised questions about the place of justice and care within a comprehensive moral theory. It also is clear how the selection of an all-male sample for research on moral judgment fosters an equation of morality with justice, providing little data discrepant with this view. In the present study, data discrepant with a justice-focused moral theory comes from a third of the women. Previously, such women were seen as having a problem understanding "morality." Yet these women may also be seen as exposing the problem in a justice-focused moral theory. This may explain the decision of researchers to exclude girls and women at the initial stage of moral judgment research. If one begins with the premise that "all morality consists in respect for rules,"[6] or "virtue is one and its name is justice,"[7] then women are likely to appear problematic within moral theory. If one begins with women's moral judgments, the problem becomes how to construct a theory that encompasses care as a focus of moral attention rather than as a subsidiary moral concern.

The implications of moral orientation for moral theory and for research on moral development are extended by a study designed and conducted by Kay Johnston.[8] Johnston set out to explore the relationship between moral orientation and problem-solving strategies, creating a standard method using fables for assessing spontaneous moral orientation, and orientation preference. She asked 60 eleven- and fifteen-year-olds to state and to solve the moral problem posed by the fable. Then she asked: "Is there another way to solve this problem?" Most of the children initially constructed the fable problems either in terms of justice or in terms of care; either they stood back from the situation and appealed to a rule or principle for adjudicating the conflicting claims or they entered the situation in an effort to discover or create a way of responding to all of the needs. About half of the children, slightly more fifteen- than eleven-year-olds, spontaneously switched moral orientation when asked whether there was another way to solve the problem. Others did so following an interviewer's cue as to the form such a switch might take. Finally, the children were asked which of the solutions they described was the best solution. Most of the children answered the question and explained why one way was preferable.

Johnston found gender differences parallel to those previously reported, with boys more often spontaneously using and preferring justice solutions and girls more often spontaneously using and preferring care solutions. In addition, she found differences between the two fables she used, confirming Langdale's finding that moral orientation is associated both with the gender of the reasoner and with the dilemma considered.[9] Finally, the fact that children, at least by the age of eleven, are able to shift moral orientation and can explain the logic of two moral perspectives, each associated with a different problem-solving strategy, heightens the analogy to ambiguous figure perception and further supports the conception of justice and care as organizing frameworks for moral decision.

The demonstration that children know both orientations and can frame and solve moral problems in at least two different ways means that the choice of moral standpoint is an element of moral decision. The role of the self in moral judgment thus includes the choice of moral standpoint, and this decision, whether implicit or explicit, may become linked with self-respect and self-definition. Especially in adolescence when choice becomes more self-conscious and self-reflective, moral standpoint may become entwined with identity and self-esteem. Johnston's finding that spontaneous moral orientation and preferred orientation are not always the same raises a number of questions as to why and under what conditions a person may adopt a problem-solving strategy that he or she sees as not the best way to solve the problem.

The way people chose to frame or solve a moral problem is clearly not the only way in which they can think about the problem, and is not necessarily the way they deem preferable. Moral judgments thus do not reveal *the* structure of moral thinking, since there are at least two ways in which people can structure moral problems. Johnston's demonstration of orientation-switch poses a serious challenge to the methods that have been used in moral judgment and moral development research, introducing a major interpretive caution. The fact that boys and girls at eleven and fifteen understand and distinguish the logics of justice and care reasoning directs attention to the origins and the development of both ways of thinking. In addition, the tendency for boys and girls to use and prefer different orientations when solving the same problem raises a number of questions about the relationship between these orientations and the factors influencing their representation. The different patterns of orientation use and preference, as well as the different conceptions of justice and of care implied or elaborated in the fable judgments, suggest that moral development cannot he mapped along a single linear stage sequence.

One way of explaining these findings, suggested by Johnston, joins Vygotsky's theory of cognitive development with Chodorow's analysis of sex differences in early childhood experiences of relationship.[10] Vygotsky posits that all of the higher cognitive functions originate as actual relations between individuals. Justice and care as moral ideas and as reasoning strategies thus would originate as relationships with others—an idea consonant with the derivation of justice and care reasoning from experiences of inequality and attachment in early childhood. All children are born into a situation of inequality in that they are less capable than the adults and older children around them and, in this sense, more helpless and less powerful. In addition, no child survives in the absence of some kind of adult attachment—or care, and through this experience of relationship children discover the responsiveness of human connection including their ability to move and affect one another.

Through the experience of inequality, of being in the less powerful position, children learn what it means to depend on the authority and the good will of others. As a result, they tend to strive for equality of greater power, and for freedom. Through the experience of attachment, children discover the ways in which people are able to care for and to hurt one another. The child's vulnerability to oppression and to abandonment thus can be seen to lay the groundwork for the moral visions of justice and care, conceived as ideals of human relationship and defining the ways in which people "should" act toward one another.

Chodorow's work then provides a way of explaining why care concerns tend to be minimally represented by men and why such concerns are less frequently elaborated in moral theory. Chodorow joins the dynamics of gender identity formation (the identification of oneself as male or female) to an analysis of early childhood relationships and examines the effects of maternal child care on the inner structuring of self in relation to others. Further, she differentiates a positional sense of self from a personal sense of self, contrasting a self defined in terms of role or position from a self known through the experience of connection. Her point is that maternal child care fosters the continuation of a relational sense of self in girls, since female gender identity is consonant with feeling connected with one's mother. For boys, gender identity is in tension with mother-child connection, unless that connection is structured in terms of sexual opposition (e.g., as an Oedipal drama). Thus, although boys experience responsiveness or care in relationships, knowledge of care or the need for care, when associated with mothers, poses a threat to masculine identity.[11]

Chodorow's work is limited by her reliance on object relations theory and problematic on that count. Object relations theory ties the formation of the self to the experience of separation, joining separation with individuation and thus counterposing the experience of self to the experience of connection with others. This is the line that Chodorow traces in explicating male development. Within this framework, girls' connections with their mothers can only be seen as problematic. Connection with others or the capacity to feel and think *with* others is, by definition, in tension with self-development when self-development or individuation is linked to separation. Thus, object-relations theory sustains a series of oppositions that have been central in Western thought and moral theory, including the opposition between thought and feelings, self and relationship, reason and compassion, justice and love. Object relations theory also continues the conventional division of psychological labor between women and men. Since the idea of a self, experienced in the context of attachment with others, is theoretically impossible, mothers, described as objects, are viewed as selfless, without a self. This view is essentially problematic for women, divorcing the activity of mothering from desire, knowledge, and agency, and implying that insofar as a mother experiences herself as a subject rather than as an object (a mirror reflecting her child), she is "selfish" and not a good mother. Winnicott's phrase "good-enough mother" represents an effort to temper this judgment.

Thus, psychologists and philosophers, aligning the self and morality with separation and autonomy—the ability to be self-governing—have associated care with self-sacrifice, or with feelings—a view at odds with the current position that care represents a way of knowing and a coherent moral perspective. This position, however, is well represented in literature written by women. For example the short story "A Jury of Her Peers," written by Susan Glaspell in 1917, a time when women ordinarily did not serve on juries, contrasts two ways of knowing that underlie two ways of interpreting and solving a crime.[12] The story centers on a murder; Minnie Foster is suspected of killing her husband.

A neighbor woman and the sheriff's wife accompany the sheriff and the prosecutor to the house of the accused woman. The men, representing the law, seek evidence that will convince a jury to convict the suspect. The women, collecting things to bring Minnie Foster in jail, enter in this way into the lives lived in the house. Taking in rather than taking apart, they begin to assemble observations and impressions, connecting them to past experience and observations until suddenly they compose a familiar pattern, like the log-cabin pattern they recognize in the quilt Minnie Foster was making. "Why do we *know*—what we know this minute?" one woman asks the other, but she also offers the following explanation:

> We live close together, and we live far apart. We all go through the same things—it's all just a different kind of the same thing! If it weren't—why do you and I *understand*.[13]

The activity of quilt-making—collecting odd scraps and piecing them together until they form a pattern—becomes the metaphor for this way of knowing. Discovering a strangled canary buried under pieces of quilting, the women make a series of connections that lead them to understand what happened.

The logic that says you don't kill a man because he has killed a bird, the judgment that finds these acts wildly incommensurate, is counterposed to the logic that sees both events as part of a larger pattern—a pattern of detachment and abandonment that led finally to the strangling. "I *wish* I'd come over here once in a while," Mrs. Hale, the neighbor, exclaims. "That was a crime! Who's going to punish that?" Mrs. Peters, the sheriff's wife, recalls that when she was a girl and a boy killed her cat, "if they hadn't held me back I would have—" and realizes that there had been no one to restrain Minnie Foster. John Foster was known as "a good man . . . He didn't drink, and he kept his word as well as most, I guess, and paid his debts." But he also was "a hard man," Mrs. Hale explains, "like a raw wind that gets to the bone."

Seeing detachment as the crime with murder as its ultimate extension, implicating themselves and also seeing the connection between their own and Minnie Foster's actions, the women solve the crime by attachment— by joining together, like the "knotting" that joins pieces of a quilt. In the decision to remove rather than to reveal the evidence, they separate themselves from a legal system in which they have no voice but also no way of voicing what they have come to understand. In choosing to connect themselves with one another and with Minnie, they separate themselves from the law that would use their understanding and their knowledge as grounds for further separation and killing.

In a law school class where a film-version of this story was shown, the students were divided in their assessment of the moral problem and in their evaluation of the various characters and actions. Some focused on the murder, the strangling of the husband. Some focused on the evidence of abandonment or indifference to others. Responses to a questionnaire showed a bi-modal distribution, indicating two ways of viewing the film. These different perspectives led to different ways of evaluating both the act of murder and the women's decision to remove the evidence. Responses to the film were not aligned with the sex of the viewer in an absolute way, thus dispelling any implication of biological determinism or of a stark division between the way women and men know or judge events. The knowledge gained inductively by the women in the film, however, was also gained more readily by women watching the film, who came in this way to see a logic in the women's actions and to articulate a rationale for their silence.

The analogy to ambiguous figure perception is useful here in several ways. First, it suggests that people can see a situation in more than one way, and even alternate ways of seeing, combining them without reducing them—like designating the rabbit-duck figure both duck and rabbit. Second, the analogy argues against the tendency to construe justice and care as opposites or mirror-images and also against the implication that these two perspectives are readily integrated or fused. The ambiguous figure directs attention to the way in which a change in perspective can reorganize perception and change understanding, without implying an underlying reality or pure form. What makes seeing both moral perspectives so difficult is precisely that the orientations are not opposites nor mirror images or better and worse representations of a single moral truth. The terms of one perspective do not contain the terms of the other. Instead, a shift in orientation denotes a restructuring of moral perception,

328

changing the meaning of moral language and thus the definition of moral conflict and moral action. For example, detachment is considered the hallmark of mature moral thinking within a justice perspective, signifying the ability to judge dispassionately, to weigh evidence in an even-handed manner, balancing the claims of others and self. From a care perspective, detachment is *the* moral problem.

> "I could've come," retorted Mrs. Hale... "I wish I had come over to see Minnie Foster sometimes. I can see now . . . if there had been years and years of—nothing, then a bird to sing to you, it would be awful—still—after the bird was still . . . I know what stillness is."

The difference between agreement and understanding captures the different logics of justice and care reasoning, one seeking grounds for agreement, one seeking grounds for understanding, one assuming separation and thus the need for some external structure of connection, one assuming connection and thus the potential for understanding. These assumptions run deep, generating and reflecting different views of human nature and the human condition. They also point to different vulnerabilities and different sources of error. The potential error in justice reasoning lies in its latent egocentrism, the tendency to confuse one's perspective with an objective standpoint or truth, the temptation to define others in one's own terms by putting oneself in their place. The potential error in care reasoning lies in the tendency to forget that one has terms, creating a tendency to enter into another's perspective and to see oneself as "selfless" by defining oneself in other's terms. These two types of error underlie two common equations that signify distortions or deformations of justice and care: the equation of human with male, unjust in its omission of women; and the equation of care with self-sacrifice, uncaring in its failure to represent the activity and the agency of care.

The equation of human with male was assumed in the Platonic and in the Enlightenment tradition as well as by psychologists who saw all-male samples as "representative" of human experience. The equation of care with self-sacrifice is in some ways more complex. The premise of self-interest assumes a conflict of interest between self and other manifest in the opposition of egoism and altruism. Together, the equations of male with human and of care with self-sacrifice form a circle that has had a powerful hold on moral philosophy and psychology. The conjunction of women and moral theory thus challenges the traditional definition of human and calls for a reconsideration of what is meant by both justice and care.

To trace moral development along two distinct although intersecting dimensions of relationship suggests the possibility of different permutations of justice and care reasoning, different ways these two moral perspectives can be understood and represented in relation to one another. For example, one perspective may overshadow or eclipse the other, so that one is brightly illuminated while the other is dimly remembered, familiar but for the most part forgotten. The way in which one story about relationship obscures another was evident in high-school girls' definitions of dependence. These definitions highlighted two meanings—one arising from the opposition between dependence and independence, and one from the opposition of dependence to isolation ("No woman," one student observed, "is an island.") As the word "dependence" connotes the experience of relationship, this shift in the implied opposite of dependence indicates how the valence of relationship changes, when connection with others is experienced as an impediment to autonomy or independence, and when it is experienced as a source of comfort and pleasure, and a protection against isolation. This essential ambivalence of human connection provides a powerful emotional grounding for two moral perspectives, and also may indicate what is at stake in the effort to reduce morality to a single perspective.

It is easy to understand the ascendance of justice reasoning and of justice-focused moral theories in a society where care is associated with personal vulnerability in the form of economic disadvantage. But another way of thinking about the ascendance of justice reasoning and also about sex differences in moral development is suggested in the novel *Masks*, written by Fumiko Enchi, a Japanese woman.[14] The subject is spirit possession, and the novel dramatizes what it means to be possessed by the spirits of others. Writing about the Rokujo lady in the *Tales of Genji*, Enchi's central character notes that:

> Her soul alternates uncertainly between lyricism and spirit possession, making no philosophical distinction between the self alone and in relation to others, and is unable to achieve the solace of a religious indifference.[15]

The option of transcendence, of a religious indifference or a philosophical detachment, may be less available to women because women are more likely to be possessed by the spirits and the stories of others. The strength of women's moral perceptions lies in the refusal of detachment and depersonalization, and insistence on making connections that can lead to seeing the person killed in war or living in poverty as someone's son or father or brother or sister, or mother, or daughter, or friend. But the liability of women's development is also underscored by Enchi's novel in that women, possessed by the spirits of others, also are more likely to be caught in a chain of false attachments. If women are at the present time the custodians of a story about human attachment and interdependence, not only within the family but also in the world at large, then questions arise as to how this story can be kept alive and how moral theory can sustain this story. In this sense, the relationship between women and moral theory itself becomes one of interdependence.

By rendering a care perspective more coherent and making its terms explicit, moral theory may facilitate women's ability to speak about their experiences and perceptions and may foster the ability of others to listen and to understand. At the same time, the evidence of care focus in women's moral thinking suggests that the study of women's development may provide a natural history of moral development in which care is ascendant, revealing the ways in which creating and sustaining responsive connection with others becomes or remains a central moral concern. The promise in joining women and moral theory lies in the fact that human survival, in the late twentieth century, may depend less on formal agreement than on human connection.

Notes

1. Gilligan, C. (1977). "In a Different Voice: Women's Conceptions of Self and of Morality." *Harvard Educational Review* 47 (1982): 481–517; *In a Different Voice: Psychological Theory and Women's Development*. Cambridge, Mass.: Harvard University Press.

2. Piaget, J. (1965). *The Moral Judgment of the Child*. New York, N.Y.: The Free Press Paperback Edition, pp. 76–84.

3. Kohlberg, L. (1984). *The Psychology of Moral Development*. San Francisco, Calif.: Harper & Row, Publishers, Inc.

4. Gilligan, C. and J. Attanucci. (1986). *Two Moral Orientations*. Harvard University, unpublished manuscript.

5. See Kohlberg, L. op. cit., also Walker, L. (1984). "Sex Differences in the Development of Moral Reasoning: A Critical Review of the Literature." *Child Development* 55 (3): 677–91.

6. Piaget, J., op. cit.

7. Kohlberg, L., op. cit.

8. Johnston, K. (1985). *Two Moral Orientations—Two Problem-solving Strategies: Adolescents' Solutions to Dilemmas in Fables*. Harvard University, unpublished doctoral dissertation.

9. Langdale, C. (1983). *Moral Orientation and Moral Development: The Analysis of Care and Justice Reasoning Across Different Dilemmas in Females and Males from Childhood through Adulthood*. Harvard University, unpublished doctoral dissertation.

10. Johnston, K., op. cit.; Vygotsky, L. (1978). *Mind in Society*. Cambridge, Mass.: Harvard University Press; Chodorow, N. (1974). "Family Structure and Feminine Personality" in *Women, Culture and Society*, L. M. Rosaldo and L. Lamphere, eds., Stanford, Calif.: Stanford University Press; see also Chodorow, N. (1978). *The Reproduction of Mothering: Psychoanalysis and the Sociology of Gender*. Berkeley, Calif.: University of California Press.

11. Chodorow, N., op. cit.

12. Glaspell, S. (1927). *A Jury of Her Peers*. London: E. Benn.

13. Ibid.

14. Fumiko, E. (1983). *Masks*. New York: Random House.

15. Ibid. p. 54.

Appendix III
Basic Rights

A Bill of Rights for Employees and Employers

Patricia H. Werhane

Employee Rights

1. Every person has an equal right to a job and a right to equal consideration at the job. Employees may not be discriminated against on the basis of religion, sex, ethnic origin, race, color, or economic background.

2. Every person has the right to equal pay for work, where "equal work" is defined by the job description and title.

3. Every employee has rights to his or her job. After a probation period of three to ten years every employee has the right to his or her job. An employee can be dismissed only under the following conditions:

   - He or she is not performing satisfactorily the job for which he or she was hired.
   - He or she is involved in criminal activity either within or outside the corporation.
   - He or she is drunk or takes drugs on the job.
   - He or she actively disrupts corporate business activity without a valid reason.
   - He or she becomes physically or mentally incapacitated or reaches mandatory retirement age.
   - The employer has publicly verifiable economic reasons for dismissing the employee, e.g., transfer of the company, loss of sales, bankruptcy, etc.
   - Under no circumstances can an employee be dismissed or laid off without the institution of fair due process procedure.

4. Every employee has the right to due process in the workplace. He or she has the right to a peer review, to a hearing, and if necessary, to outside arbitration before being demoted or fired.

5. Every employee has the right to free expression in the workplace. This includes the right to object to corporate acts that he or she finds illegal or immoral without retaliation or penalty. The objection may take the form of free speech, whistle-blowing, or conscientious objection. However, any criticism must be documented or proven.

6. The Privacy Act, which protects the privacy and confidentiality of public employees, should be extended to all employees.

7. The polygraph should be outlawed.

8. Employees have the right to engage in outside activity of their choice.

9. Every employee has the right to a safe workplace, including the right to safety information and participation in improving work hazards. Every employee has the right to legal protection that guards against preventable job risks.

10. Every employee has the right to as much information as possible about the corporation, about his or her job, work hazards, possibilities for future employment, and any other information necessary for job enrichment and development.

11. Every employee has the right to participate in the decision-making processes entailed in his or her job, department, or in the corporation as a whole, where appropriate.

12. Every public and private employee has the right to strike when the foregoing demands are not met in the workplace.

Employer Rights

1. Any employee found discriminating against another employee or operating in a discriminatory manner against her employer is subject to employer reprimand, demotion, or firing.

2. Any employee not deserving equal pay because of inefficiency should be shifted to another job.

3. No employee who functions inefficiently, who drinks or takes drugs on the job, commits felonies or acts in ways that prevent carrying out work duties has a right to a job.

4. Any employee found guilty under a due process procedure should be reprimanded. (e.g., demoted or dismissed), and, if appropriate, brought before the law.

5. No employer must retain employees who slander the corporation or other corporate constituents.

6. The privacy of employers is as important as the privacy of employees. By written agreement employees may be required not to disclose confidential corporate information or trade secrets unless not doing so is clearly against the public interest.

7. Employers may engage in surveillance of employees at work (but only at work) with their foreknowledge and consent.

8. No employee may engage in activities that literally harm the employer, nor may an employee have a second job whose business competes with the business of the first employer.

9. Employees shall be expected to carry out job assignments for which they are hired unless these conflict with common moral standards or unless the employee was not fully informed about these assignments or their dangers before accepting employment. Employees themselves should become fully informed about work dangers.

10. Employers have rights to personal information about employees or prospective employees adequate to make sound hiring and promotion judgments so long as the employer preserves the confidentiality of such information.

11. Employers as well as employees have rights. Therefore the right to participation is a correlative obligation on the part of both parties to respect mutual rights. Employers, then, have the right to demand efficiency and productivity from their employees in return for the employee right to participation in the workplace.

12. Employees who strike for no reason are subject to dismissal.

Any employee or employer who feels he or she has been unduly penalized under a bill of rights may appeal to an outside arbitrator.

The United Nations Declaration of Human Rights

Now, Therefore, The General Assembly *proclaims*

This universal declaration of human rights as a common standard of achievement for all peoples and all nations, to the end that every individual and every organ of society, keeping this Declaration constantly in mind, shall strive by teaching and education to promote respect for these rights and freedoms and by progressive measures, national and international, to secure their universal and effective recognition and observance, both among the peoples of Member States themselves and among the peoples of territories under their jurisdiction.

Article 1

All human beings are born free and equal in dignity and rights. They are endowed with reason and conscience and should act towards one another in a spirit of brotherhood.

Article 2

Everyone is entitled to all the rights and freedoms set forth in this Declaration, without distinction of any kind, such as race, colour, sex, language, religion, political or other opinion, national or social origin, property, birth or other status.

Furthermore, no distinction shall be made on the basis of the political, jurisdictional or international status of the country or territory to which a person belongs, whether it be independent, trust, non-self-governing or under any other limitation of sovereignty.

Article 3

Everyone has the right to life, liberty and security of person.

Article 4

No one shall be held in slavery or servitude; slavery and the slave trade shall be prohibited in all their forms.

Article 5

No one shall be subjected to torture or to cruel, inhuman or degrading treatment or punishment.

Article 6

Everyone has the right to recognition everywhere as a person before the law.

Article 7

All are equal before the law and are entitled without any discrimination to equal protection of the law. All are entitled to equal protection against any discrimination in violation of this Declaration and against any incitement to such discrimination.

Article 8

Everyone has the right to an effective remedy by the competent national tribunals for acts violating the fundamental rights granted him by the constitution or by law.

Article 9

No one shall be subjected to arbitrary arrest, detention or exile.

Article 10

Everyone is entitled in full equality to a fair and public hearing by an independent and impartial tribunal, in the determination of his rights and obligations and of any criminal charge against him.

Article 11

1. Everyone charged with a penal offence has the right to be presumed innocent until proved guilty according to law in a public trial at which he has had all the guarantees necessary for his defence.

2. No one shall be held guilty of any penal offence on account of any act or omission which did not constitute a penal offence, under national or international law, at the time when it was committed. Nor shall a heavier penalty be imposed than the one that was applicable at the time the penal offence was committed.

Article 12

No one shall be subjected to arbitrary interference with his privacy, family, home or correspondence, nor to attacks upon his honour and reputation. Everyone has the right to the protection of the law against such interference or attacks.

Article 13

1. Everyone has the right to freedom of movement and residence within the borders of each State.

2. Everyone has the right to leave any country, including his own, and to return to his country.

Article 14

1. Everyone has the right to seek and to enjoy in other countries asylum from persecution.

2. This right may not be invoked in the case of prosecutions genuinely arising from non-political crimes or from acts contrary to the purposes and principles of the United Nations.

Article 15

1. Everyone has the right to a nationality.

2. No one shall be arbitrarily deprived of his nationality nor denied the right to change his nationality.

Article 16

1. Men and women of full age, without any limitation due to race, nationality or religion, have the right to marry and to found a family. They are entitled to equal rights as to marriage, during marriage and at its dissolution.

2. Marriage shall be entered into only with the free and full consent of the intending spouses.

3. The family is the natural and fundamental group unit of society and is entitled to protection by society and the state.

Article 17

1. Everyone has the right to own property alone as well as in association with others.

2. No one shall be arbitrarily deprived of his property.

Article 18

Everyone has the right to freedom of thought, conscience and religion; this right includes freedom to change his religion or belief, and freedom, either alone or in community with others and in public or private, to manifest his religion or belief in teaching, practice, worship and observance.

Article 19

Everyone has the right to freedom of opinion and expression; this right includes freedom to hold opinions without interference and to seek, receive and impart information and ideas through any media and regardless of frontiers.

Article 20

1. Everyone has the right to freedom of peaceful assembly and association.

2. No one may be compelled to belong to an association.

Article 21

1. Everyone has the right to take part in the government of his country, directly or through freely chosen representatives.

2. Everyone has the right to equal access to public service in his country.

3. The will of the people shall be the basis of the authority of government; this will shall be expressed in periodic and genuine elections which shall be by universal and equal suffrage and shall be held by secret vote or by equivalent free voting procedures.

Article 22

Everyone, as a member of society, has the right to social security and is entitled to realization, through national effort and international cooperation and in accordance with the organization and resources of each State, of the economic, social and cultural rights indispensable for his dignity and the free development of his personality.

Article 23

1. Everyone has the right to work, to free choice of employment, to just and favourable conditions of work and to protection against unemployment.

2. Everyone, without any discrimination, has the right to equal pay for equal work.

3. Everyone who works has the right to just and favourable remuneration ensuring for himself and his family an existence worthy of human dignity, and supplemented, if necessary, by other means of social protection.

4. Everyone has the right to form and to join trade unions for the protection of his interests.

Article 24

Everyone has the right to rest and leisure, including reasonable limitation of working hours and periodic holidays with pay.

Article 25

1. Everyone has the right to a standard of living adequate for the health and well-being of himself and of his family, including food, clothing, housing and medical care and necessary social services, and the right to security in the event of unemployment, sickness, disability, widowhood, old age or other lack of livelihood in circumstances beyond his control.

2. Motherhood and childhood are entitled to special care and assistance. All children, whether born in or out of wedlock, shall enjoy the same social protection.

Article 26

1. Everyone has the right to education. Education shall be free, at least in the elementary and fundamental stages. Elementary education shall be compulsory. Technical and professional education shall be made generally available and higher education shall be equally accessible to all on the basis of merit.

2. Education shall be directed to the full development of the human personality and to the strengthening of respect for human rights and fundamental freedoms. It shall promote understanding, tolerance and friendship among all nations, racial or religious groups, and shall further the activities of the United Nations for the maintenance of peace.

3. Parents have a prior right to choose the kind of education that shall be given to their children.

Article 27

1. Everyone has the right freely to participate in the cultural life of the community, to enjoy the arts and to share in scientific advancement and its benefits.

2. Everyone has the right to the protection of the moral and material interests resulting from any scientific, literary or artistic production of which he is the author.

Article 28

Everyone is entitled to a social and international order in which the rights and freedoms set forth in this Declaration can be fully realized.

Article 29

1. Everyone has duties to the community in which alone the free and full development of his personality is possible.

2. In the exercise of his rights and freedoms, everyone shall be subject only to such limitations as are determined by law solely for the purpose of securing due recognition and respect for the rights and freedoms of others and of meeting the just requirements of morality, public order and the general welfare in a democratic society.

3. These rights and freedoms may in no case be exercised contrary to the purposes and principles of the United Nations.

Article 30

Nothing in this Declaration may be interpreted as implying for any State, group or person any right to engage in any activity or to perform any act aimed at the destruction of any of the rights and freedoms set forth herein.

A Global Ethic

1993 Parliment of the World's Religions
The Declaration of a Global Ethic

The world is in agony. The agony is so pervasive and urgent that we are compelled to name its manifestations so that the depth of this pain may be made clear.

Peace eludes us . . . the planet is being destroyed . . . neighbors live in fear . . . women and men are estranged from each other . . . children die!

This is abhorrent!

We condemn the abuses of Earth's ecosystems.

We condemn the poverty that stifles life's potential; the hunger that weakens the human body; the economic disparities that threaten so many families with ruin.

We condemn the social disarray of the nations; the disregard for justice which pushes citizens to the margin; the anarchy overtaking our communities; and the insane death of children from violence. In particular we condemn aggression and hatred in the name of religion.

But this agony need not be.

It need not be because the basis for an ethic already exists. This ethic offers the possibility of a better individual and global order, and leads individuals away from despair and societies away from chaos.

We are women and men who have embraced the precepts and practices of the world's religions:

We affirm that a common set of core values is found in the teachings of the religions, and that these form the basis of a global ethic.

We affirm that this truth is already known, but yet to be lived in heart and action.

We affirm that there is an irrevocable, unconditional norm for all areas of life, for families and communities, for races, nations, and religions. There already exist ancient guidelines for human behavior which are found in the teachings of the religions of the world and which are the condition for a sustainable world order.

We Declare:

We are interdependent. Each of us depends on the well-being of the whole, and so we have respect for the community of living beings, for people, animals, and plants, and for the preservation of Earth, the air, water and soil.

We take individual responsibility for all we do. All our decisions, actions, and failures to act have consequences.

We must treat others as we wish others to treat us. We make a commitment to respect life and dignity, individuality and diversity, so that every person is treated humanely, without exception. We must have patience and acceptance. We must be able to forgive, learning from the past but never allowing ourselves to be enslaved by memories of hate. Opening our hearts to one another, we must sink our narrow differences for the cause of the world community, practicing a culture of solidarity and relatedness.

We consider humankind our family. We must strive to be kind and generous. We must not live for ourselves alone, but should also serve others, never forgetting the children, the aged, the poor, the suffering, the disabled, the refugees, and the lonely. No person should ever be considered or treated as a second-class citizen, or be exploited in any way whatsoever. There should be equal partnership between men and women. We must not commit any kind of sexual immorality. We must put behind us all forms of domination or abuse.

We commit ourselves to a culture of nonviolence, respect, justice, and peace. We shall not oppress, injure, torture, or kill other human beings, forsaking violence as a means of settling differences.

We must strive for a just social and economic order, in which everyone has an equal chance to reach full potential as a human being. We must speak and act truthfully and with compassion, dealing fairly with all, and avoiding prejudice and hatred. We must not steal. We must move beyond the dominance of greed for power, prestige, money, and consumption to make a just and peaceful world.

Earth cannot be changed for the better unless the consciousness of individuals is changed first. We pledge to increase our awareness by disciplining our minds, by meditation, by prayer, or by positive thinking. Without risk and a readiness to sacrifice there can be no fundamental change in our situation. Therefore we commit ourselves to this global ethic, to understanding one another, and to socially-beneficial, peace-fostering, and nature-friendly ways of life.

We invite all people, whether religious or not, to do the same.

The Principles of a Global Ethic

Our world is experiencing a fundamental crisis: A crisis in global economy, global ecology, and global politics. The lack of a grand vision, the tangle of unresolved problems, political paralysis, mediocre political leadership with little insight or foresight, and in general too little sense for the commonweal are seen everywhere: Too many old answers to new challenges.

Hundreds of millions of human beings on our planet increasingly suffer from unemployment, poverty, hunger, and the destruction of their families. Hope for a lasting peace among nations slips away from us. There are tensions between the sexes and generations. Children die, kill, and are killed. More and more countries are shaken by corruption in politics and business. It is increasingly difficult to live together peacefully in our cities because of social, racial, and ethnic conflicts, the abuse of drugs, organized crime, and even anarchy. Even neighbors often live in fear of one another. Our planet continues to be ruthlessly plundered. A collapse of the ecosystem threatens us.

Time and again we see leaders and members of religions incite aggression, fanaticism, hate, and xenophobia—even inspire and legitimate violent and bloody conflicts. Religion often is misused for purely power-political goals, including war. We are filled with disgust.

We condemn these blights and declare that they need not be. An ethic already exists within the religious teachings of the world which can counter the global distress. Of course this ethic provides no direct solution for all the immense problems of the world, but it does supply the moral foundation for a better individual and global order: A vision which can lead women and men away from despair, and society away from chaos.

We are persons who have committed ourselves to the precepts and practices of the world's religions. We confirm that there is already a consensus among the religions which can be the basis for a global ethic—a minimal *fundamental consensus* concerning binding *values*, irrevocable *standards*, and *fundamental moral attitudes*.

I. No new global order without a new global ethic!

We women and men of various religions and regions of Earth therefore address all people, religious and non-religious. We wish to express the following convictions which we hold in common:

- We all have a responsibility for a better global order.
- Our involvement for the sake of human rights, freedom, justice, peace, and the preservation of Earth is absolutely necessary.
- Our different religious and cultural traditions must not prevent our common involvement in opposing all forms of inhumanity and working for greater humaneness.
- The principles expressed in this Global Ethic can be affirmed by all persons with ethical convictions, whether religiously grounded or not.
- As religious and spiritual persons we base our lives on an Ultimate Reality, and draw spiritual power and hope therefrom, in trust, in prayer or meditation, in word or silence. We have a special responsibility for the welfare of all humanity and care for the planet Earth. We do not consider ourselves better than other women and men, but we trust that the ancient wisdom of our religions can point the way for the future.

After two world wars and the end of the cold war, the collapse of fascism and nazism, the shaking to the foundations of communism and colonialism, humanity has entered a new phase of its history. Today we possess sufficient economic, cultural, and spiritual resources to introduce a better global order. But old and new ethnic, national, social, economic, and religious tensions threaten the peaceful building of a better world. We have experienced greater technological progress than ever before, yet we see that world-wide poverty, hunger, death of children, unemployment, misery, and the destruction of nature have not diminished but rather have increased. Many peoples are threatened with economic ruin, social disarray, political marginalization, ecological catastrophe, and national collapse.

In such a dramatic global situation humanity needs a vision of peoples living peacefully together, of ethnic and ethical groupings and of religions sharing responsibility for the care of Earth. A vision rests on hopes, goals, ideals, standards. But all over the world these have slipped from our hands. Yet we are convinced that, despite their frequent abuses and failures, it is the communities of faith who bear a responsibility to demonstrate that such hopes, ideals, and standards can be guarded, grounded, and lived. This is especially true in the modern state. Guarantees of freedom of conscience and religion are necessary but they do not substitute for binding values, convictions, and norms which are valid for all humans regardless of their social origin, sex, skin color, language, or religion.

We are convinced of the fundamental unity of the human family on Earth. We recall the 1948 Universal Declaration of Human Rights of the United Nations. What it formally proclaimed on the level of rights we wish to confirm and deepen here from the perspective of an ethic: The full realization of the intrinsic dignity of the human person, the inalienable freedom and equality in principle of all humans, and the necessary solidarity and interdependence of all humans with each other.

On the basis of personal experiences and the burdensome history of our planet we have learned

- that a better global order cannot be created or enforced by laws, prescriptions, and conventions alone;
- that the realization of peace, justice, and the protection of Earth depends on the insight and readiness of men and women to act justly;
- that action in favor of rights and freedoms presumes a consciousness of responsibility and duty, and that therefore both the minds and hearts of women and men must be addressed;
- that rights without morality cannot long endure, and that *there will be no better global order without a global ethic.*

By a global ethic we do not mean a global ideology or a single unified religion beyond all existing religions, and certainly not the domination of one religion over all others. By a global ethic we mean a fundamental consensus on binding values, irrevocable standards, and personal attitudes. Without such a fundamental consensus on an ethic, sooner or later every community will be threatened by chaos or dictatorship, and individuals will despair.

II. A fundamental demand: Every human being must be treated humanely.

We all are fallible, imperfect men and women with limitations and defects. We know the reality of evil. Precisely because of this, we feel compelled for the sake of global welfare to express what the fundamental elements of a global ethic should be—for individuals as well as for communities and organizations, for states as well as for the religions themselves. We trust that our often millennia-old religious and ethical traditions provide an ethic which is convincing and practicable for all women and men of good will, religious and non-religious.

At the same time we know that our various religious and ethical traditions often offer very different bases for what is helpful and what is unhelpful for men and women, what is right and what is wrong, what is good and what is evil. We do not wish to gloss over or ignore the serious differences among the individual religions. However, they should not hinder us from proclaiming publicly those things which we already hold in common and which we jointly affirm, each on the basis of our own religious or ethical grounds.

We know that religions cannot solve the environmental, economic, political, and social problems of Earth. However they can provide what obviously cannot be attained by economic plans, political programs, or legal regulations alone: A change in the inner orientation, the whole mentality, the "hearts" of people, and a conversion from a false path to a new orientation for life. Humankind urgently needs social and ecological reforms, but it needs spiritual renewal just as urgently. As religious or spiritual persons we commit ourselves to this task. The spiritual powers of the religions can offer a fundamental sense of trust, a ground of meaning, ultimate standards, and a spiritual home. Of course religions are credible only when they eliminate those conflicts which spring from the religions themselves, dismantling mutual arrogance, mistrust, prejudice, and even hostile images, and thus demonstrate respect for the traditions, holy places, feasts, and rituals of people who believe differently.

Now as before, women and men are treated inhumanely all over the world. They are robbed of their opportunities and their freedom; their human rights are trampled underfoot; their dignity is disregarded. But might does not make right! In the face of all inhumanity our religious and ethical convictions demand that *every human being must be treated humanely!*

This means that every human being without distinction of age, sex, race, skin color, physical or mental ability, language, religion, political view, or national or social origin possesses an inalienable and untouchable dignity, and everyone, the individual as well as the state, is therefore obliged to honor this dignity and protect it. Humans must always be the subjects of rights, must be ends, never mere means, never objects of commercialization and industrialization in economics, politics and media, in research institutes, and industrial corporations. No one stands "above good and evil"—no human being, no social class, no influential interest group, no cartel, no police apparatus, no army, and no state. On the contrary: Possessed of reason and conscience, every human is obliged to behave in a genuinely human fashion, to do good and avoid evil!

It is the intention of this Global Ethic to clarify what this means. In it we wish to recall irrevocable, unconditional ethical norms. These should not be bonds and chains, but helps and supports for people to find and realize once again their lives' direction, values, orientations, and meaning.

There is a principle which is found and has persisted in many religious and ethical traditions of humankind for thousands of years: *What you do not wish done to yourself, do not do to others.* Or in positive terms: *What you wish done to yourself, do to others!* This should be the irrevocable, unconditional norm for all areas of life, for families and communities, for races, nations, and religions.

Every form of egoism should be rejected: All selfishness, whether individual or collective, whether in the form of class thinking, racism, nationalism, or sexism. We condemn these because they prevent humans from being authentically human. Self-determination and self-realization are thoroughly legitimate so long as they are not separated from human self-responsibility and global responsibility, that is, from responsibility for fellow humans and for the planet Earth.

This principle implies very concrete standards to which we humans should hold firm. From it arise four broad, ancient guidelines for human behavior which are found in most of the religions of the world.

III. Irrevocable directives.

1. Commitment to a Culture of Non-violence and Respect for Life.

Numberless women and men of all regions and religions strive to lead lives not determined by egoism but by commitment to their fellow humans and to the world around them. Nevertheless, all over the world we find endless hatred, envy, jealousy, and violence, not only between individuals but also between social and ethnic groups, between classes, races, nations, and religions. The use of violence, drug trafficking and organized crime, often equipped with new technical possibilities, has reached global proportions. Many places still are ruled by terror "from above"; dictators oppress their own people, and institutional violence is widespread. Even in some countries where laws exist to protect individual freedoms, prisoners are tortured, men and women are mutilated, hostages are killed.

a) In the great ancient religious and ethical traditions of humankind we find the directive: *You shall not kill!* Or in positive terms: *Have respect for life!* Let us reflect anew on the consequences of this ancient directive: All people have a right to life, safety, and the free development of personality insofar as they do not injure the rights of others. No one has the right physically or psychically to torture, injure, much less kill, any other human being. And no people, no state, no race, no religion has the right to hate, to discriminate against, to "cleanse," to exile, much less to liquidate a "foreign" minority which is different in behavior or holds different beliefs.

b) Of course, wherever there are humans there will be conflicts. Such conflicts, however, should be resolved without violence within a framework of justice. This is true for states as well as for individuals. Persons who hold political power must work within the framework of a just order and commit themselves to the most non-violent, peaceful solutions possible. And they should work for this within an international order of peace which itself has need of protection and defense against perpetrators of violence. Armament is a mistaken path; disarmament is the commandment of the times. Let no one be deceived: There is no survival for humanity without global peace!

c) Young people must learn at home and in school that violence may not be a means of settling differences with others. Only thus can a culture of non-violence be created.

d) A human person is infinitely precious and must be unconditionally protected. But likewise the lives of animals and plants which inhabit this planet with us deserve protection, preservation, and care. Limitless exploitation of the natural foundations of life, ruthless destruction of the biosphere, and militarization of the cosmos are all outrages. As human beings we have a special responsibility— especially with a view to future generations—for Earth and the cosmos, for the air, water, and soil. We are all intertwined together in this cosmos and we are all dependent on each other. Each one of us depends on the welfare of all. Therefore the dominance of humanity over nature and the cosmos must not be encouraged. Instead we must cultivate living in harmony with nature and the cosmos.

e) To be authentically human in the spirit of our great religious and ethical traditions means that in public as well as in private life we must be concerned for others and ready to help. We must never be ruthless and brutal. Every people, every race, every religion must show tolerance and respect—indeed high appreciation—for every other. Minorities need protection and support, whether they be racial, ethnic, or religious.

2. Commitment to a Culture of Solidarity and a Just Economic Order.

Numberless men and women of all regions and religions strive to live their lives in solidarity with one another and to work for authentic fulfillment of their vocations. Nevertheless, all over the world we find endless hunger, deficiency, and need. Not only individuals, but especially unjust institutions and structures are responsible for these tragedies. Millions of people are without work; millions are exploited by poor wages, forced to the edges of society, with their possibilities for the future destroyed. In many lands the gap between the poor and the rich, between the powerful and the powerless is immense. We live in a world in which totalitarian state socialism as well as unbridled capitalism have hollowed out and destroyed many ethical and spiritual values. A materialistic mentality breeds greed for unlimited profit and a grasping for endless plunder. These demands claim more and more of the community's resources without obliging the individual to contribute more. The cancerous social evil of corruption thrives in the developing countries and in the developed countries alike.

a) In the great ancient religious and ethical traditions of humankind we find the directive: *You shall not steal!* Or in positive terms: *Deal honestly and fairly!* Let us reflect anew on the consequences of this ancient directive: No one has the right to rob or dispossess in any way whatsoever any other person or the commonweal. Further, no one has the right to use her or his possessions without concern for the needs of society and Earth.

b) Where extreme poverty reigns, helplessness and despair spread, and theft occurs again and again for the sake of survival. Where power and wealth are accumulated ruthlessly, feelings of envy, resentment, and deadly hatred and rebellion inevitably well up in the disadvantaged and marginalized. This leads to a vicious circle of violence and counter-violence. Let no one be deceived: There is no global peace without global justice!

c) Young people must learn at home and in school that property, limited though it may be, carries with it an obligation, and that its uses should at the same time serve the common good. Only thus can a just economic order be built up.

d) If the plight of the poorest billions of humans on this planet, particularly women and children, is to be improved, the world economy must be structured more justly. Individual good deeds, and assistance projects, indispensable though they be, are insufficient. The participation of all states and the authority of international organizations are needed to build just economic institutions.

A solution which can be supported by all sides must be sought for the debt crisis and the poverty of the dissolving second world, and even more the third world. Of course conflicts of interest are unavoidable. In the developed countries, a distinction must be made between necessary and limitless consumption, between socially beneficial and non-beneficial uses of property, between justified and unjustified uses of natural resources, and between a profit-only and a socially beneficial and ecologically oriented market economy. Even the developing nations must search their national consciences.

Wherever those ruling threaten to repress those ruled, wherever institutions threaten persons, and wherever might oppresses right, we are obligated to resist—whenever possible non-violently.

e) To be authentically human in the spirit of our great religious and ethical traditions means the following:

- We must utilize economic and political power for service to humanity instead of misusing it in ruthless battles for domination. We must develop a spirit of compassion with those who suffer, with special care for the children, the aged, the poor, the disabled, the refugees, and the lonely.
- We must cultivate mutual respect and consideration, so as to reach a reasonable balance of interests, instead of thinking only of unlimited power and unavoidable competitive struggles.
- We must value a sense of moderation and modesty instead of an unquenchable greed for money, prestige, and consumption. In greed humans lose their "souls," their freedom, their composure, their inner peace, and thus that which makes them human.

3. Commitment to a Culture of Tolerance and a Life of Truthfulness.

Numberless women and men of all regions and religions strive to lead lives of honesty and truthfulness. Nevertheless, all over the world we find endless lies and deceit, swindling and hypocrisy, ideology and demagoguery:

- Politicians and business people who use lies as a means to success;
- Mass media which spread ideological propaganda instead of accurate reporting, misinformation instead of information, cynical commercial interest instead of loyalty to the truth;
- Scientists and researchers who give themselves over to morally questionable ideological or political programs or to economic interest groups, or who justify research which violates fundamental ethical values;
- Representatives of religions who dismiss other religions as of little value and who preach fanaticism and intolerance instead of respect and understanding.

a) In the great ancient religious and ethical traditions of humankind we find the directive: *You shall not lie!* Or in positive terms: *Speak and act truthfully!* Let us reflect anew on the consequences of this ancient directive: No woman or man, no institution, no state or church or religious community has the right to speak lies to other humans.

b) This is especially true

- for those who work in the mass media, to whom we entrust the freedom to report for the sake of truth and to whom we thus grant the office of guardian. They do not stand above morality but have the obligation to respect human dignity, human rights, and fundamental values. They are duty-bound to objectivity, fairness, and the preservation of human dignity. They have no right to intrude into individuals' private spheres, to manipulate public opinion, or to distort reality;
- for artists, writers, and scientists, to whom we entrust artistic and academic freedom. They are not exempt from general ethical standards and must serve the truth;
- for the leaders of countries, politicians, and political parties, to whom we entrust our own freedoms. When they lie in the faces of their people, when they manipulate the truth, or when they are guilty of venality or ruthlessness in domestic or foreign affairs, they forsake their credibility and deserve to lose their offices and their voters. Conversely, public opinion should support those politicians who dare to speak the truth to the people at all times;
- finally, for representatives of religion. When they stir up prejudice, hatred, and enmity towards those of different belief, or even incite or legitimize religious wars, they deserve the condemnation of humankind and the loss of their adherents.

Let no one be deceived: There is no global justice without truthfulness and humaneness!

c) Young people must learn at home and in school to think, speak, and act truthfully. They have a right to information and education to be able to make the decisions that will form their lives. Without an ethical formation they will hardly be able to distinguish the important from the unimportant. In the daily flood of information, ethical standards will help them discern when opinions are portrayed as facts, interests veiled, tendencies exaggerated, and facts twisted.

d) To be authentically human in the spirit of our great religious and ethical traditions means the following:

- We must not confuse freedom with arbitrariness or pluralism with indifference to truth.

- We must cultivate truthfulness in all our relationships instead of dishonesty, dissembling, and opportunism.

- We must constantly seek truth and incorruptible sincerity instead of spreading ideological or partisan half-truths.

- We must courageously serve the truth and we must remain constant and trustworthy, instead of yielding to opportunistic accommodation to life.

4. Commitment to a Culture of Equal Rights and Partnership between Men and Women

Numberless men and women of all regions and religions strive to live their lives in a spirit of partnership and responsible action in the areas of love, sexuality, and family. Nevertheless, all over the world there are condemnable forms of patriarchy, domination of one sex over the other, exploitation of women, sexual misuse of children, and forced prostitution. Too frequently, social inequities force women and even children into prostitution as a means of survival—particularly in less developed countries.

a) In the great ancient religious and ethical traditions of humankind we find the directive: *You shall not commit sexual immorality!* Or in positive terms: *Respect and love one another!* Let us reflect anew on the consequences of this ancient directive: No one has the right to degrade others to mere sex objects, to lead them into or hold them in sexual dependency.

b) We condemn sexual exploitation and sexual discrimination as one of the worst forms of human degradation. We have the duty to resist wherever the domination of one sex over the other is preached—even in the name of religious conviction; wherever sexual exploitation is tolerated, wherever prostitution is fostered or children are misused.

Let no one be deceived: There is no authentic humaneness without a living together in partnership!

c) Young people must learn at home and in school that sexuality is not a negative, destructive, or exploitative force, but creative and affirmative. Sexuality as a life-affirming shaper of community can only be effective when partners accept the responsibilities of caring for one another's happiness.

d) The relationship between women and men should be characterized not by patronizing behavior or exploitation, but by love, partnership, and trustworthiness. Human fulfillment is not identical with sexual pleasure. Sexuality should express and reinforce a loving relationship lived by equal partners.

Some religious traditions know the ideal of a voluntary renunciation of the full use of sexuality. Voluntary renunciation also can be an expression of identity and meaningful fulfillment.

e) The social institution of marriage, despite all its cultural and religious variety, is characterized by love, loyalty, and permanence. It aims at and should guarantee security and mutual support to husband, wife, and child. It should secure the rights of all family members.

All lands and cultures should develop economic and social relationships which will enable marriage and family life worthy of human beings, especially for older people. Children have a right of access to education. Parents should not exploit children, nor children parents. Their relationships should reflect mutual respect, appreciation, and concern.

f) To be authentically human in the spirit of our great religious and ethical traditions means the following:

- We need mutual respect, partnership, and understanding, instead of patriarchal domination and degradation, which are expressions of violence and engender counter-violence.
- We need mutual concern, tolerance, readiness for reconciliation, and love, instead of any form of possessive lust or sexual misuse.

Only what has already been experienced in personal and familial relationships can be practiced on the level of nations and religions.

IV. A Transformation of Consciousness!

Historical experience demonstrates the following: Earth cannot be changed for the better unless we achieve a transformation in the consciousness of individuals and in public life. The possibilities for transformation have already been glimpsed in areas such as war and peace, economy, and ecology, where in recent decades fundamental changes have taken place. This transformation must also be achieved in the area of ethics and values!

Every individual has intrinsic dignity and inalienable rights, and each also has an inescapable responsibility for what she or he does and does not do. All our decisions and deeds, even our omissions and failures, have consequences.

Keeping this sense of responsibility alive, deepening it and passing it on to future generations, is the special task of religions.

We are realistic about what we have achieved in this consensus, and so we urge that the following be observed:

1. A universal consensus on many disputed ethical questions (from bio- and sexual ethics through mass media and scientific ethics to economic and political ethics) will be difficult to attain. Nevertheless, even for many controversial questions, suitable solutions should be attainable in the spirit of the fundamental principles we have jointly developed here.

2. In many areas of life a new consciousness of ethical responsibility has already arisen. Therefore we would be pleased if as many professions as possible, such as those of physicians, scientists, business people, journalists, and politicians, would develop up-to-date codes of ethics which would provide specific guidelines for the vexing questions of these particular professions.

3. Above all, we urge the various communities of faith to formulate their very specific ethics: What does each faith tradition have to say, for example, about the meaning of life and death, the enduring of suffering and the forgiveness of guilt, about selfless sacrifice and the necessity of renunciation, about compassion and joy. These will deepen, and make more specific, the already discernible global ethic.

In conclusion, we appeal to all the inhabitants of this planet. Earth cannot be changed for the better unless the consciousness of individuals is changed. We pledge to work for such transformation in individual and collective consciousness, for the awakening of our spiritual powers through reflection, meditation, prayer, or positive thinking, for a conversion of the heart. Together we can move mountains! Without a willingness to take risks and a readiness to sacrifice there can be no fundamental change in our situation! Therefore we commit ourselves to a common global ethic, to better mutual understanding, as well as to socially-beneficial, peace-fostering, and Earth-friendly ways of life.

We invite all men and women, whether religious or not, to do the same.

Appendix IV
When Do We Take a Stand?

When Do We Take a Stand?

Bowen H. McCoy

I wrote about my experiences purposely to present an ambiguous situation. I never found out if the sadhu lived or died. I can attest, though, that the sadhu lives on in his story. He lives in the ethics classes I teach each year at business schools and churches. He lives in the classrooms of numerous business schools, where professors have taught the case to tens of thousands of students. He lives in several casebooks on ethics and on an educational video. And he lives in organizations such as the American Red Cross and AT&T, which use his story in their ethics training.

As I reflect on the sadhu now, 15 years after the fact, I first have to wonder, What actually happened on that Himalayan slope? When I first wrote about the event, I reported the experience in as much detail as I could remember, but I shaped it to the needs of a good classroom discussion. After years of reading my story, viewing it on video, and hearing others discuss it, I'm not sure I myself know what actually occurred on the mountainside that day!

I've also heard a wide variety of responses to the story. The sadhu, for example, may not have wanted our help at all—he may have been intentionally bringing on his own death as a way to holiness. Why had he taken the dangerous way over the pass instead of the caravan route through the gorge? Hindu businesspeople have told me that in trying to assist the sadhu, we were being typically arrogant Westerners imposing our cultural values on the world.

I've learned that each year along the pass, a few Nepali porters are left to freeze to death outside the tents of the unthinking tourists who hired them. A few years ago, a French group even left one of their own, a young French woman, to die there. The difficult pass seems to demonstrate a perverse version of Gresham's law of currency: The bad practices of previous travelers have driven out the values that new travelers might have followed if they were at home. Perhaps that helps to explain why our porters behaved as they did and why it was so difficult for Stephen or anyone else to establish a different approach on the spot.

Our Sherpa sirdar, Pasang, was focused on his responsibility for bringing us up the mountain safe and sound. (His livelihood and status in the Sherpa ethnic group depended on our safe return.) We were weak, our party was split, the porters were well on their way to the top with all our gear and food, and a storm would have separated us irrevocably from our logistical base.

The fact was, we had no plan for dealing with the contingency of the sadhu. There was nothing we could do to unite our multicultural group in the little time we had. An ethical dilemma had come upon us unexpectedly, an element of drama that may explain why the sadhu's story has continued to attract students.

I am often asked for help in teaching the story. I usually advise keeping the details as ambiguous as possible. A true ethical dilemma requires a decision between two hard choices. In the case of the sadhu, we had to decide how much to sacrifice ourselves to take care of a stranger. And given the constraints of our trek, we had to make a group decision, not an individual one. If a large majority of students in a class ends up thinking I'm a bad person because of my decision on the mountain, the instructor may not have given the case its due. The same is true if the majority sees no problem with the choices we made.

Any class's response depends on its setting, whether it's a business school, a church, or a corporation. I've found that younger students are more likely to see the issue as black-and-white, whereas older ones tend to see shades of gray. Some have seen a conflict between the different ethical approaches that we followed at the time. Stephen felt he had to do everything he could to save the sadhu's life, in accordance with his Christian ethic of compassion. I had a utilitarian response: do the greatest good for the greatest number. Give a burst of aid to minimize the sadhu's exposure, then continue on our way.

The basic question of the case remains, When do we take a stand? When do we allow a "sadhu" to intrude into our daily lives? Few of us can afford the time or effort to take care of every needy person we encounter. How much must we give of ourselves? And how do we prepare our organizations and institutions so they will respond appropriately in a crisis? How do we influence them if we do not agree with their points of view?

We cannot quit our jobs over every ethical dilemma, but if we continually ignore our sense of values, who do we become? As a journalist asked at a recent conference on ethics, "Which ditch are we willing to die in?" For each of us, the answer is a bit different. How we act in response to that question defines better than anything else who we are, just as, in a collective sense, our acts define our institutions. In effect, the sadhu is always there, ready to remind us of the tensions between our own goals and the claims of strangers.

Biographical Notes

Biographical Notes

Claire André served as assistant director of the Makkula Center for Applied Ethics and is one of the founders of *Issues in Ethics*.

Aristotle (384–322 B.C.), the student of Plato and teacher of Alexander the Great, was preeminent among the ancient philosophers. His *Nichomachean Ethics*, the first book in the Western world devoted exclusively to ethics, emphasizes the importance of a virtuous character and good judgment for living a happy life.

John R. Boatright is the Raymond C. Baumhart, S.J., Professor of Business Ethics at Loyola University. In 2000, he was chosen the School of Business Administration Faculty Researcher of the Year. He has authored numerous journal articles and textbooks in business ethics. His newest book is entitled *Ethics in Finance*.

Dean L. Bottorff is the Principal for Ethics Quality, Inc. and President of Allegheny Industrial Sales, Inc. He received an MBA from Robert Morris University, Pennsylvania, and is a consultant and trainer on Ethics Quality for Organizational Excellence. He has published extensively on professional ethics.

Archie B. Carroll is professor of management and Robert W. Scherer Chair of Management and Corporate Public Affairs in the Terry College of Business, University of Georgia. Dr. Carroll is past president of the Society for Business Ethics and has published extensively. He is senior co-author of *Business & Society: Ethics & Stakeholder Management*, 4th Edition (2000).

James E. Chesher is a professor of philosophy at Santa Barbara City College. He is the co-author of *The Business of Commerce: Examining an Honorable Profession* and *A Primer on Business Ethics* with Tibor R. Machan.

Stephen Covey is co-founder/co-chairman of FranklinCovey Company, the world's largest management and leadership development organization. He is perhaps best known as the author of *The 7 Habits of Highly Effective People* and *Principle-Centered Leadership*.

David E. DeCosse is director of Campus Ethics Programs at the Makkula Center for Applied Ethics, Santa Clara University.

Thomas Donaldson is the Mark O. Winkelman Professor at the Wharton School of the University of Pennsylvania. He is director of the Wharton Ethics Program. Donaldson has published extensively in the areas of business and professional ethics. Among his books are *The Ties That Bind: A Social Contract Approach to Business Ethics*, co-authored with Thomas W. Dunfee, and *Ethics in International Business*.

Joel Feinberg (1926–2004) was an American political and social philosopher who received international recognition for his four-volume work *The Moral Limits of Criminal Law* (1984–1987). He promoted concern for individual rights and justification for state authority.

R. Edward Freeman is Elis and Signe Olsson Professor of Business Administration and director of the Olsson Center for Applied Ethics at the Darden Graduate School of Business Administration at the University of Virginia. He is also a professor of Religious Studies. Among his books are *Strategic Management: A Stakeholder Approach, Ethics and Agency Theory* (with Norman Bowie), *The State of the Act*, and *Corporate Strategy and the Search for Ethics* (with Dan Gilbert, Jr.).

Milton Friedman (1912–2006) was a senior research fellow at the Hoover Institution and the Paul Snowden Russell Distinguished Service Professor Emeritus of Economics at the University of Chicago. Friedman is recognized as the leader of the Chicago School of Monetary Economics. The Chicago School emphasizes the importance of money as a tool of government policy and a determinant of business cycles and inflation. In 1976 he was awarded the Nobel Prize for Economics and in 1988 was the recipient of both the Presidential Medal of Freedom and the National Medal of Science. He has authored many books, including *Capitalism and Freedom*.

Carol Gilligan is a professor at New York University and holds an interdisciplinary position between the Graduate School of Education and the NYU School of Law. Gilligan taught at Harvard for thirty-five years where she worked with psychologists Erik Erikson and Lawrence Kohlberg. She became a leading critic of Kohlberg's work and produced a body of work in the psychological and moral development of women that emphasized caring and human relationships. Gilligan is known as the founder of "difference feminism" and is the author of *In A Different Voice: Psychological Theory and Women's Development*.

Kirk O. Hanson is executive director of the Makkula Center for Applied Ethics at Santa Clara University and University Professor of Organizations and Society.

Richard H. Hersh is president of Trinity College and has a reputation as a highly respected scholar, educator, and community leader. He is a champion of liberal arts education and academic excellence. Hersh also served as visiting professor and director of the Center for Moral Development at Harvard University. His books include *Promoting Moral Growth, Models of Moral Development,* and *The Structure of School Improvement.*

Michael Josephson is the founder and president of the nonprofit Joseph and Edna Josephson Institute of Ethics, which he named for his parents. He conducts ethics programs for leaders in education, business, government, journalism, law, and the nonprofit community. He has designed ethics training programs and has made extensive media appearances. Mr. Josephson founded the Character Counts! Coalition and the President of the United States and the United States Congress have declared the third week in October "National Character Counts! Week."

Immanuel Kant (1724–1804) the foremost German philosopher of the Enlightenment has had a profound influence on modern ethical theory. In his *Critique of Practical Reason* and *Groundwork of the Metaphysics of Morals,* he presents morality as the product of practical reason, not feelings or "inclinations."

Daryl Koehn is the Cullen Chair of Business Ethics at the University of St. Thomas in Houston, Texas. Ms. Koehn has published numerous articles and has written several books: *The Ground of Professional Ethics, Rethinking Feminist Ethics: Care, Trust, Empathy, Trust in Business: Barriers and Bridges,* and *Local Insights, Global Ethics in Business.* She also consults with major corporations on ethical issues and helps companies establish ethics training programs.

Lawrence Kohlberg (1927–1987), an expert in developmental and social psychology and former Harvard Professor, advanced an influential theory on moral development that is widely recognized and used today. He is internationally recognized for his work on moral development and moral education.

Tibor R. Machan is a Hoover research fellow and professor at Chapman University. Professor Machan is also a nationally syndicated columnist for the *Orange County Register*. He recently co-authored *The Business of Commerce, Examining an Honorable Profession* and *A Primer on Business Ethics* with James E. Chesher. The list of Dr. Machan's publications and media appearances is extensive.

Karl Marx (1818–1883), Prussian born, was a philosopher and revolutionary theorist. Influenced by radical Hegelians, Marx placed the foundation of his thinking in the material base of economics. His most famous writings, *The Communist Manifesto* and *Das Kapital* (*Capital*), were done in collaboration with Friedrich Engels.

Dennis P. McCann is the Wallace M. Alston Professor of Bible and Religion at Agnes Scott College in Atlanta/Decatur, Georgia. He is also the executive director of the Society of Christian Ethics. Dr. McCann was named the first annual holder of the Wicklander Chair in Business Ethics at DePaul University. He has published numerous books and articles.

Bowen H. "Buzz" McCoy is a retired managing director of Morgan Stanley where he was responsible for worldwide real estate finance. He is currently president of the Urban Land Foundation and has served as president of the Real Estate Counselors, Chairman of the Center for Economic Policy Research at Stanford University, and a member of the Executive Committee at the Hoover Institution.

Margaret R. McLean is Ethics Center Associate Director and Director of Bioethics. Her combined expertise in both science and ethics makes her a top commentator and consultant on the ethical advances in medicine and biotechnology.

Michael J. Meyer is associate professor of philosophy and the Santa Clara University Presidential Professor of Ethics and the Common Good.

John Stuart Mill (1806–1873), was a famous British utilitarian philosopher and social reformer. He sat in Parliament from 1865–1868. Mill believed that a person *ought* to act in ways that would maximize human welfare. Among his major works are *System of Logic, On Liberty, Utilitarianism,* and *The Subjection of Women*.

Dennis Moberg is Presidential Professor of Ethics and the Common Good at Santa Clara University's Makkula Center for Applied Ethics. He has published four books and more than thirty articles. Moberg's "The Ethics of Organizational Politics" (1981) is the most frequently cited article in the field of business ethics.

Patrick E. Murphy is a professor in the Mendoza College of Business at the University of Notre Dame and C. R. Smith Director of the Institute for Ethics Worldwide. He has published many articles and is the editor of *Eighty Exemplary Ethics Statements*.

Nel Noddings is professor of philosophy and education at Teachers College, Columbia University, and Lee L. Jacks Professor of Child Education Emerita at Stamford University. Dr. Noddings' current research interests include caring in schools, feminist ethics in education, and moral dialogue. She has published over 125 articles and has written many books including *Awakening the Inner Eye: Intuition in Education* and *Caring: A Feminine Approach to Ethics and Moral Education*.

Robert Nozick (1938–2002) was one of the most influential thinkers of the later twentieth century. Nozick was Arthur Kingsley Professor of Philosophy at Harvard University and the author of *Anarchy, State, and Utopia* (National Book Award 1975), *Philosophical Explanations*, and *The Examined Life*. He was a champion of libertarianism and held that "the minimal state is the most extensive state that can be justified." (*Anarchy, State and Utopia*, p. 149)

Ayn Rand (1905–1982) was a Russian-American novelist, philosopher, playwright and screenwriter whose philosophy "objectivism" remains influential today. She is well-known for her major works *The Fountainhead* (1943) and the philosophical novel *Atlas Shrugged* (1957).

John Rawls (1921–2002) was perhaps the leading moral and political theorist of the twentieth century. Rawls argued powerfully for a political philosophy based on equality and individual rights. His *Theory of Justice*, one of only two books he wrote, became a contemporary classic. Rawls was the James Bryant Conant University Professor Emeritus at Harvard.

Thomas Shanks is associate professor of communications at Santa Clara University. He is also a nationally recognized expert in ethical decision-making.

David Stewart was an award-winning professor at Ohio University where he taught philosophy. He is the author or editor of nine books including *Business Ethics* and *Exploring the Philosophy of Religion*. He co-authored *Exploring Ethics*, *Medical Ethics: A Reader*, and *Fundamentals of Philosophy*.

Iwao Taka is project director, Business Ethics Research Project, Reitaku Centre for Economic Studies, Reitaku University, Japan.

Manuel G. Velasquez is the Charles J. Dirksen Professor of Business Ethics in the management department, Santa Clara University. He is the author of the highly acclaimed text, *Business Ethics: Concepts and Cases.*

Patricia H. Werhane is the Wicklander Chair of Business Ethics and Director of the Institute for Business and Professional Ethics at DePaul University and Peter and Adeline Ruffin Professor of Business Ethics and Senior Fellow at the Olsson Center for Applied Ethics in the Darden School at the University of Virginia. Professor Werhane is the founder and former editor-in-chief of *Business Ethics Quarterly*. She has numerous publications including *Ethical Issues in Business* (with T. Donaldson and Margaret Cording, Seventh Edition), *Persons, Rights and Corporations, Adam Smith and His Legacy for Modern Capitalism, Moral Imagination and Managerial Decision-Making* and, her latest book, *Employment and Employee Rights* (with Tara J. Radin and Norman Bowie).